THE WOMEN WHO BUILT BRISTOL

By Jane Duffus

Tangent Books

The Women Who Built Bristol
First published February 2018 by Tangent Books.
Reprinted May and October 2018, April 2019.

Tangent Books
Unit 5.16 Paintworks, Bristol BS4 3EH
0117 972 0645
www.tangentbooks.co.uk
richard@tangentbooks.co.uk

ISBN 978-1-910089-71-2

By Jane Duffus

Cover illustration: Tiitu Takalo
Cover design: Emily Turner
Inside illustrations: Jenny Howe, Carrie Love
Typesetting: Joe Burt (www.wildsparkdesign.com)

A CIP record of this book is available at the British Library.

Printed using paper from a sustainable source.

This book is dedicated to the memory of every single wonderful woman named within it, without whom there would be no book.

FOREWORD

By Penny Gane

The extraordinary stories of the sheroic women Jane Duffus has brought together in this collection have important implications for us today. On the one hand, at least as contemporary feminist activists, we have not had to overcome all the obstacles that stood in the way of the suffragettes and suffragists carving a path through prejudice and small mindedness – women such as Ellen Pitman, who was imprisoned and force fed multiple times despite her advancing years. And we do not have to tolerate *quite* the same level of gender bias that trailblazers in the medical profession such as Beryl Corner and Vicky Tryon endured (although the glass ceiling remains unshattered). And we have not had to fight like the women who overcame the odds to pursue meaningful careers, obtain better healthcare and acquire an education; or women such as Rosa Pease (champion of the inclusion of women in the police force), who pioneered new ways of working and took on careers traditionally held by men.

And on the other hand, how absurd it is that we activists are still having to fight for women's equality in this city, in this country, in this century… and in just about every aspect of our lives. How hard it is for us to keep women's equality on the agenda. How convenient it is for the government to assume that the battle for women's equality is won and that the female 51% of the population is 'having it all'. How hard it is for the decision makers to grasp any of this... despite the huge amount of evidence to the contrary: the shocking figures on domestic violence and abuse that fail to shock; the gender pay gap that permeates even the most respected of institutions; and the low numbers of women in parliament, on boards and in technological industries that persist despite the achievements of young women.

It would be easy for the privileged to sit back and think gender equality will happen of its own accord over time. But the truth is that at every stage success has been hard fought. Every time we take our eye off the ball, progress slows and the status quo of male privilege creeps back to the top.

It is hard to imagine that in 21st-century Britain, politicians are seriously proposing women-only carriages on our trains as the only way for women to travel safely. It is beyond belief that each week more than two women die at the hands of male partners and that this is not headline news. It is staggering that more than three centuries after Dinah Black escaped slavery from the plantations of the West Indies, women are trafficked and sold into modern day slavery both in Bristol and across the world. It is beyond comprehension that, here in Bristol, one in four children lives in poverty (many in lone-parent families headed by women). It is appalling that it should be necessary to have a new hate crime category of 'gender'. It is horrifying that homeless young single women in the city now outnumber homeless men.

So just as our predecessors were fearless, we must also be fearless. We must take our inspiration from all the women who built Bristol and carry on building a city where women live in safety, are powerful, confident, achieving their potential, not living in anyone's shadow and getting the most out of life.

That is why a group of motivated women set up Bristol Women's Voice in 2012: to be a powerful voice for women in the city to make change happen.

That is why we persuaded the elected Mayor of Bristol to sign the European Charter for Equality of Women and Men in Local Life in 2013. Bristol is still the only United Kingdom signatory to this Charter.

That is why we set up Bristol Women's Commission in 2013, so that key organisations in Bristol can work together to bring about real change for women in every part of the city, from universities to hospitals, the police to the council, and everything in between.

That is why we launched Bristol Women's Voice's 'Womanifesto' in 2016, focussing on all of the areas where more needs to be done: health, housing, education, safety, power, business, economy – essentially, *every* aspect of women's lives still needs to be vastly improved.

Women working together can achieve so much more. But women have to be brave. We have new battles to fight, such as online abuse and misogyny, the prevalence of violent pornography, a rise in hate crime... to name but a handful.

And despite all this, we are surrounded by wonderful female role models in so many areas of our lives. Bristol Women's Voice and its members are the women who are proud to still be building Bristol and in this book we pay tribute to those who laid the foundations on which we now stand.

Penny Gane is the Chair of Bristol Women's Voice and Bristol Women's Commission. Born and brought up in Bristol, she has been involved in the women's movement for decades. Penny works with individuals and organisations as an equalities consultant and executive coach. She was part of the delegation that lobbied the Mayor of Bristol to sign the European Charter for Equality for Women and Men in Local Life, which led to the establishment of Bristol Women's Commission. She chaired NHS Bristol's Equality Strategy Group as a Non-Executive Director and served for four years on a national board of the Medical Research Council, ensuring public and patient involvement. In 2016, Penny was awarded an honorary doctorate by the University of the West of England for her work regarding inclusivity and equality.

FOREWORD

By Dr Finn Mackay

I cannot claim to have built Bristol like the women in this book did but I certainly reap what they sowed. All of us, women and men, owe a great debt to the women who stepped out of line, because they expanded our room to thrive and to even exist at all in many cases.

We must not forget just how radical and difficult it must have been to clear the path that we now tread without thinking. It was a brave woman who forged into medicine, politics, art, literature and science among so many more of the causes, callings and professions that feature in the biographies of the women chronicled here. These women broke solid walls, not glass ceilings, they smashed into institutions quite dramatically, and it cannot have been painless. They broke not just professional barriers but also social conventions of what a woman should be, and in so doing they changed the rules forever, rewriting who women can be and what we can achieve.

I answered the call of Bristol in 2010 when I moved from London to undertake my PhD at the University of Bristol, at the Centre for Gender & Violence Research in the School for Policy Studies. Hackney and Clifton Wood are miles apart, 124 miles to be precise, but it felt like much more.

Moving into my rented student flat, a neighbour popped in through the propped open door, weaving in between the boxes, to welcome me to the road and invite me to dinner. People walked at a slow Pink Panther pace and shopping took much longer as everyone said "hello" and conversed. I bored my friends with photographs of my commute to the city centre along the floating harbour, my trip to the art gallery on a ferry that cost 50p, selfies on the SS Great Britain and all the sunsets over the suspension bridge. I was in love with Bristol! I still am.

It was therefore such a joy and an honour to be asked to write an introduction for this marvellous and uplifting book because, like old school graffiti on desks and jotters, I will now forever be etched in history myself as a Bristol Woman: Finn + Bristol = 4Eva!

This accessible and often humorous book is full of inspirational examples; not all were residents of the city but all have a key connection to the place we call home. Reading through it I have wondered about how many times I have walked down streets or passed unremarkable houses that possess such significant histories. I will take different routes around Bristol now I have this knowledge and it makes me love the place even more. Having been involved for many years in campaigns for the abolition of the prostitution industry, I was particularly interested to read, for example, of Bristol's connection to the reformer Josephine Butler. The number of suffragette herstories here are also an absolute delight. They serve as a humanising insight into women who can often seem more like legends than real people from a variety of backgrounds, including in social class background. Which feminist in our fair city would not feel their heart beat faster to learn the fact that Bristol had the highest volume of suffrage activity outside of London?

It is essential to find and share our own history. It is a history of women's place in the world we also built, of advances and discoveries and revolutions touched and led by women. This is a legacy that often merited barely a footnote in the hands of men, it is therefore a political act to put women back in their place, which is at the centre of everything. This book will be a heartening and affirming read for everyone, especially those who are building

Bristol today, clearing their own paths and shining a light for those who follow after.

Dr Finn Mackay has been a feminist activist for more than 20 years, living at the Menwith Hill Women's Peace Camp in the 1990s and later founding the London Feminist Network and reviving London's Reclaim the Night in 2004. She is now a Senior Lecturer of Sociology at the University of the West of England. Before this, Finn's professional background was in education and youth work, where she worked on domestic violence prevention and anti-bullying. Finn speaks and writes about feminist activism, feminist theory, male violence against women and women's liberation. In 2010, she was the individual winner of the Emma Humphreys Memorial Prize for her work about male violence against women and children. Finn's book *Radical Feminism: Feminist Activism in Movement* was published in 2015.

INTRODUCTION

By Jane Duffus

"How splendid the women [of Bristol] are.
It is wonderful to see them rise to every call that is made."
Suffragette Annie Kenney

With *The Women Who Built Bristol,* I want to tell the stories of women; women whose stories you may not be familiar with, women who may not have gone on to be the first woman Lord Mayor or to have set up a school for underprivileged children, but whose stories are nonetheless crucial for shaping the lives we live today. Which is why, alongside the stories of suffragettes and doctors and politicians, you will also read the stories of, for instance, mustard gas manufacturers, child pottery workers and charity fundraisers. Their stories are equally as important as those of their better-known sisters.

This book does not claim to be perfect (I'm not sure any book is entirely without fault). It is a compendium of 250 wonderful women who in some way shaped the way our lives are lived today and we hope they will inspire you. We obviously have not written rigorously in-depth biographies of the women, although some of them are the subject of individually published biographies, and instead we intend the synopses here to give you an introduction to these fabulous women. And while there have been a handful of books about Bristolian women before (notably: Madge Dresser, *Women and the City*; Lorna Brierly, Helen Reid, *Go Home and Do the Washing*; and Lucienne Boyce, *The Bristol Suffragettes*), and a few 'Top 100' lists (notably Shirley Brown, Dawn Dyer, *100+ Women of Bristol*; and Eugene Byrne, *Bristol's Top 100 Women*), *The Women*

Who Built Bristol seeks to celebrate the less well-known women of our past as well as the key big names. We have also welcomed contributions from contemporary women for this book, who have written pieces celebrating Bristolian women close to their own hearts and passions.

When choosing which women to include in the main A-Z section of this book, we have limited ourselves to women who are no longer with us because we were so spoilt for choice in terms of women to include that we needed a demarcation. And because I am a firm believer that we need to look at what we have achieved in the past to know what we need to do in the future. We also made a decision to focus, in this book, only on women who have made a positive impact on the city. So we will save for another time the women who were murderers, pirates, fascists and so on; we are certainly not claiming that all of the women who came out of Bristol were perfect, nor are we attempting to rewrite history by pretending all women only did wonderful things.

The ways the women in this book link to Bristol also vary. Some were born here, worked here and died here… but most do not tick all three boxes. Instead, you will find women who were born here and then moved elsewhere to achieve what has made them noteworthy. You will find women who were born elsewhere, achieved something elsewhere and moved to Bristol upon retirement. You will find women who passed through Bristol and achieved something while visiting. You will even find a woman who swam here from Wales, only to go home again the same afternoon. And you will find many other ways of linking these women to Bristol. All women are welcome in this book, provided they have some link to our city's heritage.

And while 250 women may initially seem like a large number, it really isn't. If you consider that the oldest woman in this book was born in 1184 and the most recent death was in 2017, we have covered an 833-year period. But just imagine how much bigger that number would be if this book had been written about the *men* who built Bristol during the same timeframe. There are undoubtedly many more than 250 women who built Bristol and in any future editions of this book we would be pleased to include any glaring omissions. But it stands as an ugly testament to our times that women are frequently written out of history and as such it becomes increasingly difficult to find out about the women who deserve to be remembered and celebrated.

"Inspired by your passion for freedom and right may we and the women who come after us be ever ready to follow your example of self-forgetfulness and self-conquest, ever ready to obey the call of duty and answer to the appeal of the oppressed."
Letter from Emmeline Pankhurst to suffragettes on their release from prison

My own passion is for the suffrage movement: the suffragists (the women who peacefully campaigned for decades to try and secure women the vote) and the suffragettes (who employed militancy for a short period and attracted headlines). When I first moved to Bristol, I stumbled across a tiny yet powerful Women's Social and Political Union pin badge from the 1910s in Bristol Museum and Art Gallery on Queens Road, and every so often I pop in and pay my respects to it. I look at this badge and find myself wondering who the woman was who owned it: what her story was, what her role was, did she go to prison, was she force fed, what did her family think and – more than anything – did she live long enough to see women achieve the vote? Perhaps the woman who earned it is one of the suffragettes in this book and we just don't realise.

For women to be able to cast their vote in how the country is run remains essential, not only so they can influence who governs their society but also to further the political equality of their gender. Until the 1900s, women were unable to participate in public life or to influence government and they were denied access to any of the men-only business, political and cultural institutions that ran Bristol. But that didn't stop women from quietly supporting vulnerable women and girls who were trapped by poverty, illiteracy, poor health, poor education and so on.

Outside of London, Bristol saw the highest volume of suffrage activity in the United Kingdom. In the years following the establishment of the Clifton Anti-Slavery Campaign in 1840, several Bristol women signed the first-ever women's suffrage petition in 1866, and the Bristol suffrage society was only the fifth to be established in the UK. During the 1880s, Bristol women were noisily active strike supporters and worked on campaigns leading to the creation of an organisation called Promotion of Trades Unions Among Women in 1889. These were not women to be messed with.

Indeed, none of the women in this book were women to be messed with. Whether gentle peacekeeper or militant agitator, every single woman profiled in this book was a shero who deserves to be remembered well. They are all an inspiration to us today.

Jane Duffus qualified as a journalist in 2001 and has since worked as a journalist and editor for numerous best-selling national magazines and publishers. After moving from London to Bristol, Jane set up the award-winning all-female What The Frock! Comedy project in 2012 to challenge an industry that knowingly overlooks female talent, and wrote *The What The Frock! Book of Funny Women* in 2015. In addition, she continues to work as a freelance writer, editor and public speaker. *The Women Who Built Bristol* is her third book, although Jane has contributed chapters to several others:

all of which are about women. Jane is currently researching and writing volume two of *The Women Who Built Bristol*, which will be published by Tangent Books in autumn 2019 and features another 250 amazing women from this city. She takes a break from all of the above by also being a long-distance runner. Jane's website is **janeduffus.com**

A-Z OF THE WOMEN WHO BUILT BRISTOL

MARY SOPHIA ALLEN

1878-1964, SUFFRAGETTE

Women's Social and Political Union (WSPU) Organiser Annie Kenney inspired a huge number of women during her reign as top dog in the West Country... and Mary Sophia Allen was one of the many. But this is where Mary starts and stops being part of the crowd. There was nothing generic about Ms Allen.

Hearing Annie talk in early 1909 spurred Welsh-born Mary into action. And there was no hanging about or deliberation. By February 1909, Mary was already in prison for joining a deputation at the House of Commons, and promptly endured a hunger strike and three rounds of force feeding while imprisoned. While sent to work in prison mending men's shirts, Mary took the opportunity to secretly embroider the stirring words 'Votes For Women' onto the shirt tails.

Once out of prison, Mary became Organiser of the Newport and Cardiff WSPU branch... until 29 June 1909 when she was arrested again, this time for smashing a window at the Home Office in London. Upon release, Mary came to Bristol on 4 September 1909 with fellow newly released prisoner Lilian Dove-Wilcox and they were met at Temple Meads Station with a triumphant procession led by their shero Annie Kenney.

Mary's third prison sentence of 1909 came in November when she was sent to Horfield Gaol for two weeks after breaking windows at the Board of Trade Office in Bristol during Winston Churchill's visit; the same visit that Theresa Garnett notoriously accosted him with a horse whip.

Upon her release from Horfield Gaol, the *Western Daily Press* reported that both Mary and Vera Wentworth, who was released on the same day, looked in a terrible state when they were met at the gates by a group led, again, by Annie. "Miss Mary Allen in particular looked extremely ill and emaciated in her features, while it was apparent she was very weak. Miss Vera Wentworth was also bearing ample evidence of her refusal to take nourishment," reported the paper. Mary gave a very frank interview to the reporter about her experiences in the prison where she said she was already ill when she went in so was straight away placed in the hospital wing. But her refusal to wear the prison uniform meant she was forcibly stripped by guards. She goes on to describe in great detail the horror of force feeding: "I began the hunger strike as soon as I entered the gaol and the prison authorities fed me with a tube, through the nose, three times, after which the tube was passed into my throat. This was done twice a day until today... I resisted three times and then with four wardresses and three doctors it was impossible to resist further as my strength was fast ebbing away."[1]

After all of this, Mary was deemed unfit for any further suffragette militant work and she moved to Hastings to become WSPU Organiser there. The outbreak of World War One curtailed Mary's enthusiastic plans to set fire to some empty houses in the name of suffrage... which were in clear defiance of her orders from HQ to step aside from militancy.

Mary used her experiences as an imprisoned suffragette in Holloway to highlight why a female police force was desperately needed, not least in a *women's* prison. And as soon as she heard that a women's police force was being established during World War One she joined up and quickly became second in command. Training schools were subsequently opened in Bristol and London. However, once peace was declared in 1918, the women's police force was – against Mary's wishes – disbanded. Known as 'Robert' by her friends and 'Sir' by her colleagues, Mary continued

1 *Western Daily Press*, 1909, 27 November, 'Suffragettes Leave Horfield Prison'. 9.

to wear her police uniform in public for the rest of her life.[2]

Please also see the entries for: Theresa Garnett, Annie Kenney, Rosa Pease, Dorothy Peto, Vera Wentworth and Lilian Dove-Wilcox.

LADY APSLEY

1895-1966, POLITICIAN

Few people in Bristol today know of the city's first woman MP, Lady Apsley. She was not elected until 1943 and took over her husband Lord Apsley's seat of Bristol Central after he was killed in an air accident in Malta in 1942.

Given her brief career as an MP (1943-1945) and the circumstances leading to her election, it is tempting to dismiss her as a traditional upper-class Tory wife rather than as a public figure in her own right. But Lady Apsley's unusual breadth of life experience, her disability (she was confined to a wheelchair at 35) and her sheer energy differentiates her from the rank and file of elite women in this period. Her public career raises questions about the way women of her class were involved in political activism and her political views, grounded as they were in imperialist, patriarchal and racist world views, also contain elements that would be considered progressive today.

She was born Violet Meeking into a landed family with military, trade and Oxbridge connections. Her father, Captain Christopher Spencer Meeking, served with the 10th Hussars in the Boer War and died there, along with his brother, of enteric

2 I'm choosing not to mention that in 1934 Mary reportedly visited Adolf Hitler and apparently urged him to establish a force of Nazi police women, and that she then joined the British Union of Fascists. I'm not pretending it didn't happen, I'm just not mentioning it.

fever when Violet was five. When her mother remarried in 1912, to the wealthy big game hunter and stockbroker Herbert Johnson, the family relocated to his newly built house at Marsh Court, Hampshire. At the outbreak of World War One, Marsh Court was turned over by the family for use as a military hospital run by Violet's mother. Violet and her sister Finola worked as full-time volunteer nurses and Violet was also a part-time ambulance driver.

By 1918, she was drawn into the post-war social world of the aristocracy. She became a regular visitor at Balmoral Castle, near Aberdeen, and dined with leading politicians and industrialists in London. Her surviving memoirs from that period show her to be very much part of the traditionalist right-wing Tory faction of the day. A devoted sportswoman, she took advantage of the freer mores of the post-suffrage United Kingdom to become a devotee of fishing and fox hunting. Her marriage to Allen Algernon Bathurst in 1924 (who became Lord Apsley) allied her to a family noted for their high Tory and imperialist sympathies and love of field sports.

The new Lady Apsley supported her husband, who was then MP for Southampton, by chairing the Southampton's Women's Conservative Association. When he was asked to go undercover to Australia to investigate the treatment of poor English emigrants there, she insisted on joining him and spent some months masquerading as a poor settler in spartan conditions in the Outback, an account of which she published in 1926. On her return to the United Kingdom, she became a qualified air pilot and a keen amateur driver, writing occasional articles about hunting, driving and sport for the press. She was on the board of her husband's airline company, ran their estate at Petty France in Gloucestershire and took an active part in the Cirencester Hunt. By then the mother of two sons, her world shattered in 1930 when a hunting accident confined her to a wheelchair for the rest of her life.

When her husband became Conservative MP for Bristol Central the following year, Lady Apsley became the head of the Bristol Conservative Women's Association and within five years increased its membership to nearly 8,000. These Women's Associations, although they had little say in policy making, were key to fundraising and getting out the vote.

In 1936, she visited a Nazi labour camp for the German unemployed and sang its praises in a letter to *The Times*. Neither she nor her husband (who was courted by the Nazis and was an invited guest of honour at the Nuremburg Rally of 1936) ever joined the Fascist Party in the United Kingdom, but both were much more vigorous in their repudiation of Bolshevism and British socialists than of Adolf Hitler or Benito Mussolini. The Apsleys certainly allied themselves firmly to Appeasement and organised meetings in Bristol supporting Prime Minister Neville Chamberlain well into 1939.

When World War Two broke out, the Apsleys rallied to the British cause. Bristol Central was heavily blitzed in 1940-1942, during which time Lady Apsley took over many of her husband's constituency duties while he served abroad. Since 1938, she had served as a County Commandant for the (women's) Auxilliary Territorial Service for Gloucestershire and her dynamic leadership of the women's section of the British Legion throughout World War Two made an important contribution to the war effort.

After her husband's death, she was selected as a National Candidate for her husband's seat, which was contested by Jennie Lee, a charismatic socialist who ran as an independent. Contrary to expectations, Lady Apsley increased her husband's majority and received cheers from the Commons when she made her maiden speech from her wheelchair on 25 February 1943. She was one of only 15 women MPs at the time and the first ever in Bristol.

Although less prominent in the House than some of her fellow Parliamentarians, by the end of her term in 1945 Lady Apsley made no fewer than 187 contributions to the Commons in the form of questions and speeches. Her Tory views were on occasion tempered by her personal experience as a disabled person, as a woman and as someone exposed first hand to the needs of the poor through her constituency and wider welfare work. She pushed consistently for the needs of the housewife and women in the services to be taken into account, and for the training of disabled veterans. She allied with Labour women MPs in pushing for Family Allowances to be paid to the mother, although only after she was assured this would not undermine the principle that the father was the head of the household.

After her surprise defeat in the Labour landslide victory in 1945, Lady Apsley tried unsuccessfully to re-enter the Commons until retiring from politics in 1950.

Written by Dr Madge Dresser, FRHistS and FRSA, who is Visiting Senior Research Fellow at the University of the West of England and Honorary Professor in Historical Studies at the University of Bristol. She is the editor and co-author of *Women and the City: 1373-2000*.

Please also see the entry for: Jennie Lee.

JANET ARNOLD

1932-1998, FASHION DESIGNER, HISTORIAN

If fashion is a language, then Janet Arnold was probably the world's most skilled translator. It is thanks to her work that we understand so much about historical dress today – not just their styles but also their cut and construction. She was both an artist and a scholar and, under layers of fabric, unpicked not only the technical aspects of how garments were put together but also the history of the artistry that went into making them.

Born on Clifton Down Road on 6 October 1932, Janet was the daughter of an ironmonger and a nurse. Her fascination with clothing and its construction began during her time at The Red Maids' School where, since its inception in 1634, students have always been "apparelled in red"[3]. (In fact, even today when the school celebrates its founders' day, the students continue to wear the traditional bonnets and cloaks that so intrigued Janet.) She went on to receive a National Diploma from the West of England College of Art, later graduating from the University of Bristol in 1954.

Several teaching posts followed, including at Hammersmith Day School and Royal Holloway College, and it was during this time that Janet began to amass the impressive collection of artefacts and research on historical dress that became her life's work. As well as collecting papers, books and portraits, Janet began to shoot reel after reel of colour slide film of garments, annotated with her own research and insights. She is believed to have collected 300,000 colour slides, all of which have been passed to The School of Historical Dress in London to be preserved for future generations of costumiers and enthusiasts.

Janet authored several books that have become seminal texts for students of costume and historical fashion; her world renowned *Patterns of Fashion* series, published in three volumes between 1964 and 1985, *A Handbook of Costume* (1973) and *Queen Elizabeth's Wardrobe Unlock'd* (1988) all achieved worldwide acclaim. She lectured across the globe to rapt audiences from

3 http://www.redmaidshigh.co.uk/about-us-a-brief-history

Stockholm to Tokyo and from Ankara to Washington DC.

Her extensive research and notoriety as an authority on historical dress prompted an approach from Palazzo Pitti's Galleria del Costume in Florence in the 1980s to collaborate on a groundbreaking project to document and conserve the 16th century Medici burial clothes. Few royal families have captured the public imagination quite like the House of Medici. Their meteoric rise to power makes the Boleyns look apathetic by comparison. With Janet's help, the museum was able to document with astonishing accuracy the garments they would have worn, based on what remained in their tombs, alongside historical documents and paintings. As a result, Janet's work will continue to be appreciated for years to come, not just by Italians but by the whole world.

While Janet would undoubtedly be proud that her academic work continues to be so revered, she made it clear in her will that it was her students that mattered most to her. The Janet Arnold Award from the Society of Antiquaries of London continues to provide an annual fund for new research work, allowing others to pick up the cloth where she left off and add new stitches to the rich tapestry she began all those years ago.

Written by Gina Jones, who is a Bristol-based fashion and lifestyle journalist, and director of content marketing agency 42group.

BERTHA AYLES

died 1942, SUFFRAGIST, TRADES UNIONIST

Along with her husband Walter (who would become a Labour MP in Bristol), Bertha was a strong supporter of the women's rights movement. The couple moved to Bristol in 1910 when Bertha became a Part-Time Organiser, and Walter became Secretary, of the Bristol Independent Labour Party (ILP), and together they ensured that the ILP and the Women's Labour League (WLL) had women's suffrage at the top of their agendas. The WLL had been rather slow on the uptake regarding women's suffrage until Bertha arrived in Bristol, but once in the city she worked hard to engage working women and trades unions in the important suffrage campaign.

Thanks to Annie Townley coming to Bristol in 1913 and her work with the East Bristol Women's Suffrage Society, Bertha and Walter had a focus for the WLL's suffrage energies. East Bristol was a key area because at that time the sitting MP was the Liberal Charles Hobhouse who was strongly opposed to women's suffrage and the ILP worked hard to try and oust him. Mabel Tothill, who had worked with Bertha and Walter at the Barton Hill University Settlement, already had strong links to East Bristol and stood in opposition to Hobhouse

As soon as Walter had established his plans for a socialist local council in Bristol, Bertha wasted no time in organising a South West one-day conference to try and improve housing conditions for dockers and factory workers. This was followed by a women's public meeting the same evening, where Bertha spoke on the subject of municipal lodging houses for women.

Due to a heart condition, after giving birth to a son in 1913 Bertha decided to step back from public campaigning. Their home was at 12 Station Road, Bishopston, which is acknowledged with a blue plaque.

Please also see the entries for: Mabel Tothill and Annie Townley.

FLORA BAMBERGER
1896-1975, WAR SHERO

World War Two generated quite a few sheroes and one such woman was Flora Bamberger, who worked tirelessly at the scene of bombing raids to rescue people who were trapped in the rubble. As a volunteer member of the Women's Voluntary Service in Bristol, Flora ran a mobile canteen during the war and received the British Empire Medal in gratitude for her contribution to the war effort. Flora had married Harold in 1914 and they had two sons, Louis and Cecil, who were both young men during World War Two and may well have been called up to fight. This undoubtedly would have preyed on Flora's mind while she dug through the Bristol rubble seeking survivors.

FLORENCE BARRETT
1867-1945, DOCTOR

This pioneering doctor of women's medicine was born in Henbury and began her education at University College, Bristol, from where she graduated with a first-class degree in 1895. Florence Barrett, as she became after her second marriage, went on to gain two further medical degrees from the London School of Medicine for Women, of which she would later become Dean and President. In 1916, Florence began a campaign to fundraise for an extension to the hospital to create specialist maternity, paediatric and infant welfare wings. And in 1917 she was appointed CBE: this was the first year that women were admitted to the order.

During her career, Florence, who would later be known as Lady Barrett, became one of the leading gynaecologists and obstetricians of her time, and before World War One she set up centres in London to offer food for malnourished children and pregnant women despite there being little widespread understanding at that time of the importance of a good diet for pregnant women.

Although she was a member of the Eugenics Society (which, long before the Nazis took it to the extreme, maintained a desire to promote 'high-quality' humans and wipe out 'bad' genetic features), she was opposed to contraception, believing couples should only have sex to conceive a child. She also felt that the free availability of contraception would not liberate women but instead turn them into sexual slaves for men, who she felt had no control over their desires.

In addition to medicine, Florence had an interest in the supernatural thanks to her second husband, Sir William Fletcher Barrett, who was a Professor of Physics. After Sir William's death, Florence maintained that she could communicate with his spirit and in 1937 published a book about her contact with him from beyond the grave.

AGNES BEAMISH

1890-1978, SUFFRAGETTE

When Agnes Olive Beamish's family moved to Clifton from Cork, Ireland, so that their four sons could attend Clifton College, daughter Olive (as she was known) was sent to Clifton High School. She joined the Women's Social and Political Union (WSPU) when she was just 16 and proudly wore her 'Votes for Women' badge to school. Olive recalled: "I became an ardent suffragist because in the 1905 election my brothers first became interested in politics and I felt the position keenly, that I would never be equal with them in the political world, and also I realised the inferior position of women everywhere."

She later attended Girton College, Cambridge, where she studied maths and economics. After graduation, Agnes moved to London in 1912 where she became a militant suffragette involved with pillarbox raids and was a WSPU organiser in Battersea. During the war Olive joined Sylvia Pankhurst's Workers' Suffrage Federation in the East End.

Along with Elsie Duvall, Olive was arrested in April 1913 after they were found in possession of incendiary material. The pair were arrested a second time in January 1914 when they were belatedly charged with setting fire to a house in Egham, Surrey, the previous March. Olive was convicted under the name 'Phyllis Brady', underwent hunger strike and survived the trauma of force feeding. What a woman!

CARMEN BECKFORD

1929-2016, NURSE, CAMPAIGNER

Carmen Beckford was born in St Thomas, Jamaica. At the age of 17, she travelled to the United Kingdom and trained to become a nurse. She decided to train in every aspect of nursing because she wanted to be free to travel to any country and still be able to find meaningful employment.

In 1965, Carmen moved to Bristol and was working in midwifery in Downend. In the same year, Harold Wilson (the Leader of the Labour Party) set up the Race Council in London and shortly thereafter it was introduced in Bristol. Carmen was happily working as a midwife when the Medical Officer of Health suggested that she apply for the job as Race Relations Officer for Bristol. However, Carmen had plans to move to Canada to be closer to her parents and so she refused to apply. The Medical

Officer was adamant that Carmen should apply for the post and as a last attempt to convince her he contacted the Jamaican High Commission and told them that they were experiencing problems with Carmen because she would not apply for the post and that Bristol City Council were keen to interview her.

The Jamaican High Commission and the Chief Medical Officer convinced Carmen to apply for the role of Race Relations Officer and to wait two years before moving to Canada. Carmen reluctantly took their advice. Thirty five people applied for the position (including Dr Paul Stephenson OBE[4]), of which Carmen was the only woman. She became the first Race Relations Officer in Bristol. Her role was to integrate communities and to help build young people's self esteem. Carmen recalled: "There was a lot of racism in the city and I was the last Race Relations Officer to be appointed in the UK."

In the same year, Carmen became an executive member of the Commonwealth Coordinated Committee and worked alongside Owen Henry, Roy Hackett, Leotta Goodridge, Dr Paul Stephenson OBE, Clifford Drummond, Audley Evans, Barbara Dettering, Princess Eldoris Campbell, Trevor Thompson and many other of our city's community activists. Carmen explained: "Back then there was no jealousy or malicious intent. We all had our own lives and projects and supported one another. We all shared the same vision and we worked together to make it happen."

Through her role of Race Relation Officer and as the founder of the West Indian Dance Team, Carmen organised a camping trip to Devon for young people living in Bristol and she wanted to host a fundraising event at the Colston Hall. Carmen was told that it would not be possible as the venue had never hosted an

4 Dr Paul Stephenson OBE is a community worker, activist and long-time civil rights campaigner for the British African-Caribbean community in Bristol. He was instrumental in the creation of the first Race Relations Act in 1965.

event like the one she was proposing, to which she replied: "Well, we need to change it." She duly received permission to host the fundraiser at the Colston Hall. There were Asian and Irish dance teams in addition to the African Caribbean dancers. The event was a complete success and continued to run annually for several years. Carmen states that they raised more than enough money to take the children away on camping trips and remembers that there was a European man, who chose to remain anonymous, who every year doubled the proceeds and donated it to the camping trips. Carmen stated that, while the man remained unknown, she was extremely grateful for his contributions as they made a great difference to the lives of others in the city.

The St Paul's Festival was established in 1968 and Carmen was in charge of the entertainment. This free event has achieved worldwide recognition and continues to attract crowds of approximately 100,000 people each year.

Carmen was very passionate about the integration of all ethnicities in Bristol. For her work and dedication, Carmen was awarded with an MBE in 1982 and was the first female of African Caribbean descent in the South West to receive the honour. When asked about being identified as an iconic Black Bristolian and one of The Seven Saints of St Paul's[5], Carmen said: "I never paid much attention to what other people felt was right or wrong, or whether people felt that I should be doing this or that. I just followed what was in here [my heart], as that is the only voice that matters, and [I] trust that [God] is guiding me to do the right thing." Following her death in 2016 at the age of 87, she continued to be a respected and loved elder of our city.

5 The Seven Saints of St Paul's is a series of murals about key people who shaped Bristol's black community. The project was devised by Michele Curtis. Two of the seven saints depicted are Carmen Beckford and Princess Campbell, who both feature in this book.

Written by Michele Curtis, who is a multi award-winning artist, illustrator, graphic designer and the Founder of the mural project known as Iconic Black Bristolians.

Please also see the entries for: Princess Campbell and Leotta Goodridge.

AGNES BEDDOE

1832-1914, SUFFRAGIST, EDUCATIONALIST

Born and raised in Scotland, Agnes Beddoe moved to Bristol in 1858 after marrying a doctor. She had been an ardent philanthropist since her teenage years, seeking to support women less fortunate than herself, and once in Bristol became a friend and colleague of social reformer Mary Carpenter. Both women were passionate about the welfare of young women and in 1889 Agnes helped set up lodgings in Portland Square, St Paul's, where young unmarried women could live safely and affordably.

Among Agnes' many roles, she was a representative of the Feeding Industrial School, on the Bristol School Board, a Governor of Red Maids' School, and President of the Home for Working Girls (founded by Mary Carpenter). Agnes was also a Poor Law Guardian, member of the Bristol Women's Liberal Association, the Industrial School Committee, a committee member of the Stanhope House Industrial School, a co-founder (with Mary) of the Indian Society, and in 1882 she formed the Bristol Emigration Society to help orphaned children from industrial schools and workhouses emigrate to Canada and find work there.[6] Phew!

As a founder member of the Bristol and Clifton National

6 Madge Dresser, (2016). *Women and the City: Bristol 1373-2000*. Bristol: Redcliffe Press. 114.

Society for Women's Suffrage, Agnes was a signatory of the first women's suffrage petition in 1866. She described the first meeting of the committee of the Bristol Society for Women's Suffrage as follows: "I had been very ill but was out again in a bath chair when I received an invitation from Mr Commissioner Hill[7] ... to a meeting at his house ... I found a large party of the fashionable part of the community present. He explained to us that the Society, which he wished to form, was unlike most others for it would require neither time nor money, it was so evidently fair and just too – that it only required to be properly brought to parliament to be granted. Then the time came to sign and seal. In a few minutes the audience had disappeared as quickly as a flight of birds, leaving only myself (who was lame) and Mrs Goodere, a lady so kind-hearted that she would not have left anyone in the lurch."[8] The fashionable people to whom Agnes referred included Mary Carpenter and Dr Eliza Walker Dunbar.

In spring 1871, Agnes joined Lilias Ashworth Hallett on a speaking tour for the Society, joining Millicent Fawcett[9] in Bath, Bristol, Exeter, Taunton, Plymouth and Tavistock. And on 4 November 1880, Agnes chaired a public meeting at Bristol's Colston Hall that was "crowded by women, earnest and anxious to hear what women had to tell them of the question connected with their political emancipation"[10].

Please also see the entries for: Mary Carpenter, Lilias Ashworth Hallet, Rosamund and Florence Davenport Hill, Eliza Walker Dunbar.

7 Commissioner Matthew Davenport Hill, whose daughters Rosamund and Florence are included in this book.

8 Ellen Malos, (1983), 'Bristol Women in Action 1839-1919: The Right to Vote and the Need to Earn a Living' in Bristol Broadsides, (1983). *Bristol's Other History*. Bristol: Broadsides. 100.

9 Millicent Fawcett gave her name to the Fawcett Society, which continues to this day and is the longest-running women's rights organisation in the UK.

10 Ellen Malos, (1983), 'Bristol Women in Action 1839-1919: The Right to Vote and the Need to Earn a Living' in Bristol Broadsides, (1983). *Bristol's Other History*. Bristol: Broadsides. 102

AMY BELL

dates unknown, ACADEMIC, STOCKBROKER

Alongside Marian Pease and Emily Pakeman, Amy Bell was one of the first three women to win a scholarship to the then-new University College, Bristol. Amy's parents had been killed in the Indian rebellion of 1857, which was an unsuccessful uprising against the power of the British in India. Consequently, orphaned Amy was brought back to England by her Indian ayah (nanny) to live with her uncle, Colonel Goodere. They lived at Cook's Folly, which at that time was the only house on the Downs overlooking the Avon Gorge (and would become the setting for a romantic novel written in 1886 by Victorian author Emma Marshall). Thanks to her university education and privileged upbringing, Amy went on to become a respected stockbroker. While her gender made it impossible for her to actually work inside the London Stock Exchange, Amy instead set up an office close by and operated successfully from there.

Please also see the entries for: Emma Marshall and Marian Pease.

MATILDA BENNETT

born 1830, POTTERY MAKER

Although perhaps an unusual entry for this book as we know very little about Matilda Bennett as a child, and we do not know what she went on to achieve in adulthood, her story is still important because it is a rare glimpse into the life of a pre-adolescent working-class Bristol girl engaged in full-time employment. Aged just nine years, Matilda began work at the Bristol Pottery as a painter. In 1841, when she was 11, Matilda was a case study for an inspector who came to check on working conditions at the pottery. This is his report about her:

"She is a painting girl at the Bristol Pottery. Has been so about two years, paints cups and saucers, comes from 6am to 6pm with a half hour for breakfast and one hour for dinner. Sits at her work and is employed every day there to work. Is under Mr Marsh the foreman, who superintends but never beats her or treats her ill. Is paid as much as she earns and gets 4s 6d a week at most or sometimes 2s 9d. Has her health very well and likes her work and her treatment."[11]

We do not know what happened to Matilda in the rest of her life. Although, sadly, there was a report in the *Western Daily Press* on 20 August 1906 of a woman named Matilda Bennett being found dead by the Victoria Pottery in St Philips after having been knocked down by a train. Whether or not this is the same woman and whether or not the closeness to the pottery is a mere coincidence, it is impossible to say.

PHILIPPA BETHELL
born 1816, ARTIST

Clifton-based artist and tutor Philippa Bethell, who lived at 1 Arlington Villas, regularly exhibited at the Royal West of England Academy between 1856 and 1883. Her work included 'Stone Steps Near Clifton Turnpike', 'Portrait of a Young Lady and Canary' and 'The Rescue'.

11 Helen Reid, (2005). *Life in Victorian Bristol*. Bristol: Redcliffe Press. 31.

DINAH BLACK

born 1660, FREED ENSLAVED AFRICAN

Dinah Black was an enslaved African living in Bristol who had spent five years working for a woman named Dorothy Smith. But in 1687, Smith sold Dinah to a man who wanted to transport her to work on the plantations in the West Indies against Dinah's will.

After bravely escaping from the ship when it briefly docked near Portishead, Dinah was taken in by some kind Quakers who helped her to take her new owner to court and eventually win the right to stay in England. Because her master refused to take Dinah back after the court case, Dinah was happily later granted her freedom.

This is Dinah's story of escape in her own words: "My name is Dinah and I have been a servant to my master in Bristol… He told me he wanted to ship me out to the West Indies to work on the plantations. I cried when I heard what he had done. I cried and ran away. I hid at the top of a house, but when the men found me they dragged me out. I fought them and screamed for help. The people in the street seemed upset for me. One lady said my tears fell down my face like rain. She was upset, but like all nice people, she didn't want to interfere, so I was put on a ship bound for Jamaica."[12]

Dinah's story continues: "The ship I was on sailed up the river Avon and stopped for a while near Portishead. When we were docked, the men took away my shoes but I still managed to sneak off the ship. I hid in the woods until dark and walked miles and miles back to Bristol. The people they called Quakers have taken me in, they gave me food and clothes and said that it was against the law what my mistress did. They said people like myself cannot

12 http://www.bbc.co.uk/bristol/content/madeinbristol/2004/09/blackhistory/blackhistoryintro.shtml

be forced to go abroad if we don't wish it. I hope they can help me. Life on the plantation is horrible. I do not want to go there."[13]

HELEN BLACKBURN

1842-1903, SUFFRAGIST

"This committee records with deep sorrow the irreparable loss which this society, together with all other associations working for the good of women, has suffered in the death of Helen Blackburn," stated the minutes of the Bristol and West of England Women's Suffrage Committee after the death of their comrade Helen Blackburn in January 1903. Helen had previously been Secretary of the committee and had written fondly about her time with the Bristol group in her 1902 book *Women's Suffrage: A Record of the Women's Suffrage Movement in the British Isles*. Lilias Ashworth Hallett continued to say at the meeting: "All who had the privilege of knowing Helen Blackburn realised that a truly noble spirit has passed away, and when they looked back upon the past their thoughts would ever lovingly dwell on bright and grateful memories."[14]

After her death, a generous letter in *The Times* said of Helen: "She was one of the pioneers in the movement for improving the position of women politically, industrially and educationally ... Those who worked with her were constantly indebted to her wide knowledge of all that had gone before and to her readiness to grasp what was essential to the immediate work and, most of all, to her courtesy and generous appreciation of the part taken in the work by her colleagues."[15]

13 Ibid.
14 *Western Daily Press*, 1903, 31 January, 'The Late Miss Helen Blackburn'. 9.
15 Cited in *Western Daily Press*, 1903, 13 January, Letters. 6.

In her full life, Helen was both Secretary and then Honorary Secretary to the Central Committee for Women's Suffrage in London, which were posts she assumed after having been Secretary to the Bristol branch since 1872. Helen had run the Bristol branch from her lodgings at 20 Park Street and spent her time organising large demonstrations as well as undertaking a national speaking tour.[16] She also organised the pioneering Loan Exhibition of Women's Industries in Clifton in 1885, which is written about more fully in the Women's Work section towards the back of this book. Helen had been the editor of *The Englishwoman's Review*, which was a quarterly feminist journal about women's work. She was also very keen to challenge legislations that restricted women's work and as such she co-founded the Women's Employment Defence League in 1891.

Please also see the entry for: Lilias Ashworth Hallett.

EVELINE DEW BLACKER

1884-1956, ARCHITECT

Eveline Dew Blacker was born on 28 July 1884 at 5 Unity Street in the centre of Bristol. Her parents were Arthur Edward Blacker, a GP, and Harriet Sophia Williams Blacker (née Dew). Eveline's sister Winifred was born in Unity Street in 1886. But by the time the third Blacker sister, Helen, arrived in June 1891, the family had moved to a semi-detached house called Fairlee in Richmond Hill Avenue, Clifton. George, the only son, was born there in 1893. In April 1900, Harriet died when Eveline was just 15, and the following year the family moved to 20 Victoria Square nearby.

16 Madge Dresser, (2016). *Women and the City: Bristol 1373-2000*. Bristol: Redcliffe Press. 102.

In the autumn of 1893, nine-year-old Eveline and seven-year-old Winifred started at Clifton High School for Girls. However, in 1901 the sisters transferred to Redland High School. A dissatisfaction with Clifton High can perhaps be read into the fact that Helen never attended that school, but followed her sisters straight to Redland where there was more emphasis on girls' education leading to university or a career.

In 1905, Eveline was articled to the eminent architect George Oatley (who later designed the Wills Memorial Building for the University of Bristol). Eveline completed her articles in 1909, and in the same year passed the Intermediate Examination of the Royal Institute of British Architects (RIBA). In fact, she was placed 31 out of 152 candidates, of which she was the only woman. She then continued with Oatley and his partner George Lawrence as a Junior Assistant. Jobs in the office during her time there included churches, chapels, houses, banks, offices, factories, and work for Clifton and Redland High Schools.

In the 1901 census, only six women in England and Wales had described themselves as architects, compared with 10,775 men. And by 1905 there were just two female members of the RIBA. In the 1911 census, Eveline was one of only seven women listed as architects – compared with 8,914 men. It appears she may have left the practice in 1913, when Oatley wrote her a glowing reference: "She draws with great neatness and care and with expedition. She is regular in attendance to her duties and her character leaves nothing to be desired. In our opinion she is an excellent Junior Assistant."

At the end of World War One, Eveline set up in practice with Harry Heathman in Colston Chambers at 4 Colston Street in the Centre, thereby becoming the first woman to practise as an architect in Bristol. They then moved to Wellington Chambers, 12 Bridge Street, in the early 1920s, before transferring the office to

Eveline's home in Victoria Square in about 1929, where they were based until the end of their careers.

Heathman & Blacker carried out a variety of works in the 1920s and 1930s, including a number of private houses, and alterations and additions to commercial buildings. A major source of work for architects at this time was the large amount of public housing schemes around the country that local authorities undertook after World War One. In the Welsh Agricultural Labourers' Cottages Competition, held as part of the 1918 National Eisteddfod in Neath, Harry won first prize for a design in Class B. And Eveline was jointly awarded first prize for her entry in Class C – 'Accommodation at the discretion of competitors, but with a minimum of three bedrooms, planned entirely or mainly on one floor'. *Building News* reported that: "The interest of this particular competition is increased by the fact that a lady architect, Miss E D Blacker, divided the honours of the occasion ... the judges being of the opinion that the merits of the two designs were equal, and we are inclined to confirm this judgment."

Then, in 1919, Heathman & Blacker won the first premium in Section I of a Scottish Housing Competition. This time *Building News* wrote: "This joint production is certainly the best sent in, and it is very gratifying to find a lady occupying so prominent a position in the premium list..." And the article added: "The plan is a very skilful one, well adapted to the contours and configuration of the land", and that: "All the elevations are very quiet and restful in treatment".

Also in 1919, Bristol Corporation announced a competition for 5,000 houses – one of the largest schemes in the country – comprising eight council estates. An Advisory Architect designed the layouts, and eight architectural firms, including Heathman & Blacker, were selected to form a board to design the houses, which comprise characteristic cottage types in the Garden Suburb style in areas such as Sea Mills, Fishponds and Knowle.

Perhaps Heathman & Blacker's most significant work is the Bristol cenotaph. In January 1931, after years of vacillation, a competition for local architects was launched to design Bristol's memorial to World War One. The assessor shortlisted three entries from the 18 received, and at the end of May they were published in the *Bristol Evening Times* and put on display at the Art Gallery in Queen's Road for a public vote, when the people of Bristol chose Heathman & Blacker's design. Their cenotaph now stands in Colston Avenue as a continuing monument to those lost in both World Wars and is the focus of Remembrance Day services every year.

Written by Dr Sarah Whittingham FSA, who is a historian specialising in people, buildings and gardens. She is currently writing *Remembering and Forgetting: Three Sisters and the Great War*, a biography of the Blacker sisters.

ELIZABETH BLACKWELL

1821-1910, DOCTOR

Elizabeth Blackwell was the first woman on the British General Medical Council's medical register, and the first woman to qualify with a medical degree in the United States. She was born in February 1821 in Bristol, and lived just off Portland Square, St Paul's, for the first decade of her life, before her family immigrated to the US in 1832 – initially to New York City and then Cincinnati, Ohio, six years later. Elizabeth was the third of nine children of Samuel, a sugar refiner, and Hannah.

Her father was a liberal man, believing that all his children should have access to education and opportunity, regardless of

Elizabeth Blackwell illustration by Jenny Howe

their gender. This provision of education meant that when he died in 1838 Elizabeth and one of her sisters were able to set up a school in order to provide for the family. However, after a family friend suffered a terminal illness and noted that she would feel less embarrassed if she were able to see a woman physician rather than a man, Elizabeth decided to train as a doctor.

Despite applying to every medical school in Philadelphia, she was initially unable to find an institution that would accept her, and spent a year or more undertaking private tuition in anatomy and using the library of a physician she boarded with to teach herself. She was advised to go to Europe or even to disguise herself as a man in order to be accepted on a course. Nevertheless, she persisted.

Eventually she found a medical school that would consider her and she applied. The 150 male students were given a vote as to whether Elizabeth should be allowed to undertake the course with them and, apparently as a practical joke, were unanimous in allowing her on. While enrolled she still found it difficult to secure training placements and experienced discrimination from those at the school as well as from locals, who eventually came round and turned out in large numbers to witness and celebrate her graduation.

It was something of a floodgate opening for women in medicine – within three years of her groundbreaking graduation in 1849, a further 20 women successfully graduated from American medical schools (one of whom was Elizabeth's sister Emily, the third woman to gain a medical degree in the US). Elizabeth later worked in France and the United Kingdom; in Paris she was working as an obstetrician when she contracted ophthalmia from a patient and lost an eye, ruling out her becoming a surgeon. Back in the United States, along with her sister Emily and the Polish doctor Marie Zakrzewska, Elizabeth set up the New York Infirmary for

Indigent Women and Children. After finally moving permanently back to the United Kingdom she was involved in setting up the National Health Society, an organisation designed to educate the public about health and hygiene, whose motto 'prevention is better than cure' rings as true today as it did then.

Elizabeth died in Hastings in 1910, and in 2013 the University of Bristol honoured her by naming their new Health Research Institute after her.

Written by Dr Suzi Gage, who is a psychology lecturer at the University of Liverpool. She regularly writes for *The Guardian* and presents the award-winning podcast 'Say Why To Drugs'.

VIOLET BLAND
1863-1940, SUFFRAGETTE

Not content with her lot as a kitchen maid, Violet Bland left her post in Shrewsbury and moved to Bristol where she became head of the Ladies' College of Domestic Science. But between lessons she managed to find time to support the suffrage cause. Violet joined the Women's Social and Political Union (WSPU) and offered paid hospitality to recovering suffragettes at Henley Grove, Henleaze. Among those women who came to stay were Annie Kenney, Lettice Floyd, Elsie Howey, Vera Wentworth and Mary Phillips.

To welcome the recently released hunger strikers Lillian Dove-Wilcox and Mary Sophia Allen home to Bristol in August 1909, Violet lavishly decorated her garden for a triumphant party for the returning sheroes, although Mary Blathwayt noted in her diary that guests were expected to pay for their tea. Whether this charge was a fundraising drive for the WSPU or to cover Violet's outlay is unclear. Violet herself was arrested the following year when she joined the Black Friday protest on 10 November 1910 at Parliament. This was a mass protest of women angered by the failure of the Conciliation Bill and on this occasion the police – who had been no strangers to using brute force on women in the past – really stepped up their violence. As the *Western Daily Press* put it in an understated phrase, "turbulent scenes occurred"[17]. A total of 117 women and two men were arrested that day and Violet was one of the 119. Other local women arrested included Maud Fussell from Kingswood and Mabel Hunt of Clevedon.

Not one to be deterred, in March 1912 Violet joined the West End window-smashing campaign in London and again found herself facing prosecution after smashing a window on Northumberland Avenue, Westminster. At her trial, Violet defiantly stated that she "had paid rates and taxes to the tune of nearly £1 a week for 20 years, and she had been working for citizenship for a number of years"[18]. When sent to Aylesbury Prison for a four-month stretch, Violet immediately went on hunger strike and endured forcible feeding by the authorities.

Please also see the entries for: Mary Sophia Allen, Emily and Mary Blathwayt, Lilian Dove-Wilcox, Elsie Howey, Annie Kenney and Vera Wentworth.

17 *Western Daily Press*, 1910, 19 November, 'Some Local Names'. 12.

18 Elizabeth Crawford, (1999). *The Women's Suffrage Movement: A Reference Guide 1866-1928*. London: University College London Press. 62.

EMILY BLATHWAYT and MARY BLATHWAYT
1852-1940 and 1879-1962, SUFFRAGISTS

Inevitably, the combined ordeals of prison and forcible feeding would take their toll on the suffragettes and when they were released from jail they would need time to recover. Many of these women would go to Eagle House in Batheaston to recuperate as guests of the supportive but peaceful Blathwayt family, whose pro-suffrage activities also included holding open-air meetings on their tennis courts.

In addition to offering rest and respite, Colonel Linley Blathwayt, his wife Emily and daughter Mary created a three-acre Suffragettes' Wood on their land in tribute to their political guests – most notably Yorkshire-woman Annie Kenney (who made her home in Clifton for a number of years), and as such areas in the garden were affectionately known as Annie's Arboretum and Pankhurst Pond. There was also a summerhouse called The Suffragettes' Rest where the women could write speeches, letters or simply relax. Annie Kenney and her sister Jessie, Christabel and Emmeline Pankhurst, Emmeline Pethick Lawrence, Lady Constance Lytton and Theresa Garnett were frequent guests. Many others also enjoyed the Blathwayts' hospitality, although Annie in particular remained a firm favourite of the Blathwayts'. June Hannam notes from Emily's diaries how Linley would always leave some white and purple sweet peas in a green vase (these being the suffragette colours) in Annie's room whenever she came to visit.[19] In turn, Annie noted in her autobiography: "There is just one [family] I should like to mention, that of the late Colonel Blathwayt. He and Mrs Blathwayt, of Eagle House,

19 June Hannam, (2000), 'Suffragettes are Splendid for Any Work: The Blathwayt Diaries as a Source for Suffrage History' in Claire Eustance, Joan Ryan, Laura Ugolini (eds), (2000), *A Suffrage Reader: Charting Directions in British Suffrage History*. London: Leicester University Press. 55.

Batheaston, treated me as though I were one of their own family. All my weekends I spent under their hospitable roof."[20]

The arboretum was a fascinating and unique project that was developed between 1909 and 1912 and saw more than 60 women plant a tree in the specially cultivated plot. Those who had undergone hunger strike and forced feeding were invited to plant a conifer, and non-militant suffragettes planted holly bushes. The planting of each was accompanied by a special ceremony in which the suffragette in question would dress in her finest clothes and her awarded suffrage jewellery. In the Edwardian era, ceremonial tree planting was not uncommon but has there ever been another collective work of feminist landscape design?

These particular ceremonies and the development of the arboretum were diligently documented on camera by Linley, who also ordered iron plaques for each tree or bush to record the date of planting, type of species planted and the name of the woman being honoured. These photos were often sold to raise money for the Women's Social and Political Union's (WSPU) activities. Long forgotten after the arboretum fell to ruin in the middle of the last century, these photographs and many of the plaques were recovered in the attic of Eagle House when it was being prepared for sale and conversion into flats in the 1960s. However, Bath-based historian Dan Brown archived the photos (there are around 250 available to view on the Bath In Time website[21]) in 2002, and in 2011 he curated an exhibition with researcher Cynthia Hammond celebrating the centenary of the Suffragettes' Wood.

Dan and Cynthia's work builds a vivid picture of the creation and destruction of this extraordinary political parkland. That the arboretum was allowed to become overgrown and bulldozed by housing developers is extremely sad. Just one tree remains

20 Ibid. 57.
21 http://www.bathintime.co.uk/search/keywords/blathwayt

Mary Blathwayt illustration by Jenny Howe

today – an Austrian Pine planted by Rose Lamartine Yates of the Wimbledon WSPU who was a guard of honour at Emily Wilding Davison's funeral – and it stands in the middle of a housing development.[22]

Cynthia later carried out an astounding project that she detailed in her 2012 book *Architects, Angels, Activists and the City of Bath*. In this, Cynthia retraces the steps of the suffragettes around Batheaston and Eagle House, and in the process she finds two (now very elderly) women who used to play in the Suffragettes' Wood as children, which enables her to construct a detailed map locating where all the bushes and trees would have stood and the exact location of each of Linley's photographs. Cynthia then attempted to rebuild the arboretum as far as possible, given the fact the site is now a contemporary housing estate. She bought trees and bushes and delivered them to all the residents of the Eagle Park housing development, inviting them to plant and care for the trees in their gardens and letting them know about the history of the site upon which they now live. Cynthia's respect for this task was a powerful gesture of support for the history of women in the United Kingdom.

But what of the Blathwayt family? Linley and Emily retired to Eagle House in Batheaston in 1882 after returning from India, and were closely related to the Blathwayt family who owned the nearby Dyrham Park estate (now a National Trust property and the current location of Emily and Mary's diaries). Their daughter Mary joined the WSPU in July 1906, although she was already a member of the Bath Suffrage Society for which she became Treasurer in 1908. Until 1908 Mary remained a loyal member of both organisations, and would always carry copies of suffrage

22 Three Austrian Pines were planted in Bath in March 2011 in honour of the one surviving tree from the arboretum and of the centenary of the creation of the wood. They can be found at Royal Victoria Park, Alice Park and Newton Park. Dan Brown, Cynthia Hammond, (2011). *Suffragettes in Bath: Activism in an Edwardian Arboretum*. Bath: Bath in Time. 37.

propaganda with her when she visited friends to try and recruit more women to the cause. Mary chalked pavements, ran the WSPU shop, chaired outdoor meetings and attended some of the demonstrations in London. There was also a son, William, who had worked in Germany as an English teacher but returned home to safety on the eve of World War One.

Mary and Annie Kenney became close friends and together they chalked pavements, distributed leaflets and arranged meetings, among myriad other tasks. For a period between May 1908 and October 1909, Mary moved to Clifton to live with Annie and help with her domestic duties and support her as WSPU Organiser for the West Country. Such was Mary's commitment to the WSPU that she renounced her membership of all the other societies that she had previously been involved with, including writing to the Secretary of the Secular Society to say she was not donating any more money because she was solely focussed on suffrage: "When women have votes, I shall be very pleased to subscribe again."[23] Mary only returned to live at Eagle House due to persistent health problems and failing eyesight, which were perhaps symptoms of exhaustion due to her hard work for the suffrage campaign.

Mary's loyalty to Annie was returned and Emily wrote in her diary about the kindnesses Annie would show to Mary to keep her out of trouble: "Annie is always doing kind things without letting people know. M is convinced she sent her off to Swansea so as to be out of the row in Bristol for Mr Birrell's visit, when streets were barricaded against the women. She always promised us to take care of M."[24] Augustine Birrell was the North Bristol

23 June Hannam, (2000), 'Suffragettes are Splendid for Any Work: The Blathwayt Diaries as a Source for Suffrage History' in Claire Eustance, Joan Ryan, Laura Ugolini (eds), (2000), *A Suffrage Reader: Charting Directions in British Suffrage History*. London: Leicester University Press. 56.

24 Ibid. 61.

MP who was staunchly anti women's suffrage.

Despite Annie's best efforts, Mary *was* exposed to some hostility: at one meeting on the Durdham Downs in June 1909, Mary wrote in her diary about how "the young boys sang songs and threw paper at us, and an apple which hit me on the head". And after a public meeting in Weston-super-Mare she recorded how one suffrage supporter had been given a black eye and then a group of men followed them all back to the train station.[25] Mary never took part in any violent activities herself and it was to be the intensification of suffragette militancy that eventually led to the Blathwayts' withdrawal from the WSPU.

On 2 April 1911, Mary's most militant action – albeit a peaceful one – was to avoid the national census count by hiding out in an empty house at 12 Lansdown Crescent, Bath, with 29 other women, which had been led by Bath's WSPU Organiser Mildred Mansel. Census evasion was an acceptable action for peaceful suffragists who wanted to avoid the violence of militancy yet still take a determined stand against the patriarchal government. In her diary entry for 1 April, Mary notes: "I went to Batheaston Villa [home of Aethel and Grace Tollemache] with Miss Cave who fetched a number of green branches for decorating the house in Lansdown Crescent tomorrow night", and her pocket diary adds a reminder to bring a banana and some oranges to the house.[26] What a feast!

Mary's diary entry for the day after the census evasion gives more detail about how the night was spent: "I went into Bath last night by tram and walked to 12 Lansdown Crescent, to spend the night there and so evade the census, as a protest against the Government for not giving us Votes for Women. I got there before

25 Ibid. 61.

26 Jill Liddington, (2014), *Vanishing For the Vote*. Manchester: Manchester University Press. 162.

10 o'clock. A little crowd of people were standing in the next doorway to the east side to watch us go in. I took a nightdress etc with me, and had a room to myself on the first floor and a bed [by this point, Mary was suffering from chronic health problems]. Everyone else slept on mattresses. Mrs Cave arranged everything very well and we had a charming room to hold our meeting, beautifully decorated and very comfortable. There were 29 of us.

"Mrs Mansel took the chair and spoke. Mrs Rogers came over from Bristol and recited, but left again at midnight. Grace Tollemache played the violin and Aethel accompanied on a piano. Mrs Forbes Williams gave a lecture on Clairvoyance but did not stay all night. We had food in the next room. Mrs Berriman and Miss Pavey worked very hard washing up etc. We sat up until 2am this morning. Breakfast 8am. I helped wash up afterward. Some of us went out by the back door as I found the key in a greenhouse."[27]

Mary's parents Emily and Linley complied with the census and Emily recorded her feelings about it in her own diary entry for 2 April 1911: "M went after supper to 12 Lansdown Crescent where Mrs Mansel has taken a house for the Census evaders, as women say they will not be counted if they do not count. M expected there would be about 30 in that empty house. They all subscribe towards the £5 fine [for evading the census] and all take food for the community. M pays for a bed too. She will stay in Bath till after midday. I do not blame women for taking this action. There is no justice with the rulers."[28]

Emily resigned from the WSPU in September 1909 and Mary in June 1913. At the time of her resignation, Emily wrote in her diary: "I shall continue to do what I can to help, but I cannot conscientiously say now that 'I approve of the methods' used by

27 Ibid. 163.
28 Ibid. 162.

several of the members."[29]

Emily and Mary remained in touch with Annie after she moved away from Bristol in 1911, at which point Mary returned to her former interests of swimming and cooking although Emily continued to organise house parties to raise money for the WSPU and to recruit more women to the cause. They kept up a sporadic correspondence with Annie throughout the war, during which Mary was helping the Red Cross, and when Annie married in 1920 the Blathwayts sent her a wedding present.[30] Linley died in 1919 and Emily in 1940. Mary spent the remainder of her life in Eagle House living "quite like a hermit" according to one neighbour[31], until her own death in 1961. At which point Eagle House was sold to developers and the grounds were separated from the house. By this point, the Suffragettes' Wood had become wildly overgrown and it was unforgivably destroyed by bulldozers on 3 August 1965.

Please also see the entries for: Theresa Garnett, Annie Kenney, Emmeline Pethick Lawrence and Aethel and Grace Tollemache.

BARBARA BLAUGDONE

1610-1704, PREACHER, TRAVELLING MISSIONARY

The welcoming smile of the Quaker man on packets of oats does not reflect the reception he might well have received from the population of England when Quakers (or Friends of the Truth) spread their doctrine from 1647. Their black clothing and broad-

29 June Hannam, (2000), 'Suffragettes are Splendid for Any Work: The Blathwayt Diaries as a Source for Suffrage History' in Claire Eustance, Joan Ryan, Laura Ugolini (eds), (2000), *A Suffrage Reader: Charting Directions in British Suffrage History*. London: Leicester University Press. 62.

30 Ibid. 61.

31 Dan Brown, Cynthia Hammond, (2011). *Suffragettes in Bath: Activism in an Edwardian Arboretum*. Bath: Bath in Time. 29.

brimmed hats caused alarm, which grew when many Quakers disrupted church services in an endeavour to spread their faith. But instantly converted, Barbara Blaugdone abandoned the teaching profession and took to the road as a preacher after listening to travelling Quakers who came to Bristol in 1654. The Quakers' unruly behaviour was a threat to the decorum of the Cromwellian state and consequently many Quakers, including Barbara, were repeatedly imprisoned in harsh conditions as they travelled around the country.

Little is known about Barbara's early life except that she was married and taught in Bristol, rubbing shoulders with the well-to-do who disowned her after her conversion. She then travelled mostly around the South West to spread the Quaker ideology. They believed in spiritual equality, although when female Quakers became too radical they were encouraged to become involved in more traditional feminine pursuits. Barbara carried on with little respect for any law by entering churches and preaching. Women were treated just as harshly as men when arrested and were thrown into jail. By her own account Barbara was whipped "til the blood ran down my back" but, undeterred, she continued travelling and was constantly imprisoned for confrontations when preaching. She went on hunger strikes but "fed on the word of the Lord".

Unwelcome under anyone's roof, she had to sleep in barns (even a pigs' trough during winter frosts), leading to arrest for vagrancy. At that time, male vagrants were branded with a 'V' and women were whipped. Not one to give up, and increasingly encouraged by her faith despite all setbacks including being stabbed by a man, Barbara travelled to prisons and spoke up for other imprisoned Quakers to gain their release. Feeling that the Lord "called me forth to labour abroad" she embarked on a missionary trip to Ireland. The tempestuous Irish Sea conditions led the crew to almost throw her overboard after considering her responsible for bringing on the storm. In 1681, she was imprisoned in Bristol for failing to attend the Anglican Church and was fined £60; a huge sum in those days.

Before she died at an incredible 95 years of age, Barbara left a written account of her life, some of which ends this short biography: "And much more could I declare of my Sufferings which I passed through, which I forbear to mention, being not willing to be over-tedious... For many have been the Tryals, Tribulations and Afflictions which I have passed through."

Written by Jacqui Furneaux, who has been exploring the world on the back of her motorbike since 2000. Her memoir *Hit The Road, Jac!* was published in 2017.

HELEN BLOOM

1901-1987, POLITICIAN

Helen Bloom was one of five sisters born to Bristol's Strimer family. Having had a fairly conventional, middle-class upbringing, Helen, Jeanette (later Britton) and Berta (later Sacof) became Labour councillors. In 1971, Helen became Bristol's third female and first Jewish Lord Mayor.

Having joined the Labour Party in 1940, Helen was first elected as a Councillor to the Borough Council for the Avon ward in November 1945. She later represented the St George East ward of Bristol City Council.

For more than 30 years, Helen gave continuous service to the community with a particular interest in health and hospitals. In 1948, she was appointed to the board of United Bristol Hospitals by Aneurin Bevan, who was Minister of Health at the time. She remained a member of the board for the next 26 years. In the mid 1970s, Helen was Vice Chair of the Bristol (Teaching) Community Health Board and she sat on many local, regional and national committees and gave lectures on all aspects of healthcare. She was instrumental in pioneering the establishment of health centres in Bristol, and in 1975 was National President of the Association of Sea and Air Port Authorities. Helen was also Chief Whip of the Labour group in 1974.

As well as her Council duties, Helen served as a Governor of many Bristol schools and of South Bristol College, where a building was named after her. She was subsequently Chair of the West of England College of Art when the new college was built at Ashton Court.

In her private life, Helen was married to Sidney Bloom and they shared a love of travel and the arts, visiting galleries all over the world. They were regular attenders at the Bristol Old Vic. Helen was the first woman to fly in Concorde to Hanover, Germany, and took a great interest in Bristol's twinning with the city and that of Bordeaux, France. She was also a founder member of the Bristol Fabian Society.

Written by Helen Wilde, who was the High Sheriff of Bristol from 2016-2017.

Please also see the entry for: Berta Sacof.

HELENA BORN

1860-1902, SOCIALIST

Describing her political ideas to a friend, socialist Helena Born wrote: "Equality and freedom for women is one phase of an ideal of universal freedom and equality. I have not taken up a new position without thinking it out ... The principles of Socialism as I understand them, seem to me economically incontrovertible, and to comprise spiritual ideals of unity and brotherhood which alone can transmute the materialism of our time. And I feel that the only way to convince others of the truth of one's principles, and to bring about the new times, is by living them ... It is uphill work but we cannot isolate ourselves from the mass."[32]

There were few political causes that Helena did not support. She was an executive member of the Bristol Women's Liberal Association (where she learned to organise), a member of the Bristol Socialist Society, Secretary of the Bristol Strike Committee, and Joint Honorary Secretary of the Bristol Tailoresses' branch of the Bristol District of the National Union of Gasworkers' and General Labourers' of Great Britain and Ireland. Which is something of a mouthful.

By 1889, Bristol was busy with industrial discontent and working women and men across the city were striking with increasing regularity. Keen to see some organisation and coordination among the strikers so that they would achieve the best results, Helena and sister socialist Miriam Daniell worked together to try and help unionise the strikers.

Helena spent a great deal of time searching for new recruits to the trades unions from home workers in the clothing industry who were based around Bristol. Comrade Helen Tufts described how Helena would enthusiastically set out on this gruelling task: "Week after week she laboured hopefully in the good cause. From house to house she passed, striving to arouse interest in the union. It was not an uncommon day's work for her to tramp 30 miles,

32 Ellen Malos, (1983), 'Bristol Women in Action 1839-1919: The Right to Vote and the Need to Earn a Living' in Bristol Broadsides, (1983). *Bristol's Other History*. Bristol: Broadsides. 117-118.

Helena Born and Helen Tufts illustration by Jenny Howe

scouring the country on her self-imposed mission."[33]

In November 1889, the *Western Daily Press* reported on the strike at The Great Western Cotton Factory saying: "This strike remains in about the same position ... Mrs Miriam Daniell (Treasurer) and Miss Helena Born (Secretary) have issued an appeal for help, and this has been sent to all towns in England. They say there are now 1,250 cotton workers, the majority being women, standing out for advanced wages, together with the abolition of vexatious fines. The directors, it is stated, decline to accede [but] the cotton workers shall not be starved into submission."[34]

Helena worked closely with Miriam whom she had met in 1888, and Helena moved from her comfortable Whiteladies Road home to live with Miriam, who had walked out on her husband, in St Phillips among the working-class people they wanted to support. Helena explained: "I feel that the only effectual way to convince others of the truth of one's [socialist] principles, and to bring about the new time, is to live them."[35] The two women lived in an openly lesbian relationship[36] which, although never illegal in the way that male homosexuality was, was still regarded with horror by many. To complicate matters, they also lived with a younger man called Robert Allan Nicol, for whom Miriam had initially left her husband and with whom she was also in a relationship. The trio were on the receiving end of a certain amount of hostility due to their unconventional living arrangements and this ultimately persuaded them to move to a utopian socialist community in the United States.

33 Mike Richardson, (2012). *The Bristol Strike Wave of 1889-1890: Socialists, New Unionists and New Women. Part 2: Days of Doubt.* Bristol Radical Pamphleteer 22. Bristol: Bristol Radical History Group. 6-7.

34 *Western Daily Press*, 1889, 2 November, 'The Labour Movement: The Cotton Workers'. 3.

35 Lorna Brierley, Helen Reid, (2000). *Go Home and Do the Washing!* Bristol: Broadcast. 146.

36 Ellen Malos, (1983), 'Bristol Women in Action 1839-1919: The Right to Vote and the Need to Earn a Living' in Bristol Broadsides, (1983). *Bristol's Other History.* Bristol: Broadsides. 116.

Please also see the entries for: Miriam Daniell and Helen Tufts. For more information about the strikes, please see the Working Women section towards the end of this book.

ROSA BRAIN

dates unknown, NURSE

Staff Nurse Rosa Brain of the Territorial Force Nursing Service in Bristol was awarded the Military Medal for bravery after her efforts in World War One. The medic from Dundry volunteered in 1914 and went on to nurse in France during the war.

On 25 November 1918, the *London Gazette* stated Rosa's medal was "for exceptional courage and devotion to duty during a hostile air raid, when bombs were dropped on the hospital. One of the bombs wrecked the hut in which [Rosa] was on duty, and, with the greatest coolness, she attended to all the patients in the ward, even though she herself was wounded."[37]

Staff Nurse Brain retired from work in 1920 after she married. However, upon her retirement, Queen Alexandra (who was Colonel-in-Chief of the Service) gave Rosa special permission to keep her Territorial Force Nursing Service badge in recognition of her great bravery.[38]

ADELA BRETON

1849-1923, EXPLORER, ARTIST

At the age of 50, after caring for her parents until their deaths, gentlewoman Adela Breton left her comfortable life in Bath for a

37 https://www.thegazette.co.uk/London/issue/31028/supplement/13889/data.pdf
38 *Western Daily Press*, 1935, 14 May, 'News'. 7.

more uncomfortable one in Mexico. For 18 months she travelled the length of the country on horseback with a local guide for company, painting what she saw on the wall paintings from temples and buildings in Chichén Itzá, Teotihuacan and Acancéh, and capturing the archaeological sites with vivid watercolours and unprecedented detail.

Over the following 23 years she made many more trips to the ruins, often camping in remote areas with little access to food, water and human contact. Over time her Mesoamerican work became more scientific and, as well as depictions of archaeological sites, she recorded canyons and volcanoes. By the time of her death she had produced more than 1,500 artworks, bequeathing them to Bristol Museum and Art Gallery in her will. Today the works are incredibly important, with their accurate depiction of the sites meaning they're often used as reference materials for films and academic work.

Adela's interest in archaeology had been sparked during her childhood in Bath, where she became fascinated by the town's Roman ruins. Her family travelled in Europe where her interest grew, and it's likely she studied painting in Florence, Italy. So strong was her conviction that she was meant to travel that she decided not to marry in order to maintain her independence. However, it seems the conventions of the time still stalled her ambitions, and it wasn't until her parents' deaths that Adela was able to realise her dream. Today it seems that one of the many gifts Adela left the world is her example, proving that you're never too old to throw yourself into something completely new.

Written by Amy Mason, who is a novelist, theatre maker and stand-up comedian working in Bristol and London. She is currently creating her third show with Bristol Old Vic.

SARAH ANNE BRIGHT
1793-1866, PHOTOGRAPHER

Photographer and watercolour artist Sarah Anne Bright is believed to have taken the earliest surviving photographs by a woman. However, Sarah's photographs were not attributed to her until 2015 when her initials became visible after the images were viewed under a photogram (a method of exposing photographic images to light which reveals a shadow hidden on the paper). Until 2015, the photographs were incorrectly attributed to a man.

Sarah was born in Bristol and lived here her entire life as the daughter of a wealthy merchant with an interest in science, which was presumably an influence on Sarah. Little else is known about her life, and her role as a photographer was not appreciated until a cache of photos was sold in New York in 2008 that included the 1839 photograph 'The Quillan Leaf'. This botanical image had previously been attributed to William Henry Fox but his authorship was subsequently queried by Fox expert Professor Larry Schaaf.

'The Quillan Leaf' was first sold at Sotheby's in London in 1984 where it fetched £6,000 for Bristolian merchant and MP Henry Bright, who had found it in an album and knew the image had been taken by someone in his family. After years of investigation, Professor Schaaf finally attributed the work to Sarah. Inscriptions on 'The Quillan Leaf' match the handwriting on her watercolours and other material in the Bright archive leaving "little doubt" it was by Sarah, he told *The Independent*.

The same *Independent* article continues: "While many experimented with photography at the time, 'these days we only have a tiny handful of examples, and those like this with a good pedigree and this good condition are very rare,' Professor Schaaf said. He now hopes to explore Sarah Anne's story further. 'I'm hoping to pump some life into her, that's the next step,' he said. Her only portrait is a silhouette, common in 19th-century portraiture. 'It's symbolic as we just have a shadow of who she was.'"[39]

PRINCESS ELEANOR OF BRITTANY

1184-1241, PRISONER

Born in Normandy, Princess Eleanor was orphaned in infancy and was brought up by her grandmother and uncle, King Richard of England (who had offered Eleanor, aged 11, for marriage to a man nearly 40 years her senior; fortunately the marriage never took place).

Following the disappearance of her elder brother Arthur in 1203 (at the hands of their wicked uncle John), Eleanor became the second in line to the throne and the heir to a wealth of land in England, Anjou, Aquitaine and Brittany (where the laws barring the accession of women did not apply, although the majority of men did not support it). This ruffled the feathers of a lot of powerful men who didn't want young Eleanor having all this land and power that they thought should go to a man. After King Richard died, her uncle John muscled in and took the throne for himself.

However, King John had no heirs of his own, so to prevent teenage Eleanor marrying and giving birth to an heir, he had her imprisoned in Bristol Castle from 1203 where she was kept until her death in 1241. As a result of her 39 years of incarceration, Eleanor is the longest-imprisoned member of an English royal family. She was kept in comfortable conditions, despite her confinement, and had fine clothes, servants and even a horse. When *Magna Carta* was signed, stating that King John must

39 http://www.independent.co.uk/arts-entertainment/photography/how-a-170-year-old-leaf-provoked-a-hunt-for-the-world-s-first-photographer-10367441.html

release all of his prisoners, there was a clause that exempted Eleanor from release.[40]

Upon her death, Eleanor had one last moment of victory. Although initially buried in Bristol, she was later moved to Amesbury Abbey in line with her wishes. Given that Amesbury Abbey was dedicated to St Melor, a young prince murdered by his uncle who usurped his right to the throne, it is easy to see the connection and assume that Eleanor was having a final dig at her cruel uncle. Sadly, there is no known grave for her although the remains of Bristol Castle are still visible in Castle Park.

PENNY BROHN and PAT PILKINGTON

1943-1999 and 1928-2013, CANCER CARE PIONEERS

Penny Brohn was born and educated in Bristol and met her husband David while studying sociology at Leeds University. Being married with three small children meant a busy life. David's work took them to live in Hong Kong, China, for a while and it was here that she trained as an acupuncturist. When Penny returned to Bristol she set up a practice and continued to follow her interest in complementary medicine by attending the Healing Centre on Downfield Road in Clifton. And it was here that she first met Pat Pilkington.

Pat and her husband Christopher, the vicar of St Stephen's in Bristol city centre, had long been interested in the church's ancient Ministry of Healing. Together they had established the Healing Centre, not only offering spiritual healing but also a place for alternative therapists and practitioners to meet. This was fertile ground from which much more was to arise.

40 Valerie Pitt, (2015). *Bloody Bristol*. Stroud: The History Press. 12.

Penny's life, already very full, went into overload when, at the end of the 1970s, both of her parents died in quick succession. The stress of these events was followed by her own diagnosis of breast cancer. When Penny was told there was nothing she could do to help heal herself, she declined a full mastectomy and discharged herself from hospital. She and David then left for Bavaria, Germany, where a doctor called Josef Issels was offering a complementary approach to this illness.

As David needed to return home to care for the children, Pat joined Penny and remained with her for the rest of her stay. While in Bavaria two things happened: Penny was able to re-absorb her tumour, and the trip gave Penny and Pat time to plan how to take this kind of support home with them in order to help others. So in 1980, the Bristol Cancer Help Centre was formed at the Healing Centre on Downfield Road. At first there was only a daily phone line but soon the need came for people to visit the Centre. With help from retired surgeon Dr Alec Forbes, the doors opened with Penny and Pat in attendance to support and inform people, along with other fully trained therapists and healers.

Over the next few years, the trickle of visitors became a flow. Around this time a television show aired, *A Gentle Way with Cancer*, publicising the Centre and its work. It became clear there was a need for a larger premises and also a need for a place where people could stay. In 1983 the right property was found in the heart of Clifton: Grove House, a former convent and the property of La Ratraite School. After some refurbishment, Prince Charles opened the new Cancer Help Centre. Soon the first residents came to stay – some for just one night, others for up to a week. This approach proved to be so successful that people came in endless streams, not only from the United Kingdom but also from around the world. This gave the Centre the opportunity to flourish and grow throughout the 1990s.

In the mid 1990s, Penny's cancer returned. Sadly, this was partly bought about by the infamous and devastating Chilvers Report published back in the early 1990s. With Penny having to deal with the negative publicity and media scrutiny, this put a great strain on her mentally and physically. However, she battled on bravely, still continuing to support the Centre right up until her death. Penny died peacefully at home surrounded by her family in 1999.

By this time the Cancer Help Centre was well established. Pat took over, continuing their work with energy and passion. It became apparent that even Grove House was proving to be too small. Eventually the Centre's new home was found just outside Bristol in Pill, North Somerset. This beautiful Georgian Grade II listed house with grounds was perfect. A wing was added to create the many bedrooms and therapy rooms needed. This provided all that was necessary for its continued growth and development.

Now a patron of the Centre, Prince Charles again opened the new building in 2007 and the Centre began its third life cycle. With the larger premises the Centre was able to expand, offering even more help to an even bigger number of people while still keeping the core values at its heart. It is a place where people can come to be shown how they can help themselves, to take responsibility for their own health by using such methods as meditation, healing, counselling, healthy eating, bodywork, art therapy and exercise, all of which are available on the premises. And so the work continues to grow and expand, networking out to other cancer charities and the NHS.

Sadly, Pat died in 2013. With Penny and Pat's inspirational work so deeply woven into the fabric of the staff and building, the Centre continues today with the same energy, offering the same skills, services and support as it always has done. Penny and Pat were two remarkable and inspiring women who transformed cancer care not only in Bristol but also worldwide. How appropriate that the Centre is now called Penny Brohn UK.

Written by Janet Swan, who was one of the founders of the Bristol Cancer Help Centre and later its Senior Healer. Janet had been friends with Penny and Pat since the 1970s.

DOROTHY BROWN

1927-2013, ARCHITECTURAL CAMPAIGNER

The indignities that many Bristol buildings have suffered at the hands of the town planners are widely lamented. But it could have been a heck of a lot worse if it wasn't for Dorothy Brown who became a passionate campaigner to save historic buildings in the city. She was so committed to preserving the grand architecture in Bristol that at the time of her death in October 2013 she was working in Redland Library on yet another campaign.

Born in Berwick-upon-Tweed, Dorothy moved to Bristol in 1954 after marrying her husband Tom. They settled in the city and brought up five children. When she heard about plans in 1970 to build a "monstrous" hotel complex in the Avon Gorge, Dorothy stepped in and launched a campaign to protect the Gorge from the damaging development[41], and the following year she established the Bristol Visual and Environmental Group with a view to tackling Bristol City Council's destructive plans to bulldoze the city's historic buildings and harbour area and replace them with concrete, steel and motorways: a damning proposal that ignored everything except the flow of traffic. Some 400 buildings were scheduled for demolition but because of Dorothy's hard work

41 https://www.arnolfini.org.uk/blog/dorothy-brown-tireless-defender-of-bristol2019s-historic-architecture

almost all of them were saved.[42]

In a letter to the town planners, Dorothy fumed: "I write to you in disgust and indignation, having just seen the shells of the elegant sandstone houses which are being demolished in Clifton Park. I understood that Clifton is some kind of special area and would have thought that demolitions of this type would have required planning permission."[43]

In addition to letters, Dorothy wrote numerous books about the development of Bristol as a city and in 1979 she set up the Conservation Advisory Panel to inform Bristol City Council about future planning decisions. In 1988, she was awarded an MBE for her decades of dedication.

In a piece celebrating Dorothy's achievements, Johanna Darque wrote: "During a time when the residual momentum of Modernism and a prevailing post-war ethic of accelerated redevelopment were driving town planners towards fast, concrete-based development within city centres, Dorothy Brown stood as a bastion of common sense conservation."[44]

Without Dorothy's tireless campaigning, Bristol would look very different to the city we currently know and enjoy.

FLORENCE BROWN

1899-1981, POLITICIAN

Bristol finally saw its first female Lord Mayor when Florence Brown assumed the post in 1963. She had previously been elected as a Labour councillor in 1936, and before that had been a tobacco stripper at the Wills factory in Bedminster. The Florence Brown Community School in Knowle is named in her honour.

42 https://www.theguardian.com/uk-news/2013/nov/04/dorothy-brown-obituary
43 https://www.arnolfini.org.uk/blog/dorothy-brown-tireless-defender-of-bristol2019s-historic-architecture
44 Ibid

Florence Brown illustration by Jenny Howe

MARY BRYAN

dates unknown, PUBLISHER

Following the death of her husband in 1845, Mary Bryan took over his printing press and renamed it Mary Bryan & Co. She ran the business from Corn Street between 1815 and 1823 but was starting from the back foot as her husband had left a lot of debts, meaning Mary – who also had to look after six young children – had to further support her family through writing.[45] However, this was an opportunity for her to print the poems that her husband had forbidden her to publish and she dedicated these poems to the writer Charlotte Smith who had also turned to writing to provide for her own young children.[46] Following Mary's subsequent marriage to a surgeon from the Bristol Infirmary, the newlyweds were disowned by his family who felt that he had made an unwise choice of wife and disinherited him from the family estate. The couple then moved to Suffolk where, as Mrs Mary Bryan Bedingfield, Mary forged a fair career as a novelist.[47]

BARBARA BUCHANAN

1915-2015, JOURNALIST

Journalism has the power to affect real change: a prime example being the work of award-winning journalist Barbara Buchanan, who is widely recognised as influencing a national roll-out of cervical cancer screening – a move that's undoubtedly saved lives.

Living to the impressive age of 100, Buchanan's experience as a Bristol-based journalist saw her working on two of the city's

45 Jacqueline Labbe (ed), (2010). *The History of British Women's Writing, Vol 5*. London: Palgrave Macmillan. 42.

46 Madge Dresser, (2016). *Women and the City: Bristol 1373-2000*. Bristol: Redcliffe Press. 79.

47 Ibid. 79.

main newspapers covering a range of women's and social issues as well as penning a light-hearted regular column, 'Saturday Chatterday'. She was so respected as a health writer that she went on to write for medical journals. Barbara did spend some time as a freelance journalist in London in her 20s but returned to dedicate herself to the city she grew up in.

Joining the Bristol *Evening World* newspaper as the first female trainee reporter in 1933, Barbara rose through the ranks to become Women's Editor – a position she maintained until the paper closed in 1962. She went on to work as a Feature Writer with the *Bristol Evening Post*. It was through her regular features here that she received the title of Woman Journalist of the Year in 1967 for covering "many of the major social problems of the day".

Barbara became a widow during World War Two when her first husband John Danvers-Williams died at the age of 32. She was left to raise two young sons on her own; six-year-old Charles and baby Quentin. Barbara once boasted that she took her typewriter into the hospital when she gave birth so that she could carry on working. She went on to marry the Dutch-born aircraft engineer Jan Breyer but kept the name Buchanan for work.

Speaking after her death in 2015, former *Bristol Post* colleague Quita Morgan said: "Barbara was a great role model for me and dozens more female journalists who have followed in her West Country wake. She was feisty ahead of her time, and rightly proud of her journalistic credentials."

And another thing... Rumour has it that Barbara once flung a glass full of beer over a drunken and obnoxious Dylan Thomas in a London bar.

Written by Laura K Williams, who is a Bristol-based journalist and editor, and founding member and trustee of Baby Bank Network: a women-led charity that provides baby essentials to families in need.

GEORGINA BUDGETT
1860-1944, WAR SHERO

As a rich grocer's wife from Stoke Bishop, Georgina Budgett muddled along perfectly quietly until World War One broke out… at which point she came into her own as Secretary of the Bristol Red Cross. Georgina was responsible for a massive fundraising drive and, by the end of the war, she had helped secure more than £40,000 as well as in excess of 1,000 weekly Red Cross parcels being sent to Bristolians held in prison camps. The Red Cross parcels were Georgina's invention. In this way, she helped save hundreds of lives. When the war ended, Georgina was invited to give a speech to 1,100 returning soldiers but she was interrupted before she could begin talking by a captain calling out for "three cheers for our fairy godmother" and the men responded by cheering until they had all but lost their voices.[48]

ROSA BURDEN
1873-1939, SCIENTIST

If you have ever driven down the M32 heading out of Bristol and wondered what that grand yellow house on the top of a hill near Purdown is, wonder no more. The Dower House (as the yellow building is formally known) has been in situ in one form or another since 1553 and in 1909 it changed from residential to institutional use becoming Burden's Stoke Park Colony for Mental Defectives. It evolved in 1939 to become the Burden Neurological Institute, which was a home for people with learning difficulties and

48 Eugene Byrne, (2014), '"Three Cheers for our Fairy Godmother!": Bristolians and Voluntary Work' in Bristol2014, *Bristol and the First World War*. Bristol: Bristol Cultural Development Partnership. 70.

mental health problems. The Dower House remained in medical use until 1988 when it was converted into the flats it currently is.

Rosa Burden, whose husband Reverend Harold Nelson Burden had owned the lease on the building since 1909, was the Superintendent of the Colony, which with more than 1,500 inmates was the country's largest colony of 'mental defectives' (a catch-all term that included everyone from alcoholics to schizophrenics). After her husband's death she founded the Burden Neurological Institute and repurposed the building, turning it into an independently funded research unit specialising in the human nervous system and human neurological disorders, as well as clinical and experimental neuroscience. Although Rosa died a few months after the Institute opened, it was left in the hands of director Frederick Golla to carry out her work. It was at the Burden Neurological Institute that Britain's first psychosurgical operations were carried out, as were the first British experiments with electroconvulsive therapy (ECT).

Testimonials from former patients at the Institute are unfortunately largely unfavourable about their experiences of ECT and the damaging effects this had on them throughout the rest of their lives. However, it is important to recognise the significance of Rosa and the Institute on early mental health treatment and how at the time what they were doing was considered revolutionary.

Please also see the entry for: Angela Rodaway.

FANNY BURNEY
1752-1840, NOVELIST

My favourite sentence about 18th century novelist and diarist Fanny Burney is that she educated herself by "omnivorous reading at home"[49]*. It brings to mind a remark made by a certain Mr Darcy to a certain Miss Bennett, which is – it turns out – more than an apt association. The title of Jane Austen's most famous novel,* Pride and Prejudice, *is likely from Fanny's second novel* Cecilia*. The younger Jane was reportedly a fan. And Fanny, some claim, paved the way for Ms Austen.*

Frances Burney was born in King's Lynn, Norfolk, in 1752, though moved with her family to Soho, London, in 1760. Culture touched her from an early age. Her father, the musician Charles Burney, threw soirées attended by some of England's finest literary and musical talents, including Dr Johnson and Edmund Burke. Fanny started a journal at 14 and shared her writing with her father's friend Samuel Crisp, who was to become her mentor.

Fanny had a particular talent for social observation. Her first novel, *Evelina, or The History of a Young Lady's Entrance into the World* (1778), was a huge success and is still considered her greatest novel. An epistolary 'novel of manners' based between London and Hotwells, it charts the development of a young girl who uncertainly enters society, makes mistakes but ends up in a happily ever after marriage. Although Fanny, 26, published the novel anonymously, her identity leaked out and she soon became the toast of society. Her second novel, *Cecilia, or Memoirs of an Heiress,* was published in 1782, again to great acclaim.

Fanny continued her journal writing, and in 1785 got an opportunity to observe life at the highest echelons of society. She was recruited as Second Keeper of the Robes to Queen Charlotte

49 https://www.britannica.com/biography/Fanny-Burney

(the Queen's dresser). Despite the great honour the appointment represented, Fanny was unhappy with regimented court life[50] and in 1791 retired on the grounds of ill-health.

In 1793, at 41, Fanny married for love, to impoverished and Catholic French aristocrat Alexandre d'Arblay. They had one son. In 1796 she published her third novel, *Camilla: or A Picture of Youth*, and built a house – 'Camilla's Cottage' – with the profits. After ten years living in France, they moved to Bath and in 1814 Fanny published her final novel: *The Wanderer, or Female Difficulties*. Though it was her least popular work – *The Edinburgh Review* claimed women didn't have problems that made interesting fiction – its focus on the hardships women faced in the pursuit of independence arguably makes it her most interesting work: "Burney was one of the earliest female authors to get mansplained by a famous critic."[51] After Alexandre's death in 1818, Fanny returned to London. She died in 1840, three years after her son's death. Her journals and letters were published posthumously.

My second favourite sentence about Fanny Burney is that she was considered "the least promising of the clever Burney children"[52]. Yet look at what she achieved. Marrying who she wanted, being an older mother, turning her back on royalty, inspiring "England's favourite author" Jane Austen[53], a feminist before feminism existed... And all at a time when reading novels was considered inappropriate for women, let alone writing them.

Written by Caroline Bolhoven, who is a short story writer and book lover from Bristol.

Please also see the entry for: Anne Yearsley.

50 http://www.bbc.co.uk/legacies/work/england/berkshire/article_1.shtml
51 http://flavorwire.com/442262/the-50-greatest-british-novels-of-the-19th-century
52 https://www.britannica.com/biography/Fanny-Burney
53 https://www.janeausten.co.uk/

JOSEPHINE BUTLER
1828-1906, CONTAGIOUS DISEASES ACTS REPEALER

The story of how a Victorian and Christian woman comes to be the figurehead of a campaign to overturn a cruel and patriarchal Act to vilify women who sold sex for money is a fascinating one.

Grieving the tragic death of her six-year-old daughter who had fallen down a flight of stairs (an accident that she said haunted her every single day for the rest of her life), Josephine Butler was desperate for something to occupy her mind and took up charity work at a workhouse in Liverpool. This was far from her first good deed, though. Early in her marriage, Josephine had been affected by the story of a young woman who was imprisoned for murdering her baby, which had been fathered by a married university don who had abandoned the woman and their unborn baby. Incensed that the young girl was in prison and the father was walking free, Josephine gave the woman a job in her home as a maid when she was released from prison. Unlike almost everyone else, Josephine did not see the woman as a sinner but as a victim of male behaviour.[54]

Many of the women in the workhouse had been prostitutes and, struck by their situation, Josephine fundraised to set up a refuge for these women away from the workhouse and to provide them with training schemes to find alternative employment. Unlike other middle-class do-gooders who visited the workhouse, the immaculate and pristine Josephine was not repulsed by the women she met there: "The girls and women incarcerated [in the workhouse jail] were not pretty specimens. They were dirty, dishevelled and very often diseased and yet Josephine Butler not only allowed herself to be touched but touched first. More than

54 Margaret Forster (1984), 'Josephine Butler' in *Significant Sisters: Active Feminism 1839-1939*. London: Secker & Warburg. 175.

one prostitute remembered how amazed and even shocked she was when Mrs Butler took her in her arms and held her tenderly and kissed her kindly."[55]

By 1867, Josephine was campaigning for equal education rights for women, and was organising public lectures for women that would help equip them to sit exams at the prestigious Cambridge University. Her belief was that a lack of training and a substandard education drove some women to sell sex for money, and she lamented the double standards that made it acceptable for a man to buy a prostitute's services but execrable for a woman to work as a prostitute. As Margaret Forster writes: "It seemed clear to [Josephine] that *all* women were debased by [the Contagious Diseases Acts], that the very notion of womanhood was viciously attacked. In them the buying and selling of the female body was sanctified by statute law and the whole position of women in society was degraded."[56]

Josephine identified two recurring scenarios that typically led the women into the sex trade. Either they were a domestic servant who had been seduced by a master at the house and had been sacked when she had become pregnant or the liaison discovered. Or she was a shop worker who needed to subsidise her tiny income in order to eat. In neither scenario did the women want to be prostitutes. During her time with the women from the workhouse, Josephine had gone with them to the Liverpool Docks where they prostituted themselves and saw for herself the skeletal young women hanging around in alleys, backyards and gin shops trying to make some money to stay alive: "It was a world as far away as it was possible to get from the popular image of the prostitute as an ease-loving, sex-loving vamp lolling back

55 Ibid. 178.
56 Ibid. 170.

Josephine Butler illustration by Jenny Howe

among the silks and satins of a boudoir bought with her body."[57]

But in 1869 something significant happened: the third part of the Contagious Diseases Act (CDA) was passed, which increased the scope of the previous two Acts. The CDA had been introduced in the 1860s in an effort to control the spread of sexually transmitted diseases among soldiers and sailors; it was essentially an effort to protect men from 'unclean' women. Under the Act, the police could imprison in a lock hospital for a period of three months any woman suspected of prostitution, during which time she would be forced to undergo horrific and invasive internal examinations. Notably, it was almost exclusively working-class, poor women who were targeted by the CDA. Josephine was told first-hand what happened to a woman suspected of prostitution and taken to a lock hospital (*note to the reader, what follows is pretty graphic and unpleasant so feel free to skip to the next paragraph*): "She was put on a surgical couch, her legs parted by clamps, her ankles tied in leather stirrups, and then held down while surgical instruments, dipped in boiling water, were used to inspect her. If she struggled a strait jacket was always at hand for use. Sometimes, if a girl was not only diseased but a virgin the inspection would rupture her hymen and produce a flood of blood. Then, she was usually told she was a good girl and given five shillings to buy herself a hot dinner."[58] If the woman was pregnant, the invasive examination could cause a miscarriage. And it was not unknown for a woman to pass out with pain during the procedure.

Josephine pointed out that if the women were 'unclean' it was because men had made them so and that the men were deserving of punishment as much as the women were. She also objected to the brutal examination, which she referred to as "surgical rape"[59],

57 Ibid. 179.
58 Ibid. 189.
59 Ibid. 200.

which was not only barbaric for the woman being examined but also potentially traumatising for the doctor carrying out the procedure. Her arguments fell on deaf male ears. But women heard her.

Bristol began what would become a national fight to overturn the CDA when Josephine was invited to speak at the inaugural meeting of the National Association for the Repeal of the Contagious Diseases Act in the city. It should be stated that Josephine was not the first woman to campaign against the CDA; Harriet Martineau had also taken a stand and written a number of articles in the national newspapers protesting the CDA. Various eminent male doctors had also expressed their horror at what was happening, one of whom was Daniel Cooper, who initially called the meeting in Bristol to which Josephine had been invited to speak. As Margaret Forster writes: "The impact of this elegant, lovely, utterly virtuous, upper middle-class married lady earnestly talking about prostitution was devastating. Men she addressed individually on the subject of 'natural urges' hardly knew where to put themselves."[60] As part of her work in Bristol, Josephine became good friends with women such as Mary Estlin, Mary and Anna Maria Priestman, Margaret Tanner and Mrs Charles Thomas, as well as the redoubtable Sturge sisters, whom Josephine called a "corps d'elite".[61]

As a consequence of her speech, a small group of driven women launched a national campaign to repeal the CDA, something that women of their class were not even supposed to know anything about. However, Bristol doctor Elizabeth Blackwell was the only woman allowed to attend subsequent debates about the CDA because, under archaic rules, only medical professionals were able to join the debates. However, Josephine remained a

60 Ibid. 200.

61 Lorna Brierley, Helen Reid, (2000). *Go Home and Do the Washing!* Bristol: Broadcast. 63.

key and charismatic figure in the fight to abolish the abhorrent CDA, which was finally suspended in 1882 after a 20-year fight. However, the Moral Reform Union still needed tackling, which sought to prosecute the men who purchased the sexual services of women.

Josephine had endured a long and exhausting battle and her work left her exhausted both mentally and physically, and she experienced health problems due to the stress. In February 1868 she wrote to a friend: "I am nearly blind with the pain behind my eyes."[62] Pimps and brothel owners in particular targeted her, and at one point a hotel she was staying in was attacked and she was driven out to stay elsewhere. Unusually for the era, her supportive husband George helped to ease his wife's burden by taking on several of the domestic tasks that were traditionally seen as a woman's responsibility and by actively helping out with their children.

Everything Josephine saw made her adamant that the sooner women had the vote, the sooner things would change for the better and, as early as 1873, she wrote to a friend to say that if she was not already working wholeheartedly to repeal the CDA she would be working wholeheartedly to fight for the vote.[63]

Once the CDA was abolished, Josephine turned her attention to tackling the gangs who used seemingly kindly women to trick homeless teenage virgins of 13 (the age of consent at this time) or younger into going home to tea with them... only to be drugged and raped by men to whom the gang had prostituted the children. Josephine worked with former sex worker Rebecca Jarrett to expose this awful business and they published their findings in a newspaper. As a result of their investigations and the ensuing

62 Margaret Forster (1984), 'Josephine Butler' in *Significant Sisters: Active Feminism 1839-1939*. London: Secker & Warburg. 180.
63 Ibid. 200.

publicity, the age of consent was raised to 16 in the Criminal Law Amendment Act of 1885.

In May 1928, long after Josephine had died, a special event was held at the Colston Hall to mark 100 years since her birth and the immense efforts she had made for less-fortunate women. Reporting on the event, the *Western Daily Press* wrote: "Miss Josephine Butler had splendid weapons to fight with. She had brains, great belief in the spirit that supported her, she had beauty and what was almost the most important, she had heard the trumpet call justice." It continued: "She fought for all her reforms on the grounds of justice, not sentiment, asking not for preferential treatment for women, but for equal treatment ... Her most remarkable trait was an absolute lack of bitterness against men."[64]

Please also see the entries for: Mary Blackwell, Ellen Cullinane, Mary Estlin, Anna Maria and Mary Priestman and Margaret Tanner.

CLARA BUTT

1873-1936, SINGER

National treasure Clara Butt moved with her family to live at 3 Sydney Terrace, Totterdown, in 1880. While attending the Bath Road Academy, young Clara took singing lessons and was trained to become a soprano. However, after hearing the contralto Belle Cole perform at the Colston Hall, Clara was pleased to discover she could also sing in that register as well as soprano.

Such was her talent that by 12 years old, Clara was being taught by Bristol's finest singing teacher Daniel Rootham (who

64 *Western Daily Press*, 1928, 5 May, 'Most Difficult Battle a Woman Ever Waged'. 9.

would later teach Eva Turner). Daniel famously said: "You've got gold in your throat, my child"[65] and worked hard to secure her a place at the Royal College of Music in London and build Clara's career. A judge who heard Clara's college audition later said: "I knew that even in its immature state it was the most beautiful contralto voice I had ever heard in all my long experience."[66]

Clara's career skyrocketed after this and she became famous all around the world but she never forgot her connections to Bristol, not least because her family still lived here and she continued to send money home to them. She also returned to perform in the city whenever she could and when she married baritone Robert Kennerley Rumford in 1900 the ceremony was held at Bristol Cathedral. On her wedding day, when seven-year-old Ivor Novello was one of her page boys, Clara was presented with a diamond brooch bearing the initials 'CB' (to represent both 'City of Bristol' and 'Clara Butt') by the city, which can now be seen in the Bristol Museum and Art Gallery on Queens Road. Clara was made a Dame in 1920 after having worked tirelessly for the war effort between 1914 and 1918.

Please also see the entry for: Eva Turner.

LADY BYRON

1792-1860, PHILANTHROPIST

Upon her marriage to the famed poet Lord Byron, Anne Isabella Millbanke of County Durham became known as Lady Byron. As a well-educated and religious woman, it had seemed an unlikely match when she married the agnostic and amoral poet in 1815...

65 Lorna Brierley, Helen Reid, (2000). *Go Home and Do the Washing!* Bristol: Broadcast. 106.
66 Ibid. 107.

and true enough, theirs was not a happy marriage.

Lord Byron was already a successful and admired poet at the time he met his future wife, who wrote to her mother to say that she saw it as her religious obligation to improve his morality and general bad behaviour. But she was not thanked for this gesture. Lord Byron was virtually destitute by the time of the marriage because he had managed his finances so carelessly, he drank heavily and he repeatedly cheated on his wife even during her pregnancy with their daughter Ada Lovelace. It didn't take long after this for the marriage to completely disintegrate, although Lady Byron remained obsessed with trying to save her ex-husband's soul until his death in 1824.

Lady Byron continued to do good deeds throughout the remainder of her life. One of these good deeds was to purchase the Red Lodge on Park Row, which she then gave to Mary Carpenter to use as a girls' reformatory school. Mary had wanted to open an institution for troubled young girls from poor homes that was an alternative to the harsh environments of the workhouses and the Red Lodge was her solution. The Red Lodge remained in use as a school until 1917.

And another thing... Lord and Lady Byron's daughter, Ada Lovelace, is widely believed to have been the first-ever computer programmer, although a 'computer' was called an 'analytical engine' back then. Ada Lovelace Day continues to be held annually to celebrate the achievements of women and girls in STEM subjects (Science, Technology, Engineering and Mathematics).

Please also see the entry for: Mary Carpenter.

PRINCESS ELDORIS CAMPBELL
1939-2015, NURSE, CAMPAIGNER

In the 1950s, the United Kingdom was experiencing a shortage of workers as it struggled to rebuild its economy post-war. Many people from Commonwealth countries responded by moving to the United Kingdom in search of a better life for themselves, despite the volume of discrimination they experienced on arrival. One such immigrant was Princess Eldoris Campbell from Kingston, Jamaica, who moved to Bristol in 1962.

Princess's original plan had been to spend just five years in the UK before returning to Jamaica but once her family had also moved over to England she ended up staying in Bristol for the rest of her life, working to challenge the discrimination and prejudice that she experienced.

On arrival in Bristol, Princess took a job at the Wills tobacco factory in Bedminster, becoming the first-ever black person to work for the company. After two years working for Wills, she decided to begin training as a nurse and after qualifying she started work at the Glenside Hospital in Fishponds.

Speaking of the racism she experienced at this time, Princess said: "The English nurses would have the easiest jobs. We, the black nurses, would be in the sluice cleaning bedpans and vomit boards. You couldn't complain because the ward sister made a report. You had to put up or shut up."[67]

While many other black nurses felt pushed out of their posts and left, Princess put up a fight and stayed. She applied for the post of ward sister but the position went to the other candidate: a younger, less-qualified and less-experienced nurse who was white. Not one to accept this discrimination, Princess lodged a

67 http://www.bbc.co.uk/news/uk-england-bristol-34530130

complaint and finally received an apology. Two years later she became the first black ward sister not only at Glenside Hospital but anywhere in Bristol. Princess continued to work in nursing until her retirement in the 1990s.

During her decades in Bristol, Princess became a well-known and respected activist and campaigner. One of her achievements included setting up the United Housing Association, which helped black people who experienced discrimination when looking for affordable accommodation. She was also a part of the management committee for the Malcolm X Community Centre in St Paul's and was Chair of the Golden Agers Club in Easton, both of which were established specifically to support older people from the African-Caribbean community. And as a member of the Bristol Older People's Forum, Princess was directly involved in the campaign to secure free bus passes for the over-60s. Quite rightly, in 2011 she was honoured with an MBE.

Princess's message was clear and concise – to respect yourself and others: "Use determination and your self-esteem; value yourself and let no one crush you. When you come up against challenges and adversity, don't run away; stay and fight if you want to change things. Education is a most powerful tool and it opens doors."[68]

Please also see the entries for: Carmen Beckford and Leotta Goodridge.

68 https://www.sgsts.org.uk/SupportForVulnerablePupils/EMTAS/Shared%20Documents/Princess%20Campbell.pdf

PRINCESS CARABOO
1791-1864, HOAXER

I first heard about Princess Caraboo when I was in my 20s and was immediately fascinated by this resourceful, creative young woman who audaciously clawed herself out of poverty and escaped her tragic past.

Perhaps I felt a kind of kinship with her. I was depressed, on benefits and living in Bedminster (where she ended up). I even found out that for a while she'd lived a few doors away from my previous home in London – 200 years apart. I became a serious Caraboo fan, visiting the site of her final home (on Princess Street in Bedminster, where there's a blue plaque), her unmarked grave in Hebron Burial Ground and her portrait in Bristol Museum and Art Gallery. I told her story to everyone I could.

In 1817, a cobbler in Almondsbury met a confused young woman wearing unusual clothes, including a turban, and speaking a language he couldn't understand. Worried, he took her to the local magistrate, Samuel Worrall. They spent ages looking for someone who could understand her language until eventually a Portuguese sailor claimed that he could. The sailor explained that her name was Princess Caraboo, that she came from the island Javasu in the Indian Ocean and that she had been captured by pirates before swimming ashore and finding herself in Bristol.

Hearing she was foreign royalty, the magistrate took her back to his home on the Knole Park Estate. She amazed him and his wife with her behaviour: sleeping on the floor, praying to her God ('Allah Tallah'), swimming naked, shooting a bow and arrow, and using her unknown language consistently for ten weeks. During this time she was introduced to loads of important people, was studied by doctors and linguists, and even dressed up for the portrait that now hangs in Bristol Museum and Art Gallery.

It was this unprecedented fame that eventually undid

Princess Caraboo illustration by Jenny Howe

Princess Caraboo. A drawing of her was published in the *Bristol Journal* and she was recognised by a boarding-house keeper who had known her in the past (when she was Mary Wilcocks). Confronted by the Worralls, Caraboo confessed everything. She had been desperately poor and discovered that pretending to be foreign helped when she was begging. Things had spiralled out of control. Wonderfully, instead of kicking her out in disgrace, the Worralls sent her to America to do a theatrical tour in character as Caraboo. She came back to Bristol and did the same tour in the United Kingdom. There's not much written about her life after that. Except that she married (becoming Mary Baker), had a daughter and ended up in Bedminster where she made a living selling leeches to Bristol Royal Infirmary.

There were things that Mary didn't tell the Worralls about her life before creating the persona of Princess Caraboo. People she had worked for talked about her strange tales, outrageous behaviour and periods of depression. Her parents said she became manic every spring and autumn (which is common with bipolar disorder), and records show that she had given birth to a child who died at a foundling hospital; too poor to keep him, Mary had visited the child weekly until he died. It was soon after this tragedy that she made her way to Bristol and changed her life forever in the most bizarre and wonderful way as the legendary Princess Caraboo.

Written by Amy Mason, who is a novelist, theatre maker and stand-up comedian working in Bristol and London. She is currently creating her third show with Bristol Old Vic.

MARY CARPENTER
1807-1877, EDUCATIONALIST, PHILANTHROPIST

Now portrayed as one of Bristol's most revered adopted daughters, Mary Carpenter is best remembered as pioneering educational provision for the poor and as a tireless campaigner for the more humane treatment of young offenders and child workers. She actively influenced government policy to these ends but her passion for reform also involved her in humanitarian campaigns in the United States and India.

Born in 1807 in Exeter to Lant Carpenter, a Unitarian Minister, and Anna Penn, a supervisor of a school for girls, Mary moved to Bristol with her family at the age of 10. She was the eldest of six children and at age 20 left the city to work as a governess until returning in 1829 to help her mother and sisters run a ladies' school on Great George Street.

Being a Unitarian (which was theologically radical enough to challenge the divinity of Christ), Mary was predisposed to the cause of rational reform and public service. She took an interest in the condition of the poor, especially in the area around the Unitarian chapel at Lewins Mead. By 1846, she established the city's first 'ragged school for poor children', initially in the slums of Lewins Mead and then in St James's Back.

As a reformer and non-conformist, Mary would not have seen herself as part of Bristol's old Anglican mercantile ruling class. Nor would she, as an unmarried woman in the public sphere, have been fully accepted by the professional men and manufacturers who increasingly came to dominate Bristol's newly reformed Town Council. Her hands-on experience with some of the most deprived and reviled people in the city led her to become a serious researcher about poverty, reading government reports, gathering her own data on social conditions, and ultimately publishing influential reports on child labour, the education of poor children and the treatment of 'juvenile delinquents'.

At a time when young offenders were characterised as 'street Arabs' who should be punished for their crimes, Mary focussed on the violence and deprivation affecting such children and set up the nation's first Reform Schools, with one in 1852 in Kingswood for boys and another in 1854 for girls, in what is now the Red Lodge Museum on Park Row.

Mary's Unitarianism distinguished her in some respects from the more reactionary and ethnocentric excesses of Victorian evangelicalism. She was heavily involved in the American anti-slavery movement and helped to host the former slave and eloquent abolitionist campaigner Frederick Douglass, who spoke in Bristol in 1847. Later in life, Mary lobbied for the better treatment of native Americans.

Mary's friends and supporters included leading feminists and she was a bright light in the campaign for the Repeal of the Contagious Diseases Acts (these Acts allowed for the rounding up and forcible medical examination of any woman suspected of being a prostitute; please see the entry for Josephine Butler for more information). Her involvement in this campaign took some courage, given that 'respectable women' were not supposed to discuss such subjects as venereal disease. Yet she did not publicly identify as a suffragist until a month before her death in Bristol when "...she added her voice to the cause, speaking at a meeting of the Bristol and West of England Society for Women's Suffrage".

Influenced by Raja Rammohun Roy, the Bengali reformer who had come to Bristol when Mary was in her mid-20s, Mary subsequently developed a passionate lifelong interest in India, forging friendships and working partnerships with Indian progressives, and working for women's education and prison reform there. From the late 1860s, Mary travelled to India three

Mary Carpenter illustration by Carrie Love

times visiting schools and prisons, and hosted two Hindu pupils in Bristol before her death in 1877.

And another thing... Writing about her experiences working with Mary at the ragged school, her friend Frances Power Cobbe said: "It was a wonderful spectacle to see Mary Carpenter sitting patiently before the large school gallery in St James's Back, teaching singing and praying with the wild street boys, in spite of endless interruptions caused by such proceedings as shooting marbles at any object behind her, whistling, stamping, fighting, shrieking out Amen in the middle of the prayer and sometimes rising en masse and tearing like a troop of bisons in hobnailed shoes down the gallery, around the great schoolroom and into the street. These irrepressible outbreaks she bore with infinite good humour."[69]

Written by Dr Madge Dresser, FRHistS and FRSA, who is Visiting Senior Research Fellow at the University of the West of England and Honorary Professor in Historical Studies at the University of Bristol. She is the editor and co-author of *Women and the City: 1373-2000*.

Please also see the entries for: Frances Power Cobbe, Rosamund and Florence Davenport Hill, Eliza Walker Dunbar, Elizabeth Sturge, Anna Thomas and Catherine Winkworth.

69 Frances Power Cobbe (1842) in 'The Modern Review', cited in Helen Reid, (2005). *Life in Victorian Bristol*. Bristol: Redcliffe Press. 44.

ANGELA CARTER

1940-1992, NOVELIST

Angela Carter is one of the most important and imaginative writers of the 20th century. Her well-known book *The Bloody Chamber* (1979) is taught widely in schools and universities and she has a worldwide following. Angela published novels, short stories, poetry and journalism and wrote for other media, including radio, film and television. Renowned for her fiction, a unique blend of fantasy, gothic, magic realism and feminism, Angela's writing career started and thrived in Bristol, where she lived with her husband Paul Carter from 1961 until 1969.

During the 1960s, Bristol was undergoing radical change both architecturally and culturally. It was a happening place, attracting writers and artists, yet early on for Angela, life as a bored housewife felt like living in a museum, where she complained of being unable to access the exciting things going on. A remedy for this lay in writing and studying. Besides creative writing, she produced pieces of journalism for the *Western Daily Press* and, in 1962, enrolled on an English degree at the University of Bristol. After graduating, she studied art up the road at the College of Art attached to the Royal West of England Academy.

Angela was engaged with the folk scene revival, which led to her establishing the Ballads and Broadsides folk club at The Bear in Hotwells with Paul, who was a producer for Topic Records. After leaving Bristol, her keen interest in folk song was transposed into another oral tradition, the folk tale, as indicated by her collections of fairy tales. In July 1962, she published her first work of fiction, 'The Man Who Loved A Double Bass', in *Storyteller* magazine, as the winner of a short story competition. Her poetry and earliest novels were also published while living in Bristol.

Angela's first novel, *Shadow Dance* (1966), is one of three set in the city, known as the Bristol trilogy, and these contain familiar landmarks. In *Shadow Dance*, a character views artefacts still seen today at Bristol Museum and Art Gallery, while *Several Perceptions* (1968) has a plot involving the Downs and Clifton Zoo, where Angela was employed for a short time. *Love* (1971) opens and closes in Brandon Hill Park with its Gothic Cabot Tower, and recreates the exotic Mecca Grand Locarno ballroom, where she worked for a while as a waitress.

The Carters lived at Royal York Crescent in Clifton, occupying the ground-floor flat of number 38, until July 1969 when they moved a few doors down to the fifth-floor flat of number 27. A sense of how run-down the area had become is conveyed in her Bristol trilogy with its dismal urban environment of boarded up shops, broken windows and junk shops. The dystopian *Heroes and Villains* (1969), populated by communities of Professors and Barbarians, is another novel written in Bristol and likely to have been inspired by Angela's student days. Through her clothes and the hallucinogenic surrealism of her prose, she captured the flamboyance of the hippy era.

Angela gained recognition for the books she published while living in the city. For *Several Perceptions*, she was awarded the Somerset Maugham Prize and, for her second novel, *The Magic Toyshop* (1967, film version 1987), she received the John Llewellyn Rhys Prize. The prize money enabled Angela to go to Japan, leaving behind her marriage, the folk scene and Bristol, the place where her writing career began and where it had flourished.

Written by Professor Marie Mulvey-Roberts, who lectures at the University of the West of England. She has written widely on Angela Carter and in 2016/2017 she curated a Carter exhibition at the Royal West of England Academy.

HILDA CASHMORE
1876-1943, EDUCATIONALIST

Born six miles north of Bristol at Norton Malreward Court, as a teenager Hilda Cashmore's eyes were opened to the privileged Quaker upbringing she was afforded compared to some of the less-fortunate people in the area. Hilda brought her philanthropic spirit to Bristol in 1901, when Marian Pease invited her to work at the Training College for Women Teachers. Hilda became the history teacher at the college for the next seven years.

Once the Barton Hill University Settlement was established in 1911, Hilda became its first warden and made child welfare her priority. The doors at the Settlement were kept open for the community to come and go as they wished, and toys (such as a rocking horse and a dolls' house) that were normally only to be found in wealthy homes were made available for the working-class children to play with while their parents studied in adjacent rooms.

Hilda stayed with the Settlement until 1926. During World War One, she helped Belgian refugees before travelling onwards to Poland to assist those affected by the war. In the mid-1930s, she spent four years living in India. Towards the end of her life, Hilda returned to Bristol and made her home at 107 Church Road, Redfield. The Cashmore House flats and the Cashmore Nursery are so named in her honour.[70]

Please also see the entries for: Marian Pease and Mabel Tothill.

70 With thanks to the Bristol Radical History Group: http://www.bhhg.co.uk/showfiles.php?files=Hilda+Cashmore+1934

ELIZABETH CASSON

1881-1954, DOCTOR

Bristol has no shortage of pioneering female doctors and Elizabeth Casson must be included in that category. Elizabeth, who was the first woman to obtain a doctorate from the University of Bristol, bought and established Dorset House on the Promenade, Clifton Down, for the treatment of mental illness: which was even less well understood then than now. Elizabeth favoured holistic and homeopathic treatments, and the internationally acclaimed Dorset House School of Occupational Therapy in Oxford is named in recognition of the work that Elizabeth began at Dorset House in Bristol.

However, it was nearly the case that medicine eluded Elizabeth. Her family was not a wealthy one and, initially wanting to be a teacher but being unable to afford the fees, young Elizabeth attended secretarial college so she could work for her father and later for housing reformer Octavia Hill, from whom she learned a great deal about the management of slum properties. So it was not until she was 30 that Elizabeth was able to begin studying medicine, having studied for her matriculation exams during the evenings while continuing to work as a secretary during the day. Elizabeth finally graduated in 1919 at the age of 38.

She specialised in psychiatry and worked in a variety of sanatoriums where she gained a wide experience of mental illness, going on to win the Gaskell Prize and Gold Medal in psychological medicine in 1927. Elizabeth returned to Bristol in 1920, at a time when mentally ill patients were either housed in an asylum or, if wealthy, a private nursing home. Realising there was a need for something else, Elizabeth bought the four-storey Dorset House, where she kept the windows and doors unlocked and allowed her patients the freedom they were denied in the asylums. How did she get the money to buy Dorset House? Elizabeth asked her actor brother Lewis Casson, who in turn asked his wife: the beloved actor Dame Sybil Thorndike.

At Dorset House, the staff specialised in occupational therapy for the patients and Elizabeth expected staff to join in the activities of dancing, drama and country walks alongside the patients in an effort to break down the hierarchical structures that existed in other institutions. Elizabeth had first realised how important occupational activities were to patients when she visited the Bloomingdale Hospital in New York City, saying: "The whole atmosphere of a mental hospital is completely changed whenever the boredom of its patients' lives is changed to well-ordered work and play. Never again could I settle down to see that boredom exist."[71] Plays were regularly performed at Dorset House and with several theatrical fellows – including Sybil – in the Casson family, Elizabeth had no shortage of people to assist her.

In additional to Dorset House, Elizabeth ran a small psychiatric clinic at the Bristol General Hospital and saw patients at the Walker Dunbar Hospital. But she maintained a desire to see occupational therapy spread throughout Bristol and so she worked with teams at Southmead Hospital and Ham Green Hospital to show how occupational therapy was not just for mentally ill patients but was also for those with, for example, tuberculosis or rheumatic heart disease.

During World War Two, Elizabeth sheltered refugees fleeing Hitler's Germany, and she welcomed distinguished German physicians to work at her hospitals in exchange for board and lodging. Her nephew Owen Reid wrote: "One encountered the bizarre sight of one of [Sigmund] Freud's closest associates carrying trays up to the first floor while his wife washed up in the

71 Lorna Brierley, Helen Reid, (2000). *Go Home and Do the Washing!* Bristol: Broadcast. 88.

kitchen."[72] When the military requisitioned Dorset House during the war, the 100 or so patients were transferred to two houses in Clevedon so that their care was not interrupted.

Please also see the entry for: Sybil Thorndike.

EMILY CASWILL

1884-1967, CORSET MAKER

Bristol had several large corset factories at which the vast majority of workers were female. Emily Caswill was one corset maker who decided she wasn't content simply to be an employee... she wanted to be the employer. Born Emily Jane Wollen, she was the eldest of five children in a family living at Charlton Street, St Philips, and later Bridge Street, Barton Hill. As soon as she left school in 1898 aged 14, Emily joined the corset manufacturer Charles Bayer & Company where she worked at the factory on Roman Road, Easton, learning the basics of the trade.

In 1911, aged 27, Emily married an engineer called Ernest Caswill at the Russell Town Congregational Church, Barton Hill. Spurred on by her new husband's support, Emily decided enough was enough and she wanted to be her own boss. So she established a corset business on the ground floor of their home at 2 Barrow Road from which she made and sold corsets. The shop was branded 'EJ Caswill – Corsetiere'.

A description on the specialist website Corsetiere says: "It was a small corner building with a single large display window looking out onto the busy Barrow Road. There were always two or three mannequins in the window displaying traditional

72 Ibid. 89.

lace-up corsetry and there was an orange coloured transparent blind that could be lowered to protect the merchandise from the effects of bright sunlight. As you entered the shop the door shook a small bell that would call Emily from her workroom at the back of the shop. Inside there was a large glass freestanding counter containing bras of all descriptions and other items of corsetry." The Corsetiere description continues: "The wall behind the counter was completely covered by a large mahogany storage unit having 50 or so large pigeonholes into which Emily's stock of corsets were held. A side wall was covered with shelves piled high with white cardboard boxes containing yet more stock. The shop had an old fashioned ambiance about it and it was spotlessly clean with every item of brasswork highly polished."[73]

Once Emily and Ernest's daughter Evelyn arrived in 1917, Emily's mother moved in to help with the running of the business and looking after the new baby, and the business continued to thrive in the following decades. But the family's world was shaken in 1937 when Ernest died suddenly, aged just 55. By this time, the couple had moved to a large house in Lawrence Grove, Henleaze, although Emily still ran her business from Barrow Road.

Emily's second marriage to sewing-machine representative Alfred Norton took place in August 1941, although the war years took their toll on the couple when the government issued restrictions on the clothing trade because of rationing. But even though trade picked up after fabric rationing was stopped, Emily still wasn't given an easy ride. First of all, she was devastated by the loss of her daughter Evelyn in 1946, who died while giving birth to a son – who died a few days later. Then in 1947, Emily's husband Alfred also died. Despite her profound grief, Emily carried on with her work and her corset business.

73 http://www.corsetiere.net/Spirella/Corsetiere/Caswill.htm

She continued working until 1960, even embracing the trend for rubber corsetry, which became popular after fabric shortages following the war. By the time Emily retired in the 1960s she had been trading from 2 Barrow Road for almost 50 years, which is a truly impressive feat. Thanks to Emily and her tenacity, the business of EJ Caswill – Corsetiere survived two world wars, the great depression and four terrible deaths. It was perhaps a good thing that Emily died shortly before having to see her former premises at Barrow Hill demolished by the wrecking ball to make way for St Philips Causeway.

For more information about the corset trade in Bristol, please see the 'Working Women' section towards the end of this book.

CATTELENA

died 1625, INDEPENDENT WOMAN

Cattelena, whose name suggests she has a connection to Spain or Portugal, is important for us to remember because she was a single African woman who lived independently for all of her adult life at a time when Africans in England were generally 'owned' as slaves. Cattelena is also one of the oldest-recorded black people living freely in the South West. We do not know a great deal about Cattelena but we do know that she set up home in Almondsbury on the edge of Bristol and supported herself financially until her death in 1625. Her most prized possession was a cow, who not only supplied Cattelena with milk and butter but also enabled her to earn an income by selling these products to others. At the time of Cattelena's death, her inventory values her goods at £6, 9 shillings and 6 pence, which is the equivalent of about £1,000 in contemporary money.

ALICE CHESTRE

died 1485, MERCHANT

Henry Chestre was Mayor of Bristol and a draper who imported cloth and other goods from Spain, Lisbon, Bordeaux and Brittany. Very successfully. After his death in 1470, his widow Alice, who was a property owner in her own right, inherited all of Henry's estate and she promptly took over his business. Alice further expanded it to import iron and wine alongside cloth and she did so using her own fleet of ships. It wasn't long before she had amassed a substantial fortune and she was very generous with her donations to her local church, All Saints in Clifton. Alongside monetary donations, Alice donated a house to the church, established a chantry for her husband and commissioned masses in his name. So generous were Alice's donations that the church's records refer to her as "this blessed woman". Outside of the church, in 1475 she donated a crane to the Port of Bristol on Welsh Back, which was the first ever crane recorded in the city.

HELEN PRIESTMAN BRIGHT CLARK

1840-1927, SUFFRAGIST

A mainstay of the suffragist movement in the South West, Helen Priestman Bright Clark was a Quaker who grew up in a large Rochdale household with a radical MP for a father (John Bright, who would speak in Parliament about the "assumed hostility" between the sexes as a result of women not having the vote). As the 'Priestman' part of her name suggests, Helen was a niece to Anna Maria and Mary Priestman, plus their sister Margaret

Tanner, and was a cousin of Lilias Ashworth Hallet.[74]

The family library contained copies of essays by John Stuart Mill about the enfranchisement of women and as a girl Helen found these very interesting. In May 1861 she wrote a letter to her step-cousin saying: "We have some of John Stuart Mill's essays in the house – one on the enfranchisement of women is very good. Mill I am happy to say hopes that another century will not pass without women being admitted to the franchise … How absurd to talk of representation and taxation going hand in hand, and all the while excluding wholly the one half of the population from the franchise."[75]

In 1866, Helen was one of the signatories on the original Ladies' Petition that Mill presented to the House of Commons, and shortly afterwards married William Clark (of the Street-based shoe company Clarks) and moved to Somerset. Helen's first public speech was at the 1872 Bristol and West of England National Society for Women's Suffrage meeting in Taunton, and in this she questioned the peculiar double standards of it being OK for a woman to dance in public but it not being OK for a woman to speak in public. Helen became a regular public speaker for women's emancipation, and often came to Bristol to talk at rallies at the Victoria Rooms and other venues. Her speeches were so rousing that at least one was reprinted as a pamphlet.

She travelled widely to promote the cause of women's suffrage and consequently met a great number of equally influential women, including Susan B Anthony and Elizabeth Cady Stanton, who were prominent women in the American campaign for votes for women. The eminent Elizabeth had been travelling through Europe in the early 1890s discussing her work in progress known

74 Elizabeth Crawford, (1999). *The Women's Suffrage Movement: A Reference Guide 1866-1928*. London: University College London Press. 113.
75 Ibid. 113.

as *The Woman's Bible* and as part of her tour she gave an inspiring talk in Helen's front room.

Helen and William had six children, all of whom were supportive of women's equality and became active in the National Union of Women's Suffrage Societies and they also worked to gain women's suffrage.

Please also see the entries for: Anna Maria and Mary Priestman, Margaret Tanner and Lilias Ashworth Hallett.

CLEMENTINA CLERKE
1776-1883, ABDUCTED HEIRESS

In 1791, two Bristol school teachers braved notoriety and slander to try to rescue a teenage student who had been abducted and forced into marriage. Selina Mills and her sister Mary owned a small boarding school in Park Street where they cared for, among others, Clementina Clerke, 14 years old and newly minted. One day in 1791, Clementina and her friends, out walking on the Downs, were spied by Richard Vining Perry, a local apothecary and surgeon. He fell instantly in love. Writing later, he described the moment their eyes locked. It was as if an "electrical fire shook them to their souls". Perry did not mention that he was primarily attracted to Clementina's large fortune nor that he had previously overheard her guardian saying that her money was as yet unprotected by trusts.

He set about grooming her. There was an exchange of love letters. Then he forged a note from her guardian inviting Clementina to tea with an aunt. A carriage drew up at the school. She stepped in (accompanied by a servant in Perry's pay) and was promptly whisked off to Gretna Green. In Scotland, girls could marry at 12 without parental consent.

Mary Mills and her brother set off to the rescue and encountered Perry's party heading south. "Miss Clerke, for God's sake, Miss Clerke, let me speak to you!" shouted Miss Mills. But Perry, who was armed with a pistol, just laughed and said there was no such person. He had only Mrs Perry and the servant in the carriage. The poor Miss Mills. The Bristol Elopement, as the episode was soon dubbed in the press, was the talk of the country and Mary's failed expedition to retrieve her young pupil was mocked in scurrilous cartoons, one portraying her as a "bumbrusher": a prostitute offering flagellation.

She and her brother continued the pursuit in the Low Countries, where Perry had fled with Clementina, but it was not until 1794, the French occupation of the Austrian Netherlands having forced the errant couple back to England the previous year, that she and her sister had their day in court. Selina indicted Perry for feloniously stealing a minor and marrying her against her consent, a capital charge. The trial was a tetchy and noisy affair, in which top barristers were employed on both sides. Outside, a large crowd vocalised their support of the defendant. To them he was a hero, representing the right of men to forge their own paths through life. Heiresses, however humbly born (Clementina's father was a shoemaker but her uncle had acquired a fortune from his slave estates in Jamaica), should not be reserved only for aristocrats or the super-wealthy.

Clementina, now 17 and heavily pregnant with her second child, was the last witness to appear. "Do you think it was for lucre he made himself known to you?" asked the prosecuting barrister. "No sir, I do not think it was for lucre, but out of affection for me." She said she knew exactly what she was doing when she got into Perry's carriage. At this point the case collapsed. Had Perry been convicted, the marriage would have been annulled, Clementina would have been rendered a concubine and her children would be bastards. She had no choice but to support him. Perry was carried by the jubilant mob through the streets of Bristol.

Perry soon set about spending Clementina's money. Any affection for his wife, if indeed there had ever been any, quickly dissipated. The couple separated and Clementina died in Bath in 1813 aged 38, reputedly in great poverty. Women it seemed, while still children, could be kidnapped and forcibly married with impunity. Selina and Mary Mills, dedicated to the welfare of the young girl in their care, showed that even if they lost the battle it was possible to resist.

Written by Naomi Clifford, who graduated from the University of Bristol and is the author of *Women and the Gallows 1797-1837* and *The Disappearance of Maria Glenn. The Murder of Mary Ashford* will be published in 2018.

MARY CLIFFORD

1842-1919, POOR LAW GUARDIAN

After her mother became invalided while Mary Clifford was still a young girl, household management fell on Mary's teenage shoulders and she had to prioritise domesticity and the care of her five younger siblings over her education. Once her father retired, Mary was finally able to take up other work and promptly threw herself into the welfare of poor women, becoming one of the founders of the Bristol branch of the National Union of Women Workers as well as becoming one of the first four female Poor Law Guardians elected in Bristol – and she served on the board until 1902.

The Poor Law Amendment Act of 1834 divided members

of its board into regional parishes, and within those parishes appointed guardians who were responsible for tasks such as overseeing their local workhouses. As a Poor Law Guardian, Mary undertook a wide range of work including the standard workhouse visiting but also overseeing the placement of foster children and introducing systems in the workhouse to keep orphaned girls separate from the 'rougher' women who typically inhabited the institutions, despite the poo-pooing of the idea by some male Poor Law Guardians who did not deem it necessary.

Mary was also an advocate of other charities, largely those with a swing towards women's welfare. As well as supporting the Old Park Lock Hospital (see the entry for Ellen Cullinane for more information about the lock hospital), she was also the president of the Bristol Association of Working Girls' Clubs, which arranged activities such as swimming lessons and competitions for local girls.

By the year after Mary's death, a committee had formed to arrange a memorial to her long life and many achievements. The treasurer of the committee was Elizabeth Sturge and she "reported that the amount of the subscriptions up to the present was £122, all given spontaneously by friends of the late Miss Clifford, who personally knew and valued her devoted work in connection with Poor Law and various other departments of social and religious work"[76].

76 *Western Daily Press*, 1920, 24 January, 'Mary Clifford Memorial'. 7.

FRANCES POWER COBBE
1822-1904, SUFFRAGIST, CAMPAIGNER

There were very few causes that Frances Power Cobbe did not champion. Most particularly she was an anti-vivisectionist, a social reformer and a leading suffragist. Oh, and she also wrote a number of books.

Born in Dublin, Frances attended boarding school in Brighton in 1835 and the following year visited Clifton with one of her brothers. Because the Clifton Suspension Bridge was yet to be finished, they instead travelled across the Avon Gorge in a basket suspended from an iron bar. Which sounds hair-raising. But clearly Frances wasn't one to be easily spooked: "I was ... with my brother. He bribed someone, I think, and got into the basket hanging from the bar which stretched across the Gorge, and we were pulled backwards and forwards by ropes. We thought it was great fun."[77]

After renouncing her faith, Frances was banished from the family home by her devout father and initially supported herself as a journalist. While living in Bristol, Frances befriended Mary Carpenter and the two shared a house while working together at the Red Lodge Reformatory. Frances' biographer Barbara Caine suggests the friendship disintegrated after Frances sought "a more intimate form of friendship" than Mary was interested in and after a few months Frances moved out to live with her lifelong partner Mary Lloyd, who was a sculptor, and the two women are now buried together in Wales.

While travelling in Italy in the early 1860s, Frances was appalled by experiments she saw being conducted on animals. So she cemented her commitment to animal welfare by founding the

77 *Western Daily Press*, 1902, 25 November, 'A Chat with Frances Power Cobbe'. 3.

British Union for the Abolition of Vivisection (which continues today as Cruelty Free International) and the national Anti-Vivisection Society (which is still in operation). Among those whom Frances convinced to support the cause was none other than the reigning monarch Queen Victoria.

Frances saw a clear link between men's brutality towards animals and to women and as such she wrote widely on the legal rights of married women. Her pamphlet *Wife Torture* suggested that if a husband was violent towards his wife it should be grounds for a legal separation. This ultimately influenced the Matrimonial Causes Act of 1878, which gave abused wives not only the right to a separation but also custody of any child under the age of ten.

Frances was also a member of the executive council for the London National Society for Women's Suffrage and regularly wrote for national newspapers on the subject of women's suffrage. Among those men she attempted to convince of the importance of female emancipation was scientist Charles Darwin, whose wife was a friend and ally of Frances'.

In 1902, the *Western Daily Press* ran a lengthy and fascinating interview with Frances to mark her 80th birthday, in which they looked back on all of her achievements in Bristol.[78] Segments from it are summarised below.

In answer to how her association with Mary Carpenter came about, the reporter writes: "Miss Carpenter was in need [of] a helper, and Miss Cobbe, looking about to see if there was any way in which she could be of use to the world, regarded this as a good opening for her. She came and remained at the reformatory [and] came to live with Miss Carpenter ... 'And I remained with her a couple years. She had a good deal of sympathy shown towards her efforts, and the daughter of the late Dean Elliott used to come

78 Ibid. 3.

Frances Power Cobbe illustration by Jenny Howe

and visit a great deal. She and I became great friends afterwards. We had ragged schools and used to teach in them.'"

Talking positively about the great work done by Mary, Frances said it "was a beautiful and quite new thing. She and good old Recorder Hill [Matthew Davenport Hill], a great friend of mine, were the people who introduced the notion of reforming rather than punishing, particularly in the case [of] young children. Many of the little thieves sent to them were thoroughly reformed and went into good positions in life afterwards. The very lowest now are not quite so low as they were then ... A friend of mine pointed out how marked has been the change for the better in this respect."

Frances spoke enthusiastically about all the changes to Bristol itself that she had noticed in the previous 80 years: the large shops, the new and improved houses, the electric trams, all of these things impressed her... especially the trams: "Formerly we had nothing but to walk those fearful hills: Christmas Steps and Park Street." Indeed, Frances expressed great surprise when the reporter in 1902 told her that the very steep Christmas Steps still existed and had not been demolished![79]

Talking about the changes for women that she had seen in her lifetime, Frances said that she was impressed by the new boldness of character in young women that she felt was reflected in how they carried themselves: "The young ladies here are grown taller decidedly, and at the same time they are retaining their nice, innocent, faces. They don't dress stupidly, the style which people do in many of the fashionable resorts, and they do not lace too tightly. They are wholesome, handsome, happy looking young women. I have been all my life interested in the progress of women, and therefore I am delighted see this physical progress." However, it was not all good news in Frances's opinion: "[I am]

79 Christmas Steps are still there now and are a famed historical and attractive location in Bristol. Why not walk up them for yourself and share Frances' pain?

startled when I go into bookshops and am told that ladies will not read any books except novels and such trashy things, too, and therefore it is useless to keep any serious books at all the circulating libraries."

Frances also believed strongly in the importance of a further education for women, and fought for women to be entitled to take university exams and to therefore achieve graduation at Oxford and Cambridge Universities. She says she was "the very first person to ask for degrees to be given to women. I did that in a paper at the Social Science Congress in London. Every newspaper in London the next morning had an article making fun of me ... Seventeen years after, I was invited to join Lady Stanley's deputation to Lord Granville to thank him for the granting of degrees at London University."

Confirming how indefatigable she was, Frances ended her interview by proudly telling the interviewer that, at the age of 60, she had still been capable of walking almost 3,000ft to the top of Cadair Idris near her home in north Wales, and now on her 80th birthday she continued working hard every single day. Although she still did not care for the Christmas Steps.

For Frances' 80th birthday there was a presentation where she was given an album signed by 300 well-respected names of the time. These included no lesser signatories than Florence Nightingale, Millicent Fawcett and Josephine Butler.

The effusive message of high regard began: "We, who recognise the strenuous philanthropic activity and the high moral purpose of your long life, wish to offer you this congratulatory address as an expression of sincere regard. You were among the first publicly to urge the right of women to university degrees, and your powerful pen has done much to advance that movement towards equality of treatment for them in educational and other matters, which is one of the distinguishing marks of our time."[80]

Please also see the entries for: Josephine Butler, Mary Carpenter and Rosamund and Florence Davenport-Hill.

ELIZABETH COCKS
died 1908, TEACHER

As the first headteacher of Redland High School, Elizabeth Ann Cocks was rather a radical character. Among her enlightened ideas during her 25 years as headteacher were taking the girls to Paris in 1889 for a school trip and demanding that the governors install a library for the teachers to use. She also insisted that a laboratory be built and stocked with the necessary items for science lessons. Redland High School was also novel in its election of the first woman school governor in the form of Emily Sturge.

Around 200 pupils attended a memorial service at Leigh Woods for Elizabeth in September 1908, as did her friend Emily. Rev J Gamble spoke in his eulogy about how Elizabeth had shown "immense patience, unwearying attention to details, and conscientious work" during her quarter of a century with the school. He added: "During a series of years she had shown perseverance and determination to resist every temptation, so that at last she had accomplished what had been undertaken."[81]

Please also see the entry for: Emily Sturge.

80 *Western Daily Press*, 1902, 5 December, 'Interesting Presentation to Miss Frances Power Cobbe'. 7.
81 *Western Daily Press, 1908, 21 September, 'Memorial for Elizabeth Cocks'. 5.*

CLARA CODD
1877-1971, SUFFRAGETTE

Clara Margaret Codd was born at Pill House, Bishops Tawton, Devon, the eldest of the ten daughters of Henry Codd and his wife Clara. When Henry died in 1901 the family was living at 4 Belvedere Road, Redland, but by 1908 had moved to 12 Springfield Place, Bath. Clara spent some time as a governess in Ireland and after her return to Bath in 1905 became a theosophist, as eventually did her entire family.

In 1907, she was asked to act as a steward at a meeting organised by the Women's Social and Political Union (WSPU) and addressed by Christabel Pankhurst and Annie Kenney. She immediately joined the WSPU while also remaining, until April 1908, a member of the Bath branch of the National Union of Women's Suffrage Societies. She now became Honorary Secretary of the newly-founded Bath WSPU and in the summer went to work for Annie in Bristol, eventually giving up her employment as a Governess.

In October 1908, Clara volunteered to take part in the 'rush' on the House of Commons, was arrested and sentenced to a month's imprisonment. Her 1951 autobiography, *So Rich a Life,* contains a detailed description of prison life. Although offered a position as a paid WSPU Organiser in London, Clara chose instead to work for the Theosophical Society. In 1911, she did not heed the WSPU call to boycott the census and her form reveals that, living as a boarder with one of her sisters in a house in Hampstead, London, she was working as Librarian to the Theosophical Society.

Clara spent the remainder of her life lecturing for the Theosophical Society, who held her in very high regard. She spent long periods in India, Australia, South Africa and the US and was a prolific author on matters of theosophy.

Written by Elizabeth Crawford, who is an independent suffrage researcher and the author of numerous books on the subject, including *The Women's Suffrage Movement: A Reference Guide 1866-1928* and *Campaigning For The Vote: Kate Parry Frye's Suffrage Diary*. Her latest book, *Art and Suffrage: A Biographical Dictionary of Suffrage Artists*, is published in 2018.

FANNY COKER

1767-1820, FREED ENSLAVED AFRICAN

Born into slavery on a plantation in the West Indies, Fanny Coker's mother had been purchased by the sugar and slave merchant John Pinney and the family worked as slaves on his plantation. However, Pinney was a little more benevolent than other slave owners. When she was between the ages of eight and 13, Fanny was sent by him for training as a seamstress before allowing her to attend lessons with his own children.

On 15 September 1778, when Fanny was 11 years old, Pinney freed her from slavery. She was one of the very first enslaved Africans that he freed who was neither old nor sick. However, Fanny stayed on to work as a paid maid to the Pinney family and travelled to their home at 7 Great George Street, Bristol, in July 1783 to live and work there, leaving behind her mother and siblings in the West Indies. Another of Pinney's slaves who joined the journey to Bristol was his manservant Pero Jones, for whom the footbridge outside Arnolfini is named. It is not thought that Pero was ever freed.

Fanny became very involved in the local church and joined the Broadmead Baptist Church. She was also a trusted member of the household and when Pinney's wife Jane became pregnant

Fanny worked as both nursemaid to the child and as a ladies' maid to Jane. Fanny was paid a quarterly wage by her employers and, in his will, Pinney left Fanny an annuity provided that she remained in his wife's service.

The property at 7 Great George Street is now run as The Georgian House Museum, with the interior preserved exactly as it would have been in Pinney's day. As well as showing how the Pinneys lived above stairs, it recreates how Fanny and her fellow servants lived and worked below stairs.[82]

MARIA COLBY

died 1915, SUFFRAGIST

Suffragist Maria Colby was an organiser for the National Union of Women's Suffrage Societies (NUWSS) in Bristol and in 1883 she organised 22 successive evening meetings on the Durdham Downs. Writing to the *Bristol Mercury* in 13 July 1886, Maria stated: "Sir, as organising agent for the Women's Suffrage Meetings on the Downs, will you allow me to say that the objections to our claims, based on the idea that the primary duty of woman is to darn stockings, has been advanced about ten times a night for 22 evenings successively."[83] And followed this up with a poem "protesting the idea that woman's main duty was to darn their husband's stockings, which was so often and so tediously put forward as an argument against giving [women] the vote"[84].

Along with the emancipation of women, Maria was also a believer in the temperance movement and as such was a member of the Women's Total Abstinence Union in Bristol, along with

82 https://www.bristolmuseums.org.uk/georgian-house-museum/

83 Ellen Malos, (1983), 'Bristol Women in Action 1839-1919: The Right to Vote and the Need to Earn a Living' in Bristol Broadsides, (1983). *Bristol's Other History*. Bristol: Broadsides. 103.

84 Lucienne Boyce, (2013). *The Bristol Suffragettes*. Bristol: SilverWood. 18.

Anna Maria and Mary Priestman. A sample topic for discussions at meetings was 'Woman: Her Rights, Her Responsibilities, Her Power', which emphasised the need for women to exert a moral influence over the men in their lives to steer them away from the evils of alcohol.[85]

In 1913, Maria and her sister Anne, who lived at 11 Hurle Crescent in Clifton, made a joint donation of £1,000 to the Bristol Private Hospital for Women and Children, which was in Berkeley Square, Clifton. "The gift is intended to be an expression of their appreciation of the benefits which women receive at this Hospital from treatment, medical and surgical, by qualified practitioners of their own sex," wrote the *Western Daily Press.*[86] In the days before the National Health Service, hospitals such as this were dependent on donations and subscriptions from kind benefactors.

Please also see the entry for: Anna Maria and Mary Priestman.

SARAH FRICKER COLERIDGE
1770-1845, TEACHER, POET, WRITER

Sarah (known later as Sara) Fricker was the eldest of three sisters born in Bristol. She married the poet Samuel Taylor Coleridge in 1795. Her sister Edith married the poet Robert Southey, and her sister Mary married the poet Robert Lovell. They were all part of the Pantisocracy scheme (which never materialised) to set up an ideal, free society in the United States.[87] The three sisters were well-educated and radical women, needing to earn a living as seamstresses before they married because their father, a Bristol

85 *Western Daily Press*, 1902, 24 November, 'United Temperance Crusade in Bristol'. 10.
86 *Western Daily Press*, 1913, 1 March, 'News'. 4.
87 The Pantisocracy was a form of utopian organisation where everyone is equal in status and responsibility.

merchant, went bankrupt.

Sarah was probably the most radical: she became a close friend of democrat Tom Poole when she and 'STC', as she called her opium-addicted husband, lived in Nether Stowey. The local vicar referred to her as a "democratic hoyden", which she might well have taken as a compliment. Sarah had to put up with her husband's bouts of illness related to his addiction, and also the unfriendliness of William and Dorothy Wordsworth who lived nearby. STC was touring in Germany when their second son Berkeley died as a two-year-old and STC did not hurry back to console Sarah. She had delivered both her first son, Hartley, and Berkeley herself.

The cottage in Nether Stowey was damp and, while STC philosophised with William and Dorothy, she was left to manage everything with only the help of her Bristol maid, Nanny.

Sarah later moved to the Lake District with STC and her three surviving children, Hartley, Derwent and Sara (who became a poet.) They lived with Edith and Robert, while STC stayed with the Wordsworths in Grasmere, where he fell in love with Wordsworth's sister-in-law Sara Hutchinson, or visited friends in London.

Sarah taught in the school run by Edith for the Southey, Coleridge and Wordsworth children. She corresponded with Poole and invented her own language, which the family referred to as her Lingo Grande. Sarah called her brother-in-law Robert Southey a "detesty, a maffrum, a goffrum, a chatterpye, a sillicum and a great mawkinfort". Maybe she was determined to use language as inventively as her husband. She later moved to London, where she occasionally met with STC.

Some biographers (Anna Taylor) have seen Sarah as a wife who neither understood nor loved her husband. Others (Molly Lefebure, Katie Waldegrave, Liz Cashdan) as a strong woman bringing up three children while their father neither respected her nor provided her with enough money to run her household.[88]

Written by Dr Liz Cashdan, who lives in Bristol and is a Creative Writing Tutor at the Open College of the Arts. Her most recent poetry collection is *Things of Substance: New and Selected Poems* (Smith/Doorstop, 2013).

KATHERINE ST JOHN CONWAY
1867-1950, SOCIALIST

Katherine St John Conway was motivated by the sight of striking "sister women" when they paraded around All Saints Church on Pembroke Road. The impoverished strikers wore unsuitable clothes for the weather, were wet from the rain and hungry from a lack of money to buy food. This urged Katherine to take action in support of the striking workers.[89] In 1889 she joined the strike committee and after her marriage to John Bruce Glasier became a leading figure in the Fabian Society, the Independent Labour Party and the Women's Labour League.

Please also see the entry for: Enid Stacey.

88 References for this entry: 1) Liz Cashdan, (1991). 'The Mariner's Tale' in *Troublesome Cattle*. 2) Molly Lefebure, (1988). A *Bondage of Love: a Life of Mrs Samuel Taylor Coleridge*. 3) Anna Taylor, (2005). *Erotic Coleridge, Women and Love and the Law Against Divorce*. 4) Kathryn Waldegrave, (2013). *The Poets' Daughters: Dora Wordsworth and Sara Coleridge*.

89 Ellen Malos, (1983), 'Bristol Women in Action 1839-1919: The Right to Vote and the Need to Earn a Living' in Bristol Broadsides, (1983). *Bristol's Other History*. Bristol: Broadsides. 119.

OLIVE COOKE

1923-2015, FUNDRAISER

Fishponds-based poppy seller Olive Cooke caught the nation's attention after she sadly took her own life in 2015 when, at the age of 92, she jumped from the Clifton Suspension Bridge while experiencing an episode of depression.

Olive had quietly devoted her long life to charity fundraising and was thought to be Britain's longest-serving poppy seller. She became a poppy seller at the age of 16 after her father set up a Royal British Legion branch in Bedminster.

However, the poppies took on a new meaning for Olive when her first husband Leslie was killed in World War Two after they had been married for just two-and-a-half years. Olive later said: "I had to continue working in Wills factory in Bristol, just making the best of life. We worked in the warehouse, doing the men's jobs, such as hammering the boxes to transport cigarettes to the forces. The men took the jobs when they returned at the end of the war. Women had to go to other departments. I moved to the next factory in the cigarette department in Ashton."[90]

Following the war, Olive joined the Royal British Legion and became the Standard Bearer in the Bedminster Women's Section. She also held the positions of Secretary and Chairman for the Royal British Legion at various times. Speaking in 2005, Olive said: "I carried the standard for 54 years until 1998. I sold poppies every year and was given a special medal from the Royal British Legion for 66 years of continuous selling. I still sell them now on Park Street and the Cathedral porch throughout poppy week."[91] Olive went on to receive numerous regional and national awards for her work.

90 http://www.bbc.co.uk/history/ww2peopleswar/stories/79/a4021679.shtml
91 Ibid.

Olive Cooke illustration by Carrie Love

NORAH COOKE-HURLE

1871-1960, EDUCATIONALIST, CAMPAIGNER

The Quaker Fry family were big players in Bristol with successful chocolate factories in the city centre. And Norah Fry (as was her name before she married) was born into this chocolatey dynasty. This afforded her inherited wealth and privilege, and meant she benefitted from a good education in Clifton. Evidently this stood Norah in good stead and she went on to become one of the first female Cambridge scholars to graduate with the equivalent of a double first, and she would become a founder member of the University of Bristol's Council in 1909. However, Norah used her combined powers of wealth and education for good, and she became a lifelong campaigner for children with disabilities and learning difficulties once she realised what a lack of schools and housing there was for people with special needs. The Norah Fry Centre for Disability Studies at the University of Bristol was established in 1988 and is named after her, as was the Norah Fry Hospital in Shepton Mallet (although this closed in 1990). In 1918, Norah became the first woman councillor in Somerset.

Please also see the entry for: Anna Fry.

BERYL CORNER

1910-2007, DOCTOR

A pioneer of neonatal medicine who broke down the barriers facing women in medicine, Beryl Corner from Henleaze was no ordinary doctor. Having excelled at Redland High School for Girls, she was accepted to study at London's Royal Free Hospital in 1927 aged just 17, and shone so brightly that she won a clutch of scholarships, bursaries and prizes during her education. As part of her training, Beryl had worked at Great Ormond Street Hospital and this sparked her determination to work with children and become a pioneering paediatrician.

Despite her hard work, excellent qualifications and tireless determination, Beryl endured great frustration as job application after job application was unsuccessful… and on each occasion a male applicant was given the post instead. After a particularly crushing disappointment from the Westminster Children's Hospital, Beryl received a letter from one of the consultants who had interviewed her which confirmed that she "was the best candidate by far"[92], acknowledging Beryl's suspicions that she was being overlooked simply because of her gender. In her obituary, Dr Martin Crossley Evans wrote: "She triumphed against prejudices and constraints which would have crushed a person less determined and without such deeply held convictions … she carved out a career in medicine in the face of considerable male obstruction and hostility."[93]

Despite these frustrations, Beryl secured a post as Resident Medical Officer at the Royal Hospital for Sick Children on St Michael's Hill back in Bristol. While working here, she passed the exams for both the Royal College of Physicians and to be a Doctor of Medicine: both of which she achieved within two years of qualification, which was the fastest time that anybody had ever achieved this.

Now that she had all these qualifications, Beryl moved to the Brompton Hospital for Diseases of the Chest in London, where she took an interest in treatments for tuberculosis and tuberculosis meningitis, which in the era before antibiotics or penicillin was a death sentence. Within ten years, Beryl had become a pioneer in

92 Lorna Brierley, Helen Reid, (2000). *Go Home and Do the Washing!* Bristol: Broadcast. 91.
93 http://www.bristol.ac.uk/news/2007/5352.html

Beryl Corner illustration by Jenny Howe

the use of antibiotics, having already been the first doctor to use a German drug called Prontosil (an early antibiotic) to save the life of a desperately sick child.[94]

When she heard of a post for Honorary Physician at the Children's Hospital in Bristol, Beryl applied but feared the job would go to the other candidate: a man. However, the male candidate was so sure of his successful appointment that he didn't even attend the board meeting… meaning that Beryl won the job. At this time in the 1930s, there were very few paediatricians based outside London and Beryl was the only one in Bristol. Despite this, paediatric medicine was poorly paid and, before the National Health Service came into existence in 1948, many doctors worked in hospitals on a voluntary basis, supplementing their income from private patients. Beryl became known as a specialist in treating babies and children, and was able to boost her income by privately looking after the children of those who could afford to pay.

During World War Two, Beryl received an urgent call ordering her to go to Swindon Hospital. There she was expected to treat the first casualties coming back from the Second Front and this was the first time that Beryl saw and used the golden phials of the penicillin that was being made solely for treating servicemen. During the three days Beryl spent in Swindon, she treated around 180 casualties.[95] She also served as the Air Raid Precaution doctor at the Bristol Aeroplane Company and often had to sleep on the premises to deal with emergencies.[96] After the war, the advent of the National Health Service introduced salaries for doctors and Beryl returned to paediatric work in Bristol. She became noted for her clinical research, particularly concerning tuberculosis,

94 Lorna Brierley, Helen Reid, (2000). *Go Home and Do the Washing!* Bristol: Broadcast. 92.
95 Ibid. 96.
96 http://www.bristol.ac.uk/news/2007/5352.html

meningitis, jaundice and infections of newborn babies. She also worked extensively as a lecturer and was a member of countless advisory boards, and was the first woman to be elected to the British Paediatric Association in 1945.

Paediatrics was little known in the 1930s, as was neonatal medicine. Nobody knew how to look after premature babies and as such the survival rate was very low. Upon hearing about the pioneering use of draught-proof, high-sided and heated cots (an early form of incubator) in Sorrento, Italy, Beryl introduced these heated cots to Southmead Hospital and in doing so she founded the Southmead Special Baby Care Unit in 1946, which would become a major centre of treatment for premature babies in the South West and was only the second such centre in the whole of the country, which halved mortality rates from premature birth.[97]

Timothy was a more unusual occupant of the incubator during the 1950s. During a ward round, a colleague thrust a bundle into Beryl's arms pleading with her to "keep it alive if you can". The bundle contained a tiny prematurely born chimpanzee. Treating Timothy exactly as she would any other premature baby, Beryl placed him in an empty incubator, fed him human milk and glucose water, and after five weeks he was strong enough to be released to a zookeeper who looked after the chimp at his home until he was big enough to be housed with the other chimpanzees at Bristol Zoo.[98] Following her successful experience with Timothy, Beryl provided neonatal care to other gorillas and orangutans born at Bristol Zoo, serving as the zoo's honorary consultant paediatrician between 1972 and 1980.[99]

Please also see the entry for: Dorothy Crowfoot Hodgkin.

97 Lorna Brierley, Helen Reid, (2000). *Go Home and Do the Washing!* Bristol: Broadcast. 94.
98 Ibid. 95.
99 http://www.bristol.ac.uk/news/2007/5352.html

MABEL COWLIN
1876-1960, POLICE PIONEER

With a strong education from Redland High School, Mabel Hephzibah Cowlin was set up for good things and she swiftly went on to earn one of the very first diplomas awarded at the London School of Economics. With that under her belt, as well as experience as a social worker, Mabel moved to the Liverpool Women Police Patrols and worked alongside the pioneering Dorothy Peto.

The Women's Patrol Committee was inaugurated in the early days of World War One and Mabel was appointed as Director in January 1915. The poverty and overcrowding in Liverpool were particular problems, and were exacerbated by it being a big port city and the inevitable rise in the sex trade this created. Mabel firmly believed police officers would gain a better understanding of the people they were working with if they went out and spoke with them in their own communities, in an effort to break down any hostilities. Realising that going in full uniform would create a barrier, Mabel encouraged officers to go in their own clothes and to chat to residents on their streets informally.

A lot of the work involved working with women who were trapped in the sex trade and Mabel wrote: "The patrols were given powers to inspect lodging houses frequented by common prostitutes and were enabled to take younger ones away and do really constructive work in re-establishing them. In this they were helped by the older women living on their earnings from the streets: for example, one of them brought a young girl to the office and begged the patrols to save her from the life she found so difficult to leave."[100]

100 Cited in Joan Lock, (2014), *The British Policewoman*. London: Robert Hale.

Mabel's weekly case meeting with the officers was a crucial feature of how she revolutionised police work, because it enabled her to pair up officers with a case best suited to their skills. Dorothy Peto explained: "Every person or situation dealt with on the beat was examined – their background, their individual needs and the possibilities of helping them; whilst with her trained perception and deep concern for the individual, Cowlin led the patrol concerned to seek and find the best solution. In the years between the two World Wars I met both policewomen and social workers who told me that they owed their whole conception of constructive work to Mabel Cowlin's teaching and I know how much I learned myself whenever I had an opportunity myself of sitting in at one of her case meetings at the Liverpool Patrol Office."[101] When Mabel retired from her post in Liverpool in 1927 and moved back to Bristol, her colleague Dorothy stepped up to fill her black leather shoes.

With decades of experience working with sex workers, it was not surprising that women's health and particularly tackling the spread of venereal disease were issues that greatly concerned Mabel. In the same way that Josephine Butler had worked tirelessly to fight the vexatious Contagious Diseases Acts in the 1880s, Mabel was part of the Bristol Diocesan Moral Welfare Association deputation that worked to influence the Bristol Health Committee. A newspaper article reported: "The object of the deputation was to express the concern felt in religious and welfare circles at the lack of moral guidance in the problems uncovered by the campaign against venereal disease."[102]

Ever one to give a rousing call to arms, on 16 February 1945, when there was a Women's World Day of Prayer service held at Bristol Cathedral, Mabel gave the address. She told

101 Ibid.

102 *Western Daily Press*, 1943, 7 April, 'Fight Against VD: Deputation to Health Committee'. 3.

the congregation: "It is now time for the housewife to take an intelligent interest in the things happening outside and submit her help and advice in international legislation, for we have lived too long on the traditions of the past."[103]

In addition to everything else, Mabel also served as a magistrate in Bristol for 14 years.

Please also see the entry for: Dorothy Peto.

LUCY COX
1894-1983, POLITICIAN

Lucy Cox was a schoolteacher from Keynsham who was so struck by the sacrifices she saw working-class parents make to ensure their children received an education that she became determined to enter politics to try and make the world a better place. Her belief was further cemented after seeing the loss of so many young men from her village during World War One and she subsequently became Secretary of the No More War Federation.

Lucy joined the Independent Labour Party in 1916 and became Secretary of the Keynsham branch, working closely with Walter Ayles and his wife Bertha on their plans for municipal socialism. After her marriage to James Middleton, who was the General Secretary of the Labour Party, as Lucy Middleton she was elected MP for Plymouth Sutton in 1945. In 1977, Lucy edited a book collecting the stories of women: *Women in the Labour Movement: The British Experience.*

Please also see the entry for: Bertha Ayles.

103 *Western Daily Press*, 1945, 17 February, 'Women's Service at Cathedral'. 5.

ELLEN CRAFT

1826-1891, FREED ENSLAVED AFRICAN

Bristol's historical connection to the slave trade is inescapable but Ellen Craft provides us with a positive example of an enslaved African-American who notoriously escaped slavery and found freedom in Bristol.

Ellen was born in Georgia, United States, as the daughter of a black slave and her white owner. At the age of 20, Ellen married fellow enslaved African William Craft, whom her master also owned. However, they made history by escaping in December 1848 while in disguise. Because she had a white father, Ellen had a pale complexion and so she successfully disguised herself as a powerful white man, with dark-skinned William posing as her slave servant.

They escaped to Boston, where abolitionists encouraged the Crafts to publicly share their story as widely as possible and as a result they became the most famous fugitive slaves in history. Audiences were fascinated by the young couple who had successfully carried out this most daring of escapes.

However, the Fugitive Slave Act of 1850 required all law officers in every American state to return escaped enslaved people to their owners and therefore slave catchers became a real threat to the Crafts. Given their newfound fame, the Crafts' former master knew exactly where they were and despatched two slave hunters to Boston to retrieve them. But before the hunters could arrive, Bostonians had formed the Vigilance Committee and rallied round to protect the Crafts from capture until they were able to escape the US and travel to the United Kingdom for safety.

Once in England, the Crafts were aided by Harriet Martineau who helped them to gain an education and supported Ellen to write the following statement in 1852: "I had much rather starve

Ellen Craft illustration by Jenny Howe

in England, a free woman, than be a slave for the best man that ever breathed upon the American continent." During their 19 years in England, Ellen became a vociferous campaigner for various organisations including the London Emancipation Committee and the Women's Suffrage Organisation. The Crafts also undertook a lecture tour around England, sharing their story with a wider audience. They were supported on this by the Bristolian anti-slavery campaigner Mary Estlin, who welcomed the couple to her home in Bristol. Mary ran the Bristol and Clifton Ladies' Anti-Slavery Society and the Crafts were invited to Bristol on 9 April 1851 to speak at the Broadmead Public Room, which attracted a huge crowd.[104]

Ellen gave birth to her first son, Charles, in December 1852 and the boy's full name is registered on the birth certificate as 'Charles Estlin Phillips Craft', which gives an indication of the extent to which Mary had supported and sheltered the couple. Shortly after the birth, Ellen told *The Liberator* publication that her baby was "our first free born babe", although her husband's occupation was still listed as "fugitive slave" on the child's official birth certificate.

The Crafts and their five children returned to the US in 1868 where they opened an agricultural school for the children of freed slaves.

Please also see the entries for: Mary Estlin and Harriet Martineau.

104 The full report of the meeting is available online and gives great detail of what was said and the resolutions passed. http://historyonline.chadwyck.co.uk/getImage?productsuffix=_studyunits&action=printview&in=gif&out=pdf&src=/bap/bap00023/conv/bap00023.pdf&IE=.pdf

EMILY CRAWFORD
1831-1915, JOURNALIST

Hailed as one of the best female reporters of her generation, Emily Crawford spent her final years in Clifton after a successful career as a journalist in Paris, France.

Born in Ireland in 1831 as Emily Johnstone, she and her mother and sisters moved to Paris following the death of her father. While in Paris, Emily began writing letters to a friend in the United Kingdom who suggested she pen regular pieces for newspapers in America and London, which she did. It wasn't long before the talented writer was making a living out of her journalism, writing for publications across the world including the *New York Tribune, The Fortnightly Review* and *The Contemporary Review.* Emily was also Paris correspondent for *The Weekly Dispatch, The Calcutta Englishman* and *The Chicago Daily News.* In 1864, she married her *Daily News* colleague George Morland Crawford, who was 22 years her senior, in Paris. The pair worked together until his death in 1885 at which point she inherited his position at the newspaper "for the sake of the children". The pair had four children and Emily managed to maintain a successful journalism career alongside her role as a mother.

Emily was a well-respected journalist, renowned for going the extra mile – from crossing the battle lines to interview the communard leaders in the 1871 siege of Paris, to climbing the Eiffel Tower before it was finished, and finding a way into the 17-hour-long historic debate between France and Prussia at Versailles in order to write a newspaper report from memory, to scouring Paris's hospitals to pen a report on the cholera epidemic for the *Daily News* despite battling influenza herself.

A *Mercury* newspaper report about Emily in the late 19th century noted: "Mrs Crawford knows not how to spell the word 'fear'; she is strong and courageous both in heart and head. Endowed with a grand constitution, she faces her work with a soldierly spirit, fired with the conviction that there is nothing that a man can do that a woman cannot do also."

Hailed as an example of an educated middle-class woman making her way in a male-dominated industry, Emily showed that women could combine parenting with working but warned that journalism was "not a profession for the faint hearted" and women journalists had to make themselves "mentally and physically tough".

A Life Fellow of the Institute of Journalists, Emily was appointed President of the Society of Women Journalists in 1901 before retiring in 1907. She was offered the Légion d'Honneur but declined it, asking that it be awarded to her son Robert instead, who had followed his parents into journalism. It was Robert who drew Emily to Bristol during the outbreak of World War One and she remained living in Clifton until her death in 1915 aged 84.

Written by Laura K Williams, who is a Bristol-based journalist and editor, and founding member and trustee of Baby Bank Network: a women-led charity that provides baby essentials to families in need.

GWENDOLINE CROSS

1896-1966, ARTIST

Painter, printmaker, jeweller, cutler, sculptor, illustrator and etcher. Gwendoline Cross was many things to many people. She was born in Bristol and trained at the Municipal Art College. Alongside her artist husband Fred Whicker, with whom she lived at 19 All Saints Road and who credits his wife as an influence on his own work, Gwendoline was a founder member of the New Bristol Arts Club, as well as being the club's first President in 1934.

However, Gwendoline's work was appreciated far beyond the confines of Bristol, as this news report from 1931 confirms: "A Bristol artist, Miss Gwendoline Cross, has secured the distinction of acceptances at the Royal Academy [in London] and one of her pictures, a work in oils, has been hung. Miss Cross, who studied and is a teacher at the Bristol Municipal Art School, has had much of her work purchased for foreign permanent collections."[105]

After World War Two the couple moved to Falmouth, where Gwendoline was a Teacher and Governor of Falmouth Art School.

MABEL CROSS

born 1872, SUFFRAGIST, PILGRIM

As a solicitor's wife and Honorary Secretary of the National Union of Women's Suffrage Society (NUWSS) and Organiser of the West of England Federation, Clifton-based Mabel Harriet Cross was in a prominent position to organise the Bristol contingent in the mammoth Suffrage Pilgrimage of 1913. The plan was for members of local suffrage federations from all over the United Kingdom to

105 *Western Daily Press*, 1931, 30 April, 'Bristol Painter Honoured'. 10.

walk from Land's End, Cornwall, to Hyde Park, London, for a mass rally of 50,000 protestors on 26 July 1913.

The Pilgrimage was organised by the non-militant NUWSS and was the brainchild of Society member Katherine Harley. It came shortly after Emily Wilding Davison's death following her actions at the Epsom Derby earlier the same month.[106] Passions were understandably fired up and women everywhere felt the need to take action against the Government, which was still refusing to budge on the issue of female emancipation. But the women wanted to act peacefully. Why was a pilgrimage such a good idea? Because it created a huge visual impact without resorting to the window-smashing, fence-chaining, headline-grabbing antics of the militant suffragettes. Lisa Tickner explains: "A pilgrimage refused the thrill attendant on women's militancy, no matter how strongly the militancy was denounced, but it also refused the glamour of an orchestrated spectacle."[107]

Mabel was assisted in her organisational role by suffrage songwriter Sarah Tanner from Westbury-on-Trym as well as another solicitor's wife, Mrs Hicks (unfortunately we do not know her first name so regrettably have to refer to her by her husband's name). Walter Ayles spoke at an energising rally on the Downs when the Pilgrimage crossed Bristol on 14 July 1913 and Mabel Tothill also attended. As the march progressed across the South West, people would step up and join them for as long as they were able, even if they could not commit to the whole five-week journey. Over the course of the pilgrimage, 46,000 new signatures were collected in support of votes for women.

While the march largely went well, there were inevitably a few spots of trouble from those who were opposed to women getting

106 Emily Wilding Davison was an active member of the WSPU. She famously attended the Epsom Derby on 4 June 1913 where, while attempting to fix a suffragette banner to King George V's horse, she was trampled and later died from her injuries.
107 Lisa Tickner (1988), *The Spectacle of Women*. Chicago: University of Chicago Press.142.

the vote. For instance, during a meeting at Twerton near Bath, "pilgrims were badly mobbed by hooligans … Miss Tanner was knocked down and much bruised and Mrs Cross had to escape, disguised in a man's coat and hat, from the back of a house in which they had taken refuge"[108].

Researcher Elizabeth Crawford explains: "Pilgrims were urged to wear a uniform, a concept always close to Katherine Harley's heart. It was suggested that pilgrims should wear white, grey, black, or navy blue coats and skirts or dresses. Blouses were either to match the skirt or to be white. Hats were to be simple, and only black, white, grey, or navy blue. For 3d, headquarters supplied a compulsory raffia badge, a cockle shell, the traditional symbol of pilgrimage, to be worn pinned to the hat. Also available were a red, white and green shoulder sash, a haversack, made of bright red waterproof cloth edged with green with white lettering spelling out the route travelled, and umbrellas in green or white, or red cotton covers to coordinate civilian umbrellas."[109]

On 29 July 1913, a few days after the Hyde Park rally, the leader of the NUWSS, Millicent Fawcett, wrote to Prime Minister Herbert Asquith "on behalf of the immense meetings which assembled in Hyde Park on Saturday and voted with practical unanimity in favour of a Government measure". Asquith replied that the demonstration had "a special claim" on his consideration and stood "upon another footing from similar demands proceeding from other quarters where a different method and spirit is predominant"[110]. It was fair to say the pilgrimage had been a success, not only for the women's suffrage movement but also for proving that women did not need to resort to violence to make their voices heard.

108 Madge Dresser, (2016). *Women and the City: Bristol 1373-2000*. Bristol: Redcliffe Press. 133.
109 Elizabeth Crawford, (1999), *The Suffrage Movement*. London: Routledge. 552.
110 http://spartacus-educational.com/Wpilgimage.htm

ELLEN CULLINANE
1843-1879, LOCK HOSPITAL PATIENT

The Cullinane family from Cork, Ireland, moved to Bristol during the 1850s and in the 1861 census 17-year-old Ellen Cullinane is living at 22 Bread Street, while her mother Mary later becomes a resident of the Barton Regis Workhouse (where she died in 1885). Unfortunately, by the 1871 census, 27-year-old Ellen's address has become the Old Park Lock Hospital where her occupation is listed as "charwoman/patient".[111]

Lock hospitals, being hospitals from which patients could not leave and were effectively prisoners, were exclusively for the treatment of women affected by sexually transmitted diseases and they viewed their patients as nothing more than 'common prostitutes'. The name 'lock hospital' dated from medieval institutions where lepers were kept in restraint, which gives an indication of the level of disregard with which these women were viewed. Incidentally, the 'cure' for sexually transmitted diseases in the Victorian era was mercury: a poison.

The initial Contagious Diseases Act (CDA) was passed in 1864[112], having been rushed through with little debate in a desperate effort to try and curb the number of military men infected with sexually transmitted diseases. The CDA gave the police authority to arrest women suspected of being prostitutes and bring them before a magistrate. The woman was then required to sign papers consenting to internal medical examinations and by signing these papers she was by default publicly declaring herself to be a prostitute. This was clearly an abhorrent way to treat anybody. Those who were examined and found to have a sexually

111 http://www.stantonetal.com/genealogy/getperson.php?personID=I1133&tree=maintree
112 There were three parts to the Contagious Diseases Act.

transmitted disease were sent to a lock hospital until cured, and they could be held there for up to a year. Even upon release, the women were subject to further medical examinations, often as regularly as fortnightly, as a consequence of having signed the papers acknowledging themselves to be a prostitute, even if they no longer worked in the sex trade (or indeed had never sold sex for money to begin with). In the same vein, any woman who was released from a lock hospital would find it very hard to assimilate into everyday life and find new employment because everybody would know her history and she would be tainted by the stigma. Ironically, this had the consequence of forcing financially desperate women into prostitution because few people would employ 'a fallen woman'.

It is important to note that no action was *ever* taken against the men who purchased, exploited and infected the female sex workers. The men were seen as the 'victims' in this scenario.

In response, the Ladies' National Campaign Against the Contagious Diseases Act was launched in September 1869 at the Victoria Rooms, Clifton. However, women led by Josephine Butler had been appealing the Act since 1864 and a number of women in Bristol emerged as passionate opponents to the CDA. Anna Maria and Mary Priestman and Margaret Tanner were very vocal in their support for reforming the CDA, while Mary Carpenter added her support later in the 1870s.[113]

The Ladies' National Campaign centred on the CDA's violation of women's rights, the unequal treatment of men and women under the CDA, and the implication that the government condoned the use of prostituted women by the military. The Bristol Old Park Lock Hospital opened in 1870 and had places for 16 patients. It was located at 3 Lower Park Hill and Ellen was listed

113 http://humanities.uwe.ac.uk/bhr/Main/women_routes/4_philanthropy.htm

there as a patient by 1871. Whether or not Ellen had fallen into a life of prostitution, she would by the standards of the time have been considered to have 'fallen' simply by having – presumably – contracted a sexually transmitted disease while unmarried. Sadly, Ellen died at the hospital in 1879 at the age of 34 and did not live to enjoy her freedom again.

The hospital's annual report of 1878 noted that of the 37 patients who were discharged from the hospital that year, 30 returned to the care of their friends or were sent to homes or into service, while seven were believed to have gone back to what was termed "their evil habits"[114]. An 1881 report for the Old Park Lock Hospital stated proudly: "It is the only hospital that receives women when they are suffering from diseases incident to an immoral life. And however much we may regret that there are no wards set apart in the Infirmary and General Hospital for this class of patient, there are great advantages in their being treated in a separate house, where they have constant personal attention, and are placed in healthful moral condition."[115]

By the 1880s, the attitude was still one of belittlement to the women as the 1881 report attests: "They receive the best medical care and most kind and skilled nursing. Whilst lying by, sick and suffering, they are led to see the past in a new light; they become attached to the nurse, who watches over them with motherly care, and are influenced for good by her and the ladies who help her in the work. A large proportion of those who come to be healed, without any thought of amendment, leave with an earnest desire to lead better lives and pass to Houses or Reformatories, or, in some cases, to service, under mistresses who are willing to watch over them."[116]

114 Ibid
115 https://archive.org/stream/lockhospitalsloc00lown/lockhospitalsloc00lown_djvu.txt, 18-19.
116 Ibid,18-19.

It took almost two decades of campaigning before the CDA was suspended in 1883 and repealed in 1886. The archaic Bristol Old Park Lock Hospital closed in 1886 and the institution moved to 87 Ashley Road and changed its name to the Voluntary Lock Hospital where, as the name suggests, entry was now on a voluntary basis and conditions for the patients were vastly improved.

Please also see the entries for: Josephine Butler, Mary Carpenter, Anna Maria and Mary Priestman and Margaret Tanner.

MIRIAM DANIELL

1861-1894, SOCIALIST

Much of socialist Miriam Daniell's story crosses over with that of Helena Born. The two women, who met in 1888, were key players in the unionisation of striking workers at the various factories around Bristol.

Miriam shocked polite society when she left her middle-class husband – solicitor Edward Daniell – and their comfortable Clifton home to live with her younger lover, medical student Robert Allan Nicol, in a simple house in the working-class area of St Philips. The thinking behind this decision was so that they could live among the people they wanted to support. Mike Richardson and Sheila Rowbotham write: "They created aesthetic simplicity amidst the bees-waxed bare boards at 9 Louisa Street and an over-attentive rat."[117]

The couple were soon joined by fellow socialist Helena Born, with whom Miriam was also in a romantic relationship. And

117 Madge Dresser, (2016). *Women and the City: Bristol 1373-2000*. Bristol: Redcliffe Press. 120

when Miriam became pregnant by Robert, the scandal of their unconventional living arrangement *and* of being pregnant out of marriage pushed the trio to move to the United States where their daughter Sunrise was born in November 1890.

Please also see the entry for: Helena Born.

ROSAMUND DAVENPORT HILL and FLORENCE DAVENPORT HILL

1825-1902, 1829-1919, SUFFRAGISTS

Rosamund and Florence Davenport Hill were the daughters of Commissioner Matthew Davenport Hill, who worked closely in Bristol with Mary Carpenter to achieve prison reform and improved welfare for pauper children. It was at his home at 3 West Mall, Clifton, and on the request of Florence, that the city's first ever women's suffrage meeting was held in 1868. Florence had already been a signatory of the 1866 suffrage petition and was a subscriber to the London-based Enfranchisement of Women Committee.[118] The strangely worded, although perhaps not so strange for a time when men were perceived to be in control, invitation to the 1868 meeting read: "Commissioner Davenport Hill permits his daughter, Miss Florence Davenport, to issue [the invitation]."[119] *Permits!*

However, Matthew was one of the good guys. He had publicly endorsed the notion of women's suffrage as early as 1832, and in 1856 he had helped women's rights campaigner Barbara Bodichon to draft a report outlining the reasons why women's suffrage

118 Elizabeth Crawford, (1999). *The Women's Suffrage Movement: A Reference Guide 1866-1928*. London: University College London Press. 129.
119 Lorna Brierley, Helen Reid, (2000). *Go Home and Do the Washing!* Bristol: Broadcast. 144.

was necessary. Consequently his daughters had a supportive home in which to develop their opinions and campaigns around suffragism.

Rosamund followed in her father's footsteps and taught in Mary Carpenter's Ragged School in St James's Back during the 1850s and later became a Co-Founder and Treasurer of the Stanhope House Industrial School. Florence was similarly concerned with improving the welfare of those less fortunate and joined the Poor Law's Board of Guardians.

Florence went on to write *Children of the State* in 1889, in which "she urged the abolition of the old system of herding [poor children] together in workhouses, and proposed to restore them to a natural life by boarding them out in cottage homes and by other means"[120]. This led to the creation of a children's aid society and in 1908 Florence drafted a Bill for the establishment of children's courts.

"They took a great interest in all movements for the amelioration of the condition of women, political and social, as well as in many minor movements of reform," wrote the *Western Daily Press* about the sisters upon Rosamund's death in 1902.[121]

Rosamund and Florence left Bristol for London in 1872 after the passing of their beloved father. For 15 years, Rosamund sat on the London School Board, where she was known on several occasions to pay from her own purse for the best medical treatment for some of the poorest boys under her care, and as such she "won their affection by the kind and motherly interest she took in them"[122]. The Brentwood School was subsequently renamed the Davenport Hill Home for Boys in Rosamund's honour.

It's curious that when Florence died in 1919 (17 years after her

120 *Western Daily Press, 1919, 6 November, 'A Noted Woman Reformer'. 5.*
121 *Western Daily Press, 1902, 8 August, 'The Late Miss Rosamund Davenport Hill'. 6.*
122 Ibid. *6.*

sister and 47 years after their father) the *Western Daily Press* chose to report her passing by focussing largely on her father Matthew's achievements, in much the same way that contemporary news reports about a famous woman seem to feel they must always identify the woman via the man to whom she 'belongs'. The paper began the news report about Florence's death saying: "Those of our older readers who remember Mr Commissioner Hill ... may have recollections of those bygone days revived by learning that his daughter, Miss Florence Davenport Hill, has just passed away at the ripe age of 90 years."[123] Which, frankly, seems an insulting way to honour the memory of this magnificent woman.

GERTRUDE DIX

1867-1950, SUFFRAGIST, NOVELIST

A committed socialist, writer Gertrude Dix used her novels to bring societal issues to a new audience. As a member of the Clifton and Bristol Christian Society, Gertrude advocated for the workers caught up in the labour unrest in Bristol between 1889-1890 and her popular 1900 novel *The Image Breakers* is a fictionalised account of the strike at the Sanders' sweet factory on Redcliff Street. Gertrude later abandoned the literary societies of Bristol and London to up sticks and emigrate to a Californian ranch where she had a family with Robert Allan Nicol, following the death of his partner Miriam Daniell.

Please also see the entry for: Miriam Daniell. For more information about the strikes, please see the Women's Work section towards the back of this book.

123 *Western Daily Press, 1919, 6 November, 'A Noted Woman Reformer'. 5.*

LILIAN DOVE-WILCOX
1877-1963, SUFFRAGETTE

Lilian Mary Dove-Willcox was born in Clifton, one of several children of Alfred Dugdale and his wife Elizabeth. Following his family's seafaring tradition, her father had been Captain of a merchant ship, before losing both ship and cargo in a fire and becoming obliged to take a position as the Clerk of Bristol Market. Lilian married Arnold Dove-Willcox, a leather manufacturer, at Westbury-on-Trym in 1903, the couple then living at Yatton until Arnold died in 1907.

By October 1908, when she was the host for a suffrage 'At Home', Lilian was a member of the West of England branch of the Women's Social and Political Union (WSPU). When arrested the following June, after taking part in a WSPU deputation from Caxton Hall to Parliament, Lilian mentioned that it was hearing Emmeline Pankhurst speak that had inspired her to join the WSPU. The idea of 'votes for women' was not new to her because her mother had been a suffrage supporter for 40 years, however Lilian thought the lack of progress made by the older generation necessitated more militant action.

Lilian was sentenced to a month's imprisonment, went on hunger strike and was released. She was subsequently charged with striking a wardress and was sentenced to a further ten days, again went on hunger strike and again secured an early release. Her father-in-law, who had been a subscriber to the 19th century Bristol suffrage society, wrote a letter to *Votes for Women* (3 September 1909) commenting that, while he was a supporter of women's suffrage, he was against militancy and repudiated Lilian's actions, while remarking how much care she had given to his son in his final illness.

Lilian succeeded Annie Kenney as Honorary Secretary of the

Bristol branch of the WSPU in autumn 1911. Earlier in the year, when she boycotted the census, Lilian was lodging at 50 Bradley Road, Trowbridge, Wiltshire. Her census form was completed by an official, who wrote on it that she had spent census night "in a caravan at Bristol". Lilian's country cottage, on a hill overlooking the Wye and Tintern, provided a place in which suffragettes could recuperate after imprisonment.

By 1913, she was a member of Mrs Pankhurst's 'bodyguard' and on 9 March attempted to protect her from the police at a meeting in St Andrew's Halls, Glasgow, which descended into violence. A couple of days later, back in London, Lilian was arrested while attempting to petition the King at the opening of parliament and was sentenced to a month's imprisonment.

In 1914, Lilian remarried. She had met her new husband, Reginald Buckley, at Stratford-on-Avon. He was a dramatist associated with the composer Rutland Boughton and the pre-war 'Arthurian Revival' and was co-founder of the 1914 Glastonbury Festival. Buckley was a regular reviewer for *TP's Weekly* and in the issue of 30 June 1911 had reviewed Sylvia Pankhurst's *The Suffragette* and had read there something of Lilian's suffragette exploits. He had worked with Mary Neal, friend and sometime co-worker of Emmeline Pethick Lawrence, who had become a leader in the folk-dance revival movement. The couple lived in London but the marriage did not last. Buckley was not happy with Lilian's continued suffrage activity, latterly, during World War One, as a member of the East London Federation of the Suffragettes. After the birth of a daughter, Diana, in 1915, and a subsequent suicide attempt, Lilian returned to her mother, who was living close by in a Bloomsbury flat.

In her 1988 memoir, *Tracing Papers,* Lilian's daughter Diana Rowntree suggests that her mother had suffered from a degree of mental instability. Buckley died in 1919, leaving what money he had to his mother, who took responsibility for Diana's education. Support also came from Buckley's wealthy cousin Marjory Lees who, with her mother Sarah Lees, had before the war run the National Union of Women's Suffrage Societies' Oldham branch. Although it was an unlikely pairing, Lilian, the volatile suffragette, and Marjory, the measured suffragist, appear to have had a harmonious relationship.

Shortly before she died, Lilian subscribed to the Pethick Lawrence Memorial Appeal Fund and in her will left £10 to the Suffragette Fellowship. At the time of her death she was living at 44 The Park, Ealing, London.

Written by Elizabeth Crawford, who is an independent suffrage researcher and the author of numerous books on the subject, including *The Women's Suffrage Movement: A Reference Guide 1866-1928* and *Campaigning For The Vote: Kate Parry Frye's Suffrage Diary*. Her latest book, *Art and Suffrage: A Biographical Dictionary of Suffrage Artists*, is published in 2018.

Please also see the entry for: Emmeline Pethick Lawrence.

ELIZA WALKER DUNBAR

1845-1925, DOCTOR

One of the first 'lady doctors' in Bristol, Eliza Walker Dunbar was "very highly respected by medical practitioners in Bristol and was greatly esteemed by her patients"[124]. While Bristol's Elizabeth Blackwell is well known to be the first British woman to qualify as a doctor, less is known about Eliza Walker Dunbar.

124 *Western Daily Press*, 1925, 28 August, 'Death of Dr Eliza W Dunbar'. 7.

Born in Bombay, India, and educated at Cheltenham Ladies' College, Eliza grew up with a father and sister who were both doctors. Add in the surrounding influence of women such as Elizabeth Blackwell and Elizabeth Garrett (under whom Eliza would later study), and Eliza clearly had strong images of successful doctors and women around her and this surely influenced her own decision to study medicine.

Eliza studied the medical degree course at the University of Zurich, Switzerland, which had welcomed women since 1864 because at this time women still could not study medicine in the United Kingdom. Her thesis, written in German, about embolism in arteries of the brain secured Eliza her medical doctorate and after a further year of study in Vienna, Austria, Eliza moved to Bristol where she was to remain for the rest of her life.

Once in Bristol, alongside work as a doctor, Eliza joined a circle of friends that included Mary Carpenter and she became an ardent campaigner for women's suffrage. In addition, she broke new ground at the Hospital for Women and Children on St Michael's Hill when they appointed her as the first ever female Resident Medical Officer in 1873, deciding "there would be a peculiar fitness in electing a lady to the vacant office"[125].

However, Eliza quickly had a large disagreement with one of the hospital physicians resulting in his male colleagues rallying around him in support and Eliza, as the lone woman, bitterly handed in her notice. Medical journal *The Lancet* took up the story and seemingly expressed disapproval that Bristol had ever thought it was a good idea to have appointed a woman in the first place, writing: "We cannot affect surprise at the result which has been attained, and do not see how any other could have been expected … Women are neither physically nor morally qualified

125 Lorna Brierley, Helen Reid, (2000). *Go Home and Do the Washing!* Bristol: Broadcast. 77.

for many of the onerous, important and confidential duties of the general practitioner; nor capable of the prolonged exertions or severe exposures to all kinds of weather which a professional life entail."[126] Ouch.

Nevertheless, supported by her friends, Eliza persisted. When Miss Read founded the Read Dispensary for Women and Children in St George's Road, Hotwells, in 1874, Eliza was the Honorary Medical Assistant. Women and children were charged a sum to attend and seek medical support, but given the impoverished state of Hotwells – and the size of many families there – access to vital medical care was an expensive burden to a lot of the neighbouring families. This gave Eliza the inspiration to gather the funds required to open an alternative dispensary in Berkeley Square in 1895: the Bristol Private Hospital for Women and Children. However, *The Lancet* remained opposed to the idea of women doctors, writing in 1892: "The idea of female attendants is positively repulsive to the more thoughtful women of this country!"[127] Again, ouch.

Regardless, the hospital thrived and rapidly outgrew its original premises, relocating to a larger house on Clifton Down Road and adopting the name of the Walker Dunbar Hospital where the staff was entirely female.

None of this was enough for Eliza. In addition, she was the visiting medical officer for both the Red Lodge Reformatory School and the Bristol Training College for teachers, she was a sponsor of the Bristol suffrage movement, a co-founder of the Bristol Association of Working Women and much more.

Despite *The Lancet*'s long hostility towards Eliza and her sister doctors, *The Medical News* was far more supportive and following her death in 1925 it wrote: "This wonderful and kindly old lady

126 Ibid. 79.
127 Ibid. 81.

will be much missed by all who had the good fortune to know her or be under her care."[128]

Please also see the entries for: Elizabeth Blackwell and Mary Carpenter.

HELEN DUNMORE

1952-2017, NOVELIST

Novelist, children's author, poet and short story writer Helen Dunmore was more than a writer. She was a champion of creative work, particularly women's. Her enthusiasm for literature, history and storytelling was infectious, and her generosity towards younger or emerging writers was as inspiring as it was helpful.

Helen's literary life began as a poet, with her first collection *The Apple Fall* published in 1983. She remained loyal to the publisher Bloodaxe Books throughout her career; they were to publish her final collection *Inside the Wave* (which won the Costa Book Prize for Poetry in January 2018) just before her tragically early death from cancer in 2017. But it was through her novels that I got to know and love Helen's work.

Helen never restricted herself to one genre. She wrote thrillers, historical fiction, horror, contemporary fiction – reaching back into Roman times, turn of the century Finland and Stalinist Russia; exploring ideas of obsession and unresolved conflict, adultery, family, war and feminist politics. From the creepy thriller *Your Blue Eyed Boy* to the oppressive *House of Orphans,* Helen's work is that of a novelist who is concerned with telling a story – the right story – regardless of genre or trend. The breadth of her work

128 Ibid. 82.

shows a writer who refused to be put in a pigeonhole, one who wanted her imagination to roam across time and space, and who invited her readers to go on that journey right along with her.

Helen's first novel, *Zennor in Darkness*, examines the life of DH Lawrence and his German wife Frieda after they moved to Cornwall in World War One. It explores the impact of war on men returning home to visit family as the conflict raged across the Channel. Helen writes with sensitivity about the juxtaposition between the trauma of the trenches and the apparent normality of home – that clash of violence and peace – and the struggle returning soldiers faced to articulate or share the horrors they had endured. Helen returned to the secrets and unspeakable narratives of World War One in her 2014 novel *The Lie*.

In 1996, Helen's third novel *A Spell of Winter* won the inaugural Women's Prize for Fiction (then known as the Orange Prize), set up by Kate Mosse after an all-male Booker shortlist in 1991. This was followed by the disconcerting and confrontational *Talking to the Dead*, which explores the conflict between sisters, childbirth and adultery.

A prolific writer, more novels and children's books followed, and in 2002 Helen wrote the Whitbread Prize shortlisted *The Siege*, surely one of her masterpieces. This chilling novel tells the frightening story of a family's desperate fight for survival during the Leningrad siege. The novel evokes the cold, the hunger and the blank fear of war and starvation. The reader lives the pain of the characters – the writing is so vivid that you feel the intense cold of the Russian winter as the Levin family cooks shoe leather in boiling water to try and extract the tiniest bit of protein to stay alive. A sequel, *The Betrayal*, followed in 2010, with its exacting description of life under Stalin's totalitarian regime.

Helen's final novel, *Birdcage Walk*, was published shortly before her death in 2017. Named after the path through Clifton's

Helen Dunmore illustration by Jenny Howe

beautiful cemetery, the story takes place in the city during the years that followed the French Revolution. It's a remarkable book: one that explores radical politics, the history of Bristol and the forgotten stories of women. It's a novel about care and devotion and motherhood. But perhaps most importantly of all, it's a novel about male violence and the creeping, insidious nature of emotional abuse. Dunmore deftly explores the slow build-up of coercive control and threatening behaviour shown towards the protagonist Lizzie by her husband as the story builds towards its terrifying denouement.

I was lucky enough to work with Helen when I organised the first Bristol Women's Literature Festival. Her warmth, encouragement and wisdom, as well as her enthusiasm for promoting women's writing, has remained with me. The impact of the poetry group she set up includes the work of prolific poet Tania Hershman among others. Helen leaves behind an incredible body of work and a legacy of generosity to writers in Bristol and beyond.

Written by Sian Norris, who is a writer and feminist activist. Sian is the Founder and Director of the Bristol Women's Literature Festival, where Helen spoke in 2013.

MARIA EDGEWORTH

1768-1849, EDUCATIONALIST, NOVELIST

A contemporary of Hannah More, bluestocking Maria Edgeworth was a Clifton-based writer who shared Hannah's concerns about the poor education given to girls. In 1798 she co-authored the book *Practical Education* with her father, stating: "It will tend to the happiness of society in general that women should have their understanding cultivated and enlarged as much as possible … Let a woman know one thing completely and she will have sufficient understanding to learn more."[129] Maria strived to raise the standard of writing among girls and women and wrote a number of morally improving books to further this cause.

Please also see the entry for: Hannah More.

AMELIA BLANFORD EDWARDS

1831-1892, EXPLORER

Amelia Blanford Edwards wasn't your average Victorian child. From an early age, she was headstrong and funny despite her father being a dour ex-military man. Her Irish mother, however, recognising that her daughter was gifted, judged that Amelia was destined for great things and educated her herself, delighting in her daughter's eccentricities. An only child, Amelia began writing stories, one of which was published at the age of 12. She later wrote ghost stories (how the Victorians loved those!) eventually becoming a successful journalist and novelist. Her novel *Lord Brackenbury* went to 15 editions. When her parents died in 1864, Amelia moved from London to Westbury-on-Trym and by this time she was living from her income as a writer.

Nile travel was quite the fashionable thing to do in the 1800s, and in 1873 Amelia and some friends embarked on a voyage down the Nile. Smitten by the new sights during their six-week stay at Abu Simbel, Egypt, Amelia's destiny was fixed. Arriving at a tomb, they reportedly found a small opening in the sand and Amelia started digging with her bare hands while wearing her

129 Lorna Brierley, Helen Reid, (2000). *Go Home and Do the Washing!* Bristol: Broadcast. 54.

skirts. As a Victorian lady, any vigorous physical activity must have been difficult with such restrictive clothing but, undeterred by sandstorms filling eyes, mouth, hair and ears, she and her friends excavated a chamber. Amelia later wrote and illustrated a book, *A Thousand Miles up the Nile*, which was a vivid description of what she found. It was an immediate success.

Amelia was appalled at the destruction of the things she was seeing: "The tourist carves it all over with names and dates ... the 'collector' buys and carries off everything of value and the Arab steals for him. There is no one to prevent it; there is no one to discourage it." She learned to read hieroglyphics and became an advocate for the ancient monuments and artefacts by co-founding the Egypt Exploration Fund (now Society) in 1882.

She also found time to become Vice President of the Society for Promoting Women's Suffrage and was an active supporter of the suffrage movement ignoring those in her circle who called it a 'fad'. She never married and instead of the male chaperone expected of a Victorian lady, she travelled and lived with a female partner who accompanied her on an American lecture tour from 1889-1890 leading to honorary degrees from American colleges.

Amelia kept most of her collection of Egyptian antiquities in her home, and in a charming 1891 article written for *The Arena* journal she describes how her hundreds of artefacts are kept out of sight in her personal library. While legend has it that Amelia kept an Egyptian mummy in her wardrobe, the truth is rather more gruesome: "There are stranger things... fragments of spiced and bituminized humanity to be shown to visitors who are not nervous, or given to midnight terrors. Here is a baby's foot (some mother cried over it once) in the Japanese cabinet in the ante-room. There are three mummified hands behind *Allibone's Dictionary of English Authors* in the library. There are two arms with hands complete ... in a drawer in my dressing-room; and grimmest of all, I have the heads of two ancient Egyptians in a wardrobe in my bedroom, who, perhaps, talk to each other in the watches of the night, when I am sound asleep."[130]

Amelia died from influenza in Weston-super-Mare in 1892, and in her will she bequeathed her extensive collections to University College London together with the sum of £2,500... because it was the only university that awarded degrees to women.

And another thing... Amelia reportedly had a ménage-à-trois with clergyman John Rice Byrne and his wife Ellen, of 7 Cambridge Park, Redland. Amelia also enjoyed a relationship with the artist and traveller Marianne North, and passionate love letters between the couple are kept at Clifton Hill House (now part of the University of Bristol). Amelia is buried in the same grave as her "very dear friend" Ellen Drew Braysher, with whom she lived at The Larches, Westbury-on-Trym, for 25 years. Their burial plot (a Grade-II listed grave in the churchyard at St Mary's Church in Hengrove) is marked by a large Egyptian ankh.[131]

Written by Jacqui Furneaux, who has been exploring the world on the back of her motorbike since 2000. Her memoir *Hit The Road, Jac!* was published in 2017.

GLADYS ELLIS

1906-1995, NURSE

On 2 December 1940, at 8.45pm, three German bombs hit Bristol Children's Hospital. Matron Gladys Ruth Ellis was standing on the hospital's steps at the time the bombs hit. This is her story

130 Amelia B Edwards, (1891). 'My Home Life' in *The Arena*, Vol IV. Boston: Arena Publishing Company. 308-309.

131 http://www.symondsinbristol.co.uk/?p=1084

in her own words, as originally told to the *Bristol Post* in 1995[132]: "When the blast took me, I sailed through the air with the greatest of ease. My flight was only stopped by my tin hat and the pair of front doors." Gladys spoke effusively about the bravery of the nursing staff that night, even though they were only young student nurses who didn't have a wealth of experience behind them. The children and staff were all evacuated to the Homeopathic Hospital at the top of St Michael's Hill, despite the bombs continuing to fall around them.

Gladys went on: "Eventually we got all 86 children up to the Homeopathic Hospital, with great difficulty; you could see the bombs coming down and the fires going up everywhere. Then I said we must do a roll call. And there was a child missing. Everyone was very shaken and they said 'Matron, we think you've made a mistake '. And I said, 'Well I don't think I have. You gave the list and there are 86 children. How many do you have?' They replied, '85, Matron.' I said, 'We must go back.'"

Despite everyone warning Gladys of the dangers of returning to the hospital to look for the missing child, she was adamant: "I started walking down to the hospital. I must say, I was a bit apprehensive, but it was my duty to find that child. And before I got to the front door I heard pattering feet behind me and it was one of the fire-watchers. We couldn't get in the front door because of a great big hole – I fell in it!"

After clambering out of the hole, Gladys made her way inside the hospital and up to the children's floor but there was no sign of the missing child, although she had a gut feeling that he was in there somewhere: "I don't know, from that day to this, what made me go into my office, which was on the left-hand side as you go into the front hall. And underneath my dining room table was this

132 Cited in Chloe Headdon, 'Heroic Matron Rescued Boy in Blitz' in *Bristol Times*, 25 October 2016, 4.

little boy, sound asleep, wrapped up in a long bed mackintosh. I picked up this child and gave thanks, and we carried him out to the Homeopathic Hospital."

Reporting on Gladys being awarded an MBE in recognition of her actions in 1941, the *London Gazette* wrote: "In spite of the fact that she had been severely shaken by the blast the Matron took command of the situation and the staff, under her direction, behaved magnificently."[133]

Gladys had trained at the Bristol Children's Hospital between 1922 and 1926, before she went to the Bristol General Hospital. After a few years as the sister in charge of the Milk Laboratory, Great Ormond Street Hospital, London, Gladys became Lady Superintendent of the British Red Cross and was appointed as Matron of the Bristol Children's Hospital in April 1940.[134]

MARY ESTLIN

1820-1902, SLAVERY ABOLITIONIST, SUFFRAGIST

Bristol-based Mary Estlin was a leading figure in both the British anti-slavery and anti-prostitution campaigns. She joined the committee of the Ladies' Anti-Slavery Society in 1851 and progressed to the role of Treasurer in the Women's Suffrage Society in subsequent years.

Such was Mary's commitment to the causes she championed that she never married and instead devoted her life to her campaigns, including travelling to the United States to meet with leading American abolitionists. Among her many roles, Mary was Secretary of the Bristol and Clifton Ladies' Anti-Slavery Society, and she welcomed the fugitive American ex-slave Ellen Craft to

133 https://www.thegazette.co.uk/London/issue/35143/supplement/2335/data.pdf
134 *Western Daily Press*, 1941, 26 April, 'Bristol Hospital Matron Awarded an MBE'. 5.

her Bristol home during Ellen's lecture tour. Mary also formed strong links with suffrage sisters in America, including Elizabeth Cady Stanton[135], who visited Bristol in 1883 in a show of solidarity with her British sisters.

In terms of suffrage work, Mary was a founding committee member of the Bristol and West of England branch of the Women's Suffrage Society in 1868, becoming Treasurer in 1870. And in line with her suffrage work, Mary recognised that the vote alone was not enough to liberate women so she also joined the executive committee of the Ladies' National Association for the Repeal of the Contagious Diseases Act (CDA).

Work on the CDA needed particular care and tact since it concerned women working as prostitutes, as Anna Priestman observed at the 1870 Social Science Conference when she said: "Our cause is a secret one." The topic was delicate and one that many Victorians found distasteful and considered to be no concern of theirs. As such, Women's Franchise League co-founder Elizabeth Wolstenholme was moved to say about Mary: "How brave and true she [was] to CDA when so many were timid."[136]

Please also see the entries for: Josephine Butler, Helen Priestman Bright Clark, Ellen Craft and Anna Priestman.

135 As a crude comparison, Elizabeth Cady Stanton could perhaps be seen as the American counterpart to Millicent Fawcett, in that she was the leader of a peaceful, non-militant campaign to secure votes for women in the United States. Prior to her suffrage campaigns, Elizabeth had been an active campaigner to end slavery, which was how she met Mary Estlin.

136 Sandra Stanley Holton (1996), *Suffrage Days: Stories from the Women's Suffrage Movement*. London: Routledge. 31.

DOROTHY EVANS
1888-1944, SUFFRAGETTE

When Annie Kenney stepped down as Organiser of the Women's Social and Political Union (WSPU) in Bristol, her shoes were filled by Dorothy Evans who had previously been WSPU Organiser in Birmingham and who came to Bristol on 29 August 1913.

Dorothy originally joined the WSPU in 1909 and her frequent arrests for militancy quickly saw her lose her job as a school PE teacher. Not one to be deterred, Dorothy threw herself into campaigning for votes for women, was arrested numerous times, experienced force feeding, endured great police brutality during the Black Friday demonstration in London in 1910 and much more. For instance, in May 1911 Dorothy was imprisoned for two weeks for refusing to pay her dog tax, claiming "no taxation without representation". What we're learning here is that Dorothy was a strong woman, indeed WSPU stalwart Sylvia Pankhurst even called her a "sturdy, handsome young woman".

But Bristol was only to have the benefit of Dorothy for a mere month because just four weeks later she was dispatched to Belfast to set up a WSPU office in Northern Ireland, and this she did until April 1914 when she was arrested yet again. One of the charges against her was that she had failed to attend a previous court hearing… although she was sort of there: Dorothy apparently drove backwards and forwards past the court during the hearing in a brightly coloured car!

Dorothy's time in Bristol may have been brief but her presence in the militant campaign was certainly frenetic.

MARJORIE EVANS

1905-1996, CAMPAIGNER

A member of the Labour Party from 1922 until her death, there were not many causes that Marjorie 'Marge' Evans did not support. Even in her later years, she was marching in support of striking miners in Bristol in the mid 1980s. She was relentless.

Born into a hard-working and working-class Bristolian family, and with both parents involved in the trades union movement, Marge had a strong socialist ethic from day one. However, after her mother died in the Spanish Flu epidemic of 1918, 13-year-old Marge suddenly had to grow up a lot quicker than expected… and say goodbye to her school education in order to stay home and look after her younger siblings. But given the school's insistence on glorifying war in history lessons, future peace campaigner Marge wasn't so sure that leaving school was a bad thing.

In 1922, Marge joined the Independent Labour Party (ILP) after being recruited by Florence Brown, who would become Bristol's first female Lord Mayor in 1963. Marge joined a few other organisations as well: the Co-operative Women's Guild, the National Council of Labour Colleges, the Peace Pledge Union (who pioneered the white peace poppies for Remembrance Sunday) and the Bristol Athletics Club (where Marge was a keen runner and swimmer). The guilds were particularly important for women in the 1920s because, at that time, women were much less active in the political parties than they are today so the guilds offered them a platform to speak. Talking about the Co-operative Women's Guild, Marge said: "It was a most democratic organisation, they did a lot for women; before you obtained any particular office you had to go through the lower offices; you couldn't just come in and be Vice President or Chairman; you earned your way. The guilds were interested in issues like child welfare and peace: they were affiliated to the Peace Pledge Union." On the subject of the local political parties she added: "The [ILP] was dominated by men. They didn't even take up the issue of votes for women at first – we've still got a terrific fight about getting women representatives on to committees and for women's rights."[137]

As time progressed and Marge proved herself to her comrades, she became much more involved in the campaigns and achieved positions of higher office. However, like most other women, she still didn't have the vote herself until 1928[138]: "Women didn't have the vote then. I worked for the Labour Party and didn't have the vote, and you only had a vote if you were a householder; lots of people that were lodgers didn't get one. So the odds were heavily against us."[139]

Marge became frustrated with the ILP and considered it "parochial" in outlook, so when some of her friends went to fight in the Spanish Civil War she joined the Bristol Committee for Spain, despite still being a peace campaigner. Initially the committee collected money for the republic, but later organised homes for Spanish refugee children from Bilbao and San Sebastian to stay safely in Bristol and she took in several refugees herself. Marge recalled: "I said… how many [children] do you want me to have? So she said you could have four or five children. We put up a placard in the garden saying 'Support Spain'. The kids were here all through the war."[140]

When World War Two was declared, peace campaigner

137 David Parker, (1986), 'A Proper Joiner: Marge Evans – Memories of the Bristol Labour Movement', in Bristol Broadsides, *Placards and Pin Money: Another Look at Bristol's Other History*. Bristol: Broadsides. 7.

138 The Representation of the People Act 1918 widened suffrage by enabling all men over 21 to have the vote (regardless of whether they owned property), and granting the vote to women over 30 who owned property. Many suffragists and suffragettes were angered by this half-hearted compromise offered by the Government.

139 Ibid. 18.

140 Ibid. 13.

Marge was again stirred into action to find safe homes for refugee German Jewish children, and in 1939 took a young German Jewish boy into her family home for the duration of the war. In addition, Marge worked hard to try and bring the boy's Jewish parents to Bristol from Germany and tried to find work for them in the city, but sadly the boy's parents died in a German concentration camp before she was able to bring them to England.

A lifetime of politics and campaigning was to follow for Marge, who fought for all causes ranging from women's suffrage to peace and the trades unions. Even in 1984, when she was 79, Marge supported the striking miners, saying simply: "I walked with the miners in 1926 and I walked with them again in 1984"[141], as if there was nothing else to do but keep on marching. Indeed, speaking in 1986 Marge lamented the general sense of apathy that she felt surrounded the contemporary generation: "I wonder what's happened to all the enthusiasm which in my youth was for change. I can only think that we had nothing to lose, we were in that position, the working class in the '20s and '30s… Now the first thing they think about is I've got a mortgage and I've got a car, I've got all these possessions, it's something to hang on to. People have come to value their possessions more than their principles."[142]

Please also see the entry for: Florence Brown.

ANNA-MARIA FALCONBRIDGE

1769-1816, TRAVEL WRITER, ABOLITIONIST

Born on All Saints Lane (next door to what is now St Nicholas Market), when she came of age Anna-Maria Horwood married

141 Ibid. 19.
142 Ibid. 21.

Alexander Falconbridge – who was a surgeon on a slave ship, although later became a staunch abolitionist and wrote about the horrors he witnessed aboard the slave ships – who gave his wife a taste for international travel. Anna-Maria twice accompanied her husband on lengthy trips to the embryonic Sierra Leone, West Africa, and published her eyewitness account of the slave trade in her book *Narrative of Two Voyages* (1794). At a time when most travelogues were written by men, Anna-Maria offered an exclusively feminine view of what she experienced.

After seven years as a slave ship surgeon, Alexander came to the belief that the slave trade should be abolished and began working to set up a colony for freed slaves on the banks of the Nile. And in her book, Anna-Maria – who also came to be an abolitionist – refers to the slave ships as "floating cages, without room either to walk about, stand erect, or even to lay at length"[143]. The link to Anna-Maria's home city remains, though, as many of the entries in her book start as a letter to a "dear friend" in Bristol. The amount of detail in Anna-Maria's writing is extraordinary, and offers an unparalleled glimpse into a time that is thankfully behind us. On one occasion, she describes being a guest at a grand dinner hosted by a slave owner and being able to view the slave yard from the dining table: "Judge then what my astonishment and feelings were, at the sight of between two and three hundred wretched victims, chained and parcelled out in circles, just satisfying the cravings of nature from a trough of rice placed in the centre of each circle."[144]

Alexander died in 1792 while the couple were in Sierra Leone, and just a few weeks later Anna-Maria married again, this time to Isaac DuBois.

143 http://www.sierra-leone.org/Books/
144 Ibid

ELIZABETH FARLEY
1710-1779, JOURNALIST

The Bristol media landscape has not always been male dominated. Rewind a few hundred years and women had a huge role to play in publishing, editing and leading the city's respected newspapers. Elizabeth Farley was one of these women. Taking over the reigns of *Felix Farley's Bristol Journal* when her husband and journal owner Felix Farley died in 1753, Elizabeth ran an impressive business, not only covering the publication of the journal but also undertaking printing and distribution for others, as well as the selling of patent medicines, which was a common practice for newspapers back then.

Religion played a big role in Elizabeth's life: a devout Wesleyan Methodist, she was also a disciple of the High Tory cause, which led to some questionable coverage in her newspaper including a propaganda campaign against Jews. She also had links to John Wesley, the co-founder of the Methodist Church. As well as publishing the *Journal*, Elizabeth released many books from poetry to hymns and more than 20 Methodist books, including pamphlets with sermons by Wesley.

Famed for being the first newspaper proprietor to be prosecuted for libel, after running a series of articles on Whig corruption in which the paper referred to them as a "plague of locusts", Elizabeth stood her ground and won the case with the journal found not guilty of libel.

Elizabeth's brother-in-law died the same year as her husband and he left his *Bristol Journal* newspaper to his niece Sarah Farley (who later renamed it *Sarah Farley's Bristol Journal*). The two women were effectively rivals and, while Sarah ran a similar operation and business model, she was the opposite of Elizabeth in a lot of ways; not least because Sarah was a Quaker and a

Whig supporter. Interestingly, Sarah bequeathed her paper to Elizabeth's daughter Hester, who ran it briefly before selling to proprietors the Routh Brothers in 1775. Upon Elizabeth's death a few years later, *Farley's Bristol Journal* was also sold to William Routh.

Written by Laura K Williams, who is a Bristol-based journalist and editor, and founding member and trustee of Baby Bank Network: a women-led charity that provides baby essentials to families in need.

MARY FEDDEN

1915-2012, ARTIST

Mary Fedden was born in Bristol in 1915 and attended Badminton School. She developed a passion for art at an early age and became the youngest student to study at the Slade School of Art in London in 1932, which was an experience that she loved. Although the use of bright colours was not encouraged, Mary pursued her love for them and became a prolific painter.

In her early years, Mary painted sets for ballet performances at Sadler's Wells in London but eventually returned to Bristol to make a living selling portraits and teaching art. After selling one of her paintings to the editor of *Woman* magazine at her solo show at Mansard Gallery in Heal's Department Store, London, Mary was commissioned to paint covers for the magazine for three years. Her colourful and exuberant paintings depicted her surroundings – rolling hills, birds and other local wildlife, crockery, fruit, flowers and many beautiful paintings of cats. The vivid colours in most of her pictures display an excitement for her subjects and her painted animals are full of character and charm.

Mary became the first female painting tutor at the Royal

College of Art in 1956 and she taught both David Hockney and Allen Jones. Between 1984-1988, Mary was President of the Royal West of England Academy (which had been established by Bristol artist Ellen Sharples in 1844) and was very active in Bristol's art scene. She was elected a Royal Academician in 1992 and made an OBE in 1997. Her celebrations of the everyday are beautiful compositions and poignant reminders of the ways in which women's art is often devalued.

Written by Ellie Vowles, who is a trustee of Bristol Women's Voice and an artist/maker.

Please also see the entry for: Ellen Sharples.

'MICHAEL FIELD': KATHERINE BRADLEY and EDITH COOPER

1846-1914 and 1862-1913, WRITERS

"Michael Field? What's he doing in a book about Bristol women?" you ask. Well, not only was he no man but this wasn't exactly a woman either. Michael Field was, in fact, the pen-name of two women: Katherine Bradley and Edith Cooper, two poets as interesting for the way they boldly fashioned a life together in Victorian Britain as they are for their work. Together they became self-described "poets and lovers", writing (as novelist George Meredith described it) with "a voice of one heart".

Katherine Bradley was born into a moneyed tobacco family in Birmingham in 1835. She was well-educated at home and lived the free life that only a woman of her class could during that period: studying in Paris, taking summer schools at Cambridge, writing (under the name 'Arran Leigh') and befriending many of the leading (male) intellectual lights of the time. She was also Edith Cooper's aunt. Edith was born to Katherine's sister in 1862 in Kenilworth. She wrote poetry since childhood and was translating the classics by the time she was a teenager.

In the 1870s, both women moved *en famille* to Bristol, living in solid villas on Ivywell Road in Sneyd Park. It was in Bristol that the women came alive. They would walk the two miles over the Downs to attend classes at University College, Bristol, on Park Row. They acted as a couple (sharing a bedroom), which seemed to attract scant attention, perhaps because they were cushioned by wealth, family relationship and the sanitising idea of 'romantic friendship'. Both were involved in the political life of the city, speaking at suffrage debates, and Katherine was Secretary of the Clifton Anti-Vivisection Society.

It was also here, in 1884, that they chose the pen name 'Michael Field' for their shared writing. Initially they used a male name, like many peers, so publication would be easier. But even after their secret was out (poet Robert Browning, it seems, let slip) they continued with this name. At home, they would also refer to each other as "he" sometimes and use male pet names.

Their first work was *Callirrhoë and Fair Rosamund*, published in Clifton by J Baker of The Mall in 1884. Like most of their output, it was high Victorian verse looking over its shoulder to a classical past. But the pair were not backwards looking in everything: their female characters are all strong and uncompromising and, moreover, they deal with love between women head-on, rhapsodising breasts and the naked forms of women in Renaissance paintings and – who else? – Sappho. In this, their heyday, Michael Field was hugely popular in literary circles, garnering rave reviews and enthusiastic readers.

Three years and six verse dramas later, Katherine and Edith left Bristol – again, in their extended family – and moved to Reigate, then Richmond. As the century ticked on, their popularity declined and by the late 1890s they were finding it hard to get a publisher as they were viewed as cranky and too prolific. And though they carried on writing into the new century, they got published less: their books were circulated in small, exquisitely illustrated quantities, until Edith and then Katharine was diagnosed with cancer. Edith died on 13 December 1913 and Katherine on 26 September 1914.

In total, they published 19 volumes of plays and five of verse, and filled 30 volumes of diaries, which documented their lives intimately, in every sense: as lovers, writers and late Victorian women. While Joseph Bristow writes that they "maintained a deliberately vexed relationship with contemporaneousness," and they did poetically look to a long-gone golden age, they were also massively modern women: active in the political and intellectual movements of the day, and actually living independent, authentically lesbian lives.

Written by Kim Renfrew, who is a South Walian, ex-Amsterdammer and adopted Bristolian who writes (especially from an LGBT angle) and edits things.

DORIS FLINN

1892-1977, ARTIST

Doris Kathleen Flinn was an artist, and one half (with Joan Tuckett) of a mid-century Bristolian lesbian power couple. Born in Chorlton, Lancashire, on 15 October 1892, Doris was the solidly middle-class daughter of a drapery and fancy goods merchant and she went to study sculpture at Manchester School of Art in 1914. Not long after her studies finished, Doris upped sticks to Bristol where, in 1917, she met the woman who would be her companion for the next 40 years. By 1923, Doris and Joan were living at 5 Beaufort Buildings in Clifton, a tall Georgian townhouse overlooking Christchurch Green, where they stayed until 1927.

Around the same time, Doris took a studio just down the road on Boyce's Avenue, where she worked and sometimes exhibited. She sculpted in bronze, silver, stoneware and earthenware. She made many studies of female heads and explored the idea of the mask. She also created intimate, rather intense, sculptures of her own face: one photo shows Doris, handsome and pomaded in a white warehouse coat, wryly holding the gaze of an unamused self-portrait. Perhaps her most thrillingly titled piece, though, is 'Lawyer, Athlete, Aviator, Woman, 1935': it is of Joan Tuckett, who happened to be all these things (as was another remarkable Bristol woman, Joan's sister Angela).

Doris exhibited widely: at the Royal West of England Academy on Queen's Road, and in London, Edinburgh, Manchester, Paris and New Zealand. She also made the city of Bristol her canvas: sketching all around town, creating busts for the University of Bristol, and some of the carvings on the Wills Memorial Building are hers. She also worked at Bristol Potteries, modelling porcelain figures.

When she wasn't creating, Doris was throwing herself into Bristol's left-wing life. She mixed with other politically committed intellectual lesbians, like Clevedon's Doris Hatt and Margery Mack Smith. She was involved in the co-operative movement. She sat on Dundry Parish Council as the member for the Communist Party and was part of the local chapter of the Committee for the Defence of Spanish Democracy. Doris wanted to refashion the Theatre Royal (now Bristol Old Vic) into a People's Theatre. Her politics suffused much of her art: one work is called 'The Rich and the Poor'. The relief panels of 'In England's Green and Pleasant Land' is an almost Soviet-style depiction of gaunt and huddled working classes. Another sculpture, 'Unemployed', shows a man in a flat cap, eyes downcast, fists balled in rage.

Doris made her last home with Joan in Dundry, at the Rookery, a sprawling stone house dating back to the 17th century, tucked down a track off East Dundry Lane. The couple moved there in 1930; Doris' tiny, navy blue Charles Letts's appointments diary for that year on 24 February notes: "Saw Rookery and like it very much." On 4 April she jotted that a deposit of £70 had been paid on the house. She continued creating in the studio she built there, now complete with her own kiln. Four pieces of her work are in Bristol Museum and Art Gallery's collection: 'Meditation', 'Mermaid' and 'Boy With Grapes' – but perhaps the most interesting is 'Sostenuto': a flat, Art Deco plaster portrait of Joan, described in the museum's catalogue as a "Female Face with Dutch Boy Hairstyle".

Joan died in 1957 and Doris continued living in Dundry until her own death 20 years later at the age of 85. At Doris' funeral on 22 September 1977, her coffin was played out by the Red Army Choir singing 'The Song of Departure.'

Written by Kim Renfrew, who is a South Walian, ex-Amsterdammer and adopted Bristolian who writes (especially from an LGBT angle) and edits things.

Please also see the entries for: Angela Tuckett and Joan Tuckett.

ANNA FRY

1719-1803, BUSINESSWOMAN

Joseph Fry's chocolate and cocoa business propelled the Quaker family to the leagues of big business hitters. And when Joseph died in 1787 his widow Anna Fry – and son Joseph Storrs Fry – carried on the business under the name Anna Fry & Son until Anna's death in 1803. In an article acknowledging 200 years of the Bristol business, the *Western Daily Press* noted that Anna "must have been a remarkable lady"[145]. I think that is an understatement.

Please also see: 'The Chocolate Factory' in the Women's Work section towards the back of this book.

KATHARINE FURSE

1875-1952, MILITARY PIONEER

Clifton-born Katharine Furse was largely educated at home by governesses. She married painter Charles Furse in 1900 only to be widowed four years later and left as a single mother with two young children. Given that she was already a member of the Territorial Army, when World War One broke out Katharine was selected to lead the Voluntary Aid Detachment of Red Cross nurses to Boulogne, France, in October 1914.

Realising that the existing number of nurses was totally insufficient to handle the volume of wartime casualties, Katharine set up the Voluntary Aid Detachment (VAD), which soon became recognised as a part of the Red Cross and through this she helped to create paid jobs for women. However, despite the successes of

145 *Western Daily Press*, 1928, 5 July, 'Fry's Chocolate'. 4.

the detachment, by 1917 Katharine was so frustrated about her lack of powers (as a woman) to implement change, and disappointed that her repeated concerns about the living conditions of her volunteers were ignored, that she reluctantly resigned. Although it should be noted that due to Katharine's influence, by the end of the war there were more than 90,000 female VADs.

Katharine promptly became Director of the Women's Royal Naval Service (the WRNS), which she had been asked to set up, and she was able to continue working for the war effort in this way. She remained the head of the WRNS until it was demobilised at the end of the war. The Royal Navy was the first branch of the armed forces that recruited women, and this was so successful that the Women's Army Auxiliary Corps and Women's Royal Air Force swiftly followed.

After the war ended, Katharine continued to develop her skills. In addition to becoming an accomplished skier, she helped set up the travel agency that would become Lunn Poly, and she also headed up the World Association of Girl Guides and Girl Scouts.

FANNY FUST
1764-1827, HEIRESS

Bristol-born Fanny Fust was the only surviving child of Denton Fust of Clifton, a family long established in Gloucestershire. In the language of the day she had 'an imbecility of mind'. These days we might say she had learning impairments or special educational needs. According to her family, she was someone who needed constant care – otherwise she might "walk into the pond" – and being oblivious to danger and of a trusting nature she was inclined to wander off with anyone.

What made Fanny especially vulnerable was her wealth. She

had inherited not only her father's fortune but also, through her uncle, the vast and lucrative Hill Court estate in Gloucestershire. Before the age of 21, living in Clifton with her widowed mother, Fanny was reasonably safe from predators as the law prevented her from marrying without the permission of a guardian, but after that she was considered fair game for unscrupulous men wanting to get their hands on her money. At the time, a woman's property passed to her husband on marriage.

In 1785, Henry Pawlet Bowerman, about whom little is known, made Fanny, now 21, his target, showering her with attention and 'gallantry' and whispering 'love-tales' into her 'unsuspecting ear'. Perhaps he was a music teacher or had worked his way into the Fusts' social circle. What *is* known is that once her mother was alerted to his behaviour, Bowerman was sent packing. However, he managed to gain the trust and cooperation of some of Fanny's friends in the neighbourhood, in particular two sisters from the Payne family who were friends of Mrs Fust's.

Bowerman arranged to bring a carriage and horses to the Paynes' house while Fanny was visiting and the Payne sisters persuaded her to get in it, upon which Bowerman, along with his brother, a man called Matthew Willick and one of the Paynes, rapidly drove away with the prize. They crossed the Channel to Belgium where, according to Bowerman, he and Fanny went through two marriage ceremonies and then headed south through France.

The Fust family sent a Mr Lewis to the English Ambassador at the court of Versailles to request a warrant to apprehend Fanny and sometime later Lewis caught up with the couple at Lisle in the Dordogne, France, where Bowerman "claimed possession of the lady, as his true and lawful wife". Despite these protestations, and after checking with the authorities in Tournai, Belgium, where the monks were adamant that they had refused to marry the couple, Lewis brought Fanny back to England.

A protracted court case ensued. Bowerman failed in his attempt to overturn the Lord Chancellor's decision to declare Fanny incompetent to decide to marry and to place her fortune in the hands of a committee, and the marriage was annulled. Fanny returned to Bristol and later lived at Hill Court where, after her mother's death, she was cared for by her cousin Flora Langley, who inherited Fanny's fortune when she died at the age of 63.

What does this distressing tale, in which Fanny was at all times powerless and voiceless, tell us? Forced marriage is nothing new of course. It persists and, despite well-intentioned efforts, will probably do so for as long as marriage partners regard each other as commodities for sale or trade. The story also highlights issues of disability rights. Fanny's brief experience of marriage reminds us that while a match such as Fanny Fust and Henry Bowerman was based on Bowerman's cynical exploitation and was rightly ended, people with cognitive disabilities can and do have romantic and sexual relationships just like anyone else.

Written by Naomi Clifford, who graduated from the University of Bristol and is the author of *Women and the Gallows 1797-1837* and *The Disappearance of Maria Glenn*. *The Murder of Mary Ashford* will be published in 2018.

THERESA GARNETT
1888-1966, SUFFRAGETTE

If you have ever wished you could whack a misogynistic politician around the head with a horse whip, give praise to suffragette Theresa Garnett who did just that – and to no less than future Prime Minister Winston Churchill, who was steadfast in his refusal to support votes for women and adamant in his endorsement of force feeding for hunger striking suffragette prisoners.

On 15 November 1909, Churchill was due in Bristol to speak at the Colston Hall and Theresa arrived at Temple Meads Station to welcome him to the city. Armed with a horse whip, she set about striking Churchill while shouting: "Take that in the name of the insulted women in England!"[146] When taken in by the police, Theresa bluntly told them her name was 'Votes For Women'.

The *Western Daily Press* reported: "The assault on Mr Churchill created a considerable sensation, not only in Bristol, but also through the country", and the London evening papers thundered: "Winston Churchill flogged in Bristol". It even reached the United States where the *New York Herald* ran with the headline: "Mr Winston S Churchill Lashed by Suffragettes".

With an overly dramatic tone, an hysterical story in the *Western Daily Press* referred to "the sensational assault made upon Mr Winston Churchill," before squealing that "Mr Churchill, in his struggle with Miss Garnett, disarmed her, and subsequently presented the whip to his wife, who was witness of an extraordinary scene".[147] Poor old Mr Churchill, eh?

When Churchill stood up to speak at the Colston Hall later that day, he experienced severe heckling from members of the

146 The scene was recreated by members of the Bristol Radical History Group on the 100 year anniversary of the event. A video of the recreation can be seen on YouTube: youtube.com/watch?v=i__V0G4-UYo

147 *Western Daily Press*, 1909, 23 December, 'The Whip! Application by Bristol Suffragettes'. 9.

crowd. Security guards had already been instructed to prevent any women from entering and a man was thrown out for asking why the government didn't give votes to women. Another man who asked "They have tortured female political offenders during the past six months – why doesn't the Liberal Government put its principles into practice?" was promptly beaten by stewards.[148] So while we do not endorse Theresa's physical attack on Churchill, it must also be noted that the authorities were considerably more violent to anyone who opposed them.

Despite Theresa, of 5 York Place, being arrested, Churchill later dropped the charges because he did not want to have to appear in court himself. So instead of assault, Theresa was charged with disrupting the peace and sentenced to one month in Horfield Gaol. In protest at her sentence, Theresa immediately set fire to her prison cell and went on hunger strike, for which she later endured force feeding. Vera Wentworth was in Horfield Gaol at the same time as Theresa and told the *Western Daily Press*: "She is now in the punishment cell, that dark place I told you of, for 15 days for that. She set fire to her cell, but they discovered the flames before much damage was done and put out."[149] Theresa's sisters at the Women's Social and Political Union later awarded Theresa with a brooch for her imprisonment and a medal for her hunger strike, as was customary for all incarcerated suffragettes.

Other activities Theresa got up to in the name of suffrage included chaining herself to a statue in the Houses of Parliament in protest at the 'Brawling Bill'[150] and biting a warden during a previous stay at Horfield Gaol. Theresa was also one of the many suffragettes who would visit Eagle House at Batheaston (run by the Blathwayt family) while recovering from hunger strike and on

148 http://museums.bristol.gov.uk/narratives.php?irn=3985

149 *Western Daily Press*, 1909, 27 November, 'Suffragettes Leave Horfield Prison'. 9.

150 The 'Brawling Bill' was a way of penalising anyone who behaved in a disorderly manner in the Palace of Westminster while Parliament was in session.

Theresa Garnett illustration by Jenny Howe

7 November 1909 she planted a tree in their suffrage arboretum.

Although Theresa's attack on Churchill is well documented, what is less well remembered is that she was not the first suffragette to accost a misogynistic politician at Temple Meads Station. In March 1909, Elsie Howey and Vera Wentworth confronted Bristol North MP Augustine Birrell as he disembarked from a train and they demanded "Votes for Women!" They were met with a condescending "Tut tut" from the unimpressed elected (by men) representative of the people.

And another thing... Theresa worked as a nurse on the frontline in France during World War One and her former adversary Winston Churchill subsequently decorated her with a medal for bravery.[151]

Please also see the entries for: Emily and Mary Blathwayt, Elsie Howey and Vera Wentworth.

LEOTTA GOODRIDGE

1939-2015, COMMUNITY LEADER

Known as the 'Queen of St Paul's', Leotta 'Leo' Goodridge worked hard for equality and social justice in Bristol and was a founding member of the Bristol City Council Race Forum. Leo arrived in Bristol from the West Indies as part of the Windrush generation and she eventually became a part of Bristol's welcoming committee to greet future immigrants to the city: she was "more a mother than a friend" wrote broadcaster Roger Griffith in his obituary for Leotta.[152]

151 Lorna Brierley, Helen Reid, (2000). *Go Home and Do the Washing!* Bristol: Broadcast. 153.
152 http://www.ujimaradio.com/2016/01/tribute-leotta-leo-goodridge-18th-may-1939-15th-december-2015/

Leo was concerned with the health and social welfare of the diverse communities located in Bristol, and young people were a particular group she wanted to support. She also worked for decades alongside her good friend Carmen Beckford, who in her eulogy for her "icon" Leotta said: "We shared a lot of laughter which helped us face the future challenges in a more relaxed, but very determined focus going forward."[153] Both Leo and Carmen were also members of the St Paul's Carnival committee, founded in 1968, which better enabled them to help young people.

Please also see the entries for: Carmen Beckford and Princess Campbell.

CATHERINE GRACE

1907-1986, EDUCATIONALIST

When Catherine Grace from Clifton, who had trained as both a teacher and a nurse, set up St Christopher's School in Westbury Park in 1945 for children with learning and physical disabilities, she had just six pupils and one rented room. However, from small acorns big oaks grow and at one point St Christopher's was the largest school of its kind in the United Kingdom, largely thanks to Catherine's vision, hard work and dedication. Her goal had simply been to educate the "non-educable". At the time of writing, St Christopher's is still operating and offers year-round support to 38 pupils from all over the country who have a range of complex learning difficulties.

153 Ibid.

JANE GREEN

1719-1791, ACTOR

Alongside her sister Elizabeth Hippisley, Jane Hippisley was a celebrated comic actor in the Bristol, Bath and London areas. Their father John Hippisley had run a theatre on the Jacob's Well Road since 1729, which doubtless gave them the taste for a life treading the boards. After her father's death, Jane took over the running of his theatre. Such was Jane's popularity that she performed at the opening night of the King Street Theatre (now Bristol Old Vic) in 1766 and received the written equivalent of a standing ovation in the press.

However, a cloud hung over Jane's head. Rumours abounded that her illegitimate son Samuel, born 1747, was fathered by actor-manager David Garrick. Despite this perceived scandal, Jane later married a Mr Green and was finally deemed a respectable lady. Their artist son John composed a dignified epitaph for her memorial, which sits in St Andrew's Church, Clifton. It reads: "As a comedian she was ... deservedly admired in public, while in private life her virtues gained her distinguished esteem."[154]

Please also see the entry for: Elizabeth Hippisley.

ELSIE GRIFFIN

1895-1989, SINGER

"Oh, Danny boy..." If you automatically responded to that with: "... the pipes, the pipes are calling...", then you have Kingsdown operetta sensation and proto-Forces sweetheart Elsie Griffin

154 Madge Dresser, (2016). *Women and the City: Bristol 1373-2000*. Bristol: Redcliffe Press. 73.

to thank for it. Elsie was born in 1895 on St Michael's Hill and lived with her mother on Tankard's Close (the house they lived in is long superseded by university buildings), while her father, a joiner, worked in London.

They went to live with him in the capital in 1903 for three years, then came back to Bristol, where Elsie lived an unremarkable life and looked set to do what every other ordinary girl of her era did: a basic education (at St Michael's on the Mount school, where a blue plaque was unveiled in her honour in 2012), then onto a job at the factory at 14. In Elsie's case it was the Fry's factory on the Pithay where she began packing chocolates.

But there was something that set Elsie apart: a voice. A contralto voice that was discovered when she began singing at the chocolate factory's morning prayer meetings, then with the factory choir, then the local Temperance choir, with whom she performed at a landmark Colston Hall concert where she sang the solo, backed by a 500-strong choir. While she was at Fry's she won a singing scholarship. "I then had to choose between taking up singing seriously – or staying at Fry's," she said in an interview in 1926. Naturally, singing won. Elsie trained her voice and performed around the West Country.

Then World War One broke out. She joined a company of troop-entertaining performers, formed at the behest of King George V to boost morale on the battlefields. It was during the war that she sang 'Danny Boy', the song that made her famous – and that she made famous in turn. Around this time she was introduced to the man who would seal her fate as a celebrity: Rupert D'Oyly Carte, doyen of the Gilbert and Sullivan opera company and owner of the Savoy Hotel, London. She joined his troupe as a soprano, making her first appearance in 1919 at the Prince's Theatre as Josephine in *HMS Pinafore*, conducted by Sir Malcolm Sargent.

She went on to play numerous other leading roles, including Yum-Yum in the *Mikado*, which was captured in a 1926 short film commissioned by the D'Oyly Carte to promote their sets and costumes for the show: two nitrate prints of this film are at the British Film Institute, London. Another career high came in 1929, when she won a Best British Gramophone Solo award for her performance on a record of the *Pirates of Penzance*. While with the D'Oyly Carte, she met fellow singer (and fellow Bristolian) Ivan Menzies; they fell in love and married in 1923 – at a register office in Sheffield between performances.

In the 1930s, Elsie left Gilbert and Sullivan behind (although she performed at their 1975 centenary celebrations) and joined the Carl Rosa Opera Company, which was set up to take classical music to the provinces at affordable prices. Here, Elsie sang opera proper, taking the lead soprano parts in *Carmen, The Barber of Seville, Die Fledermaus* and many others. Although Elsie left Carl Rosa in 1937, she continued performing and touring internationally well into her 60s. Her last role was in a 'musical morality play' called *The Vanishing Island* in 1957.

Elsie died in Blackheath, London, on 21 December 1989 at the age of 94: it's a testament to the impact she had on the performing arts that her papers are kept in the Victoria & Albert Museum's Theatre and Performance Archives.

Written by Kim Renfrew, who is a South Walian, ex-Amsterdammer and adopted Bristolian who writes (especially from an LGBT angle) and edits things.

Please also see: 'The Chocolate Factory' in the Women's Work section towards the back of this book.

SARAH GUPPY
1770-1852, INVENTOR, ENGINEER

Sarah Guppy: engineer, inventor, designer, campaigner, reformer, writer, environmentalist and businesswoman, to name but a few of her skills. She was born in Birmingham in 1770 – as the Industrial Revolution revved its engine – the daughter of a wealthy brass manufacturer. In 1795 she married a Bristol merchant called Sam Guppy, and they made their home in Queen Square where most of their six children were born. Their fortune they made from copper sheathing nails in the Napoleonic Wars. Copper deters barnacles and the navy bought the Guppys' nails in bulk. War is remarkably good for business and Sam and Sarah surely knew it. Two nail patents in 1796 and 1804 (for machinery to make them cheaply, quickly and in large quantities) were promptly registered in Sam's name. How much Sarah contributed is unknown but Sam was already 40 when they married and the 1796 patent – the following year – was his first. In the light of Sarah's own subsequent patents, it seems likely that she had a hand in it somewhere.

In 1811, Sarah patented a form of suspension bridge that she intended should be built at Clifton but the principle could be applied anywhere. Although women simply didn't design bridges in 1811 and hers was never built. However, 200 years later it's still a hot topic and in 2016 Sarah Guppy finally made the national newspapers and the *Oxford Dictionary of National Biography*. *The Independent* called her "the woman behind Britain's most famous bridge"[155] (ie Clifton Suspension Bridge, which is famously attributed to Isambard Kingdom Brunel). She wasn't; they got it wrong. Although she may have offered advice to the young

155 http://www.independent.co.uk/news/uk/home-news/sarah-guppy-the-woman-behind-britains-most-famous-bridge-isambard-kingdom-brunel-clifton-suspension-a7057506.html

Brunel on his Clifton one, and to Scottish civil engineer Thomas Telford on his Menai Bridge in North Wales.

Sarah is said to have made models for Brunel and models of her own bridge were exhibited in London although none survive. She also proposed innovative solutions to agricultural and environmental issues, writing to the Earl of Liverpool, Leader of the House of Lords and future Prime Minister. She had studied the set-up at London's Smithfield Market (a wholesale meat market that still trades today), which she considered a disgrace: "Economic interests prevail over the good of society, and certainly over the comfort of mere animals." Her proposal was radical: a new network of local markets to get people moving out of the city, rather than all crushing in. And a market every day in one of the districts to suit even the most distant farmer. Her letter ended with a PS: "I have not mentioned the sufferings of the poor animals, because man where his interest and convenience is served (generally speaking) feels little for any animal, but if observed their eyes sufficiently indicate that they do severely suffer both in mind and body." She suggested that the Smithfield Market could become a park, so still a public meeting place but also a much-needed source of health and recreation.

But Sarah, housewife and "amateur inventor" (and that was what the papers called her in 2016!), was marginalised and patronised – or completely ignored and not allowed off the starting blocks. So she invented domestic appliances instead: an early Teasmade that prepared your breakfast, and the Cook's Friend, a portable oven with hood – tasks much better suited to a woman! And she wrote books for little children. Nobody had a problem with that. She did charitable work, advised on housing for single women and campaigned to *lower* the wages of female servants – considering them overpaid, badly behaved and likely to cause all kinds of social problems.

Later Sarah moved to Clifton's Richmond Hill, where her heritage plaque remains. Her son Thomas's plaque is in nearby Berkeley Square. Thomas was Brunel's business partner: he funded Brunel's projects and designed the engines for the SS Great Britain. The Guppys did a lot for Bristol and for the Brunels. Sarah's bridge may never have been built but she created something much better: a virtual bridge between the 19th and the 21st centuries and that's very modern indeed.[156]

Written by Sheila Hannon, who is Creative Producer of the Bristol theatre company Show of Strength. She wrote and produced 'An Audience With Sarah Guppy' in 2006, which will be revived in 2018.

LILIAS ASHWORTH HALLETT

1844-1922, SUFFRAGIST

Bath-based Quaker Lilias Ashworth Hallett, who was the niece of Anna Maria and Mary Priestman and Margaret Tanner, was a founder member of the Bristol and Clifton National Society for Women's Suffrage and later became a generous benefactor to the Women's Social and Political Union. She joined the cause early on, having signed an Enfranchisement of Women Committee petition and joined the London Society for Women's Suffrage back in 1867.

With Bristol being such a hub for suffrage activity, Lilias knew all of the prominent women in the South West community and was also friends with the Blathwayt family at Batheaston. In addition to visiting the house and planting a tree in the Suffragette Wood there, she also chaired a meeting at Eagle House in May 1908 at

156 With thanks to Madge Dresser and Peter Revelle.

which Annie Kenney spoke. Historian Elizabeth Crawford writes: "[Lilias] was herself a valuable and busy speaker for the suffrage cause. It required considerable courage then for a woman to sit on a public platform and actually to speak from [a platform] was regarded as almost indecent."[157]

Lilias became well known as a speaker for suffrage and in spring 1871 she joined Agnes Beddoe on an early speaking tour and described the meetings as such: "The novelty of hearing women speakers brought crowds to the meetings. Invariably the doors were thronged with people unable to obtain seats. The tours of meetings, consisting of six or seven in a fortnight, were a great nervous effort in those early days. They were, however, a source of much interest, and even pleasure in the retrospect, for we never failed to carry out resolutions affirming the principle of suffrage and adopting petitions to Parliament."[158]

On another occasion, in 1892, when the National Union of Women's Suffrage Societies' leader Millicent Fawcett came to speak at 69 Park Street, the throngs were so huge to see Millicent that the audience spilled out of the rooms, down the stairs and onto the street... indeed, it was so crowded that even the chairwoman Agnes Beddoe could not get into the room and Lilias, who had arrived early, was called upon to step in and introduce the star speaker to the platform. The *Western Daily Press* reported: "Owing to the number of ladies who accepted the society's invitation, and to the comparative smallness of the accommodation afforded, many ladies were unable to obtain admission to the meeting. The crowds in the passage on the staircase rendered the difficulty so great that many, with great regret, gave up the attempt of reaching the room at all."

157 Elizabeth Crawford, (1999), *The Suffrage Movement*. London: Routledge. 260.
158 Ellen Malos, (1983), 'Bristol Women in Action 1839-1919: The Right to Vote and the Need to Earn a Living' in Bristol Broadsides, (1983). *Bristol's Other History*. Bristol: Broadsides. 101-102.

Lilias Ashworth Hallett illustration by Carrie Love

The article continued: "Amongst the number was Mrs Beddoe, who should have taken the chair. Her place was ably supplied by Mrs Ashworth Hallett of Bath, a lady whose name is well known in this part of England for the indefatigable efforts she is ever making in the furtherance of the interests of her own sex ... Mrs Ashworth Hallet after having apologised for the unavoidable absence of Mrs Beddoe downstairs addressed the meeting, remarking that she had much pleasure as a worker of over 20 years' standing, in introducing Mrs Fawcett to those who had come to visit them that afternoon. They all knew that there was no woman of our day who had done so much for the improvement, the enlargement and the advancement of her sex as Mrs Fawcett."[159] It is interesting how much more supportive the local papers were of the suffrage campaign in the early days than they were to become after the turn of the century.

In 1908, Lilias was again welcoming Millicent Fawcett to the South West when she was expected to speak at the Bath Victoria Rooms on 11 March. "We may readily admit that the second reading of a Women's Suffrage Bill by no means ensures us immediate final success," began Lilias. "Nevertheless, the second reading of the Bill has significance which former events have lacked. Many quote Mrs Fawcett's own words to the feeling of the country on the subject. In Women's Franchise ... we look forward tonight to a meeting which will demonstrate anew both the justice of our claim to the suffrage and the enlightened political era in Bristol."[160]

Please also see the entries for: Agnes Beddoe, Emily and Mary Blathwayt, Anna Maria and Mary Priestman and Margaret Tanner.

159 *Western Daily Press*, 1892, 9 November, 'The Bristol and West of England Society for Women's Suffrage'. 3.
160 *Western Daily Press*, 1908, 11 March, 'The Women's Suffrage'. 9.

JOAN HAMMOND

dates unknown, GREENHAM CAMPAIGNER

Greenham Common Women's Peace Camp in Berkshire was where Kent-born Joan Hammond found her feminist sisters. Previously a county councillor in Hertfordshire for the Labour Party with a focus on issues affecting women and children, Joan and her family moved to Bristol after attending the first Greenham March and she joined the Greenham supporters group in the city. They would meet at the Women's Centre or at the Quaker Meeting House and one of their actions was creating lifesize puppets of judges and businessmen, known as 'the power team', which were attached to Bristol Bridge.

But it was Greenham that was to become central to Joan's life, despite being aged 60 at the time of her first visit there. Greenham Common Women's Peace Camp was established in September 1981 to protest about the nuclear weapons located at RAF Greenham Common, Berkshire. The camp remained active until 2000. During the 19 years of the camp, the women protestors took actions including chaining themselves to the fences, and forming a 14-mile human chain when 70,000 protesters held hands with each other as they stood all around the perimeter of the RAF base. It was important for the peace camp to be women-only because it had been instigated by mothers protesting about the dangers nuclear missiles posed to their children. However, it was not always peaceful. The RAF continually called in the police to evict the women, which led to fires, fighting and assault. And the constant hostility from the RAF and some neighbours was exhausting for the campaigners. A memorial to the peace camp can now be seen at the site.

Women from Bristol would visit the camp on two Sundays every month and then split into either support or action groups.

Action might involve sitting by the road shouting "missiles out!" or putting bolt cutters in their handbags and setting off to cut the perimeter fence. But while there was a huge sense of camaraderie and sisterhood among the women at Greenham, Joan recalled that it wasn't always pleasant and that it could be "a horrifying experience, noisy and nasty".

In an interview with the Feminist Archive South, Joan admitted that she felt more afraid at Greenham than she had during World War Two, saying "being bombed [in the war] was remote not personal" whereas at Greenham the treatment of the women was both personal and distressing. She added that a lot of women were often "not good for anything much" after Greenham, such were the demands on their physical and mental health.[161]

FLORENCE HANCOCK

1893-1974, TRADES UNIONIST

Florence Hancock was a trades union organiser in Bristol in the interwar years who also played a national role in her own union, the Transport and General Workers Union (TGWU), and in the Trades Union Congress (TUC).[162]

She was born in Chippenham, the eldest of four children of a cloth weaver and his second wife who already had ten children when Florence arrived. Her early life was difficult. Florence started work at the age of 12 and when her parents died before she was 18 she had to look after her siblings. When she was 14, she was employed for 55 hours a week for 6s at the Nestle Condensed

161 Based on an interview with Joan by Viv Honeybourne, stored at the Feminist Archive South.

162 For a more detailed account of her activities, see June Hannam, 'Hancock, Dame Florence May (1893–1974)', *Oxford Dictionary of National Biography*, Oxford University Press, 2004; online edition, January 2011 [http://www.oxforddnb.com/view/article/31193, accessed 6 Oct 2017]

Milk Company. A turning point in her life came in 1913 when Julia Varley, a representative from the Workers' Union, held a recruitment meeting in the factory. Florence was the only woman who attended. She joined the union, took on the role of Dues Collector and then became Secretary of the branch. In 1917 she was appointed a full-time Organiser for the Workers' Union and was District Officer for Wiltshire. She also thought that trades unions should take part in politics and was Chair and Secretary during the 1920s for the Gloucester Independent Labour Party, a socialist group, as well as being active in the Labour Party.

Trades unionism, however, was Florence's main focus and when the Workers' Union merged with the TGWU in 1929 she was made Women's Officer in Bristol, a post she held until 1942. She worked hard to organise women in the newly expanding light engineering and consumer industries such as confectionary and laundry work where it was difficult to retain members. With her soft West Country voice and neat appearance, usually wearing a tailored suit and blouse, Florence was recognised as an effective trades union leader. Nonetheless, she found that male colleagues in mixed-sex unions often had little interest in organising women or in prioritising their needs. She therefore joined with other female union leaders to press the TUC to set up a women's advisory committee composed of women members. This was established in 1931 and Florence became a member.

She took part in other movements to improve women's work conditions, including a campaign in 1937 against legislation that proposed to allow women and children to work excessive overtime and a TUC agitation for a national maternity service. During these years she was gaining prominence at a national level. From 1935-1958, Florence was a member of the general council of the TUC and visited numerous countries as a TUC nominee on the International Labour Organisation.

Florence's work in Bristol ended when she was promoted to Chief Woman Officer of the TGWU in 1942. Nonetheless, she did not sever her ties with Bristol, returning to the city to support causes she found important. In 1947, for example, she addressed a public meeting in support of the candidature of Berta Sacof, who was standing as a Labour candidate for Clifton ward, attended a Temperance Education Conference at the Old King Baptist Church, and opened a Yule fayre at Kingswood to raise money to renovate the mission premises of the Bristol East Temperance Band. When giving evidence to the Royal Commission on Equal Pay in July 1945, she drew her examples from the Bristol aero engine factory.[163]

Florence's long years of trades union organising and campaigning were recognised in 1947-8 when she became only the third woman to be made chair of the general council of the TUC. She was also awarded a CBE in 1947 and was accompanied to Buckingham Palace by two Bristol friends, Mrs L and Miss W Harris.[164] In 1951, she was made a Dame of the British Empire. By this period Florence had lost some of her earlier militancy and emphasised her loyalty to the trades unions and Labour Party leadership, which could mean putting women's interests in second place. She was, for example, a strong advocate of equal pay but supported the Labour Party when it refused to implement the recommendations of the Royal Commission on the grounds that it would hamper economic recovery. These attitudes meant she had to face strong criticism from a younger generation of trades union women who felt their interests were being ignored.

With her long experience of industrial affairs, Florence was frequently called upon to sit on public bodies and to give evidence to investigations. She was a Governor of the BBC between 1956

163 *Western Daily Press* (1947) 22 October, 17 November, 18 December.
164 *Western Daily Press* (1945) 28 July.

and 1962, a director of the *Daily Herald*, a Justice of the Peace and President of Hillcroft College. She continued with many of these activities after her retirement from the TGWU in 1958.

In 1964, aged 71, Florence married John Donovan whom she had known as a colleague for 30 years in the TGWU and they lived in Bristol. Florence died while visiting her sister in Chippenham on 14 April 1974.

Written by June Hannam, who is Professor Emerita of Modern British History at the University of the West of England. June has written extensively on the relationship between socialism and feminism in the late 19th and early 20th centuries.

Please also see the entry for: Berta Sacof.

MRS HAND

dates unknown, BUS CONDUCTOR

During World War Two, Gwen Hand's grandmother was a clippie (a bus conductor) for the Bristol Omnibus Company. Recalling one occasion when her grandmother was making her way home from work during an air raid and ended up narrowly escaping death, Gwen said: "Passing through the centre of the city the air raid sirens started. She made for the nearest shelter. When she went in she was confronted by a gang of [drunken] blokes – she made a quick decision that she was safer in the streets. She got home safely but next day discovered that the shelter had taken a direct hit and there were no survivors." On a separate occasion, the air raid siren sounded while Mrs Hand was working on the buses. The driver parked up and everybody went and hid in the nearest shelter...

only for the bus to be destroyed by fire after a bomb hit it directly.[165] Mrs Hand was clearly like a cat with nine lives.

ANNE RAIKES HARDING

1779-1858, NOVELIST

'Anonymous' took the credit for Anne Raikes Harding's novels, which is a crying shame given their popularity. Even more of a shame is the fact that her books would doubtless have been a lot less popular had readers known the books were by a woman. Her published work includes *Realities* (1825) and *Dissipation* (1827). Upon marriage to Thomas Merchant, Anne and he moved to Bristol where they lived for many years until relocating to Boulogne, France.

MINNIE HASKINS

1875-1957, SOCIOLOGIST, POET

Sociologist, poet and (now not so) mystery author of some famous lines in King George VI's 1939 Christmas speech... Minnie Louise Haskins, we salute you. The Warmley-born writer was a Sunday School teacher who informally studied at University College, Bristol. Minnie's voluntary work for the church took her all over the globe, including to Madras, India. After returning to England in her early 40s, Minnie trained as an economist and also became published as a poet, with her poem 'The Gate of the Year' becoming her most famous work – largely because the King used it in his festive message. King George VI was alerted to the poem by his

165 http://www.bbc.co.uk/history/ww2peopleswar/stories/75/a2410075.shtml

wife, Elizabeth the Queen Consort, who felt the opening lines would strike a chord with a nation on the brink of a second world war. Minnie had not known her poem was going to be used in the speech so when she heard the King's message on the radio that Christmas Day she thought how familiar the words seemed… and then realised why. They were *her* words in his mouth!

GLADYS HAZEL
1880-1959, SUFFRAGETTE

After working as an Organiser for the Women's Social and Political Union (WSPU) in Birmingham and Leicester, Gladys Hazel became the Bristol Organiser in 1914. By this point she had already been arrested and imprisoned numerous times and had had great fun in Birmingham on the night of the 1911 census evasion by organising "a meeting, speeches, dancing and probably a play", followed by a "chalking party" (presumably to chalk suffrage slogans on the pavements) before breakfast.[166]

Gladys was imprisoned in Holloway at the same time that Emily Wilding Davison[167] made one of her two suicide attempts in the jail, both times by throwing herself over the railings. Emily's belief was that by sacrificing herself she would be drawing attention to the brutal and agonising force feeding that she, Gladys and hundreds of other women were being tortured with in prison by the authorities. In her memoirs, Gladys wrote: "My cell door was open and a warden hurried to me calling: 'Come quick!' I followed her out to the gallery. And there was Emily Davison. She was sitting with her feet hanging down over

166 https://womanandhersphere.com/tag/birmingham-suffragettes/
167 Emily Wilding Davison was an active member of the WSPU. She famously attended the Epsom Derby on 4 June 1913 where, while attempting to fix a suffragette banner to King George V's horse, she was trampled and later died from her injuries.

the stairway her face closed and set. The warden said, 'Speak to her and stop her doing it.' I felt suddenly full of [emotion] and in a sort of rage and I said, 'Why? She'll be well out of it.' And I turned away. I heard [Emily] fall and saw her lying across the steps as they hustled me into my cell."[168]

Following the attacks on the Bristol WSPU shop on Park Street by university students in 1913 (please see the entry for Alice Walters for more information), Gladys led the group of volunteers tasked with repairing and restocking the shop. She also organised a collection of furniture and book donations to replace those that had been destroyed. And on 9 March 1914, Gladys led a deputation to the Bishop of Bristol, the Right Reverend George Forrest Browne, to protest against the church's inability to act on the inhumane horror of force feeding experienced by suffrage prisoners.

DOROTHY HAZZARD

died 1674, DISSENTER

Both of Dorothy Hazzard's husbands were Separatists. With her first husband, grocer Anthony Kelly (they kept their shop open on Christmas Day, which in itself was an extremely radical act for the time), she was at the centre of a group of Separatists who allowed women to preach, regardless of the ridicule they received from Bristol's "more conservative male majority among its political-religious elite"[169]. Her second marriage to vicar Matthew Hazzard enabled her to use St Ewen's parsonage as a refuge for other radical women who "wished to escape churching, the process of purification of women 40 days after childbirth that most of

168 Cited on http://blewbury.co.uk/blewburys-secret-suffragette/

169 Madge Dresser, (2016). *Women and the City: Bristol 1373-2000*. Bristol: Redcliffe Press. 41-42.

the city's Anglican clergy insisted upon"[170]. By 1640, Dorothy had become a signatory to the newly formed Broadmead Baptist Church, which was the first dissenting church in Bristol.

The arrival of Royalist troops in Bristol in 1643 upset the status quo in Parliamentarian Bristol and it was clear the Royalists had the strength and numbers to take Bristol. On hearing that the Royalists had breached the outer defences and reached the Frome Gate, Dorothy rallied 200 women and headed to the gate. The women were tooled up with shovels and promptly began the business of strengthening the defences with dirt and woolsacks. Dorothy then assured Bristol's Colonel Nathaniel Fiennes that she and the other women, with their young children in their arms if necessary, would stand in front of the gates to act as human shields. However, Fiennes felt the Royalists would still win and to save Bristolian lives being lost in the inevitable fight he surrendered to the Royalists.[171]

RUBY HELDER

1890-1938, SINGER

Despite her humble beginnings in Easton, thanks to her powerful tenor voice Ruby Helder went on to become a renowned international opera singer. Born as Emma Jane Holder, her father was the landlord of the Glasshouse pub on Brooklyn Terrace, Lawrence Hill, and his talented daughter would regularly sing to entertain the customers. After being encouraged to take formal singing lessons, Emma changed her name to Ruby Helder and a superstar was born.

Known as 'The Girl Tenor', owing to how extraordinary it

170 Ibid. 41-42.
171 Valerie Pitt, (2015). *Bloody Bristol*. Stroud: The History Press. 37.

was for a woman to have the range she did, Ruby's singing teacher Charles Santley said: "Miss Ruby Helder possesses a natural, pure tenor voice of great beauty and power. She also possesses what few can boast, a thoroughly artistic temperament. In my opinion, she has no rivals among the artists of the day."[172] By 1911, Ruby had a recording contract with HMV and her reputation had gained an international following. American audiences adored her and she regularly sang in New York, Philadelphia and Chicago. One American millionaire is said to have paid Ruby £10,000 (approximately £190,000 in contemporary money) to travel across the Atlantic and sing at a private party in 1913. Not bad for a girl from a pub in Easton.

Sadly, Ruby's star began to fade and she was reduced to working as a singing teacher and by 1935 she announced her retirement. Following a battle with alcoholism, Ruby died at the young age of 48 in Hollywood. However, she is remembered with a blue plaque outside her former home at 114 Easton Road (as Brooklyn Terrace is now known) and some digitised recordings of her singing are available to buy on CD.

SARAH ANN HENLEY

1862-1948, BARMAID

Sarah Ann Henley was the heartbroken barmaid from Easton who in 1885 tried to commit suicide by jumping off the Suspension Bridge, only for her voluminous Victorian skirts to billow out into a parachute and save her.

The *Bristol Magpie* reported the event on 16 May 1885: "The rash act was the result of a lovers' quarrel. A young man, a

172 https://www.thestage.co.uk/features/2005/the-lady-tenor-ruby-helder/

porter on the Great Western Railway, determined to break off the engagement, wrote a letter to the young woman announcing his intention. This preyed on the girl's mind, and she, in a state of despair, rushed to end her life by the fearful leap from the Suspension Bridge ... There being a slight breeze blowing on Friday the young woman's clothes were inflated and her descent was thereby considerably checked and the wind also prevented her falling straight into the water, and she was carried into the mud on the Gloucestershire side."

Sarah's subsequent fame ironically led to a rash of marriage proposals from young men who had read her sad story. One wealthy suitor even bribed a hospital official to ensure that Sarah received his offer of a life of luxury as his wife. While a showman offered her a contract to tour with him, with £400 upfront and a share of the profits; and yet another showman approached her father with an offer of £1,000 to take her on tour with him.

At the time of Sarah's jump, fewer than 20 people had tried to take their own lives by jumping off the bridge, which had opened in 1864. Sarah was the only one who survived. She later married in 1890, although whether or not her husband was one of her newspaper suitors is unconfirmed.

ALMINA HERBERT, COUNTESS OF CARNARVON

1876–1969, EGYPTOLOGIST

Born into tremendous wealth as the daughter of banker Alfred de Rothschild, Almina Herbert inherited a vast fortune upon his death, some of which her archaeologist husband, the 5th Earl of Carnarvon, used to finance the discovery of Tutankhamun's tomb in Egypt. Along with other members of her family, Almina was present at the opening of the tomb in November 1922 and her first husband is said to have died at the tomb as a victim of the Curse of Tutankhamun. Following much scandal, rumours of illicit affairs (including suggestions that her first husband's best man, Prince Victor Duleep Singh, was the real father of her son Henry) and a second marriage, Almina spent the final years of her life living in relative poverty (and with no hot water) in a terraced house in Redland, having been declared bankrupt after her son squandered all of her wealth. In an undignified ending, Almina died alone after choking on a chicken bone.

ELIZABETH HIPPISLEY
died 1766, ACTOR

Like her sister Jane Green, Elizabeth Hippisley was an actor, having grown up under the influence of their theatre-owning father John Hippisley. Although less popular than Jane, Elizabeth still enjoyed a long career. She first took to the stage as Angelina in *Love Makes a Man* in 1742 and shortly after played Rose in *The Recruiting Officer*, which was a part she was to assume many times during her career. While establishing herself at a theatre in London's West End, Elizabeth would return to Bristol to spend summer seasons at her father's theatre on the Jacob's Well Road. Towards the end of her career she worked as a dresser in Bath.

Please also see the entry for: Jane Green.

DOROTHY CROWFOOT HODGKIN

1910-1994, SCIENTIST, NOBEL PRIZE WINNER

Dorothy Mary Crowfoot was born in 1910 in Cairo, Egypt. Her father was an archaeologist who worked for the education service in Egypt and Sudan while Dorothy was growing up. Her mother was also a scientist, working on the archeological sites with her husband. Dorothy and her three sisters mainly grew up in England, and lived with friends or relatives while their parents were away working.

From an early age Dorothy developed an interest in and a passion for chemistry – she appealed to her secondary school to be allowed to study chemistry, despite it being a 'boys' subject', and in 1928 successfully gained a place at Somerville College, Oxford University, to study chemistry. After graduating, she moved to Cambridge to study for her PhD with the scientist JD Bernal, so she could pursue her interest in X-ray crystallography. The technique involves firing X-rays through a crystal of a particular molecule and observing how they scatter, using photographic film. Interpretation of the scattering reveals the 3D structure of the molecule in question, down to the atomic level. Bernal had been the first to use this new method to successfully photograph a protein, and Dorothy was able to work on this state of the art technology while she cut her teeth as a scientist.

After being awarded her PhD, she moved back to Oxford in 1934 and set up her own lab within the Oxford University Museum of Natural History. It was here that Dorothy used the X-ray crystallography to discover the atomic structures of insulin, vitamin B12 and, during World War Two, she made a hugely important discovery when she revealed the chemical structure of penicillin. In 1964, she made history by becoming the first (and, to date, only) British woman to win a Nobel Prize for science for this groundbreaking work. Alongside her extremely successful scientific career she married Thomas Hodgkin and had three children, while still maintaining her prolific academic achievements. She lived with arthritis from the age of 28, which must have been extremely challenging for her given the precision required to set up the crystallography photograph experiments.

Dorothy used her platform as a Nobel Prize winner to campaign against nuclear weapons and to support organisations trying to bring peace to Vietnam. She was appointed Chancellor of the University of Bristol in 1971, and held the post for more than 15 years. While holding the post she campaigned against university budget cuts. In 2001 she was honoured by the University when it named its new research centre for endocrinology after her.

Written by Dr Suzi Gage, who is a psychology lecturer at the University of Liverpool. She regularly writes for *The Guardian* and presents the award-winning podcast 'Say Why To Drugs'.

Please also see the entry for: Beryl Corner.

VERA HOLME

1881-1969, SINGER, SUFFRAGETTE, CHAUFFEUR

Vera Holme was born on 29 August 1881 in Birkdale, Merseyside. She became a professional performer in her early 20s, joining D'Oyly Carte Opera Company at the Savoy Theatre, London, and appearing in a number of Gilbert and Sullivan operas as part of the ladies' chorus.

Vera became interested in the suffrage movement and joined both the Actresses' Franchise League (AFL) and the Women's Social and Political Union (WSPU) in 1908. She took part in marches, demonstrations, deputations and processions, and initiated the selling of suffrage newspapers on the streets by members. She also became involved in direct action for the suffrage cause.

In May 1909 Vera and fellow WSPU member Elsie Howey managed to sneak into the Colston Hall a few hours before an anti-suffragist MP and member of the Cabinet was due to chair a meeting there. They hid in the huge pipe organ, biding their time until the meeting began, and interrupted his opening speech by calling out "Votes for women!" It took nearly ten minutes for the stewards to find the women and they were escorted out of the building, apparently in front of an amused rather than hostile crowd. The *Bristol Times* reported that "the incident was taken in good part by the audience, who could not fail to recognise the ingenuity of the women to secure their end". Theirs wasn't the only suffragist interruption to the meeting, however, as a man in the audience was also thrown out and there was a protest from two women in a house opposite the Hall, who used a megaphone to shout from their top window into an open window of the Hall. A few days after the Colston Hall event, Vera was photographed with other prominent WSPU members at Eagle House in Batheaston, the home of the Blathwayts, planting a Gold Margined Holly in their Suffragette Arboretum.

Vera became the chauffeur to WSPU leader Emmeline Pankhurst in 1911 and was, according to *The Chauffeur* magazine, Britain's only female chauffeur at that time. Dressed in a smart uniform and wearing her Royal Automobile Club badge of efficiency, Vera drove Emmeline around in an Austin Landaulette owned by the WSPU. She remained active in the campaign, and was one of more than 200 women arrested in November 1911 in London for taking part in suffrage protests. Charged with breaking through a police cordon and trying to take hold of the mounted policemen's horses to pull them round, Vera said that "as the Government would not accept them as citizens no one could blame them for acting as outlaws". She was given five days in Holloway Prison.

Soon after the start of World War One, Vera joined the Women's Volunteer Reserve, a group founded by the Women's Emergency Corps and the AFL, and became a Major in the 1st London Battalion. In 1915, she and her companion Evelina Haverfield joined the Scottish Women's Hospitals in Serbia, and Vera used her motoring expertise to be an ambulance driver. In 1918 she was awarded the Samaritan Cross by the King of Serbia in recognition of her work with the Scottish Women's Hospitals, and a Russian Medal for Meritorious Service. At the end of the war she helped set up the Haverfield Fund for Serbian Children and, after Evelina died in 1920, Vera maintained her connections with the Serbian people. In 1943, she was awarded the Order of St Sava 5th Class by the Royal Yugoslav Embassy.

Known to her friends as Jack, Vera maintained her theatrical and suffragist connections in her later life, and died in Glasgow in 1969 aged 88. Her brother Gordon named his children Vera and Jack after her, and her extensive archives are housed in the Women's Library at the London School of Economics.

Written by Dr Naomi Paxton, who is a suffrage historian, specialising in the contribution of theatre professionals to the movement, and has published two books in this area. She is also an actor and, as Ada Campe, a comedian and magician.

Please also see the entries for: Emily and Mary Blathwayt and Elsie Howey.

SUSIE HOPES
1881-1976, TEACHER, REVOLUTIONARY

The Collegiate School in Redland was founded as a dame school[173] in 1903 by three sisters: Dora, Florence and Susannah (Susie) Adams. Susie had only recently left school herself and Dora was still studying at the University College, Bristol. Following a few moves to accommodate a growth in pupils and the disruption of World Wars One and Two, in 1946 the school settled at Winterbourne House and took students up to the age of 18, with many as boarders. After her sisters married and moved away, Susie was left running the Collegiate School with her husband, the poet and artist Rex Hopes, whom she had married in 1928. They kept the ecumenical Collegiate School at a small size, believing this was of greater benefit to the girls who attended it and pupils from a range of faiths were accepted from all over the world.

Susie's dream was: "To establish a place where lots of happy people were all working together. Teaching and learning were to be a shared joy in discovering treasure left by great minds of the past and present."

By the 1940s, the Adams sisters had taken on more staff, including Fraulein Schlenker, whom Susie later called one of the great influences in her life and she was devastated when World War Two forced Fraulein Schlenker back to Germany. Susie became a supporter of all movements working for world peace, such as the League of Nations (now the United Nations). She loved poetry, elocution, music and dance, and she combined these when she oversaw a Peace Pageant in the Victoria Rooms, Clifton, performed by the entire Collegiate School. Girls wore national costumes and sang in an array of languages.

173 A dame school was a small school, typically run by older women from their homes.

On Christmas Day 1946, Susie arranged entertainment for 60 German prisoners of war from a nearby camp and as soon as peace was declared after World War Two, she re-established contact with her exiled German friends and invited them to spend Christmas at Winterbourne House in 1947. Alongside her teaching, Susie continued to campaign for world peace by attending conferences for the United Nations Association and becoming a member of The Wyndham Place Trust, which was founded in 1959 to promote global peace.

Susie's teaching career lasted 68 years, during which time she offered a multiracial, moral and social education to numerous young women, while also passing on her passions for fresh air, vegetarian food and natural medicines. After supper, Susie would call the schoolgirls to get their coats and come for a walk around the gardens of Winterbourne House to look at the stars. She led the way, a rather stooped figure in a long drooping coat, and stopped from time to time to point upwards at the constellations. Susie was continually extolling the virtues of fresh air and would regularly remind the girls to take long, deep breaths.

In the early 1950s, the Collegiate School became a public school with a charitable trust and a governing body, which was impressive considering its humble origins as a dame school. In 1991, the Collegiate School merged with Colston's School (a fee-paying school founded by slave trader Edward Colston and still supported by the Society of Merchant Venturers) with the new school being called Colston's Collegiate School, although the name reverted to Colston's School in 2005.[174]

Written by Caroline Mornement, who was a pupil at the Collegiate School between 1957-1961 and is now an artist and publisher.

174 With thanks to an obituary in a 1977 copy of the *Collegiate School Chronicle*, written by then-headteacher Joan Cable.

ELSIE HOWEY
1884-1963, SUFFRAGETTE

Elsie Howey was born in Nottinghamshire in December 1884 and grew up in the Malvern area. She spent two years at St Andrews University and became interested in the suffrage movement after a trip to Germany. Along with her mother and elder sister, Elsie joined the Women's Social and Political Union (WSPU) in 1907.

Elsie quickly became an active, visible and vocal campaigner for votes for women. She was first arrested, with her sister, in February 1908 for hiding in a van to gain access to the House of Commons, and after being released from prison spoke on a platform for the Women's Sunday rally in Hyde Park in June 1908. She dressed as Joan of Arc and rode in full armour on a white horse for a welcome procession to greet Emmeline Pethick Lawrence upon her release from prison in April 1909. A month later, Elsie and fellow WSPU member Vera Holme hid in the pipe organ at Colston Hall and interrupted the speech of a Cabinet Minister with shouts of "Votes for women!". Elsie spent the next few months in the South West. She was attacked at a public suffrage meeting in Bristol in June 1909, and arrested in July for demonstrating at a meeting in Penzance, Cornwall. She was sentenced to seven days in prison, went on hunger strike and after her release recuperated at Eagle House in Batheaston, where she planted a Caucasian Fir tree in the Suffragette Arboretum.

Her friendship with the Blathwayts at Eagle House became strained when, in September of 1909, Elsie became involved in an attempted physical assault on the Prime Minister Herbert Asquith and Home Secretary Herbet Gladstone while they were playing golf on the south coast. Elsie, Jessie Kenney and Vera Wentworth had disguised themselves earlier in the day to gain access to the grounds of Lympne Castle, Kent, by boat via a canal, and after the altercation on a nearby golf course, headed back to the Castle and disturbed the Prime Minister at dinner. Elsie shouted through an open window: "Mr Asquith, we shall go on pestering you until you give women the vote." Although police were called to the scene, the women escaped into their boat and got away before being caught.

Despite evading arrest many times, Elsie was imprisoned at least six times for her militant direct action for the cause. As was customary among WSPU militant prisoners, she went on hunger strike and was forcibly fed on several occasions. In 1910, she was given six weeks hard labour in Walton Gaol, Liverpool, for causing six shillings of damage when she broke the gaol governor's windows with a purple, white and green flag so she could be imprisoned in support of Lady Constance Lytton.[175] The WSPU described her at the time as someone "who gives the whole of her services and the whole of her life to the cause… a beautiful, refined, and charming girl". When she was imprisoned for the final time in December 1912, the WSPU newspaper *The Suffragette* reported that 75 Malvern "working men and farmers" wrote to their MP to demand a reduction in her two-month sentence. She again went on hunger strike and was forcibly fed. This time the process of the feeding broke most of her teeth.

Elsie took the symbolic role of Joan of Arc once more at the funeral of Emily Wilding Davison in 1913, but seems to have retired from public life after WSPU militancy was suspended at the outbreak of World War One. Little is known about her life after 1914. She died in March 1963 in Malvern from health

175 Lady Constance Lytton was a prominent suffragette who was appalled at the way upper-class suffrage prisoners were treated so much better than those from the working classes. So in January 1910 she disguised herself as a seamstress called Jane Warton, threw rocks at an MP's car in Liverpool and experienced prison as a working-class woman. She later wrote accounts of her differing experiences of prison for the national newspapers and helped expose the barbaric ways in which the prison authorities were treating women. It is thought that Lady Lytton's work helped to end the appalling ordeal of forced feeding for hunger striking prisoners.

complications that were mostly likely caused by the numerous forcible feedings she had endured as a suffrage prisoner. She requested that no funeral be held for her and left most of her estate to the English Theosophical Trust.

Written by Dr Naomi Paxton, who is a suffrage historian, specialising in the contribution of theatre professionals to the movement, and has published two books in this area. She is also an actor and, as Ada Campe, a comedian and magician.

Please also see the entries for: Emily and Mary Blathwayt, Vera Holme, Emmeline Pethick Lawrence and Vera Wentworth.

VERA HUGHES

dates unknown, BUSINESSWOMAN

In the post-war years, Bristolian women largely returned to the trades they had worked in before the war: shop work, factory work and so on. But one or two pushed the envelope. In Vera Hughes' case, quite literally. Vera founded a mail fulfilment business called Mail Marketing International above a shoe shop on Park Street in 1950 and by the 1960s her business had grown so large that it was considered a key Bristolian employer. Mail Marketing International still exists, although its range has expanded to move with the times. After outgrowing its Park Street office, Vera moved the business into the former Colodense factory in Bedminster (which had made cellophane), where the staff would sometimes play netball on the roof.[176]

176 https://www.flickr.com/photos/brizzlebornandbred/2129935515

VICTORIA HUGHES
1897-1978, TOILET ATTENDANT

Published in 1977, Victoria Hughes' memoir *Ladies' Mile* caused quite a stir because it is "the remarkable and shocking story of twilight Bristol" as seen through the eyes of Victoria, who was a toilet attendant on Durdham Downs from 1929 to 1962. The reason why Victoria's work is so important is that she kept diaries and notebooks in which she logged the comings and goings of the characters visiting her toilets, as well as some bizarre scrapes she found herself in due to befriending these people – including having to cycle home down Blackboy Hill one night wearing nothing but her raincoat after becoming infested with lice.

As you can imagine, working on the Downs in the small hours meant that the bulk of Victoria's customers were sex workers, for whom the Downs was a key site in the pre- and post-war years. But all the while she comes across as a kind and matronly lady who passes her time by knitting and who keeps the kettle handy for anyone who needs a warming brew.

Ladies' Mile was published when Victoria was enjoying her retirement but even in the late 1970s the subject matter was shocking to some readers. Those being readers offended by talk of women being forced to sell their bodies to feed their children, pensionable women who had no alternative but to prostitute themselves beneath a tree and the grim realities of dealing with sexually transmitted diseases in unenlightened times.

Victoria recalls an anecdote about a young woman who goes into a cubicle and doesn't emerge for some time. When she does, she looks shaky and upset but refuses offers of help. When Victoria goes into the cubicle she finds a dead premature baby wrapped in newspaper and left inside the toilet bowl. Victoria's written response is very revealing about her own nature and her

Victoria Hughes illustration by Jenny Howe

determination to be kind to whomever uses her facilities: "The noonday miscarriage left me with conflicting thoughts. I hated the cold-blooded way [the woman] had brazenly confronted us and walked out as though nothing had happened. But I wanted to sympathise with her at the same time. I was haunted by her chalk-white face and hands that were trembling."

Victoria's seemingly throwaway references to the "whores" and "tarts" who used her facilities, and the casual tone in which she recalls the women who threatened or achieved suicide due to their utterly miserable lives, betrays the kindness she showed night after night. While this disrespectful language is shocking to a 21st-century reader, please remember that the book was written at a time when attitudes were not as understanding as they are now. Victoria states that she tried never to moralise or to tell the women who sold sex for money to give up their trade, she simply tried to support them as best she could.

ELIZABETH INCHBALD

1753-1821, ACTOR, JOURNALIST

Elizabeth Inchbald made her acting debut at Bristol Theatre Royal (now Bristol Old Vic) in 1772 playing Cordelia in a production of *King Lear*. Her two published novels are *A Simple Story* (1791) and *Nature and Art* (1796), and she developed her writing career by becoming the first-ever female professional theatre critic in 1806. Given that her link to Bristol is extremely tenuous we won't dwell on her in these pages but, if you'd like to know more, a quick search online will point you in the right direction.

LADY JANET INSKIP
1897-1974, POLITICIAN

Lady Janet Inskip became a magistrate in Bristol in 1934 and worked for reform to the juvenile criminal justice system and better rehabilitation for ex-prisoners. Lady Janet also felt it was important that women who were returning to Bristol after working away during World War Two had a place to go and receive support. And so in her role as Chairwoman of the Young Women's Christian Association she lobbied to buy the American Red Cross Club on Great George Street and transform it into a club for the women of Bristol. She told a deputation about the "overwhelming feeling prevalent of having something ready at the end of the war for the women and girls of Bristol" to counteract post-war "restlessness"[177].

MAUD ISAACS
dates unknown, FACTORY WORKER

Initially employed at Fry's chocolate factory, when Maud Beatrice Isaacs from Barton Hill was around 20 she was called to work at a mustard gas manufacturing and shell-filling site at Chittening, near Avonmouth, during World War One. Her entry in this book represents all of the women who left their usual jobs to take up dangerous work in support of the war effort. Alarmingly, 1,300 women were injured at the Chittening factory, including 140 on just one morning.[178]

Like many women at the site, Maud unfortunately sustained a

177 *Western Daily Press*, 1945, 18 May, 'Central Club for Women: Scheme Inaugurated in Bristol'. 3.
178 http://museums.bristol.gov.uk/narratives.php?irn=12121

debilitating injury during her work when the mustard gas leaked from a shell and dripped onto her feet causing severe burns. Consequently, between July and September 1918, Maud received just over £1 a week as compensation for her injury. For the rest of her life, Maud found it difficult to walk long distances and once a fortnight she needed to see a chiropodist to have the bright yellow suppuration cut from her feet.

Mustard gas, or dichloroethyl sulphide, was first used by the Germans in 1917 in artillery shells and nobody in Britain had any previous experience of the substance, which explained why so many accidents occurred during its manufacture. Once fired from a gun, the gas returns to liquid form where it can retain its toxicity for weeks or even months afterwards, causing harm to anyone who comes into contact with it.

Historian Clive Burlton explained the horrific effects of working with the substance: "The human cost of the plants at Avonmouth and Chittening was considerable. Physical contact caused blisters over all of the body, the gas seeping through all clothing, protective or otherwise. Inhalation caused bronchitis, tracheitis, gastritis and bronco-pneumonia. Conjunctivitis was common among all workers." In the six months that mustard gas was produced at Avonmouth, there were 1,000 workers in the factory – of whom 710 were poisoned by the gas, some fatally.[179] The risks were so great that the factory had its own hospital. Due to its high carcinogenic factor, those who came into contact with mustard gas faced a much higher risk of contracting cancer. So the civilian women who gave up their regular jobs to work in these potentially deadly factories in order to further the war efforts were true sheroes, ones whose bravery went unrewarded. Bristol

179 Clive Burlton, (2014), 'Mustard Gas Production At Avonmouth' in Bristol2014, *Bristol and the First World War: The Great Reading Adventure 2014*. Bristol: Bristol Cultural Development Partnership. 48-49.

Maud Beatrice Isaacs illustration by Jenny Howe

City Council's Archaeological Officer Peter Insole said in 2014: "What we do know about Britain's production of mustard gas is that we actually caused more casualties producing the stuff in this country than we did on the front, which is a crazy statistic."[180]

Fortunately, we do know that in Maud's case she survived her agonising injuries and went on to get married and have a family.[181] Although shockingly, when builders began work to develop the derelict former mustard gas factory at Chittening into housing in 2012, work was halted after they suffered nosebleeds and respiratory problems, which was found to be a direct result of the site's former use and a confirmation of the long-lasting effects of the gas, almost a century after production ceased.[182]

Maud's experiences reached a wider audience when, in 2014, the Bedminster community theatre company acta dramatised her story in its play *Gas Girls*, which was performed to sold-out audiences. A ten-minute documentary, which contains a lot of information about the women who worked in the mustard gas factory in Chittening, can be viewed on the acta website.[183]

DOROTHY IVORY

dates unknown, CRICKETER

We don't have many sportswomen in this book sadly but we do have Dorothy Ivory, who was the first captain of the Downend Ladies' Cricket XI, founded in 1925. Her unconventional but delightful wedding photo, taken on 17 April 1933, shows her beside her husband George Lant behind the wicket. Pleasingly,

180 http://www.bbc.co.uk/news/uk-england-25053155

181 Eugene Byrne, Clive Burlton, (2014). *Bravo, Bristol! The City at War 1914-1918*. Bristol: Redcliffe Press. 119.

182 http://www.bbc.co.uk/news/uk-england-bristol-18069000

183 https://www.acta-bristol.com/gas-girls-2/

subsequent references to Dorothy in the *Western Daily Press* announce her also winning whist and tennis tournaments. So she was clearly a sporting all-rounder.

MARY JEFFRIES
born 1851, EMBROIDERER

After the deaths of both of her parents from cholera, Mary Jeffries was admitted to the New Orphan House at Ashley Down in 1857. During her time there, which was one of the Müller Homes orphanages in Bristol, Mary became an adept embroiderer and several of the samplers that she and other girls at the institution made are now on display at Bristol Museum and Art Gallery.[184]

Samplers were important tools for the girls because they could be used as an example of their needlework skills, which would be necessary if they were to work as domestic servants in adulthood (in contrast, samplers made by girls from well-off families were often framed and hung decoratively on the wall). The teachers at the Ashley Down Orphanage followed a template and consequently the girls made endless almost identical samplers, with rows of stitching depicting the alphabet and numbers in a range of fonts, below which the girls could add motifs of their choice from the template.

The girls were also taught sewing and knitting.[185] However, despite her embroidery skills, when Mary left the orphanage in 1870 it was to work as a nursemaid in Birkenhead, Merseyside.

184 Shirley Brown, Dawn Dyer, (2002). *100+ Women of Bristol*. Bristol: Bristol City Council. 8.
185 https://hands-across-the-sea-samplers.com/bristol-orphanage-samplers/

THEODORA JOHNSON
died 1939, SPORTSWOMAN, SUFFRAGIST

At a time when physical exertion was deemed bad for girls, Theodora Johnson and her colleague Foken Dahl broke the mould. In the 1880s, Theodora opened the Swedish Gymnasium and Institute for Massage and Medical Movements in her garden at 20 Vyvyan Terrace, Clifton, which was the first such Swedish institute in the west of England.

In 1897, Theodora wrote a book encouraging physical exercise for women and girls, which was based on the teachings of Professor Ling, who established this particular form of gymnastic exercise. Theodora wrote: "Ling desired by this arrangement to ensure close attention, to strengthen the sense of order, discipline and strict obedience, and further, to increase brain impressionability and promptness of action on reception of the mental stimulus. Brightness and cheerfulness are evolved by the joy of energetic work in unison, and the fellowship of rhythmic movement infuses a glow which transforms work into pleasure."[186]

The institute thrived with Theodora as Principal, and patrons included the Bishop of Bristol, the Duchess of Beaufort and several well regarded doctors. There were departments specialising in medicine, education and dancing. Theodora believed that selected exercises would correct various physical defects, and she also used medico-massage and electricity to relieve the symptoms of her clients. Lectures were given about physiology and hygiene to accompany the physical and mental exercise classes.

Theodora also taught Swedish drill and gymnastics at Clifton High School, which was extremely unusual for the time. In 1894, she addressed the British Medical Association when they met in

186 Theodora Johnson (1897) in Janet Horowitz Murray et al, (1980), *The Englishwoman's Review of Social and Industrial Questions*. London: Routledge.

Bristol. And in 1920, the institute changed hands and became the Bristol School of Dancing.

Alongside her commitment to physical exercise, Theodora was also a staunch supporter of votes for women. The campaign for women's suffrage inevitably attracted a lot of hostility from those who felt threatened by the possibility of women achieving political equality with men, so letters of support from men were very welcome. One such letter to the *Western Daily Press* came from a John Strong, who wrote: "Sir, Anyone who has the pleasure of the acquaintance of Miss Theodora Johnson will realise at once the absurdity of withholding the Parliamentary vote from a lady of her mental capacity, and she is representative of thousands of others. The majority of men I have met are agreed that women ought to have the vote. A few have stated that they do not possess the capacity, but that has never been tested."[187]

DIANA WYNNE JONES

1934-2011, NOVELIST

By the time Diana Wynne Jones passed away in 2011, she had invented countless impossible worlds over the course of more than 40 books, thrilling young people with her stories of magic, myth and mystery. Her *Chrestomanci* series is arguably a precursor to *Harry Potter*, while her most widely known work is *Howl's Moving Castle* (1986), made famous by the film adaptation by Studio Ghibli in 2004.

Born in 1934, Diana had a difficult childhood in London. Her parents kept their three daughters at arm's length, often leaving them with someone else while they went on holiday. The girls

187 *Western Daily Press*, 1908, 15 November, 'Letter: Women's Suffrage'. 3.

were forced to live in a damp lean-to shack rather than the main house. Illnesses they developed – including chickenpox, German measles and appendicitis – were dismissed for as long as possible as 'psychological'. It seems likely that seeds were sown during this time which led Diana to write about outsiders in her stories, creating characters who are neglected or cast out and forced to fend for themselves. She began writing "mostly to keep my sanity" during the 1960s, starting with three plays and then an adult satirical novel in 1970.

In 1976 Diana moved to Bristol, where she wrote the majority of her books. She became firmly established as a writer of magical fiction for young people, occupying an important position in the canon of children's fantastical literature. Her work bridges the gap between traditional fantasy, whose witches, dwarfs, elves and talking beasts inhabit settings like Narnia and Middle Earth (she heard both CS Lewis and JRR Tolkien speak during her time at Oxford), and today's deadlier, more duplicitous invented worlds, where children fall victim to lethal spells or murder each other in *Hunger Games*. Although her books abound with magicians, wizards, talking beasts, demons, celestial beings and every imaginable fantasy trope, Diana tends to deconstruct and question them, a process culminating in her satirical *Tough Guide to Fantasyland* (1996).

When you consider Diana's body of work, perhaps the most impressive aspect is her sheer power of invention. This is a writer who created multiple multiverses, each with its own logic, rules and politics. Sometimes they are presided over by benign authorities, or there can be something rotten at the top. As with all fantasy, her concepts are lenses through which we can examine our own power structures, both domestic and public.

The seven *Chrestomanci* books spanned her career, with the first published in 1977 and the last in 2006. The initial volume features a boy with mystical powers, who is sent to a school to learn how to master them, and because of this and other similarities it is often compared to the *Harry Potter* series. Diana herself thought that JK Rowling may have read her books – written some 20 years earlier – as a child, though she added that, not having met the author, she had been unable to ask her.

Writing in Bristol, Diana drew on the area's topography both implicitly and sometimes overtly, locating one or two scenes at landmarks such as the Clifton Suspension Bridge. In *Deep Secret* (1997), a character peers through the uneven windows of a Bristol house and claims they offer "glimpses of a great alternate universe called Bristolia". Through the eyes of this exceptional and much-missed author, even the most ordinary view is multidimensional.

Written by Heather Child, who is a Bristol-based author of literary sci-fi crossover fiction. Her debut novel *Everything About You* is published in 2018.

SARAH JONES

born 1610, WRITER

Identifying herself as "a poor widow of Bristol", in 1650 Sarah Jones wrote an epistle with the whimsical title 'This Is Light's Appearance in the Truth to all the Precious Dear Lambs of the Light'. By this, she was including all of the Quakers close to her in Bristol and in the wider area. The message of Sarah's epistle was that the light was within you and you should share it by doing good deeds and not living a selfish life.[188]

188 Grace M Jantzen, (2005), 'Choose Life! Early Quaker Women and Violence in Modernity' in *Quaker Studies*, Vol 9, No 2. 150-151.

JULIANA

died 1946, CANINE WAR SHERO

There are two suffragette dogs in this book and Juliana adds to the canine count. This Great Dane became an unlikely saviour in April 1941 when the Luftwaffe was dropping bombs on Bristol. Desperate for a wee, Juliana relieved herself where she stood in the house and in the process her urine extinguished a smouldering incendiary bomb that had fallen through the roof of the family's home and gone undetected on the floor. By extinguishing the bomb, Juliana saved the lives of her family as well as those in the vicinity.[189] She was awarded a Blue Cross medal in 1941 for her valour and in November 1944 Juliana received a second Blue Cross after her barking alerted people to a fire that was tearing through her owners' shop.[190] Blue Cross medals were awarded to military horses during World War One but this was extended to include other brave animals during World War Two.

CHARLOTTE KEEL

1888-1955, COUNCILLOR, ALDERMAN

The Charlotte Keel Health Centre in Easton, opened in 1956, is named in honour of this Councillor and Alderman who worked hard throughout her life to improve community health services. Charlotte, who lived in St Werburgh's, was a councillor from 1934 for 20 years, and Alderman from 1945 for ten years.

189 Valerie Pitt, (2015). *Bloody Bristol*. Stroud: The History Press. 120.
190 http://www.bbc.co.uk/news/uk-england-bristol-23985116

ANNIE KENNEY
1879-1953, SUFFRAGETTE

Famously, Annie Kenney (also known as 'our Captain') was a rare member of the Women's Social and Political Union (WSPU) elite who had come up from the working classes. Annie was originally a cotton-mill worker in Lancashire before being welcomed into the Pankhursts' inner circle. Indeed, such was her charismatic personality that by the time she had moved to Bristol in 1907 to lead the WSPU in the West Country, the nearby Blathwayt family was so enamoured by her that they nicknamed their wonderful suffrage garden 'Annie's Arboretum' in her honour (please see the entry for Emily and Mary Blathwayt for more information on the arboretum). After a number of Bristol homes, in 1910 Annie settled at 23 Gordon Road in Clifton where her good friend Mary Blathwayt also moved in for 18 months. The address is now marked with a blue plaque.

In her essay, June Hannam writes about the Blathwayt diaries: "After giving details of a day full of suffrage activities Mary would note, for example, that she had paid 8d to have Annie's stockings mended or that a young speaker needed to borrow a nightgown when she stayed for the night. The Blathwayt diaries are also full of references to Annie Kenney's health problems, which included toothache, loss of voice and extreme tiredness. This gives a useful reminder of how exhausting the life of suffrage activists could be."[191]

Shortly before her move to Bristol, Annie gave a speech at the Victoria Rooms, Clifton, with Christabel Pankhurst and granted an interview to the *Western Daily Press*. The reporter described

191 June Hannam, (2000), 'Suffragettes are Splendid for Any Work: The Blathwayt Diaries as a Source for Suffrage History' in Claire Eustance, Joan Ryan, Laura Ugolini (eds), (2000), *A Suffrage Reader: Charting Directions in British Suffrage History*. London: Leicester University Press. 56.

her saying: "Miss Kenney's personality offered a striking contrast to the popular conception of the suffragettes. Slight – even frail – in figure, one finds it difficult to reconcile her with the strenuous part which has to be played by those who lead a cause which only now, after years of incessant effort, is being regarded as a serious factor in political life." They continued: "Yet this lady, ordinarily gentle in manner, and possessing a temperament responsive and sympathetic, has been one of the most fearless in the rough pioneer work of the movement, and four times has preferred prison walls to the forsaking of her principles."[192]

In the interview, Annie assured the reporter that the WSPU was definitely making progress in its cause, explaining how it was spending upwards of £250 a week on marketing (approximately £280,000 in contemporary money) and that the number of women volunteering every week in the London office had exploded from 30 to 300. She also felt that men were starting to be more sympathetic, saying: "Men are beginning to take an intelligent interest in the subject and instead of creating disorder ask questions with a real desire for knowledge." She refused to speak on any other political issues and concluded: "We are firm and fixed in our purpose to press forward to our one and only goal – votes for women."[193]

Annie's time in Bristol coincided with a general election, which gave many opportunities for suffrage activity throughout all of the city and it was not unusual for Annie to be speaking at three or more different meetings in just one day. As well as organising meetings, Annie coordinated the selling of *Votes For Women* magazines, a huge theatrical event at the Princess Theatre in 1910 (including a pageant, play and concert with a combined

192 *Western Daily Press*, 1909, April 1, 'Interview with Miss Annie Kenney'. 5.
193 Ibid. 5.

Annie Kenney illustration by Jenny Howe

cast of hundreds and an audience of 3,000[194]) and a mass refusal to sign the 1911 census. After all, if women could not be recognised as citizens worthy of a vote, why should they indulge the government by being recognised as citizens at all? As well as this, day-to-day activities for Annie and her comrades included door-to-door canvassing, meetings for working women, jumble sales and lectures.

In the run up to the national census evasion in April 1911, there were activities to draw suffragists' attention to the campaign and to let them know how they could avoid the census in their area and where they could go to hide safely. In Bristol, Annie organised teams to go out with a costermonger's cart selling cakes, sweets and fruit in Clifton and on the Downs to help fund the campaign; and star speakers came to the city including Scottish suffragette Jane Brailsford who managed to secure promises to evade the census from at least half of those in her audience.[195]

Due to the 100 year rule, the exact details of 1911 citizens' census returns was not expected to be made public until 2012 but a surprise Freedom of Information ruling saw them released early in 2009. Suffragist researcher Jill Liddington embarked on a mammoth project to track and trace as many suffragist census returns as she possibly could (with the assistance of Elizabeth Crawford), and her findings are recorded in her absorbing 2014 book *Vanishing for the Vote*.

Unlike previous census reports that had been made public, the 1911 census was the first to be released exactly as it was: meaning that researchers could see the handwriting, smudges, crossings-out and so on of the people who had filled them in a century previously. How exciting to see the handwriting of Annie Kenney

194 For more information about the great pageant, please visit this website: http://www.historicalpageants.ac.uk/pageants/1009/

195 Jill Liddington, (2014), *Vanishing for the Vote*. Manchester: Manchester University Press. 160.

and her sisters! Jill wrote: "The 1911 census offers for the very first time a unique opportunity to eavesdrop right into the heart of Votes for Women homes."[196]

On the night of the 1911 census, Annie stayed at 9 Whatley Road, Clifton, and simply wrote "suffragette" as her occupation. The summary page for Annie in the census suggests that she was the only person at the property but in an interview with the *Bristol Times & Mercury* she proudly said that she had put up a poster on her front door announcing "No Vote, No Census" and told the reporter: "I have had my house crowded out all night. They are just beginning to leave now, so they cannot reach home before noon. We commenced a bridge party as soon as Monday morning broke, and some played bridge all night. Others ... played other games, or went and got what rest they could."[197]

Given there were only four rooms in the Whatley Road flat, exactly how many secret suffragists could Annie squeeze in there? We do not know, but we do know that Annie was not the only host of a census evasion party in Bristol. Information is sketchy but based on information Annie told the same reporter about a caravan of refuge, he wrote: "There was a caravan with upon one side [a poster] 'A Few Census Resisters' and upon the other 'No Vote, No Census'. In this ark of refuge from the flood of census questions some members of the local 'militants' spent the night, taking a drive in the night air over the [Clifton] Suspension Bridge ... Miss Kenney says it would not do to give the number of parties held or the total number of guests, else she would be supplying her friends at the Census Office with information they would like to get hold of. And that she would be very sorry to do."[198] No other news of this caravan has ever come to light, so there is

196 Ibid. 4.
197 Ibid. 166.
198 Ibid. 167.

the possibility that Annie simply invented it for the purpose of entertaining the reporter.

Annie left Bristol in 1912 to take over from Christabel Pankhurst as organiser of the WSPU in London, after Christabel went into hiding in France. Along with the other suffragettes, Annie ceased militancy during the war and in 1920 she got married before starting a family.

Please also see the entry for: Emily and Mary Blathwayt.

DEBORAH KERR

1921-2007, ACTOR

Born in Scotland, Deborah Kerr went to school at Northumberland House, Clifton, where her acting contemporary Joan Sanderson was also a pupil. Deborah's aunt Phyllis Smale ran the Hicks-Smale Drama School in Bristol and took her niece under her wing to mentor her. Deborah's acting work began with BBC Radio in Bristol and in local amateur theatre before she moved to London, and then her career skyrocketed and her numerous awards included a Golden Globe for her role in the 1956 film *The King And I*. "There was little to interest gossip columnists or to shock the public and, at least on the surface, she seemed rather serene in the midst of such a frantic profession," wrote *The Guardian* in Deborah's obituary, praising her "career that sailed on rather majestically, like an elegant ocean liner, only occasionally hitting a squall or rough passage".[199]

Please also see the entries for: Joan Sanderson and Phyllis Smale.

199 https://www.theguardian.com/news/2007/oct/19/guardianobituaries.obituaries1

AETA LAMB
1886-1928, SUFFRAGETTE

Having already proved her worth when working at the Women's Social and Political Union (WSPU) headquarters in London, Aeta Lamb was dispatched to Bristol in 1907 to help Annie Kenney set up the Bristol and West of England branch. When Bristol medical students threatened to break up a meeting in the Victoria Rooms, Clifton, on 3 April 1908, Aeta hired six professional boxers to protect the speakers. She was the first suffragette to plant a tree in the Suffragettes' Wood in Batheaston and was later also the last to plant a tree there. Aeta had misgivings about the rapidly escalating WSPU militancy but continued to support the Pankhursts and was still working at WSPU headquarters in London when World War One broke out.

Please also see the entries for: Emily and Mary Blathwayt and Annie Kenney.

VIOLET LAMB
1911-2009, ACTOR

An actor through and through, Acton-born Violet Lamb lived her whole life in performance. Whether on stage in a Shakespeare play or touring the country with an educational production, Violet simply loved to perform.

In 1937, she joined the Bristol Little Theatre, which was run by Peggy Ann Wood, where she proved herself to be a thoroughly versatile actor and achieved a little notoriety for one mishap: "She became well-known for walking onstage through the fireplace during a performance of [George Bernard] Shaw's *Major Barbara* when she thought the curtain was down," wrote *The Stage* in her obituary.[200]

In the *Bristol Bellman* magazine in March 1939, there is a curious piece by Violet (who is, correctly, listed under "interesting people") about her time touring Shakespeare's plays to schools. In this, her writing vividly creates a fantastical picture of what life was like on tour in the early 1930s and you are left with the impression of a woman who truly loved life and was great fun to be around. She wrote: "We played Shakespeare to schools, going round in a plain van and taking it in turns to sit by the driver. Inside, you couldn't see out and there weren't enough seats, so someone had to sit on the oil-can: we took that in turns, too. As well as the company, the van carried round all the props which were continually falling on our heads. It was marvellous. I just completely fell in love with this bus-life. We spent most of our time rehearsing in the van. When we arrived at schools, a master would emerge to contemplate our van and call it a 'Thespian Wagon'."[201] She goes on in this style for several paragraphs, taking the reader through all sorts of villages around the UK and making you wish you could join her in that van.

After marrying fellow actor Cyril Luckham in 1940, Violet had to leave the Bristol Little Theatre. In those days, there was a rule that married actors were not allowed to work for the same company, so the couple moved to Coventry where the rule was less strictly enforced. Violet acted throughout her entire life and impressed her colleagues with her continued energy and enthusiasm well into her 80s.

Please also see the entry for: Peggy Ann Wood.

200 https://www.thestage.co.uk/features/obituaries/2009/violet-lamb/
201 Violet Lamb (1939), 'The Bus-Life' in *Bristol Bellman*, Vol 1, No 1, page 8.

LADY GORE LANGTON

1820-1879, PRESIDENT OF THE NUWSS

After Katharine Russell died in 1874, Lady Gore Langton stepped up as President of the Bristol branch of the Central Committee of the National Society for Women's Suffrage, having been President of the Bath committee since 1871. Lady Gore Langton, also known by her first name of Anna, had strong suffrage credentials having been a signatory to the 1866 Women's Suffrage Petition, supported John Stuart Mill's 1867 amendment to the Representation of the People Act and in 1873 presented Benjamin Disraeli (then the Leader of the Opposition) with a petition signed by 11,000 women in favour of female enfranchisement.[202]

Praising Anna's oratory skills, Bristol suffragist Helen Blackburn wrote: "Her speaking was thoroughly practical and carried with it great earnestness and conviction – perhaps it was all the more convincing because it was quiet and unassuming. Her fine presence and noble face lent great dignity to all she said."[203]

In June 1877, Anna joined a deputation (including Lilias Ashworth Hallett) to the Chancellor of the Exchequer requesting his support for votes for women. The Chancellor said he was "in favour of the bill" and that he had voted for the measure, but never spoken upon it, and that he thought the ground taken by Miss Ashworth was "quite sound and proper"[204]. The debate was drowned out by noisy protests when it was raised in the House.[205]

Please also see the entries for: Helen Blackburn, Lilias Ashworth Hallett and Katharine Russell.

202 Elizabeth Crawford, (1999). *The Women's Suffrage Movement: A Reference Guide 1866-1928*. London: University College London Press. 251.
203 Ibid. 251.
204 *Western Daily Press*, 1877, 6 June, 'Female Suffrage'. 7.
205 Elizabeth Crawford, (1999). *The Women's Suffrage Movement: A Reference Guide 1866-1928*. London: University College London Press. 251.

EMMELINE PETHICK LAWRENCE
1867-1954, SUFFRAGETTE

Emmeline Pethick was born at Gluckstein, Apsley Road, Clifton, the eldest surviving child of the 13 born to Henry Pethick, a merchant, and his wife Fanny. Five of the children died in infancy. By 1881, the family had moved to Trewartha, Bristol Road, Weston-super-Mare. Although her younger sisters, Dorothy and Marie (who later became a doctor), were sent to Cheltenham Ladies' College, Emmeline received a more conventional education at a local day school with 'finishing' at a small boarding school, followed by extended visits to Nancy, France, and Wiesbaden, Germany, in order to polish her language skills. She was brought up as a Nonconformist, first as a Methodist and then as a Congregationalist, before her father joined an evangelical Church of England congregation. She noted her father's "deep strain of religious mysticism", a characteristic she also shared.

In 1890, Emmeline decided that there was more to life than waiting for marriage as a 'daughter at home' and went to London as a volunteer with the Sisterhood of the West London Mission. With Mary Neal, whom she met there, she left the Sisterhood in 1895 and began working among the poor in an area around Euston Road. They set up the Espérance Working Girls' Club in Cumberland Market and, in 1897, opened a dressmaking business, Maison Espérance, in Great Portland Street, paying their employees double the usual wage and providing them with very much better working conditions than most employers did. They also opened The Green Lady Hostel at Littlehampton, to allow working girls a brief holiday by the sea.

In 1901, Emmeline Pethick married Frederick Lawrence, who was active as a social reformer and who, in 1905, launched a new monthly publication, the *Labour Record and Review.* The couple

Emmeline Pethick Lawrence illustration by Carrie Love

owned a Lutyens-designed house, The Mascot, at Holmwood outside Dorking and during the week lived in a serviced apartment in Clement's Inn off the Strand, London. It was here, in 1906, that they provided an office for the Women's Social and Political Union (WSPU), having been introduced to Emmeline Pankhurst by the Labour MP Keir Hardie. Emmeline Pethick Lawrence, an astute businesswoman and good organiser, became the WSPU's Treasurer. When Christabel Pankhurst completed her university degree and left Manchester for London, she lived with the Pethick Lawrences in London and Surrey.

In October 1906, Emmeline was arrested after taking part at a protest at the opening of parliament and was sentenced to two month's imprisonment. She immediately collapsed with a nervous breakdown and was released from Holloway after only two days. In 1907, the Pethick Lawrences, as co-editors, launched the WSPU newspaper *Votes for Women.* Emmeline's articles tend towards the exhortatory and by all accounts her oratory followed the lines of her written style, uplifting and theatrical. She was one of the WSPU's star speakers, travelling round the country delivering her brand of moral uplift.

Emmeline had a flair for publicity and, in May 1908, it was she who chose purple, white and green as the colours by which the members of the WSPU should be unified and recognised while taking part in a procession through London on 21 June. This 'branding' of the WSPU is as strong now as it was more than 100 years ago. On 24 February 1909, she was once again arrested after leading a WSPU deputation from Caxton Hall to the House of Commons and sentenced to two months' imprisonment. It had taken considerable courage to place herself again in the position which had resulted previously in a deeply felt humiliation, and on her release on 16 April from Holloway she was given a rapturous reception by the WSPU.

On 21 November 1911, Emmeline led another deputation from Caxton Hall, was arrested, and received one month's imprisonment for assault. In March 1912, she did not take part in the WSPU window-smashing raid on West End shops but, on 5 March, was arrested and charged with conspiring to cause damage. As a result she was sentenced to nine months' imprisonment and, with her husband and Emmeline Pankhurst, ordered to pay the cost of the prosecution, which was an unprecedented penalty. In late June, Emmeline joined the prisoners' hunger strike and endured one forcible feeding before being released two days later.

She and her husband then travelled abroad to allow her to recuperate, meeting Emmeline and Christabel Pankhurst at Boulogne, France. In the course of this meeting it became clear that a deep division had arisen between the two parties. The Pethick Lawrences thought the WSPU should not alienate the public by committing further damage to property, hoping instead to stage a series of large popular demonstrations. As a result, when they arrived back in England they discovered they had been ousted from the WSPU, which had moved out of Clement's Inn and into a new building in Kingsway.

The Pethick Lawrences retained their paper, *Votes for Women*, around which grew another group, the Votes for Women Fellowship, which aimed to promote the paper and its policies. In July 1913, Emmeline was back in Holloway having been arrested while taking part in a deputation against the 'Cat and Mouse Act'[206], although the Home Office reduced her sentence from 14 days to four. A year later, Emmeline and

206 The 1913 'Cat and Mouse Act' was the common name for the 1913 Prisoners' (Temporary Discharge for Ill-Health) Act. In this way, the government could release hunger-striking prisoners to their homes, in order for them to regain their strength. This prevented the prisons having to deal with any deaths of hunger-striking women. However, the released prisoners were monitored and as soon as they were deemed well enough they were sent back to prison. Many women released under this Act went into hiding in order to avoid returning to prison. In this sense, the suffragettes were the mice to the prison's cat.

Frederick joined the United Suffragists, giving *Votes for Women* to this new organisation.

After the outbreak of war in 1914, Emmeline campaigned in the United States for the idea of a negotiated peace. In February 1915, with representatives of the National Women's Peace Party of America, she sailed from the United States to the Hague to attend the Women's Peace Congress. Because the government had prevented women from the United Kingdom from crossing the Channel, Emmeline was one of only three British women present. In autumn 1915, she became Honorary Treasurer of the newly-founded Women's International League of Great Britain (later the Women's International League for Peace and Freedom). At the 1918 general election, she stood as the Labour candidate in Manchester but was defeated. She devoted the rest of her life to campaigning for peace and, from 1926, was for nine years President of the Women's Freedom League. She published her autobiography, *My Part in a Changing World,* in 1938.

And another thing... Owing to the strict ban on commercial activities imposed on the relatively new (opened to the public in 1891) Victoria Park in Windmill Hill, Emmeline was refused permission to hold a WSPU meeting in the park or to sell copies of the *Votes for Women* newspaper.[207]

And another thing... There is a colourful memorial to Emmeline and the suffrage campaign painted on the tiles of the Bristol-bound platform at Weston-super-Mare train station.

Written by Elizabeth Crawford, who is an independent suffrage researcher and the author of numerous books on the subject, including *The Women's Suffrage Movement: A Reference Guide 1866-1928* and *Campaigning For The Vote: Kate Parry Frye's*

207 Barb Drummond, (2008). *Victoria Park: The People's Park*. Bristol: Barb Drummond. 13.

Suffrage Diary. Her latest book, *Art and Suffrage: A Biographical Dictionary of Suffrage Artists*, is published in 2018.

JESSIE LAWS

dates unknown, SUFFRAGETTE

While we don't have an awful lot of information about Jessie Laws, we do know that she had the gumption to hurl stones at the Colston Hall from the top deck of a tram while Winston Churchill was dining inside the Hall. And based on that information, it seems churlish to miss her out of this collection.

HARRIET LEE and SOPHIA LEE

1757-1851 and 1750-1824, NOVELISTS

Sisters Sophia and Harriet Lee moved to Clifton via London and Bath. Sophia was a popular writer thanks to books such as *The Recess* (1783-1785), while Harriet had enjoyed success with *The Errors of Innocence* (1876), a novel in five volumes written in the style of letters. They were friends with another pair of Bristolian writer siblings, Jane and Anna Porter.

The Lee sisters lived at Vyvyan Terrace, Clifton, and together wrote a series of *The Canterbury Tales* (1797), one of which was dramatised by Lord Byron. While we're talking about Byron, Harriet also wrote an adaption of *Kruitzner* before Byron published his. So there! In addition, Harriet wrote one of the earliest gothic novels, *The Mysterious Marriage* (1798), which the London theatres flatly refused to put on.

Sophia died at Vyvyan Terrace and is buried in St Andrew's Churchyard, which is now Birdcage Walk (as immortalised in the 2017 novel of the same name by Helen Dunmore). Harriet remained at Vyvyan Terrace until her own death 27 years later.

And another thing... A year after the death of his wife Mary Wollstonecraft, widower William Godwin proposed marriage to Harriet Lee. She turned him down.[208]

Please also see the entries for: Lady Byron, Helen Dunmore, Jane and Anna Porter and Mary Wollstonecraft.

JENNIE LEE

1904-1988, POLITICIAN

Scottish Labour Party politician Jennie Lee, aka Baroness Lee of Asheridge, was an MP between 1929-1931 and again from 1945-1970. During the gap when she was not in the House of Commons, Jennie remained politically active. And in 1943 she stood in the Bristol Central election, losing out to Lady Violet Apsley by just 1,379 votes: in the process, Lady Apsley became Bristol's first female MP. Although she was disappointed to lose the 1943 election, in 1945 Jennie won the seat in Cannock, Leicestershire, and held it until 1970.

Jennie may have been too young to have been a suffragette herself but she was still hugely influenced by the dynamism and determinism of those women. Julie Gottlieb writes: "Jennie Lee recalled how the [Glaswegian] suffragette Helen Crawfurd was a regular visitor to her childhood home, telling the young Jennie tales of 'window-breaking adventures and prison exploits' which made her 'wonder ... ruefully if anything at all would be left to

208 Marie Mulvey-Roberts, (2015). *Literary Bristol: Writers and the City*. Bristol: Redcliffe Press. 52.

do by the time I had finished with school'."[209] Alas, there was still plenty left to do by the time Jennie had left school.

How would you know that Jennie was in town? Because rather than using a loudspeaker to publicise her meetings, Jennie trundled a barrel organ from street to street to bring people to their doors so she could meet them and find out what they wanted from their councillor. Just as contemporary female politicians are frustrated about why their appearance seems to take precedence over their actions, Gottlieb writes: "The young Jennie Lee fumed that she 'simply could not understand why what I looked like, what I wore… had anything to do with the serious political purposes that engaged my working hours'. Her irritation reflects her recognition that this was an issue for outside observers."[210]

Among Jennie's achievements was helping to set up the Open University, which linked back to her earlier training as a teacher. She didn't particularly connect herself to women's groups or campaigns, believing that true equality would only be achieved by everyone working together from the off.

And another thing... Jennie's husband was Welsh MP Aneurin Bevan, who spearheaded the establishment of the National Health Service. What a team!

Please also see the entry for: Lady Apsley.

209 Julie V Gottlieb, Richard Toye, (2013), *The Aftermath of Suffrage: Women, Gender and Politics in Britain 1918-1945*. London: Palgrave Macmillan. 208.
210 Ibid. 218.

CAROLINE LEHMANN
1859-1956, SUFFRAGETTE

Caroline Edith Lehmann was born in Kidderminster, daughter of William Mayne, a former captain in the 10th Dragoons, and his wife Edith. In 1883, Caroline married John Watson, a minor Kidderminster industrialist, with whom she had two daughters. Ten years later, in 1893, Watson filed a petition for divorce, citing a Weston-super-Mare pharmacist. While the divorce case was being heard, Caroline was only allowed access to her children once a week – at her mother's Kidderminster house. It is clear that her husband was trying to prevent her having any access at all and after the divorce the two daughters remained in Kidderminster with their father.

Three years later, in London, Caroline married journalist Ernst Lehmann, and gave birth to a son, Heinz Maurice Talbot Lehmann in November 1897. Four years later, when the 1901 census was taken, mother and son (who was now known as 'Henry' rather than 'Heinz') were living without Ernst in St Albans. At some point between 1901 and 1911 mother and son moved to Shirehampton, to a house in Station Road that went under the name of Rockmount.

Caroline's interesting marital history and the separation from her two daughters may well have coloured her views on votes for women and certainly, by 1910, she was an active member of the Women's Social and Political Union (WSPU). That November, she was part of a Bristol delegation arrested when Emmeline Pankhurst led a deputation to Downing Street in the aftermath of the 'Black Friday' violence in Parliament Square, London. In 1911, she followed the WSPU call to boycott the census, writing firmly across her form: "Being an unrepresented ratepayer I refuse to give any information respecting myself or my household for the benefit of an Un-Liberal government. CE Lehmann." Caroline travelled to London at the beginning of March 1912 to take part in the WSPU's window-smashing campaign and subsequently served a two-month prison sentence in Holloway. She joined the hunger strike and on her release was presented with a WSPU hunger-strike medal.

Caroline's involvement with the suffrage movement may have encouraged her son, a pupil at Clifton College, to take up the position in 1913 of 'hon sec pro tem' of Bristol's Men's Political Union. He enjoyed a most colourful and unorthodox career, at one point making headlines when he kidnapped one of his daughters from her mother, from whom he was separated. Caroline lived in Shirehampton for the remainder of her long life, her later address being Talbot Cottage, 27 Grove Leaze.

Written by Elizabeth Crawford, who is an independent suffrage researcher and the author of numerous books on the subject, including *The Women's Suffrage Movement: A Reference Guide 1866-1928* and *Campaigning For The Vote: Kate Parry Frye's Suffrage Diary*. Her latest book, *Art and Suffrage: A Biographical Dictionary of Suffrage Artists*, is published in 2018.

LILIAN LENTON

1891-1972, DANCER, SUFFRAGETTE

Dancer and suffragette Lilian Lenton from Fishponds became known as the 'Pimpernel Suffragette' owing to her skill at slipping away in camouflage to evade the police: her ingenious disguises included those of a grocer's boy, nurse and crippled old woman.

A prolific arsonist, the first property Lilian set fire to was the tea house in Kew Gardens, London, with Olive Wharry on

20 February 1913. Before the trial took place, Lilian and Olive were held in custody, where Lilian went on hunger strike and experienced force feeding carried out in such a violent and forceful manner that some of the food entered her lungs causing her to develop pleurisy. Consequently, Lilian was too ill to attend her trial and Olive went to court alone. This caused questions to be asked in the House of Commons about the nature of forcible feeding, and the Home Secretary Reginald McKenna was criticised for not being able to control the suffragettes *and* for allowing the barbaric procedure of force feeding to take place at all.

Long after full suffrage was achieved in 1928, Lilian remained the Honorary Secretary of the Suffragette Fellowship and in 1970 she unveiled a memorial to her sisters near Caxton Hall, London. However, she was unimpressed by the terms under which votes for women were won in 1918 (being to women householders, the wives of householders or women over 30), telling the BBC: "Personally, I didn't vote for a very long time because I hadn't either husband or furniture, although I was over 30."[211]

VICTORIA LIDIARD

1889-1992, SUFFRAGETTE

Victoria Lidiard was born Victoria Simmons in Windsor. She had five sisters and three brothers, and her father was an antiques dealer. By 1901 the family had moved to 21 Regent Street, Clifton. Victoria was educated in a dame school[212] and left school at the age of 14. She learned shorthand at evening classes and got a job in a photographic studio. Two of her sisters, Florence and Ethel,

211 Elizabeth Crawford, (1999). *The Women's Suffrage Movement: A Reference Guide 1866-1928*. London: University College London Press. 341-342.

212 A dame school was a small primary school, typically run by older women from their homes.

had already taken up photography as a career.

With her mother and sisters, Victoria joined the Women's Social and Political Union (WSPU) in 1910, despite their father's opposition to women's suffrage. She later explained that one of the reasons she became a suffragette was because the education of girls was not considered important. Her father had invested in her brothers' education but not Victoria's or her sisters'.

Victoria worked hard for the WSPU in Bristol under the leadership of Annie Kenney. She sold the WSPU newspaper, *Votes for Women,* and although she was never a speaker, she chaired many open air meetings, often enduring insults from men in the audience. Another of her tasks was chalking pavements to advertise suffragette meetings, for which she was once arrested and cautioned. She was also a member of the National Union of Women Workers (NUWW), which was formed in 1895 by the affiliation of a number of groups around the country. In 1918, the NUWW was renamed the National Council of Women.

In the 1980s, Victoria recalled interrupting a speech which she thought was made by Winston Churchill at Clifton College. I have been unable to find any record of Churchill speaking at Clifton College but Lord Haldane, Secretary of State for War, did address the school during the jubilee celebrations in 1912. So far, though, I have not found any mention of a suffragette interruption during the proceedings.

Victoria took part in the WSPU's London West End window-smashing campaign on 4 March 1912. She stood next to a policeman on Whitehall in order to avoid being set upon by the crowd as many other women had been. She threw a stone through a War Office window, causing £2 worth of damage (approximately £115 in contemporary money). The policeman was too surprised to react but two of his colleagues and a mounted officer rushed up and arrested her and they all escorted her to Bow Street Police

Station. She still had seven stones left in her pocket and on her way to Bow Street she dropped them. It was Victoria's turn to be surprised when they arrived at the police station and she discovered the policeman behind her had picked up the stones.

Victoria was sentenced to two months' hard labour in Holloway Prison and served six weeks of this. Probably at her mother's request, she did not go on hunger strike. As a vegetarian, she remembered being fed on butter beans. In the evenings, one of her sisters stood outside the prison and shouted encouraging messages. Victoria was later awarded a WSPU Holloway medal but sadly it was stolen during a burglary.

When militancy was suspended in 1914, Victoria moved to London where she ran a guest house and worked in a munitions factory in Battersea. In 1918, she married Alexander Slater Lidiard in Croydon. Before the war, he had been a member of the Men's Political Union for Women's Enfranchisement and had trained as a pharmacist. After the war, the couple trained as opticians. They worked at the London Refraction Hospital (now the Institute of Optometry) and set up practices in Maidenhead and then High Wycombe.

By 1959 the couple were living in Hove, Sussex. Victoria joined the campaign for the ordination of women priests and took an interest in animal rights, having been a vegetarian since she was a girl. She published her first book at the age of 99: *Christianity, Faith, Love and Healing* and a year later *Animals and All Churches.*

One of Victoria's proudest memories was of meeting Britain's first woman Prime Minister, Margaret Thatcher. The last surviving suffragette, Victoria died in Hove in 1992 at the age of 102. In 1996, a plaque was unveiled at her home at 14 Palmeira Avenue by Betty Boothroyd MP, the first female Speaker of the House of Commons.

Written by Lucienne Boyce, who is a historical novelist and author of *The Bristol Suffragettes*.

Please also see the entry for: Annie Kenney.

FLEUR LOMBARD

1974-1996, FIREFIGHTER

When she joined the Avon Fire Brigade as a trainee in the early 1990s, Fleur Lombard was one of only eight women in a team of 700 firefighters. By the time of her graduation in 1994, Fleur received the Silver Axe Award in recognition of being the most outstanding recruit from her training school. However, on 4 February 1994, Fleur was killed while attending a fire at a supermarket in Staple Hill, becoming the first female firefighter in the United Kingdom to die while on duty. She was only 21 at the time of her death. Fleur was posthumously awarded the Queen's Gallantry Medal in 1998 in recognition of her bravery. Chief Fire Officer Kevin Pearson said: "Every year since Fleur's death, our staff mark the anniversary and there is no doubt in my mind that she will never be forgotten."[213]

BLANCHE LONG

1927-1999, ST GEORGE'S MUSIC TRUST

As well as being the centenary for when (some) women got the vote, 2018 is also a landmark year for St George's Bristol on Great George Street. Formerly a church, now a celebrated concert

213 http://www.bbc.co.uk/news/uk-england-bristol-35492183

Fleur Lombard illustration by Carrie Love

venue, the building turns 195 this year. One woman entwined in the history of this remarkable establishment is Blanche Long.

Wiltshire-born Blanche had suffered from polio as a child and as such was encouraged to study music as a child, which led to her spending four years at Trinity College of Music, London, where she honed her passion for the piano. After marriage, Blanche moved to Redland where her interests expanded to see her become the Director of a small engineering company, a key fundraiser for the Camphill Village Trust charity (supporting people with disabilities, for whom Blanche had an affinity following her own experience with polio) and to retain the talent that had seen her train as a pianist for 15 years. Blanche later said she had lacked the discipline to be a professional concert pianist as she enjoyed socialising too much.

In 1976, it was announced that St George's was closing as a church, and so – along with John Funnell and Harry Edwards – Blanche approached the BBC with the idea of using the building for chamber music and forming the St George's Music Trust. Fortunately, the BBC jumped at the chance and the first concert was broadcast live on 15 December 1976, although the building continued to also operate as a church for a few years more. A Friends of St George's Brandon Hill newsletter from the early 1980s stated: "[Blanche's] enthusiasm and optimism provides St George's Music Trust with a pillar of strength which is so essential to the future survival and prosperity of the Trust."

In an interview with Blanche for *Bristol Illustrated* in September 1985, reporter Chris Beaver wrote: "[Blanche] recalls the mood of triumph she felt at the end of 1976 after the first concert had been given at the church by the BBC West of England Academy Orchestra. 'That was very exciting. We knew it was the right thing to do'." Beaver also comments on the large piano that resided in Blanche's home, and writes that "she still plays 'when there's nobody listening', to amuse herself, but now feels that she can do more for music through her involvement with St George's".

Following Blanche's death in 1999, a celebration concert was held for her at St George's on 15 October 2000. The Trust's then director Jonathan Stracey wrote: "[Blanche's] kindness and care knew no bounds, and this was immediately recognised by artists who came to St George's in the late 1970s and 1980s. She knew exactly how to support and encourage them, both from an informed musical standpoint as well as in a more fundamental human way." He continued: "She had the great gift of open-mindedness. She never pre-judged anything or anyone, and her opinions, when called for, came from the wisdom of acute observation and a rare ability to see the largest picture. She could defuse a tense or difficult situation with instinctive skill and she would always emphasise the positive view ... Hooray for Blanche!" Hooray, indeed.[214]

SARAH MACREADY

1789-1853, THEATRE MANAGER

I was about 35 minutes into my first working day at Bristol Old Vic when a colleague turned to me and said: "Have you heard about Sarah? She's our resident ghost. You'll know if you've met her because you'll smell lavender."

Sarah Macready was an actor and she fell in love with theatre manager and famous tragedian William Macready. Their marriage meant that Sarah stayed in the city and became devoted to the beautiful Theatre Royal on King Street (now home to the Bristol Old Vic theatre company).

214 With thanks to Michael Beek and the St George's Bristol Archives.

I've heard the story that one day William handed her the keys to the theatre and said: "Honey, I'm off to do a bit of acting... can you look after the old gaff while I'm gone?" This of course is a delightfully anecdotal bastardisation of actual events. In real talk, William died and the care of the theatre was handed into two sets of incompetent hands in quick succession, before Sarah was called upon to save the day.

Not one to stand by and allow the artistic endeavours of the building to fall into further disrepute, Sarah worked alongside her daughter's husband, James Henry Chute, to redefine the theatre's direction. The Macready/Chute family were an absolute Bristol institution; an actor-manager dynasty of the highest order. Dominating the local theatre scene throughout the 19th century, they ran the Bristol Theatre Royal and the Prince's Theatre, as well as shuttling south to manage the Theatre Royal and the Assembly Rooms in Bath, in a reign that lasted 112 years. Sarah's position made her one of, if not *the* most, important women in Bristol – and she was more than capable of holding her own in a city led by men. Sarah managed the theatre through 20 of its most turbulent years. Her business prowess was second to none; she turned the theatre's fortunes around, attracting huge audiences and the finest actors of her generation. She was inventive, resourceful and astute.

It's said that Sarah's ghost still walks in the auditorium at Bristol Old Vic. As a member of staff, you can't show anyone around without telling a ghost story. It's a rite of passage to reiterate, embellish and pass on your own folkloric version of the tale. Sarah is a manifestation of the theatre's past but she's also very much part of its present. She has become this mythic figure, someone who loved the building so much that she even dedicated her afterlife to making sure the curtain goes up on time.

I'm pleased that I didn't wait until I caught a whiff of lavender in the pit passage post-show to get better acquainted with Sarah. She clearly kicked some major Bristol butt.[215]

Written by Charlie Coombes, who is Communications Officer at Bristol Old Vic. She is almost always reading post-apocalyptic books written by badass women, or watching horror movies.

JANET McNEILL

1907-1994, NOVELIST

Prolific Irish novelist Janet McNeill settled in Bristol from the mid-1960s and remained in the city until her death 30 years later. In her long career, Janet wrote more than 20 children's books, plus around ten adult novels, three plays and two opera libretti.

EMMA MARSHALL

1830-1899, NOVELIST

Once upon a time, Emma Marshall's books were read by every savvy young Bristolian, the best-known book being *In Colston's Days* (1884), which praises the slave trader Edward Colston for investing charitable money into education "when it was thought a grave error in judgement to teach the son and daughter of the mechanic and tradesman to read and write"[216]. Emma wrote more than 200 novels, short stories and poems, and would write for everyone from women's magazines to Christian journals.

Born into a Quaker family who moved to Victoria Square,

215 Charlie is yet to see Sarah's ghost herself but says that every time she goes into the auditorium she checks to see if Sarah is watching what's happening.

216 Shirley Brown, Dawn Dyer, (2002). *100+ Women of Bristol*. Bristol: Bristol City Council. 27.

Clifton, Emma converted to Christianity when she came to Bristol and married Hugh, the son of the reverend who baptised her. They later moved to Cotham and began their family, which would extend to an impressive nine children. Inspired by her sister Hannah, who had been a novelist until her early death, Emma took up writing and became part of the Clifton literary circle. Emma's typical writing style was of gentle romance, adventure and piety and her books featured jaunty titles such as *A Lily Among Thorns* (1874) and *Bristol Diamonds* (1892).

When Hugh's bank failed and left the family with enormous debts, it was down to Emma to write and write and write to keep the family's heads above water. Constant house moves and nine demanding children, plus the pressure of being the family breadwinner, must have meant Emma was under enormous strain. But she did succeed in rescuing the family's finances, so much so that they were eventually able to take a large house called Ferncliffe in Leigh Woods; the house still stands today but is divided into flats.

MARY PALEY MARSHALL

1850-1944, ACADEMIC

The University of Bristol welcomed its first female lecturer in 1878 in the form of Mary Paley Marshall, who co-founded the economics department with her fiancé Alfred Marshall who was already a tutor there and a strong supporter of women's higher education. The couple agreed to remove the word "obey" from their marriage vows to show their equality with one another.

Mary had already proved herself academically by being one of the first five students to study at the all-female Newnham College at Cambridge University... although being a woman she was unable to graduate, despite achieving top marks for the Moral Sciences Tripos in 1874 and despite being the first woman to ever sit her final exams at Cambridge. However, her inability to graduate did not stop Newnham from later enlisting Mary as its first-ever female lecturer.

Mary's move to Bristol in 1876 led to the foundation of the economics department at University College, Bristol, as the university was then known. The university property at 12 Priory Road is still known as the Mary Paley Building in her honour, while Cambridge University has a Mary Paley Room in the Marshall Library, which Mary helped to establish.

Please also see the entry for: Mary Sturge.

JANE MARTIN

1729-1835, BUSINESSWOMAN

Never underestimate the importance of getting your five a day. For more than 50 years, Jane Martin ran a fruit stall on Peter Street (this was destroyed in the Blitz but was close to Castle Park in the centre). Thanks to a heady combination of days spent in the great outdoors and unlimited access to fruit, Jane lived to the ripe old age of 107. Which is an impressive enough feat now but even more so for a working-class woman with no easy access to healthcare in the Georgian era. While recording Jane's death, *The Gentleman's Magazine* in 1835 noted: "She possessed all her faculties and could walk up and down stairs to the last."

HARRIET MARTINEAU

1802-1876, SOCIOLOGIST, WRITER

Not much fazed Harriet Martineau. Despite being deaf and losing her senses of taste and smell, she had no fears about anything and in her later years she greatly enjoyed travelling. In the 1830s she explored Egypt and later went to the United States to find out more about the slave trade of which she was strongly opposed.

As a teenager with a string of health problems, Harriet was sent to Bristol to stay with an aunt to benefit from a change of scene and this worked so well she stayed for 15 months. When the Martineau family business failed, Harriet took to writing to earn an income and became so successful that she was able to earn enough money to support herself and remain independent, which was highly unusual for a woman in the Victorian age – not least because writing was considered man's work. One subject on which she wrote numerous times was the Contagious Diseases Act (CDA) and the campaign led by Josephine Butler to repeal this (for more information on the CDA, please see Josephine's entry in this book).

Harriet's writing was so popular that she could count a young Princess Victoria among her admirers and as such Harriet received an invitation to the coronation of the future Queen Victoria. Harriet's first commissioned book *Illustrations of Political Economy* (which explained the convoluted free-market concepts of economist Adam Smith to the general public) was so popular that it outsold works by novelist Charles Dickens. Future topics she would write about included political economics, rent law and population control.

Please also see the entries for: Josephine Butler and Ellen Craft.

HANNAH MORE

1745-1833, WRITER, PHILANTHROPIST

Bristol born and bred, Evangelical philanthropist Hannah More was not a woman to cross. From her early years in Fishponds to her later years in Brislington, Hannah was one of the original bluestockings (an influential group of 18th century women intellectuals) and she retained Bristol at her core.

Hannah's older sister Mary opened the Academy for Young Ladies on Park Street, where Hannah was initially a pupil and later a teacher. Through teaching, Hannah indulged her passion for the theatre and wrote several plays for the girls to perform, while also spending much of her spare time at the Theatre Royal (now Bristol Old Vic).

After tiring of her fiancé's inability to set a date for their wedding, Hannah eventually broke off their six-year engagement and accepted his offer of a £200 annuity (equivalent to approximately £13,000 in contemporary money) – not least because it afforded her the freedom to quit teaching, move to London and immerse herself full-time in writing: one of her plays, *Percy,* was staged at the Covent Garden Theatre in 1777. However, she became increasingly drawn to Evangelical Christianity and began writing moral works and encouraged the establishment of Sunday schools.

Upon leaving London in 1785, Hannah moved to live with her sisters in the Mendip Hills, where she became a staunch anti-slavery campaigner, and offered educational, spiritual and financial help to miners and agricultural workers. Hannah remained committed to her work improving rights for women and her 1799 book *Strictures of the Modern System of Female Education* (which complained that women had been short-changed with a substandard education that did not equip them

Hannah More illustration by Jenny Howe

for the tasks they faced in life) has been compared in tone to Mary Wollstonecraft's seminal 1792 proto-feminist text *Vindication of the Rights of Woman*, although Hannah was not a fan of Mary.

Hannah also took the former milkmaid Ann Yearsley under her wing and nurtured Ann's talent for poetry, although Ann later felt patronised and belittled by Hannah and the relationship turned very sour.

In her final years, Hannah moved to Clifton where, despite being retired, she continued to campaign for the abolition of slavery and shortly before her death she saw that the Act finally abolishing slavery in the British Empire had at last been passed. At the time of her death, Hannah's estate was valued at £30,000, which is a huge sum today and was a colossal amount in 1833 (this is the equivalent of approximately £1.5 million in contemporary money). This meant that Hannah was one of the most successful writers of her day, regardless of gender.

And another thing... The Hannah More Primary School in St Philips opened in the 1840s and is, obviously, named in her honour. During her life, Hannah had been instrumental in setting up 12 schools in Bristol.

And another thing... In 1906, the anti-suffrage Bristol North MP Augustine Birrell was so incensed by Hannah's writing that he buried all 19 volumes of her work in his garden.

Please also see the entry for: Ann Yearsley.

SUSANNAH MORGAN

dates unknown, REFORMER

Susannah Morgan was a wealthy spinster who anonymously published a revelatory exposé of the state of Bristol's jails in 1815.

Although she had not put her name on the paper, Susannah used her own name to write to the local press to urge the adoption of the panopticon plan for a new prison: this being the model where a prison has a central point from which the guards can easily see down all of the corridors that are built off it, in a shape a bit like a clock, for increased safety of the prisoners.

As well as influencing prison reform, Susannah was involved in the Prudent Men's Society, which encouraged thriftiness among the poor. While the Society was led by men, Susannah worked behind the scenes and was Secretary of the Society's Women's Management Committee. She was clearly concerned with economic welfare because Susannah also served on the Management Committee of the Savings Bank, which fundraised for "distressed manufacturers" and helped find employment for prisoners.[217]

ADELA NICOLSON

1865-1904, POET

To create an air of mystery – or to boost sales among those who thought women made unsatisfactory poets – Stoke Bishop writer Adela Florence Nicolson published under the name of 'Laurence Hope'. Adela was raised by relatives in Bristol while her parents were stationed in Lahore, India, where her father served in the army. Consequently, Adela travelled to India to join them in 1881, where she promptly married a man twice her age and developed a passion for Indian culture that influenced her poetry.

Reportedly, Adela would dress as a young Afghan groom in order to travel alongside her husband to military camps in the northwest frontiers of Afghanistan. This would undoubtedly

217 Madge Dresser, (2016). *Women and the City: Bristol 1373-2000*. Bristol: Redcliffe Press. 83.

colour her opinions of gender and cross-dressing, which can be detected as an undercurrent in some her work.[218] Adela's 1901 poem 'Garden of Karma', like much of her work, relied on Indian and Persian imagery and symbolism, and consequently she became one of the most popular romantic poets of the Edwardian era. Unrequited love and grief were recurrent topics in her writing, and Adela's 1916 poem 'Less Than The Dust' inspired the Mary Pickford film of the same name. Following her husband's death, a distraught Adela committed suicide at the age of 39.

And another thing... Adela's sisters were also writers. Annie and Isabel Nicolson co-wrote saucy novels under the pseudonym 'Victoria Cross'.

CATHERINE NORRIS

1814-1885, SUFFRAGIST

Alongside Mary Estlin, Catherine Norris presented two large petitions to Parliament on 5 March and 5 May 1870 calling for the emancipation of women.[219] Catherine was the widow of Reverend Robert Norris and lived in their family home at Worcester Avenue, Clifton. Reporting her passing, the *Western Daily Press* solemnly stated: "The deceased lady was highly respected on account of her amiable and benevolent disposition."[220]

Please also see the entry for: Mary Estlin.

218 Anindyo Roy, 'Gold and Bracelet, Water and Wave: Signature and Translation in the Indian Poetry of Adela Cory Nicolson' in Rachael Langford, ed, (2005), *Depicting Desire: Gender, Sexuality and the Family in Nineteenth Century Europe*. Switzerland: Verlag Peter Lang. 199.

219 Elizabeth Crawford (2006), *The Women's Suffrage Movement in Britain and Ireland: A Regional Survey*. London: Routledge. 129.

220 *Western Daily Press*, 1885, 2 November, 'Obituary'. 5.

FRANCES NORTON

1644-1731, POET

Writer Frances Norton, from Abbots Leigh, was an essayist and poet who was a bit of a rapscallion, which is surely the best type of scallywag. In 1714, Frances published a collection of a poems in a *Miscellany* ... poems she described as ones "to embroider on chair backs". She once said that "unhappy marriage is to tear each other's flesh and gnaw their bones,"[221] which must have been a bit jarring for her husband Sir George Norton to read.

CAROLINE OLIPHANT

1806-1831, POET

In the time-honoured patriarchal tradition of women not being able to achieve anything under their own steam without being hailed as the new *insert appropriate-for-the-occasion male name* pubescent poet, Caroline Oliphant was nicknamed 'Girl Chatterton' in a nod to Thomas Chatteron, who had also achieved success as a poet in his teenage years.

Caroline began writing at the age of 13 and, as the favourite niece of Lady Carolina Nairne (also a poet), she travelled abroad extensively. However, Caroline was in Bristol at the time of her premature death in 1831, staying at 10 St Vincent's Parade, Hotwells (now 386 Hotwell Road). Her body is buried in what used to be called 'the strangers' burial ground' on Clifton Hill, Clifton Churchyard.

221 Lorna Brierley, Helen Reid, (2000). *Go Home and Do the Washing!* Bristol: Broadcast. 113.

MARIAN ORMEROD
1872-1946, WAR SHERO

Owing to her generosity of goodwill and kindness, not to mention her outstanding bravery, Marian Grace Ormerod was awarded an OBE for her efforts in World War One. Reporting on her death, the *Western Daily Press* wrote: "Mrs Ormerod, who was 74 years of age, was a native of Cleeve and after studying singing in Frankfurt took part in choral work in Bristol and at various festivals in other parts of England."

The paper continued: "Throughout the Great War she was Commandant of the 8th Detachment of the Bristol Red Cross, her work being chiefly concerned with the supervision of trainloads of wounded and the transfer of the men to hospitals. It was in recognition of those services that Mrs Ormerod received the OBE."[222]

ADELA PANKHURST
1885-1961, SUFFRAGETTE

Although her stay in Bristol only lasted a few months, it is fair to claim Adela Pankhurst as a brief Bristolian. Emmeline Pankhurst's youngest daughter is her least well known, which is rather unfair as Adela's contributions are just as interesting and important as those of her better-known family members.

Adela was one of the first militant suffragettes to be arrested and forcibly fed, although she grew to resist the Women and Social Political Union's (WSPU) more militant antics. However, she came to Bristol in the summer of 1908 to help Annie Kenney

222 *Western Daily Press*, 1946, 31 May, 'Death of Mrs M G Ormerod: The Services During the Great War'. 3.

Adela Pankhurst illustration by Jenny Howe

in her role as Organiser of the South West branch of the the WSPU before moving on to become WSPU Organiser in Yorkshire that autumn. Like the rest of her family and their friend Annie, Adela was a frequent visitor to the Blathwayts' home in Batheaston and planted her own tree in the Suffragettes' Wood there.

Although Emmeline and Christabel Pankhurst rejected any association with the Labour movement, Adela and Sylvia Pankhurst maintained a belief in the party, which would eventually cause both sisters to be expelled from the WSPU in a bizarre family rift. And when Adela moved to Australia in 1914 aged 29 to join the newly formed Australian Communist Party, Emmeline disowned her youngest child. Adela never saw her mother or sisters again but she continued to fight for women's rights from Australia.

Please also see the entries for: Mary and Emily Blathwayt, and Annie Kenney.

TILLY PARKER

dates unknown, TRADES UNION SECRETARY

In her role as Secretary of the Bristol Trades and Labour Council, in the early part of the 20th century, Tilly Parker would go all around the nearby towns of Swindon, Bridgwater and so on to try and persuade other workers to join the Trades and Labour Council movement and to let them know there was power in a union.

Sid Hobbs worked alongside Tilly on the Council and sometimes accompanied her on these recruitment missions. He recalls: "You hear people say that they won't join on principle. Some claim it's not Christian like. But I claim, without the trades union movement you'd have little boys on the shoulders of their fathers, going down the pits at five years of age."[223]

EMMA PATERSON
1848-1886, TRADES UNIONIST

As a teenager, Emma Paterson was forced to abandon her apprenticeship to a bookbinder after her father died, necessitating her to take a paying job as Secretary at the Working Men's Club and Institute Union in her home city of London. The club founder's wife had been a signatory to the 1866 Women's Suffrage Petition, as had some other colleagues at the club, giving young Emma an instant awakening to feminist politics.

By the time the National Society for Women's Suffrage was seeking a new Secretary in 1873, Emma had become an obvious candidate. In 1874, she wrote an article advocating the setting up of trades unions for women workers and, true to her word, in the same year she founded in Bristol the first ever trades union exclusively for women: the National Union of Working Women.

Emma argued that girls went into service to escape low pay in factories but in doing so found another kind of slavery and they therefore needed the protection of a union. Sadly, Emma died at the young age of 38 through complications from diabetes.[224]

223 Sid Hobbs in Bristol Broadsides, (1977), *Bristol as We Remember It*. Bristol: Broadsides. 15.
224 Elizabeth Crawford, (1999). *The Women's Suffrage Movement: A Reference Guide 1866-1928*. London: University College London Press. 530.

ELIZABETH PEARCE
died 1925, BUSINESSWOMAN

A canny businesswoman with a heart of gold and a chauffeur-driven car, Elizabeth Pearce ran the fish market (which was built by her grandfather) near St Nicholas Market and which is now a large pub. As well as her business acumen, Elizabeth was also known for being a good Samaritan to anybody in a spot of bother and became known as 'the soldiers' friend'.

During World War One, Elizabeth rose to the occasion by fundraising for Belgian refugees and the welfare of soldiers, and by contributing her own money to the funds, which sent care packages of chocolates, socks, cigarettes, books and more to the troops. And fish, obviously.

The Bristol2014.com project writes: "Just before Christmas 1917, a company of infantrymen received a box of kippers from her, a great luxury in the cold misery of the Western Front. That evening the men set about toasting them, causing envious groans from neighbouring soldiers. It was even said that the Germans on the other side of No Man's Land held up a sign written in English begging for any leftovers."[225]

The story continues that when a corporal returned to Bristol on leave, he went straight from Temple Meads train station to the fish market and told Elizabeth: "I have been sent by my pals in France, mum, to thank you – for the kippers, mum, they were grand." He then added, sheepishly: "I've got something to give you, mum, from my officer, but do not like to tell you what it is." Elizabeth coaxed the corporal to go on and he explained that his commander had instructed the corporal saying: "Look here, when you get to Bristol, find out the lady who sent those kippers

225 http://www.bristol2014.com/assets/files/war-stories/Old-City-Walk.pdf

and thank her for me. And look here, just you give her a kiss for me." After accepting the commander's kiss, Elizabeth instructed the corporal to return the kiss on her behalf. Whether or not he did, we will never know.

Marking her death, the *Western Daily Press* wrote in 1925: "Mrs Pearce, during the war, did an enormous amount of charitable work, and her persistent efforts in sending comforts to troops and in providing help in kind for wounded soldiers, won her the admiration of hundreds of Bristol lads who served."[226] The newspaper continued the next day: "She was known as the soldiers' friend, because of what she did in the Great War for our Bristol fighting men. Really, however, she was the friend of everybody who was down and out. Ask the people in the market, where she had spent nearly all her life; ask the humble folk who hawked fish around the street. An elderly man who had grown up among the hustle and bustle of the Bristol market found it hard, very hard, to speak without breaking down of this lady's tenderness of heart, her never-failing sympathy with those in trouble, and her prolific benefactions."[227]

MARIAN PEASE

1859-1954, EDUCATIONALIST

When Bristol's University College opened in 1876, one of the first students through its doors was 17-year-old Marian Pease. That spring, Marian had been due to sit the London University women's entrance exams (at that time, this was the only London exam open to women) but an attack of scarlet fever caused her to miss out. As compensation, her parents allowed her to apply for

226 *Western Daily Press*, 1925, 28 September, 'A Friend to Many Soldiers'. 5.
227 *Western Daily Press*, 1925, 29 September, 'A Loss to Bristol'. 5.

one of the three scholarships to the new University College in Bristol. Needless to say, Marian got in, alongside Amy Bell and Emily Pakeman who earned the other two places.

Marian came from a large Quaker family and along with her siblings took a great interest in education. She listened enviously as her elder sisters talked about the lectures they had attended and became determined to seek an education for herself. Describing her morning commute to the university, Marian wrote: "I left home a few minutes after eight o'clock carrying my heavy bag of books – there were no lockers there – walked across Durdham Down, met Amy Bell who came in a cab from Stoke Bishop and then we took the horse tram from the bottom of Blackboy Hill to the top of Park Street ... The journey had its difficulties on dark, wet and windy winter mornings and afternoons."[228]

Marian was particularly inspired by the economics lectures given by Mr Marshall, which she attended with her cousin Mary Fry and other women. Lecturer Mary Paley Marshall also impressed Marian, as she had been one of the first five students at the women-only Newnham College, Cambridge. Via the university's debating society, Marian met Katharine Bradley and her niece Edith Cooper, who wrote under the name 'Michael Field'. Although she completed her studies with honours, Marian was not able to graduate and receive her doctorate until 1911.

The death of Marian's father when she was just 24 forced her to go to teacher training college and subsequently she took the post of Mistress of Method (on the advice of Emily Sturge) at the Day Training College, 21 Berkeley Square. Marian took a keen interest in the girls she tutored and in academic breaks she would take them on trips to the Quantocks to be near where William Wordsworth and Samuel Taylor Coleridge had lived and written.

228 Lorna Brierley, Helen Reid, (2000). *Go Home and Do the Washing!* Bristol: Broadcast. 66-67.

One of her students wrote: "She was to us a new kind of person. Everything seemed turned upside-down as there unfolded before our astonished eyes a new and larger world of mind and spirit than any we could have imagined."[229]

Despite her growing deafness, Marian went on to open a School for Mothers in addition to the Day Training College. She also founded the first antenatal clinic in the city and supported the opening of the first open-air school. With her sisters Rosa and Dora, in 1880 Marian opened a club for girls working at the Great Western Cotton Factory in Barton Hill and with the purchase of three nearby houses in 1911 they had laid the foundation for the University Settlement at Barton Hill, which would be run by the University of Bristol. Free lectures were given, with Marian leading those on English Literature. After retiring in 1912, the sisters moved to Almondsbury where they supervised a holiday cottage for undernourished children.

Please also see the entries for: Amy Bell, Sarah Fricker Coleridge, 'Michael Field', Mary Paley Marshall, Rosa Pease and Emily Sturge.

ROSA PEASE

dates unknown, PHILANTHROPIST

A descendent of the reformist Pease family that was closely associated to women's rights and social reform campaigns in Bristol, Rosa Pease came from solid stock. Rosa's father Thomas Pease was Chairman of the Board of Guardians which presided over the workhouses to ensure residents were treated as well as possible. As such, his three daughters (alongside Rosa there was

229 Ibid. 68.

also Marian and Dora) all became politically active in adulthood and in 1920 Rosa stepped into her father's shoes when she became Chair of the Board of Guardians.[230]

The National Union of Women Workers (NUWW), of which Rosa was a member, saw that the looming shadow of World War One would bring with it opportunities for women to prove themselves as capable as men, most notably by performing the roles that were vacated by men who were being sent abroad to fight. The Bristol branch of the NUWW was instrumental in the establishment of the Bristol Training School for Women Patrols and Police, which was the first of its kind in England and opened in September 1915. Rosa was very involved with the police training school in Bristol, as were Helen Sturge and Emily Smith. With the formidable Dorothy Peto as director of the Bristol Training School from 1917, the establishment was settled as a force to be reckoned with.

The goals of the school were to train women volunteers to patrol public places and uphold the good moral behaviour of young women and, once volunteers had gained the necessary experience, the school wanted to assist them with finding paid roles in the police force. Shockingly, it was not until the Police Act of 1916 that women were given the authority to make arrests.[231] As a result, by 1918 there were eight women in paid and uniformed roles in the Bristol police force. And a lot of this is due to the hard work of pioneers in women's policing, such as Rosa Pease.

Please also see the entries for: Marian Pease, Dorothy Peto and Helen Sturge.

230 Madge Dresser, (2016). *Women and the City: Bristol 1373-2000*. Bristol: Redcliffe Press. 126.
231 Ibid.

ANDRÉE PEEL
1905-2010, SECRET AGENT

Born Andrée Virot in Brittany, France, this courageous woman was running a beauty salon in her hometown when World War Two broke out. But following the German invasion of France in 1940, she joined the French Resistance, was promoted to Sergeant and became one of two women known as 'Agent Rose'. In this role, Andrée distributed secret newspapers and signalled to Allied planes with torches to guide them to improvised landing sites.

In her obituary, *The Guardian* noted: "She also helped a total of 102 allied aircrew to evade capture by the Germans and to get back to Britain by small boat, submarine or night-time collection by RAF Lysander aircraft, which were favoured for SOE [Special Operations Executive] operations. This was the contribution of which she was most proud."[232]

Upon arrest in 1944, Andrée was beaten, tortured and sent to the notorious German women's concentration camp Ravensbrück, and then Buchenwald concentration camp where she contracted but survived meningitis. In an interview many years later, Andrée revealed she still suffered with pain from the torture she experienced.[233] At the same time as the United States' troops arrived to liberate the camp, Andrée was being lined up to be shot dead by a firing squad. Fortunately, she was saved by the United States' forces, although she kept her blue-and-white striped Buchenwald pyjamas for the rest of her life.

After the war, Andrée married English academic John Peel and the couple relocated to Long Ashton, Bristol, where they lived out their lives. Andrée published her autobiography *Miracles Do Happen* in 1999 in order to tell the stories of those who had not

232 https://www.theguardian.com/world/2010/mar/10/andree-peel-obituary
233 http://www.nytimes.com/2010/03/14/world/europe/14peel.html

been so fortunate to survive the horrors that she had endured. A few years before her death she said: "We [the freedom fighters] were defending freedom. It's an extremely precious thing. It is only when you do not have it that you begin to appreciate how important it is."[234]

Andrée added: "You don't know what freedom is if you have never lost it. The only fear we had was of being tortured and of speaking under torture. I rarely thought of my personal safety. I just acted and did what I believed was the right thing."[235]

In acknowledgement of her great bravery during World War Two, Andrée received a clutch of medals including the Croix de Guerre, the Medal of the Resistance and the Order of Liberation by France. President Eisenhower presented her with the Medal of Freedom and Andrée received a personal letter of thanks from Prime Minister Winston Churchill, which she then had to destroy for security reasons.

HANNAH PENN

1671-1726, STATE LEADER

Hannah Penn could be summed up by the phrase: 'Behind every great man there is a great woman.' This particular great woman reached the upper limits of political power for women in early 18th-century Anglo-America, despite being the product of a society that unquestioningly assumed men were the heads of households and a family's only political participants.

As Hannah Callowhill, she was born in Bristol to a staunchly Quaker family at a time when the Quakers were being persecuted

234 http://www.independent.co.uk/news/obituaries/andree-peel-french-resistance-fighter-who-helped-allied-airmen-evade-capture-in-occupied-europe-1936038.html
235 http://www.bristolpost.co.uk/news/War-heroine-Andree-Peel-celebrates-104th-birthday/article-667495-detail/article.html

for their beliefs. Hundreds of people, including Hannah's father, were sent to jail simply for following their faith, and by 1682 there were so many Quakers in prison that even the schools were closed as there were no teachers free to work. As a result, Hannah had to leave school at the age of 11. Quakers believed in "instructing girls and young maidens in whatsoever things were civil and useful", and despite her lack of schooling Hannah did achieve good literacy and maths skills.

Along with her mother, Hannah became a leading member of the Quaker's Women's Meetings in Bristol, which gave the women a sense of separate authority from the men's meetings. The idea was to uphold the Quaker belief that women were spiritually equal to men, and the Quaker teachings called on women and men alike to "bring forth the inner light". Hannah had always maintained that she did not plan to marry and instead intended to devote her life to the Quakers. But in 1696, at the age of 25, she married William Penn (24 years her senior), who was perhaps the most famous Quaker of the day. He was the founder of "the green country town" of Pennsylvania in the United States, to which he gave his name, and in 1699 he took his wife out to live in style on his colony there. It had taken William a year to convince Hannah that the marriage would be a good idea, that he was not simply after her family's money and that their age gap was irrelevant.

Owing to William's ill health, Hannah secretly acted as the proprietor of Pennsylvania for six years, maintaining the impression that she was simply carrying out her husband's wishes. Initially, Hannah was nervous about running Pennsylvania on her husband's behalf because she was "but a woman", but Penn's advisors had great confidence in her abilities and helped her enormously. After his death she openly acted as proprietor for a further eight years until her own death in 1726, at which point her sons assumed guardianship of Pennsylvania.

Her tenure as proprietor was not easy: Hannah presided over two changes of deputy governor, negotiated the Pennsylvania/Maryland border controversy, resolved conflicts with England about Pennsylvanian laws and fought her stepson in court over the details of her late husband's will. But her grounding and belief in Quaker values saw her behave in a kind and considered manner at all times. Indeed, such was Hannah's impact that she is the first woman to be granted the status of Honorary Citizen of the United States, given to her by Presidential Proclamation upon an Act of Congress by Ronald Reagan in 1984.

DOROTHY PETO
1886-1974, PIONEERING POLICE OFFICER

Historian Eugene Byrne writes: "Early on in the [Great] War, amid fears about the consequences of local girls flirting with men in uniform, voluntary patrols of women took to the streets during the evenings. Usually working in pairs, the patrols would try to put a stop to female behaviour that was likely to get girls into trouble. This, along with the demand for manpower from the forces, would lead to Bristol appointing some of the first women police officers in the world."[236]

Until World War One, women had zero presence in the police force. But following 1918 (the same year that some women got the vote), there began to be a grudging acceptance of women in the force. The dawn of the war had a big impact on why, since most young men were being sent away to fight on the battlefields. Women's police pioneer Dorothy Peto wrote in her diary: "The strength of police forces fell rapidly as men of all ranks left to

236 https://www.bristol247.com/news-and-features/features/bristols-war-britains-first-policewoman/

join the Colours. Everywhere problems of order and decency in public places cried out for an urgent solution."[237] Given that the suffragettes had stood down from their campaigning in respect for the war, there was a clear pool of strong women to tap into and, as early as 1914, advertisements were appearing in *The Vote* newspaper looking for women to work as special constables in the Women Volunteer Police: this later became the Women Police Service and subsequently the Women's Auxiliary Service.

England's first training school for women police officers, the Bristol Branch of the Federated Training School for Policewomen and Patrols, was set up at 6 Berkeley Square during World War One, and former National Union of Women Workers member Dorothy was Director from 1916-1920. The school, along with others like it around the country, closed when the war ended and Dorothy moved to Birmingham, where she became England's first woman detective in 1920, the same year that she received the OBE.

Announcing her role, the *Western Daily Press* wrote: "Miss Dorothy Peto ... who took up her duties a fortnight ago as Staff Officer in charge of the Metropolitan Women Police at Scotland Yard, is making a detailed examination of the duties which are performed by the women police in London. She will report to the Commissioner and will put forward suggestions for the improvement of the Service. It is probable that changes will be effected in the uniform."[238] Please note, Dorothy did rather more than just make changes to the uniform.

In 1930, Dorothy was the first woman Commissioner of the Metropolitan Police. In addition to the above, she also worked to ensure that women reported crimes of a personal or indecent nature, that they were seen by female police officers whenever

237 https://www.metwpa.org.uk/history.html
238 *Western Daily Press*, 1930, 25 April, 'New Woman Police Chief'. 4.

possible, and she used the Children and Young Persons Act 1933 to carve out a special role for female police officers.

Dorothy retired from the force in 1946, and Peto House (for the training of women police officers) in Aybrook Street, London, is named after her.

LILIAN PHEYSEY

died 1940, COUNCILLOR, ALDERMAN

Lilian Maude Pheysey was one of the first women to be elected to Bristol City Council after World War One and served continuously as a Councillor and then Alderman until her death in 1940.[239] Born in London, she lived in the Midlands and Liverpool before coming to Bristol in 1914. She became involved straight away in the Adult School movement, of which she was already a member, and the associated Brotherhood Federation. The Adult Schools aimed to provide moral and religious instruction along with entertainment to the 'respectable' working-class, and in 1908 Bristol had 50 such schools. The Brotherhoods also began to discuss social problems and aimed to connect working-class ideas of brotherhood and solidarity with religion.

Lilian's abilities were soon recognised and she held the chairmanship of the Joint Social Service Committee of the Adult School Union and the Brotherhood. The other 'social service' areas in which she became involved reflected the interests of these two bodies. For example, she spoke and worked for the Mothers' Union and the Bristol Women's Temperance Association, supporting absolute prohibition, took a Bible class every Sunday afternoon and was an active member of the Workers' Educational

239 See obituary in *Western Daily Press* (1940) 11 June.

Association. It was this work that led to her appointment as one of the first women Justices for the Peace in Bristol in 1921.

A number of men involved in the Labour Party were also active in the Adult Schools Union and it is perhaps through them that Lilian was drawn to Labour politics. She was associated with the North Bristol Labour Party and was selected in 1920 to stand as a councillor for St Philip and St Jacob North ward when the sitting councillor died. She was unopposed on this occasion and became the second woman in Bristol to take a seat on the council. In subsequent elections she was returned with increased majorities. Her abilities as a speaker, hard worker and organiser must have been evident, since it was unusual for a woman to be selected for a winnable seat after only a short period of activism in the Labour Party. The author of a profile of her in the *Bristol Times & Mirror* wondered when she ever took any rest, since she had eight children, seven of whom still attended school and "she employs no help in the home".[240]

Lilian seemed to be a hardworking, conscientious councillor, attending up to 15 council committee meetings each month and, in the interwar years, raised far more questions, motions and petitions than any other woman. Throughout the 1920s she was a member of committees dealing with Education, Visitors to the Mental Hospital, Blind Persons Act and Museum and Art Galleries. In the 1930s she was no longer on the Education Committee but was selected for the important Sanitation and Improvement Committee.[241] As a woman Lilian had had to work hard to establish her reputation on the council. When she stood for election to the aldermanic bench in 1926, she came bottom of the poll but in 1932 was selected unopposed when there was

240 *Bristol Times & Mirror* (1921) 30 August.
241 C Haskins (1981) 'Elected Women in Local Government in Bristol during the InterWar Years', MA Dissertation, University of the West of England.

a vacancy caused by an alderman's death. In the subsequent elections she came joint top of the poll.

For most of the interwar years, the Labour Party was in a minority on the council and it was difficult to make an impact on policy but Lilian was instrumental in 1921 in persuading the council to cover part of the River Frome to improve public health and to provide work for the unemployed.[242] She also campaigned for more public open spaces and for amenities on housing estates, such as public baths, washhouses, parks and libraries. She was keen that working-class children should be able to enjoy the art gallery and museum and asked the Education Committee to pay for free transport. In the late 1930s, Lilian argued for greater secondary school provision in North Bristol. Lilian was consistent therefore in pressing for reforms that would improve the quality of working-class life, including education and housing, and claimed that she was a citizens' candidate because "as a woman she knew exactly what the conditions of the majority were".[243] Nonetheless, she was never identified with support for more controversial issues such as birth control that raised in an explicit way the question of gender inequalities.

Alongside her council activities, she remained committed to the cause of temperance, was Branch Secretary of the Workers' Educational Association and was a member of the Central branch of the Women's Cooperative Guild. She was a frequent speaker to women's organisations on topics ranging from public health and housing to the importance of support for the League of Nations. She was frequently a guest speaker at Labour women's rallies and women's section meetings.

Lilian was unusual in this period, as a married woman with a large family, in taking such an active role in public life. She was

242 *Western Daily Press* (1921) 14 September.
243 Ibid. 21 October.

keen to promote the importance of Labour politics which she saw as the way forward for the causes she held dear, in particular temperance, education and decent housing. She continued as an active alderman until her death in 1940.

Written by June Hannam, who is Professor Emerita of Modern British History at the University of the West of England. June has written extensively on the relationship between socialism and feminism in the late 19th and early 20th centuries.

ELLEN PITMAN

born 1857, NURSE, SUFFRAGETTE

Nurse Ellen Pitman didn't take any nonsense from any passing misogynists, even if they happened to be a prominent politician. The day before Winston Churchill was due to speak at Colston Hall in 1909, she sent him a message… on a brick… via the plate glass window of the Post Office on Small Street. While sitting in her police cell afterwards, Ellen sang suffragette songs with Vera Wentworth and Mary Sophia Allen who had also been arrested for militancy on the same day. Ellen got 14 days' hard labour in prison and while in court she stated that "the blow was against the Government and that it would not be the last"[244]. While in prison, she underwent hunger strike and, presumably, force feeding.[245]

Shortly after her release, Ellen joined a convoy of suffragettes en route to Newcastle to protest against the Chancellor of the Exchequer, David Lloyd George. Although Ellen and all other women were barred from Lloyd George's meeting, they went

244 http://francesca-scriblerus.blogspot.co.uk/2014/07/spotlight-onellen-w-pitman-c1857.html
245 *Western Daily Press*, 1909, 12 October, 'Suffragists Prosecuted: Sentences of Hard Labour'. 6.

on a spate of window smashing in Newcastle and again found themselves imprisoned. Ellen was in her mid-50s by this point, and the alarmingly regular episodes of imprisonment and force feeding were taking their toll on her health as well as her career as a nurse. So much so that when Ellen volunteered to take part in yet another Bristol protest, Women's Social and Political Union organiser Annie Kenney asked for other women to take her place because Ellen "has already done more than her share"[246]. Good for you, Nurse Pitman!

Please also see the entries for: Mary Sophia Allen, Annie Kenney and Vera Wentworth.

JANE and ANNA MARIA PORTER

1776-1850 and 1780-1832, NOVELISTS

So much about the lives of sister novelists Jane and Anna Maria Porter resonates with the modern day. Celebrity lifestyle; the battle for intellectual property rights between artist and publisher; a successful woman's struggle to find a partner; the lauding of a man's achievement over a woman's... and yet history has almost erased them. They are part of what researcher Clifford Siskin calls "the great forgetting"[247], ie "the removal from the literary canon of early women novelists not named Brontë or Austen"[248]. The Porter sisters' contribution to literature, let alone the richness of their lives, shows this treatment to be quite unjust.

Jane and Anna Maria were born in 1776 and 1780, two of four siblings. Following the death of their army surgeon father in 1779,

246 http://francesca-scriblerus.blogspot.co.uk/2014/07/spotlight-onellen-w-pitman-c1857.html
247 http://bq.blakearchive.org/34.2.johnson
248 https://illumination.missouri.edu/s10/novelists

their mother moved the family from Durham to Edinburgh, in the hope they would receive a better education. Here, they made the acquaintance of a young Scottish writer called Walter Scott, who regaled the children with stories. It's perhaps unsurprising that, their imaginations now sparked, both sisters became writers.

Anna Maria started young, writing her first book, *Artless Tales* (1792), at age 13. She went on to produce approximately 30 works of historical romance, including collaborations with Jane, and poetry. Though both sisters became well-known in the early stages of their careers, it was Anna Maria who enjoyed this fame the most; her exploits reportedly bordering on the infamous.[249] Anna Maria died aged just 52 from typhus while visiting her brother William in Bristol.

Jane, though a later starter, was the more critically acclaimed author. She achieved success with her first novel, *Thaddeus of Warsaw* (1803), which tells the story of a Polish refugee's flight to London from the foreign occupation of Poland in the 1790s. Although Scott's *Waverley* (1814) has long been held as the first work of historical fiction[250], some argue that Jane should wear that mantle instead. Jane's second novel, *The Scottish Chiefs* (1810) – the story of William Wallace's fight for Scottish independence – won fame across Europe, and was reportedly banned by Napoléon Bonaparte. The novel deals with "political controversy, gender warfare, violence, and revolution" and suggests women are crucial agonists in the formulation of national identity.[251] One commentator writes that it is the product of "a little girl whose daydreams were of knights and battles when other children played with dolls"[252].

Despite their early fame, the Porter sisters began to disappear

249 Ibid.
250 http://www.cityofliterature.com/a-to-z/waverley-novels-sir-walter-scott/
251 https://broadviewpress.com/product/the-scottish-chiefs/#tab-description
252 http://www.reformation.org/jane-porter-bio.html

from the spotlight in their mid-40s. Because they received one-off payments rather than royalties for their works, they never made a good living from their writing. Jane spent her later years forced to live with a succession of friends and relations, and was described as "totally destitute or nearly so"[253]. Neither sister married, with Anna Maria commenting that "a woman's public fame is the death blow to her private happiness"[254]. No man wanted to be second fiddle to a successful woman, she believed.

Jane died in Bristol in 1850, two months before her brother William, with whom she had been living. Following their deaths, it was revealed that a novel believed to be authored by Jane, *Sir Edward Seaward's Narrative of his Shipwreck*, was actually by William. As a doctor, William had thought it unprofessional to appear as a fiction writer and persuaded his sister to go along with the subterfuge. A contemporary inscription in Bristol Cathedral attests to the work's true authorship and Jane's editorship: a permanent reminder of her literary contribution, despite history's attempts to make us forget.

Written by Caroline Bolhoven, who is a short story writer and book lover from Bristol.

CHRISTINE PREECE

dates unknown, BUS DRIVER

Bristol doesn't have the best track record when it comes to bus politics. The famous Bristol Bus Boycott in 1963 was the result of the refusal of the Bristol Omnibus Company to employ black

253 Devoney Looser, (2008). *Women Writers and Old Age in Great Britain, 1750-1850*. Baltimore: John Hopkins University Press. 157.
254 https://illumination.missouri.edu/s10/novelists

Christine Preece illustration by Jenny Howe

or Asian drivers. A four-month boycott of the buses led to the company overhauling its colour bar and employing its first non-white conductor later that year. However, it would be 1971 before it employed Bristol's first female bus driver: Christine Preece.

ANNA MARIA PRIESTMAN and MARY PRIESTMAN

1829-1914 and 1831-1914, SOCIALISTS, SUFFRAGISTS

Anna Maria and Mary Priestman, along with their older sister Margaret Tanner, were involved in a variety of women's rights causes in Bristol in the 19th century.[255] Born in Newcastle, they were brought up in a Quaker household that encouraged women to take an interest in politics. Their mother, born Rachel Bragg, was involved in the anti-slavery movement and was an active preacher, undertaking a speaking tour in America when her children were still young. The Priestman sisters also took part in the anti-slavery movement and the campaign against the Corn Laws.[256] Their attraction to radical liberal causes was reinforced through the marriage of their eldest sister Elizabeth to the Manchester MP John Bright. Most members of the Bright family circle, apart from John Bright himself, were prominent in the 19th-century women's movement and in 1866, both Anna Maria and Mary signed the Women's Suffrage Petition. After the death of their father they moved to Bristol in 1869, possibly to be near to Margaret.

They set up home at 9 Durdham Downs and then at number 37, called The Nook. They soon became part of a circle of women

255 For an account of their different activities, see June Hannam (1996). 'An Enlarged Sphere of Usefulness': The Bristol Women's Movement c. 1860-1914. Madge Dresser and Philip Ollerenshaw, eds. *The Making of Modern Bristol. Tiverton: Redcliffe Press.* 184-209.

256 The Corn Laws were tariffs and restrictions on imported food and grain enforced in the United Kingdom between 1815 and 1846.

who took an interest in radical politics and women's rights, including the Unitarian anti-slavery activist Mary Estlin, with whom they formed a close friendship. Members of their family who lived close by also shared their views. Their nieces Anne and Lilias Ashworth (later Hallett) and Helen Bright Clark, the daughter of Elizabeth and John Bright, who lived in Street, were particularly active.

The Priestman sisters were also involved in women's rights at a national level and were close friends with women such as Josephine Butler, leader of the Ladies' National Association to Repeal the Contagious Diseases' Acts, and Elizabeth Wolstenholme Elmy, leader of the Women's Franchise League, who was radical in her politics and unconventional in her private life. Sandra Holton describes the Priestman sisters as radical suffragists, since they were impatient with social conventions, were committed to radical politics outside the women's movement and took up controversial questions, such as opposition to the state regulation of prostitution and votes for married women.[257] In 1870, for example, they refused to pay their taxes as a protest against women's exclusion from the franchise and so their household goods were seized by bailiffs.

From 1870, the Priestman sisters played a significant role in the Bristol women's movement. Anna Maria became a committee member of the West of England Society for Women's Suffrage and was responsible for raising £1,000 (approximately £45,700 in contemporary money) to carry out organising work in the region.[258] As well as the vote, she took an interest in the work conditions and wages of working women. In 1874, Anna Maria

257 Sandra Holton (1996). *Suffrage Days. Stories from the Women's Suffrage Movement.* London: Routledge.
258 Bristol & West Society for Women's Suffrage, Annual Reports, Women's Library. Beddoe, AM (1911) *The Early Years of the Women's Suffrage Movement.* Bradford on Avon. Tanner, SJ (1918). *How the Suffrage Movement Began in Bristol Sixty Years Ago.* Bristol: The Carlyle Press.

presented a paper on 'The Industrial Position of Women as Affected by their Exclusion from the Suffrage' to the annual congress of the National Association for the Promotion of Social Science, and joined other suffragists in helping to form a trades union for working women – the Bristol Working Women's Association. In the period of labour unrest in the city in 1889, the Priestman sisters set up a soup kitchen for women on strike.

Anna Maria was keen to link women's suffrage to Liberal politics and, along with Emily Sturge, established the Bristol Women's Liberal Association (BWLA), the first of its kind in the country.[259] As President of the BWLA, she aimed not only to promote liberal politics but also to ensure that the Liberal Party supported women's suffrage. She promoted these ideas at a national level when she was elected as Vice President of the Women's Liberal Federation (WLF), formed in 1886. After an unsuccessful attempt in 1896 to commit the WLF to work only for candidates who supported women's enfranchisement, Anna Maria established and became President of a new organisation, the Union of Practical Suffragists, and under its aegis published a pamphlet on *Women and Votes*.

Mary was also active in all of these organisations, usually as a member of their executive committees and she was a Vice President of the WLF after 1893. Nonetheless she gave most of her energies to the Ladies' National Association (LNA) and its campaign to repeal the Contagious Diseases' Acts (CDA). She was a member of the executive committee of the LNA at a national level and in 1870 was a founder member and Honorary Secretary of the Bristol branch. The Bristol LNA was often characterised as feminist and independent in its views.[260] More than 40 per cent

259 Bristol Women's Liberal Association, Annual Reports, Bristol Reference Library.
260 Judith Walkowitz (1980). *Prostitution and Victorian Society: Women, Class and the State.* *Cambridge: Cambridge University Press.*

of its members were single women and large public meetings were held for mixed-sex audiences. Efforts were made to involve working-class women in the campaign and Mary suggested to Josephine Butler that working women should be issued with cards to show their support even if they could not afford the subscription. There were strong links with the suffrage campaign and a number of women, including Mary, were office holders in both movements. Even after the CDA was repealed in 1886, the Priestman sisters remained active in the Bristol LNA and took an interest in international developments. In the 1890s, for example, they joined the campaign to protest against government attempts to regulate prostitution in India and, in 1898, Mary attended the Congress of the International Federation for the Abolition of the State Regulation of Vice.

The commitment of the Priestman sisters to linking the demand for women's suffrage to Liberal Party politics brought them at various times into conflict with Liberal Party organisations and with mainstream suffrage societies. In 1905, Anna Maria was ousted as President of the BWLA when some members declared that women's suffrage should not be pursued ahead of loyalty to the Liberal Party. With their closest supporters from the BWLA, the Priestman sisters formed yet another group, the Moral Reform Union, which placed suffrage in the context of other social reforms. They subscribed to the Women's Social and Political Union (WSPU) in 1907, and helped Annie Kenney when she arrived in Bristol as WSPU Organiser for the region. As militancy increased, however, they became disenchanted with the WSPU and, in 1909, the Moral Reform Union amalgamated with the local branch of the National Union of Women's Suffrage Societies. The following year the Priestman sisters signed a letter with other Quakers, many of whom were their relatives, to express their commitment to constitutional methods of achieving the vote. As life-long pacifists and outspoken opponents of the Boer War they were distressed by the outbreak of World War One and died, five days apart, in October 1914. War had been declared on 14 July 1914.

Anna Maria and Mary Priestman, along with their widowed sister Margaret Tanner, played a leading role in the 19th-century women's movement both in Bristol and at a national level. For them, women's suffrage was inextricably linked to other causes, such as the repeal of the CDA and improved women's education, and was an integral part of their commitment to liberal politics. They were radical in their outlook, supporting married women's right to vote and taking an interest in the conditions of women workers whom they saw as allies and potential voters, rather than the subject of rescue schemes. They were at the heart of an energetic group of middle-class women campaigners who helped to ensure that Bristol was one of the key centres for the women's movement in the 19th century.

Written by June Hannam, who is Professor Emerita of Modern British History at the University of the West of England. June has written extensively on the relationship between socialism and feminism in the late 19th and early 20th centuries.

Please also see the entries for: Josephine Butler, Helen Bright Clark, Mary Estlin, Lilias Ashworth Hallett, Annie Kenney, Emily Sturge and Margaret Tanner.

GRANDMA PUGSLEY
1620-1700, WELL WOMAN

Grandma 'Gammer' Pugsley presided over a well on Ninetree Hill in Stokes Croft that she maintained had healing qualities. She became so intrinsically linked to this well, which stood on land that had been owned by her husband, that it was known variously as Mother Pugsley's Well, Dame Pugsley's Well and simply Pugsley's Well.

Widowed at the age of 25, after her beloved husband was killed in the siege of Bristol in 1645, when she died at the age of 80, Gammer had requested that her funeral be a happy occasion because she would finally be reunited with her true love and, as such, she was buried in her wedding clothes. Gammer had spent her life in devotion to her deceased husband who was buried beside the well and she wore full mourning clothes every day for the rest of her life.

Mother Pugsley's Well consisted of two stone basins in a field on their land, one of which had "an infallible remedy for the eyes"[261], while the other was renowned for making excellent tea. Given that the well was beside her husband's grave, Gammer erected a small hut over the well so that she could sit close to her late husband's remains in all weathers.

At her funeral on 4 August 1700, herbs were scattered at the head of the funeral procession and a fiddler led the way to the grave, while the church bells from St Nicholas Church rang out. However, there were some who believed Gammer to be nothing but a witch and they later trampled on her grave and dug up her husband's skull.

Some 28 years after her death, Gammer's beloved well and

261 JF Nicholls, John Taylor, 1882, *Bristol, Past and Present*, Bristol: Arrowsmith.

field were sold to a property developer who attempted to build houses on the site and when they dug up the graves they found the two bodies (one now headless) intertwined. These houses were beset with problems – the foundations kept crumbling and the houses were uninhabitable – so much so that they were pulled down and a small fountain was created on the site of the well, bearing the inscription: "To ever blooming connubial affection". Did Gammer's troubled spirit continue to have a hold on her beloved well from beyond her grave?

In 1845, the council planned to build again on the site and ignored protests from locals who tried to defend the right to keep the well, which was their main source of water – and who perhaps feared more reprisals from an angered Gammer's spirit. But the council persevered and Fremantle Square was built, despite locals clubbing together and trying to buy the land themselves.

And another thing... Gammer's will dictated that bread should be given to the poor and needy women who were living in the Almshouses on King Street on both Easter Sunday and Twelfth Night.[262]

BARBARA PYM

1913-1980, NOVELIST

The popular novelist Barbara Pym lived in Clifton from 1941-1943 at The Coppice (now called Leigh House), which overlooks Clifton Suspension Bridge. The Coppice was home to a small group of women and children who, despite wartime conditions, appeared to have had a splendid time.[263] She was drawn to the city after her younger sister Hilary was evacuated here during

262 With thanks to http://brisray.com/bristol/bmapug1.htm

263 Lorna Brierley, Helen Reid, (2000). *Go Home and Do the Washing!* Bristol: Broadcast. 133.

the war and Barbara began to envy her sister's quality of life. Barbara wrote to a friend at the time saying: "Walking back over the Suspension Bridge, lovely in the moonlight."[264] Barbara, who could speak fluent German, worked for the Censorship office in Bristol during World War Two, which was before she became a best-selling novelist thanks to her social comedies including *Excellent Women* (1952) and *A Glass of Blessings* (1958). Sadly, given that the bulk of her life and career was outside of Bristol, we won't dwell on Barbara although we think she's fantastic. And we advise you to read her novels, especially *Excellent Women.*

ELIZABETH RALPH

1911-2000, ARCHIVIST

As Bristol's City Archivist from 1937 to the 1980s, Miss Ralph (as Elizabeth Ralph was affectionately known) did a phenomenal amount to save Bristol's heritage during the Blitz. She also worked on a large number of books about the history of the city. Miss Ralph was the third City Archivist in Bristol and interestingly all three archivists were women. During her 34 years in post, Miss Ralph helped secure historically important collections relating to the city's history in a wide range of areas.

Susan Greenwood was a colleague of Miss Ralph's from the Soroptimists, of which Miss Ralph was twice President and once Secretary. Despite being bombed out of her family home in Henleaze during World War Two, Miss Ralph spent three years helping the Soroptimists to run 15 Upper Belgrave Road as a club for 300 service people, and provided bed and breakfast accommodation for 70 service women every week.

264 Hazel Holt, (1990). *A Lot to Ask: A Life of Barbara Pym* London: Bello. C9.

Susan adds: "During the bombing, she reputedly took charge of the city insignia and medieval swords storing them for safety in the Pier Railway Tunnel at Hotwells ... Elizabeth was a truly remarkable lady and in the last five years of her life moved to St Monica's [care home], being collected from her flat, full of books, to spend one day a week at the Records Office continuing with her researches right to the end."[265]

SARAH PARKER REMOND

1824-1894, ABOLITIONIST

Agreeing to undertake an international speaking tour in the 1800s when you are a single black American woman is no small task. But that is what Sarah Parker Remond from Salem, United States, did. She was born to two former slaves, so was familiar with the anger and horror of slavery but her family was unusual in that they were financially secure and used this power to campaign vociferously against slavery.

The purpose of Sarah's speaking tour was to outline the dehumanisation of American chattel slavery in order to consolidate the British anti-slavery sentiment, with the aim of linking British abolitionists to American abolitionists. Sarah said that women were "sold into slavery with cheeks like the lily and the rose, as well as those that might compare with the raven", pointing out that white women sold into slavery commanded a higher price.[266]

Between 1859 and 1861, Sarah gave 45 lectures in 17 towns and cities in England, as well as further talks in Scotland and Ireland.

265 http://sigbi.org/bristol/2017/07/12/elizabeth-ralph-commemorative-plaque-replaced/
266 Sarah Parker Remond in Maurice McInnis, (2011), *Slaves Waiting For Sale*. Chicago: University of Chicago Press.

She was well received and the press reported on her favourably. As part of the tour, Sarah visited Bristol when she spoke at Mary Carpenter's Red Lodge on Park Row.

Please also see the entries for: Ellen Craft and Mary Estlin.

MARY RENAULT

1905-1983, NOVELIST

Mary Renault (the pen name of Eileen Mary Challans) was born on 4 September 1905 in West Ham, London. With the encouragement of her godmother, she was sent to Clifton High School from 1919 to 1925.

Mary returned to Bristol, where her parents now lived, in 1928 after graduating with a third in English from St Hugh's College, Oxford, where she had been taught by the popular fantasy novelist JRR Tolkien. She hoped to be able to support herself from temporary jobs that would allow her the free time in which to concentrate on her true passion: writing. She worked in a Clark's shoe factory, a chocolate laboratory and as a Civil Service counter clerk while socialising with theatrical friends in the city and neighbouring Bath. This bohemian milieu would later feature in some of her fiction.

Mary rented a basement flat in Charlotte Street off Park Street, but ill health and dwindling finances brought an end to her independence and a return to her parents' home in 1931. The family moved to Stoke-on-Trent in 1932. The following year she enrolled as a Trainee Nurse at the Radcliffe Infirmary, Oxford. It was here that she met and fell in love with fellow student Julie Mullard, who became her lifelong partner.

In 1936, Mary qualified as a State Registered Nurse and

continued to combine her nursing career with her writing. Her first published novel, *Purposes of Love* (1939), was a hospital romance featuring depictions of lesbianism and heterosexuality that were unusually explicit for the time. Her sixth novel, *The Charioteer* (1953) – and her last with a contemporary setting – centred upon male homosexual relationships, a theme that would recur in the works of historical fiction for which she is better known. The novel drew upon her experiences of nursing Dunkirk evacuees while assigned to Winford Hospital in Bristol during the early stages of World War Two. Mary was finally able to give up nursing at the end of the war and write full-time.

In 1948, Mary and Julie emigrated to South Africa. The move was partly prompted by tax issues that resulted from her being paid more than £30,000 by MGM film studios for the rights to her fourth novel *Return to Night* (1947), which was her first American bestseller and another hospital-set romance.

The couple remained in South Africa until Mary's death on 13 December 1983. Although not well known for her political activism – and by temperament inclined to be reclusive – Mary did become a member of the Black Sash (a women's anti-apartheid group) and served as the President of the writers' association PEN in South Africa, championing freedom of speech and condemning all forms of censorship.

The first of her eight novels of ancient Greece was *The Last of the Wine* (1956), the story of two male lovers during the time of the Peloponnesian War; the last was *Funeral Games* (1981), which concluded her trilogy about Alexander the Great. It has been said that the classical background gave her the ability to explore the issues of heroism, the nature of love, male and female homosexuality, gender fluidity, difference and the role of women that were her chief concern with greater freedom than in her contemporary fiction. She could calmly introduce them in this context with naturalness and a lack of sensationalism. Many of her readers, happily immersed in her page-turning plots and evocative descriptions of Mediterranean life, accepted a subject matter they might otherwise have found controversial.

Frequently marginalised for being a female writer of popular genre fiction, in recent years Mary's work has come to be reassessed for its literary merit, its scholarship and its subtle challenging of conventions.

Written by Melanie Kelly, who is Research Director and Project Manager at Bristol Cultural Development Partnership.

MARY RICHARDSON
1882-1961, SUFFRAGETTE

Mary Richardson is largely infamous for slashing 'The Rokeby Venus' painting by Diego Velázquez at London's National Portrait Gallery on 10 March 1914. But before then...

On 4 July 1913, King George was visiting Bristol to see a statue of his father Edward VII that was outside the Victoria Rooms, Clifton. As his carriage travelled up Park Street, Canadian suffragette Mary Richardson (who had popped down to Bristol from her home in London) rushed out of the crowd and tried to drop a suffrage petition onto his knees. But one of the riders escorting the King's carriage struck out at Mary with the flat of his sword and sent her flying. Mary was duly arrested, although the police struggled to remove her from the excited crowd.

Bristol suffragette researcher Lucienne Boyce writes: "One woman slapped her face, and another struck her on the head with an umbrella. The police hustled her onto a tram and took her to Bridewell Police Station. She was later released without charge at the King's request."[267] Less than a year later and Mary was back in Bristol on 15 March 1914. This time she was with Emmeline Pankhurst and the two women interrupted evensong at All Saints Church, Clifton, to pray loudly for suffragette prisoners. On the same day, down at Bristol Cathedral, suffragettes interrupted a sermon to pray vociferously for Emmeline's wellbeing and good health (the continuous cycle of imprisonment and force feeding, plus the constant stress of the suffrage campaign, was understandably taking its toll on Mrs Pankhurst's health). After the service at the cathedral, the suffragettes gave a copy of Christabel Pankhurst's book *The Great Scourge and How To End It* (1913) to the preacher, who accepted it with apparent interest.

MARY ROBINSON

1758-1800, ACTOR, WRITER

The daughter of a whale merchant, Mary Robinson was born at Minster House near the bottom of Park Street and educated at the school established by Hannah More's sister on Park Street. After her father lost his money and disappeared, Mary felt a sense of duty to please her mother and marry well to secure her future. As such, she was married at the age of 16 and quickly became a mother. However, her husband (who had lied about his inheritance and in fact had very little money) was a cad and a bounder who openly had numerous affairs and was living a lifestyle far beyond his means. The marriage was doomed to failure after the couple and their young daughter were thrown into a debtor's prison. After Mary and her daughter were released, the marriage was over, although Mary did publish a book of poems

267 Lucienne Boyce, (2013). *The Bristol Suffragettes*. Bristol: SilverWood. 52-53.

entitled *Captivity* about her experience, thanks to the patronage of Georgiana Cavendish, Duchess of Devonshire (whose own sad life, also ruined by men, is depicted in the 2008 film *The Duchess*, in which she is played by Keira Knightley).

Mary's natural beauty meant that a life on the stage was achievable and after her spellbinding performance as Perdita in *The Winter's Tale* captivated the 18-year-old Prince Regent (later King George IV), Mary became his mistress despite being four years his senior. The £20,000 payment he offered her was no doubt tempting to the struggling single mother (it is equivalent to around £1,250,000 in contemporary money), although he later refused to pay her the promised sum. As the Prince's mistress, her portrait was painted by everyone from George Romney to Thomas Gainsborough and Mary became a high society belle. However, reigning King George III tired of the bawdy satires in the press about his son's philandering with the beautiful actor and forced the affair to an end by offering to pay Mary an annuity in exchange for her silence on the matter, and also in exchange for her agreeing not to publish letters the Prince had sent her. However, the King rarely honoured this annuity and Mary continued to struggle financially.

For the next stage of her life, Mary assumed the name 'Tabitha Bramble' and wrote novels and poems that inspired Samuel Taylor Coleridge to call her an "undoubted genius".[268] Her debut novel in the Gothic style was *Vancenza: or the Dangers of Credulity* (1792), which warned against incest and sees the female protagonist about to unwittingly marry her half-brother. The book was littered with thinly veiled allusions to Mary's former romance with the Prince, which her readers found delightful.

A friendship with Marie Antoinette ensued despite Mary's

268 Lorna Brierley, Helen Reid, (2000). *Go Home and Do the Washing!* Bristol: Broadcast. 101.

support of the French Revolution but ultimately Mary died poor and alone at the tender age of 44. Hers had been a life made tough by the broken promises of the men she had known: her father, her husband, the Prince, the King.

ANGELA RODAWAY

1919-2012, CAMPAIGNER

In her 93 years, Angela Rodaway got a heck of a lot done. Born in London to a working-class family, Angela felt frustrated watching her hard-working mother struggle to look after her children, which fired Angela's determination that women deserved a much better deal from society.

After tiring of work as a teacher and grieving the loss of her partner, Angela moved to Bristol in 1959 with their young son and lived in an archaic house on Upper Wells Street (long since demolished) where the rent was the princely sum of £100 a year (this equates to approximately £1,630 in contemporary money, which means it would still be an absolute bargain). But it was a vibrant area just behind Park Street that attracted interesting and creative people and Angela felt she was finally at home. She quickly became involved with feminist circles in Bristol, such as consciousness-raising groups, the Women's Abortion and Contraception Campaign, the Bristol Women's Centre (which she helped found in 1979) and the feminist theatre group Sistershow.

Sistershow was "a feminist theatre and arts group that used humour and mischief to mobilise social change," writes historian D-M Withers. "Women's everyday experiences were the starting point for their sketches, most of which were improvised … Contemporary stories about women's experiences also needed to be quickly invented. Unruly and anarchic, disorganised and confrontational, Sistershow used theatre as a strategy to raise feminist consciousness, whether on the street or a more traditional stage."[269] All of which was extremely unusual at the time. The idea of feminist performance was rare, and to have a whole troupe of women performing and sending up the state was virtually unheard of. Angela recalled: "Men frequently take off women … women never do it to men. Whereas we did … some of the men in the audience, really nice men, were absolutely squirming at some of the things that we did."[270]

In 2011, a retrospective exhibition, programme of workshops and accompanying book were produced in Bristol by D-M Withers to celebrate the achievements of these second wave women's libbers who made so much possible for contemporary women in the city.

Angela led a varied career that, as well as being a teacher, included becoming trained in drama and working in the theatre, radio and arts. Indeed, Angela's 1964 play *Death of the Jelly Baby* was performed several times on BBC Radio and was revolutionary in its use of EEG brainwaves: a technique Angela developed at the Burden Neurological Institute in Bristol.[271] Her drama group DAT performed at the first-ever St Paul's Carnival in 1968.

Talking about the importance of the Women's Abortion and Contraception Campaign (WACC), Angela told historian Ilona Singer: "Our first concern then was contraception because we felt that if you couldn't regulate your own body then you couldn't regulate anything."[272] It was extremely difficult to obtain contraception in the 1960s and early 1970s, making the work of

269 Deborah M Withers, (2011). *Sistershow Revisited: Feminism in Bristol 1973-1975*. Bristol: Hammer-On. 17.

270 http://feministarchivesouth.org.uk/wp-content/uploads/2013/02/Personal-Histories-of-the-Second-Wave-of-Feminism.pdf

271 https://www.theguardian.com/culture/2012/nov/15/angela-rodaway-obituary

272 http://feministarchivesouth.org.uk/wp-content/uploads/2013/02/Personal-Histories-of-the-Second-Wave-of-Feminism.pdf

WACC absolutely crucial, until eventually it was superseded by the National Abortion Campaign. Even when abortion became legal it was still a difficult process trying to obtain one, which Angela attributed to the way politics worked against women, telling Ilona: "This is what happens frequently, you demand things and then you are given half which just weakens the demand. It's terribly difficult to go on demanding when you have been given just a bit … It happened with the suffragettes and women over 30 getting the vote, whereas men over 21 had it and it was a long time before women got it equally."[273]

When asked about the general achievements of the second wave period of feminism, Angela told Ilona: "We've only half achieved everything typically … we haven't got equal pay for equal work. I know that people can bring an action against an employer where it can be shown that the work they do is equal but we haven't really got that and women's pay is only about 70 per cent of men's overall. Equal job opportunities we wanted as well and we certainly haven't got that, we've got a glass ceiling instead." Her answer to the question of what women need was simply: "I think it's a daft question. Women want what everybody wants practically from birth: to have control over their own lives."[274]

In her later years, Angela joined her friend Monica Sjöö in the feminist spirituality group Ama Mawu (named after an African goddess: 'Amu' meaning 'mother', 'Mawu' meaning 'the goddess'), which celebrates the earth, fertility, the female body and the evolution of humankind.

For the final 40 years of her life, Angela lived in a basement flat in Windsor Terrace, where she shunned modernisation and central heating: her only indulgences being a Bakelite telephone

273 Ibid
274 Ibid

and a radio. A bust of Angela, sculpted by her friend Barry Flanagan, is kept at the Arnolfini.

Please also see the entries for: Rosa Burden, Monica Sjöö, Beverley Skinner, Jackie Thrupp and Pat VT West.

IDA ROPER

1865-1935, BOTANIST

Clifton cultivated a number of botanists but the first woman from the area to command the same respect as her male colleagues was Ida Roper, who worked for decades to catalogue the thousands of species of flora within the county borders of Avon.[275]

In 1913, Ida became the first female President of the Bristol Naturalists' Society, established in 1862, and she was also among the first female members of many other scientific bodies. Among her various roles, Ida maintained a Wardian case at the Dame Emily Smyth Room at Bristol Museum and Art Gallery for 13 years, this being a case of living plants. Ida often updated her Wardian several times a week, such was her commitment to the plants. Ida's displays were a very popular museum attraction throughout the war, possibly because the botanical displays had absolutely nothing to do with the horrors of fighting that had overwhelmed every other aspect of everyone's lives and therefore it offered them a refreshing moment of escape. The *Western Daily Press* wrote: "Throughout the war the display was continued, amidst many other distractions in order to provide a pleasant relief for the citizens in their anxieties, and for the delight of the

275 Until 1996, Avon was the county name for the area that includes Bristol, Bath and parts of Somerset and Gloucestershire.

Ida Roper illustration by Jenny Howe

convalescent soldiers amongst us."[276]

Wardian cases in museums around the country were almost exclusively the domain of female volunteers, making them a visible area of female control and expertise; perhaps women were well-suited to the task, since women were accustomed to arranging flowers in the home. Researcher Kate Hill explains: "Botany had long been an acceptable feminine hobby and even the site of articulation of a feminist counter-science. Women involved in this work may therefore be seen as attempting to make space for themselves in the public places and institutions of science by inserting feminine practices alongside those of men."[277]

As well as her botanical lectures, Ida also gave papers on archaeology and was an accomplished embroiderer. Examples of her needlepoint could be seen in the chancel at St George's Church, Brandon Hill, for which she also wrote a commemorative brochure at the time of the church's centenary in 1923.[278]

ANNE ROSCO

dates unknown, EMBROIDERER

Originally from London, embroiderer Anne Barbara Rosco moved to Bristol with her husband in 1749, when they opened a boarding school on St Michael's Hill for "little masters as well as misses" after placing an advertisement in the *Bristol Weekly Intelligence* journal. After she was widowed in 1762, Anne and her daughters opened a companion school where embroidery

276 *Western Daily Press*, 1923, 2 July, 'The Lady Botanist of Bristol Museum'. 5.

277 Kate Hill, (2016), *Women and Museums 1850-1914: Modernity and the Gendering of Knowledge.* Oxford: Oxford University Press.

278 Ida M Roper, (1923). *The Church of St George's, Brandon Hill, Bristol: Prepared at the Centenary in Aid of General Repairs of the Church.* Bristol: T&W Goulding, Ecclesiastical Printers & Publishers.

featured heavily on the curriculum.[279] Some of the pieces created by Anne and her pupils at the school now fetch several hundred pounds at specialist auctions.

HANNAH ROSE

1718-1791, BRASS WORKER

Along with Mary Sarjeant, Hannah Rose was involved with the large brass works at Baptist Mills, Bristol and Coalbrookdale, Shropshire. Through the writings of these liberated and independent women we have been able to gain a good understanding of the impact of the Industrial Revolution in England. Hannah was a keen diarist, despite her modest Quaker attitude leading her to think that her words might not be of interest to others. She wrote: "I have had it on my mind for some years past to leave behind me something concerning my ancestors as far back as I have any account from my parents. Some may object and say it is pride for thee to write of thy ancestors who were all poor people, but as they were honest and sober, and my parents brought me up to read and write, I ought to employ my pen in their behalf for the Scripture says the Righteous shall be had in everlasting remembrance."[280]

Her diary also suggested that Abraham Darby, who founded the brass works at Baptist Mills with his wife Mary Sarjeant, had previously travelled to the Netherlands to hire Dutch workmen to establish the Baptist Mills works. If so, this is an interesting development for the sharing of knowledge across countries.[281]

Please also see the entry for: Mary Sarjeant.

279 Madge Dresser, (2016). *Women and the City: Bristol 1373-2000*. Bristol: Redcliffe Press. 71.
280 https://barstew.wordpress.com/thomas-family/
281 http://www.brassmill.com/linked/1984_-_continetal_origins_-_day.pdf

IRENE ROSE
1883-1965, DANCER, SINGER

Dancer and singer Irene Rose from Totterdown started young. Even at the age of 16 she was the star turn at a summer show at Bristol Zoo, to be accompanied by the zoo band no less, where the advertising billed her as "Miss Irene Rose (Clever Child Vocalist)"[282]. Four years later and she was also the highlight in the spring show at the Theatre Royal (now Bristol Old Vic): "A favourite from the Theatre Royal pantomime appears in the person of Miss Irene Rose. This dainty little versatile vocalist contributed four songs last evening, and she has evidently made a lasting impression upon Bristol."[283] Irene continued to work in showbusiness and went on to become President of the Music Hall Ladies' Guild.

KATHARINE RUSSELL
1842-1874, SUFFRAGIST

In 1872, Katharine Russell, the Viscountess Amberley, became the President of the Bristol branch of the Central Committee of the National Society for Women's Suffrage, which was the first national group in the United Kingdom to campaign for votes for women and was founded in 1867. Along with the vote, Viscountess Amberley demanded equal pay for women, equality for wives, equality of education for boys and girls and for all professions to be open to women. Which was very forward thinking for 1872.

When Viscountess Amberley read out a paper on women's suffrage at the Mechanics Institute in Stroud, Queen Victoria

282 *Bristol Mercury*, 1899, 22 August, 'Promenade Concert'. 4.
283 *Western Daily Press*, 1903, 7 April, 'The People's Palace'. 6.

was so enraged with the speech that she famously ranted against "this mad, wicked folly of 'women's rights' with all its attendant horrors, on which her poor feeble sex is bent, forgetting every sense of womanly feelings and propriety". The unamused monarch added that "Lady Amberley ought to get a good whipping" for her speech.[284] Ouch!

While we are on the subject of Queen Victoria, she is – at the time of writing – one of only two women to be honoured with a statue in Bristol (the other belongs to the goddess Sabrina[285]). Queen Victoria's regal statue stands on College Green and was unveiled in 1888 by her grandson Prince Albert Victor, although in January 2016 it experienced a feminist makeover by queenly Fishponds-based street artist Vaj, who added noble legs and majestic pubic hair to the sovereign stone. Unimpressed, Bristol City Council removed the august additions within 24 hours.

Please also see the entry for: Sabrina.

SABRINA
GODDESS OF THE SEVERN

There are are precious few statues of women in Bristol, so that of Sabrina, Goddess of the Severn (located in the courtyard of Broad Quay House), must be treasured. The Roman name for what we now call the River Severn was Sabrina, which derives from a folk story where a nymph named Sabrina drowned in that stretch of water. The 1980 statue by Gerald Laing is named 'The Apothesis

284 http://www.historyofwomen.org/suffrage.html
285 Since we're really short statues of females in Bristol, we could add a wooden sculpture at Bristol Zoo based on Wendy the elephant, who died in 2002. But frankly, since the three female statues in Bristol represent a fictional goddess, an elephant and a queen (who visited Bristol once, very briefly), it's an insult to all of the women in this book that none of them have a statue in their honour. You can't move for statues of men, though.

of Sabrina' and depicts the goddess in a sea shell supported by three young attendants.

And another thing... While we are on the subject of mythical beings, let us remember Avona. According to folklore, brothers Goram and Vincent were besotted by a woman who promised her affections to whoever could drain the lake that, reportedly, once filled the Avon Valley. Goram drank too much ale and fell asleep with the task unfinished. But Vincent achieved his goal and won Avona's heart. This is an explanation for the dramatic landscape of the Avon Gorge that we can admire today. Apparently.

BERTA SACOF

1899-1989, COUNCILLOR

Born Berta Strimer, she grew up on Cranbrook Road, Redland with her sisters Helen and Jeanette (who became Helen Bloom and Jeanette Briton after marriage). The three Strimer sisters (who had two further sisters) had a collective political awakening in the 1940s and at one point all three were Bristol City Councillors, and shaped everything from Bristol's health and education to criminal justice systems.

Please also see the entries for: Helen Bloom and Florence Hancock.

JOAN SANDERSON

1912-1992, ACTOR

Fawlty Towers, Upstairs Downstairs, Rising Damp, Please Sir... these classic TV sitcoms just scratch the surface of the long list of shows that Bristol-born actor Joan Sanderson graced during her long and illustrious career. Indeed, Joan was working on the TV version of *After Henry* alongside Prunella Scales right up until her death in 1992. She also worked extensively on the stage in London's West End and was often cast in Shakespearian productions.

Born into a Bristol family, Joan attended Northumberland House school in Henleaze, where fellow actor Deborah Kerr would also study. Celebrating her achievement of joining the Royal Shakespeare Company, Joan's mother told the *Bristol Evening Post* that her daughter "was always very keen on dramatics and took part in the school breaking-up plays. On her own initiative, she studied for and got a Leverhulme scholarship at the Royal Academy of Dramatic Arts and has finished her term by winning the Academy's most coveted prize"[286].

Because of her impressive height of 5ft 10, once she graduated from the Royal Academy of Dramatic Arts, Joan was frequently cast as imposing, matronly figures and did not suffer from the problem that many contemporary female actors have in their later years when the parts suddenly disappear. Joan had a good career playing grandmothers right up until her death.

Please also see the entry for: Deborah Kerr.

CECIL IVRY SANDWITH

1871-1961, BOTANIST

Clifton-based Cecil Ivry Sandwith was a respected botanist and botanical collector. She was known for her intensive study of the spermatophye; which is a large plant that bears seeds. She also made a collection of local grasses for a Home Office Laboratory

286 *Bristol Evening Post*, 1939, 27 February, 'Bristol Girl's Dramatic Triumph'. 15.

in Bristol and published a study of 717 foreign plants growing on the city's docks. Her son Noel followed in her footsteps to become a renowned botanist and they regularly worked together.

MARY SARJEANT

1678-1718, BRASS WORKER

Like Hannah Rose, who would follow her, Mary was involved with the brass works at both Baptist Mills in Bristol and Coalbrookdale in Shropshire. With her husband, Mary co-founded the Bristol Brass Wire Company near Temple Meads in 1702.

Originally from Worcestershire, Mary married Abraham Darby in 1699 and the couple moved to Philip's Place, Bristol. Via his apprentice John Thomas, Mary's husband experimented with making hollow iron pots from sand rather than loam, which was a process that made the production of cast iron and brass goods continuous, and was the first time that cast brass and ironware were not made on an individual basis. This was important because it paved the way for future factory style mass production methods and therefore goods could be made available to a wider range of people around the world.

Please also see the entry for: Hannah Rose.

EMMA SAUNDERS

1841-1927, RAILWAYMEN'S FRIEND

Born in Manchester, Emma Saunders' family moved to Bristol when she was just six years old. Emma's mother was a busy philanthropist, who was a committee member for the Industrial

Emma Saunders illustration by Carrie Love

Home for Destitute Girls, as well as the Park Row Asylum for discharged women prisoners. And seeing the good work her mother did clearly had an influence on young Emma.

After working as a teacher at the Industrial Home for Destitute Girls and the Ragged School, in 1878 Emma began a Bible class for Bristol's railwaymen, which would lay the foundation stone for her future as 'the railwayman's friend'. Emma went on to run a mission for railwaymen, to visit sick railwaymen in hospital, and to found the Bristol and West of England's Railwaymen's Institute, which provided educational and spiritual classes for the workers in an effort to steer the men away from the temptations of alcohol. Emma also encouraged the men to foster a sense of kindness by urging them to read the 1877 Anna Sewell novel *Black Beauty*, which teaches a message of human kindness via a story about animal cruelty.

Emma would visit railwaymen wherever they were to be found, and was anxious to provide spiritual and material help to the workers whose lives of drudgery and danger was often only made bearable by evenings spent in the pub. Emma would be known to visit six railway stations along the Clifton line in one afternoon, walking from one to another and not miss out one single railwayman. In addition to passages from the *Bible* and details of religious meetings, she would give each man a gift from the bag tied around her waist: usually a flower picked from her Sion Hill garden, some seaweed, some shells or a bag of lavender. If a man had succumbed to drunkenness and been suspended from his work, Emma would visit him at home.

The men held Emma in extremely high affection and for her 80th birthday more than 5,000 people contributed to a gift of a Chesterfield armchair.[287] And when she died in 1927, her small

287 *Western Daily Press*, 1921, 13 September, 'Railwaymen's Token of Gratitude'. 7.

coffin was proudly carried by four high-ranking uniformed railwaymen who led a procession of hundreds of workers. At her memorial service, Canon Vining said: "One thing that strikes me in her life was her joy in living. Wherever she went she radiated happiness because she was so happy herself. She did not work among the railwaymen because she thought they were depraved; she admired them and loved them and could not refrain from going out and seeking her railway friends."[288]

A plaque to Emma's memory has been posted at the main entrance to Temple Meads Station. And her work lives on in the National Association of Railway Clubs, which evolved from the Railwayman's Institute that she set up.

MARY ANNE SCHIMMELPENNINCK
1778-1856, NOVELIST

Birmingham-born Mary Anne Galton moved to Bristol in 1806 after marrying Berkeley Square-dwelling merchant Lambert Schimmelpenninck, whose surname is of Dutch ancestry. Mary had always been deeply religious and once in Bristol she became acquainted with Hannah More, who inspired Mary's interest in the Port-Royalists, which would become the subject of her first book in 1813. This book proved very popular and Mary ultimately wrote five volumes of this work, as well as several anti-slavery texts. Although described as "an excellent writer with a horrid name", Mary was well respected.

After being struck down by a mystery illness that caused temporary paralysis, Mary and Lambert moved to 4 Harley Place, Clifton, in 1837 and once she began to recover, Mary enjoyed daily

288 *Western Daily Press*, 1934, 12 March, 'The Railwaymen's Friend: Memorial Service to Miss Emma Saunders'. 5.

walks on the Downs, which she said were "useful and refreshing alike to mind and body".[289]

Please also see the entry for: Hannah More.

ELLEN SHARPLES
1769-1849, ARTIST

Ellen Sharples was part of the group that founded the Bristol Academy for the Promotion of Fine Arts. Upon her death in 1849, she left the Society £2,000 (approximately £117,000 in contemporary money), which enabled the building of the first art gallery in Bristol: the Royal West of England Academy (RWA). The Bristol Academy was ahead of its time in terms of gender, and accepted both women and men from its day of opening, possibly because of its benefactor. According to an article printed in the *Western Daily Press* on 11 January 1899, Ellen believed that women should have the means of earning their own money and she certainly exercised this view in her own life.

In her practice, Ellen specialised in portraiture and miniatures, and alongside her husband she set up a successful portraiture business in the United States. She painted portraits of American leaders, original pastel portraits and miniatures on ivory. Her children and step-children all pursued careers in art, including her daughter Rolinda Sharples, whom she taught to paint. On their journey back from the United States to the United Kingdom, the ship that Ellen and her family were on was captured by a French privateer and they were interned at Brest for seven months, which she wrote about in the diary that she keenly kept.

289 Shirley Brown, Dawn Dyer, (2002). *100+ Women of Bristol*. Bristol: Bristol City Council. 21.

In 1853, a school of art was established at the RWA, built on the foundations established by Ellen. The school eventually became the Bristol School of Art, which enables hundreds of students every year to become familiar with various disciplines to this day. The RWA gallery still stands and has hosted many famous artists over the years, including Tracy Emin and Louise Bourgeois. The institution's annual open exhibition attracts thousands of applications and showcases Bristol's enormous artistic talent – a legacy that Ellen would doubtless be very proud of.

Written by Ellie Vowles, who is a trustee of Bristol Women's Voice and an artist/maker.

Please also see the entry for: Rolinda Sharples.

ROLINDA SHARPLES

1793-1838, ARTIST

Rolinda Sharples was born in Bath in 1793. She was taught to draw and paint by her mother Ellen Sharples and, by the time she was 13, she had begun to contribute to the family portraiture business. In 1811, the Sharples family moved to Bristol, where Rolinda began to earn a living from painting portraits and groups of people in oil paint. Her work captures the character of its subjects in perfect detail. One of Rolinda's favourite people to paint was her mother; 'The Artist and her Mother' depicts the pair together, Rolinda at her easel and her mother watching approvingly as she paints. The painting now sits in Bristol Museum and Art Gallery, alongside some of her other works.

Another of Rolinda's famous works was a depiction of the trial of Colonel Brereton, who was court martialled for sending his troops away from the chaos on the night of the Bristol Reform Riots in 1831. Some believed him to be a scapegoat for the failure of city magistrates to give solid orders to cope with the rioting and he tragically shot himself four days after the trial began. Rolinda used both realistic portraits of those who were present at the trial and her artistic licence to put together the scene, which included her mother as one of the onlookers.

In 1827, she was elected an honorary member of the Society of British Artists and she painted prolifically throughout her life. In her later years, she lived with her mother Ellen in Hotwells, until Rolinda died of breast cancer in 1838. A plaque marks the family house in Canynge Road, Clifton.

And another thing... Rolinda's painting 'The Cloak Rooms, Clifton Assembly Rooms, 1819' has been used for numerous book covers including *A Portrait of Jane Austen* by David Cecil and *Austen's World* by Maggie Lane.

Written by Ellie Vowles, who is a trustee of Bristol Women's Voice and an artist/maker.

Please also see the entry for: Ellen Sharples.

MARY SHELLEY

1797-1851, WRITER

Best known for her Gothic novel *Frankenstein* (1818), London-born Mary Shelley can also stake a claim on Bristol alongside her mother, Mary Wollstonecraft. Mary Shelley had been living in Hotwells during the year prior to beginning work on *Frankenstein*. At the time, she was pregnant with Percy Bysshe Shelley's son and she was missing her partner terribly. Academics have claimed that the legendary literary monster Mary created is an embodiment of her moral struggle with the concept of slavery. And although slavery had been abolished by the time Mary came to live on Sion Hill, Hotwells, in 1815, she would not have been able to escape the consequences: whether in seeing freed enslaved Africans, or the wealth of her neighbours generated by both the slave trade and the work done by former enslaved Africans. Mary refused to consume sugar because it was a direct result of slavery.

And another thing... Mary Shelley's stepsister Claire Clairmont was born and lived in Brislington, and was rumoured to have had a child with Mary's partner Percy Bysshe Shelley, as well as an affair with Lord Byron.

Please also see the entry for: Mary Wollstonecraft.

WINIFRED SHEPLAND

dates unknown, UNIVERSITY REGISTRAR

The University of Bristol flourished in the interwar years and also developed in terms of its attitudes towards women, both as students and staff. As such, in 1928 Winifred Lucy Shepland was appointed as the first female registrar of any British university when she took up the post in Bristol.

SARAH SIDDONS

1755-1831, ACTOR

The most famous tragic actor of her day was Sarah Siddons. The Bath-based performer came from a theatrical family and was used to appearing on the stage even as a child. Sarah frequently

Sarah Siddons illustration by Jenny Howe

worked in Bristol, often staying at the Princes Buildings and performing at the Bristol Theatre Royal. Sarah commanded the top salary of the day, which was £3 per week and she felt she had earned every penny: "Hard labour indeed it was done after the rehearsal at Bath on a Monday morning I had to go and act at Bristol in the evening of the same day … a drive of 12 miles."[290]

Some people believe that Sarah's ghost continues to haunt both the Bath Theatre Royal and the Bristol Old Vic; architect Andrzej Blonski, who claims to have seen her ghost, told the BBC in 2010: "[Bristol Old Vic has] got a very strong spirit – the spirit of the people who have passed through it and I connect to that."[291]

MONICA SJÖÖ

1938-2005, ARTIST, CAMPAIGNER

"Monica was a writer, feminist, formidable networker and activist, eco-witch, anarchist, founder member, in 1969, of Bristol Women's Liberation and inspiration behind Amu Mawu[292], a Bristol women's spirituality group," wrote Monica Sjöö's friend Pat VT West in her 2005 obituary in *The Guardian*. "In the 1980s, with 100 Greenham [Common Women's Peace Camp] women, she walked across prohibited land to celebrate on the sarsen stones at Stonehenge at the full moon's eclipse."[293]

Born in Sweden to artist parents, Monica had a different view of the world to her British sisters. In Sweden, women kept their names when they married and single mothers were given support. After marrying a British man and moving to Bristol in the mid-1950s, Monica was shocked to discover that not everywhere was

290 Lorna Brierley, Helen Reid, (2000). *Go Home and Do the Washing!* Bristol: Broadcast. 100.
291 http://news.bbc.co.uk/local/bristol/hi/people_and_places/newsid_8803000/8803333.stm
292 Please see Angela Rodaway's entry in this book for a little more about Amu Mawu.
293 https://www.theguardian.com/news/2005/sep/23/guardianobituaries.artsobituaries1

as enlightened as Sweden. After nine years of marriage, Monica had had enough of repression and returned to Sweden with her two sons and joined the feminist movement there.

By 1969, Monica was back in Bristol where she had joined with other women involved with the emerging feminist movement in the city. Burdened by a constant sense of anger and resentment at the appalling way women were treated generally, Monica began to channel her energies into art and painting. The topics of motherhood and abortion were close to her heart, and these became areas she specialised in both as a writer and an artist, and she traced the history of abortion back to early Egyptian and Goddess cultures. Viv Honeybourne wrote in an article about Monica: "She also made the connection between 'witches' being early healers and midwives, at a time when nobody in this country was making that kind of connection."[294]

While in Bristol, Monica's activities ranged from founding the Women and Contraception Campaign, starting the Bristol Gay Women's Group (by the 1970s, Monica had fallen in love with a woman), helped establish the Matriarchy Resource and Research Study Group in London, joined Wages for Housework, and been a part of the Sistershow theatre group[295]. Throughout all of this, Monica continued making art centered on her devotion to the Goddesses and exhibiting it whenever the situation arose, preferably at all-female exhibitions. The tragic deaths of two of her three sons (one killed in an accident, another by cancer) fuelled her creativity. A meeting with the African-American writer Alice Walker (most famously the author of *The Color Purple* in 1982) when she visited Glastonbury in 1990 led Alice to sponsor Monica and consequently have her art displayed in

294 http://feministarchivesouth.org.uk/wp-content/uploads/2013/02/Personal-Histories-of-the-Second-Wave-of-Feminism.pdf
295 Please see Angela Rodaway's entry in this book for more information about Sistershow.

Berkeley, United States, as part of an exhibition entitled 'The Stones and the Goddess'.

Viv wrote: "Monica acknowledged that many women found it hard to devote energy and time to painting. Affording the materials, finding the physical space to create, was still hard for women who had been made to feel guilty and selfish for pursuing their creative needs. Patriarchal society had drained women of their creativity."[296]

One of the highlights of Monica's activism was storming Bristol Cathedral with 15 other women from End Patriarchy Now and interrupting a church mass to protest about "the non-recognition of female spirituality by the Church of England"[297], which Monica described as "a great liberatory experience"[298].

Monica's friend Pat should have the final word here: "She was a loyal friend, a prodigious letter-writer, powerful, compassionate, intimidating, blunt and dogmatic. But the love and admiration flowing around her drew people towards her."[299]

Please also see the entries for: Angela Rodaway, Beverley Skinner, Jackie Thrupp and Pat VT West.

BEVERLEY SKINNER

died 1999, CAMPAIGNER

Part of the Sistershow theatre group in Bristol in the early 1970s[300], Beverley Skinner had a prolific creative output. In addition to

296 http://feministarchivesouth.org.uk/wp-content/uploads/2013/02/Personal-Histories-of-the-Second-Wave-of-Feminism.pdf
297 https://www.theguardian.com/news/2005/sep/23/guardianobituaries.artsobituaries1
298 http://feministarchivesouth.org.uk/wp-content/uploads/2013/02/Personal-Histories-of-the-Second-Wave-of-Feminism.pdf
299 https://www.theguardian.com/news/2005/sep/23/guardianobituaries.artsobituaries1
300 Please see Angela Rodaway's entry in this book for more information about Sistershow.

her dramatic performances, she was also writing and creating art right up until her death from cancer in 1999. Beverley described herself as "the daughter of the English Renaissance", and after she died her son found a large manuscript among her possessions entitled *The Paradise on Earth Project*. This manuscript was based on 30 years of messages that Beverley believed she had received from the spirit world. As such, her son donated the manuscript to the Theosophical Society... who promptly returned it believing it to be cursed.[301]

Please also see the entries for: Angela Rodaway, Monica Sjöö, Jackie Thrupp and Pat VT West.

PHYLLIS SMALE

dates unknown, DRAMA TEACHER

Actor Phyllis Smale ran the Hicks-Smale Drama School on Durdham Downs with her friend Mrs Cutherbert Hicks. One of their most memorable students was the (then unknown) actor Deborah Kerr, who was Phyllis' niece and was persuaded to travel 20 miles each day from her home in Weston-super-Mare to attend classes in Bristol. It was Phyllis who would introduce a young Deborah to radio work and who would direct Deborah in her debut stage performance in 1937.

Please also see the entry for: Deborah Kerr.

301 Deborah M Withers, (2011). *Sistershow Revisited: Feminism in Bristol 1973-1975*. Bristol: Hammer-On. 101.

EMMA SMITH
1848-1886, TRADES UNIONIST

Schoolteacher's daughter Emma Smith moved to Bristol after her marriage to philosopher Thomas Paterson, who was a Secretary of working men's clubs in the city. After reading a paper about the plight of working women, Emma set up the first trades union for women workers: the Women's Protective and Provident League. Emma decided to avoid the controversial word 'union' initially, so as not to deter the fragile middle-class egos who wouldn't like to think of working women being empowered to unionise. However, in 1874 the League nailed its colours to the mast and changed its name to the National Union of Working Women.

After teaming up with intellectual Edith Simcox, who ran a workroom for Bristol shirtmakers, Emma was able to strengthen the reach of the league/union. This was doubtless aided by the fact Edith was good friends with the novelist George Eliot (the pen name of Mary Anne Evans), who had excellent connections.

This indomitable trio made great strides for working women. They would ruffle the feathers of employers and industrialists by, for instance, turning up at the all-male Trades Union Congress in 1875 and demanding equal pay for women. Although it took another century for some change to be affected in real terms (thanks in no small part to the strike by the women workers at Ford's Dagenham factory in 1968), the work of Emma and Edith undoubtedly set the wheels in motion. In 2018, equal pay for women is still a long way off for many but the situation is vastly improved from what it was.

Despite her lifetime of fighting for working women's equality, Emma herself lived a modest existence and ended her short life in poverty, surviving on just sixpence a day (equivalent to approximately £5 in contemporary money). Despite dying at the young age of 34, Emma was instrumental in starting 30 unions covering the same number of women's trades.[302]

EMILY SMITH

dates unknown, SUFFRAGIST, PIONEER

Suffragist Emily Harriet Smith of Richmond House, Clifton, had quite an impressive string of 'first woman to…' credits to her name. They include being the first woman to be a Unionist Councillor in Bristol; serve on the Housing, Libraries and Watch Committees of the City Council; take the chair in the magistrates' court; be appointed a Visiting Justice of His Majesty's Bristol Prison; and be one of the first three female Magistrates in the city. And in 1933, she became Bristol's second female Alderman. All of which definitely makes her a pioneer.

JESSIE SMITH

1865-1944, SUFFRAGETTE

Jessie Smith was born in Scotland but lived for most of her life with her elder sister at Florenceville, 81 Sommerville Road, St Andrews. Little is known about her early life but in 1908-09, advertising in the *Western Daily Press* and in the suffragette paper *Votes for Women*, she stated that she gave classes in "Voice Culture and Elocution", and added that she had been a "pupil of Mr Hermann Vezin, Shakespearean actor". This suggests that, at the end of the 19th century, she may have spent some time in London where Vezin, a renowned teacher, was based.

302 Lorna Brierley, Helen Reid, (2000). *Go Home and Do the Washing!* Bristol: Broadcast. 148.

In 1907, Jessie was one of the signatories to the petition organised by the Women's Franchise Declaration Committee calling for women's enfranchisement. She was probably at that time still a member of the Bristol and West of England Suffrage Society (which was affiliated to the National Union of Women's Suffrage Societies) but soon joined the Women's Social and Political Union (WSPU), and over the next few years became one of that society's speakers, particularly at outdoor meetings.

Jessie donated money to the WSPU and was prepared to put her professional skills at their service by, for instance, acting in the suffrage play *Man and Woman* at the Theatre Royal in Bath in May 1909. The *Bath Chronicle*, 3 June 1909, described her performance as "winning and effective". Jessie was also willing to involve herself in the WSPU's increasing militancy, and a month after taking part in the play volunteered to take part in a deputation to the Prime Minister Herbert Asquith, with the attendant risk of arrest.

In November 1910, Jessie travelled from Bristol to London with the WSPU to demonstrate against the government's decision to dissolve parliament without giving time to the Conciliation Bill, on which the women's suffrage societies had pinned their hopes. She was a member of one of the deputations that set out from Caxton Hall, attempting to speak to the Prime Minister. Once they reached Parliament Square, the women became engaged in a ferocious battle with the police and Jessie was one of 115 women arrested. She was served with a bail notice requiring her to appear at Bow Street Police Court on 19 November on a charge of "wilfully obstructing Police whilst in the due execution of their duty". However, doubtless embarrassed by the tales of police brutality that a court case would reveal, the charges against Jessie and all the others who had been arrested were dropped.

In April 1911, Jessie followed the WSPU call to boycott the census, writing across the form "No Vote No Census. As a householder I refuse to fill in the above until the Bill for the Removal of the Sex Disability is passed", and in November was back in London to take part in another WSPU demonstration. She was again arrested, this time charged with breaking a window in the Treasury. When she appeared in court on 29 November, she said "she was a tax-paying woman and had tried by peaceful propaganda to work for the emancipation of her sex, but after Mr Asquith's last proposal she threw the stone where she thought she ought to have some entrance – into the Treasury window". As a result she spent five days in prison.

As well as her involvement with the WSPU, Jessie was a member of the Bristol Fabian Society and in later years presided over the Discussion Class run by the Congregational David Thomas Memorial Church. These discussions concentrated on radical social issues. Jessie died in Bristol.

Written by Elizabeth Crawford, who is an independent suffrage researcher and the author of numerous books on the subject, including *The Women's Suffrage Movement: A Reference Guide 1866-1928* and *Campaigning For The Vote: Kate Parry Frye's Suffrage Diary*. Her latest book, *Art and Suffrage: A Biographical Dictionary of Suffrage Artists*, is published in 2018.

LADY EMILY SMYTH

1835-1914, LANDOWNER

With more than 1.6 million visitors each year, Ashton Court in south Bristol is one of the United Kingdom's most beloved country parks.[303] The majestic Grade I listed mansion house that

303 A large chunk of whom regularly visit Ashton Court every Saturday at 9am for the weekly parkrun in the beautiful grounds.

sits in the middle of the landscaped grounds (designed by the admired Humphry Repton) is the former home of Bristol's Smyth family after merchant John Smyth bought the land in 1545.

Widowed Lady Emily Edwards came to live at Ashton Court upon marrying her first cousin Greville Smyth, who donated the land for the Southville park bearing his name. Reportedly, Emily was having an affair with the Prince of Wales both before and during her marriage to Greville. When Greville died in 1901, he left everything to Emily. And with no eligible male heirs, Emily became lady of the manor. It seems that she shared her wealth and was generous to those who were less fortunate that her. For instance, she commissioned a row of eight almshouses to be built in Long Ashton between 1901-1902. The sign above the central gable reads: "Rest after toil, peace after stormy seas, doth greatly please."

The Smyth family owned much of Bedminster and Southville and had made their money from coal mines. When the Dean Lane colliery closed in 1909, Lady Emily donated the land to the community to use as a park and it was named the Dame Emily Smyth Park in her honour (Lady Emily was made a Dame towards the end of her life). The location of the main pit head can still be seen beneath a large concrete cap in the centre of the park. In 1907, Lady Emily had laid the foundation stone for what would become the Salvation Army building next door to the park and this building still stands today.

ENID STACY

1868-1903, SOCIALIST

Enid Stacy was born in Westbury, Gloucester, the eldest child of Irish artist Henry Stacy and his wife Rosina Julia Deeley, who was the daughter of a hardware merchant from the Midlands.[304] The family moved to Bristol in 1881, where Henry had a studio in Cotham. Enid studied at the University College, Bristol, winning the Whitworth Scholarship and in the late 1880s had a job as a tutor at Redland High School for Girls. It was here that she met Katharine St John Conway, who shared her interests in John Ruskin, Robert Browning and high-church Anglicanism and they became firm friends. They were later to be active in the labour and socialist movement both in Bristol and at a national level.

Enid was a member of the Bristol Women's Liberal Association in 1884 but was already taking an interest in socialist ideas. Her brother Paul was joint founder of the Bristol and Clifton Christian Socialist Society, and her father, who tried to revive the Bristol Society of Arts, was a friend of the socialist leader and textile designer William Morris. Morris gave a controversial talk at Bristol Museum and Art Gallery in 1885 on Art and Labour, and his visit stimulated Enid to read more about socialist ideas.

Her life was to take a new direction when she became involved, along with Katharine, in a wave of strikes that took place in Bristol in 1889. They were attending a service at All Saints Church in Clifton when women cotton workers who were on strike arrived at the door wet and bedraggled. Enid was so moved by their plight that she joined the Gas Workers' Union and threw herself into organising work.[305] She was able to link up with two other women, Helena Born and Miriam Daniell, who played a key role in the Workers' Organising Committee, set up to give support to men and women on strike, and they also formed the Association for the Promotion of Trades Unionism Among

304 June Hannam, 'Stacy, Enid (1868–1903)', *Oxford Dictionary of National Biography*, Oxford University Press, 2004; online edition, May 2007 [http://www.oxforddnb.com/view/article/51602, accessed 6 Oct 2017]
305 For more details on the strike, see Mike Richardson (2016). *The Maltreated and the Malcontents. Working in the Great Western Cotton Factory, 1838-1914* Pamphlet 37. Bristol: Bristol Radical History Group, Part 3.

Women (APTUW). When Helena and Miriam left for America in 1890, Enid became Secretary of the APTUW. Katharine St John Conway recalled that she often came home at midnight "with draggled skirt and swollen feet after hours of patient standing about in the effort to win laundrywomen to a trades union".[306]

In 1892, Enid led a long strike among Bristol confectionery workers at the Sanders factory. Enid's participation in strikes and her frequent clashes with police meant that she lost her job as a schoolteacher, and began to make her living as a propagandist for socialism and women's rights.

By the early 1890s, Enid was a member of the Bristol Socialist Society and the Clifton and Bristol Fabian Society, which had grown out of the Christian Socialist Society. She spoke for the Fabian Society and the Labour Church several times a week – often on the topic of women and the labour movement. In 1893, however, her activities shifted away from Bristol. Enid attended the founding conference of the socialist group, the Independent Labour Party (ILP), in Bradford in 1893 and in the same year began to live in the controversial Starnthwaite home colony for the unemployed near Kendal, Cumbria. Here, she was involved in a dispute between colonists and a clergyman who had founded the colony, and her reputation as a speaker began to grow.

In 1895, Enid was employed as a travelling lecturer for the ILP and was tireless as a propagandist, returning to Bristol in 1895 in support of the socialist candidate standing in the Bristol East by-election. For the rest of her short life she was a key figure at a national level in the ILP, becoming a member of its National Administrative Council and speaking at meetings throughout the country. She was one of the few socialist leaders who spoke out in favour of women's suffrage and wrote an influential essay, 'A

306 *Labour Leader*, 1903, 12 September.

Century of Women's Rights', published in the socialist anthology *Forecasts of the Coming Century* (1897) edited by Edward Carpenter. Here she argued that women's equality as citizens could only come about through socialism. She was forward thinking in calling for fairer divorce, equality within marriage and women's right to choose whether or not to have children, at a time when the labour movement tended to see these questions as personal rather than political matters. She married the Reverend Percy Widdrington, a devout Anglo Catholic and ILP member, in 1897, and lived at first in Newcastle and then in Lancashire. Even after the birth of her son, Enid continued to spend around six months of the year on speaking tours. She died suddenly of an embolism in 1903 at Littleborough near Rochdale.

Enid was one of a small group of women who made a significant contribution to trades unionism and to the socialist movement in Bristol in the late 1880s and early 1890s. They had all left the city before 1895 but in linking together women's rights, trades union organisation and socialism they left an important legacy for future generations to take up in the next period of labour unrest before World War One.

Written by June Hannam, who is Professor Emerita of Modern British History at the University of the West of England. June has written extensively on the relationship between socialism and feminism in the late 19th and early 20th centuries.

Please also see the entries for: Helena Born, Katherine St John Conway and Miriam Daniell.

ELIZA STEELE
born 1867, COBBLER

When bootmaker Walter Steele died in 1924, his widow Eliza Steele picked up the reins and continued the family business as a bootmaker and cobbler at 248 North Street, Southville. After all, what choice did she have? Walter's death left Eliza a widow with five daughters to support, and it was not uncommon for widows and fatherless children to end up in the workhouses. Nevertheless, Eliza persisted for the sake of her daughters and as the head of a family of six she must have worked all hours of the day to avoid that dreaded fate. Although the elder daughters Alice, Edith and Kate were just about old enough to work (as a music teacher, milliner and domestic servant respectively), there were still two younger mouths to feed. Younger daughters Gertrude and Ivy remained at school and were entirely dependent on Eliza to look after them. Local trade directories show that the Steel family's boot business operated from North Street until at least 1934, and this is testament to Eliza's plucky determination to persevere for the sake of her young female family in the face of unimaginably hard times.[307]

307 With thanks to Mark Small.

MARGUERITE STEEN
1894-1975, NOVELIST

Marguerite Steen's life reads like a heroine in her pacey historical novels. Born in 1894, this daughter of a captain killed on the battlefields of Ashanti (now Ghana, West Africa) was adopted by Joseph and Marguerite Steen and grew up in Liverpool and the Lake District.

Her first job was as a teacher at a private school, a role soon shaken off when she ran away to work in theatre. Thwarted – for now – in her ambition, she moved northwards again, becoming a dance teacher in Yorkshire, a job that paid well: enough to let her travel widely in Europe.

Refusing to give up her dreams of the stage, Marguerite joined a repertory company in 1921, which gave her the *entrée* she desired: she became friends with Ellen Terry and was photographed by Madame Yevonde (whose picture of Marguerite is in the National Portrait Gallery, London). It was Ellen who suggested that Marguerite take up writing when acting dried up again in 1926. By 1927 she had written and published her first novel, *The Gilt Cage*.

Many more were to follow: she churned out a book a year, including biographies (Ellen's and two autobiographies), plays and 30 novels. Her breakthrough was *Matador* (1934), a success in the United Kingdom and United States but her reputation was made by a saga set in Bristol. Published in 1941, *The Sun Is My Undoing* is a brick of a book: 1,000 extensively researched pages (although Marguerite rather grandly lodged in Bath to do her groundwork) about the 18th century Flood family – Bristol timber-merchants turned slave-traders set around the Bristol-Gold Coast-Cuba slaving axis. It starts with anti-hero Matthew Flood, whose head is turned by the wealth promised by the slave trade and ends with his mixed-race granddaughter, who comes to Bristol from Havana, is initially shunned by high society and then makes her mark on the city.

Let's not pretend the book isn't problematic. While clearly against the racism of slavery it is also *steeped* in racism. Slaves roll their eyes and faces are "split in half" by "beaming smiles". Flood's (captured) African wife (who of course falls in love with him) is a simplified version of a woman and continually described in animal terms: she is a panther, jackdaw, tigress. Marguerite has a cloth ear for black vernacular and most of the black characters are poor, helpless, child-like creatures deserving our pity. Its clunking racism is even more stark set against the work of Marguerite's black contemporaries: Langston Hughes and Zora Neal Hurston were already published and James Baldwin's first work was just a few years off.

The Sun Is My Undoing is a book about black people for white people. But it cannot be denied that its enormous success forced white readers to confront the role slavery played in their wealth and power. The Society of Merchant Venturers' toxic masculinity of cockfighting, drunkenness and brawling is inextricable from their obscene riches.[308] Everything is a tradeable commodity to the merchants: Africans are resources to be plundered, while beautiful young daughters are promised to the sons of colleagues to consolidate fortunes in Bristol and Havana.

"Everyone in Bristol" has an interest in the slave trade, writes Marguerite, explicitly coupling the city's prosperity to the misery

308 The Society of Merchant Venturers was established in Bristol in the 13th century to ensure that outsiders did not benefit from trade generated in the city and has been granted a Royal Charter since 1522. As well as its dealings with trade, the Society also has a philanthropic arm. It still exists today and is located in Clifton. However, some controversy exists around the Society for reasons including: women were not able to become full members until 2003; a 2009 report showed there had never been any members who were not white; a *Venue* article claimed that despite the Society's philanthropic aims most members were not involved in charity work; and that the Society remains inherently elitist.

of Africans and lays bare terrible things that happened here, often in places still standing. For example, she describes an auction at the Llandoger Trow on King Street, where people are sold alongside ships' chandlery.

Marguerite followed up her novel with two others books about the same characters: *Twilight of the Floods* in 1949 and *Phoenix Rising* in 1952. Neither were as popular as the first, nor did any of her other books capture readers' imaginations in the same way. She died in Oxfordshire in 1975 and, although her works have never been part of the literary canon, she was made a Fellow of the Royal Society of Literature in 1951.

Written by Kim Renfrew, who is a South Walian, ex-Amsterdammer and adopted Bristolian who writes (especially from an LGBT angle) and edits things.

Please also see the entry for: Ellen Terry.

JESSIE STEPHEN

1893-1979, SUFFRAGETTE, POLITICIAN[309]

Suffragist, trades unionist, politician, pacifist, lifelong women's rights campaigner. Even at the age of 85, Jessie Stephen was attending up to three women's rights meetings each week. The woman was unbreakable.

Born in 1893 in Glasgow to a socialist family, Jessie was the eldest of 11 children. Although hoping to become a teacher, she was obliged to leave school at the age of 14 and go into domestic service

309 An earlier version of this article by Jane Duffus appeared on http://www.theheroinecollective.com/jessie-stephen/ on 4 October 2015 and is reproduced here with permission.

when her father lost his job. And it was as a maid in 1912 that she received her first taste of activism by organising maidservants in Glasgow into the Scottish Federation of Domestic Workers. Jessie would knock on the back doors of the wealthy homes in Glasgow and enlist her sister maidservants to fight against exploitation.

By the age of 16, she was also Vice Chair of the Independent Labour Party in Glasgow, as well as a militant member of the Women's Social and Political Party (WSPU) in the city. While wearing her maid's uniform, Jessie blended into the bustling street scene, putting her in an easy position to join the WSPU in their campaign to destroy the contents of letterboxes in protest at their voices not being heard. "I was able to drop acid into the postal pillar boxes without being suspected because I walked down from where I was employed in my cap and apron ... nobody would ever suspect me of dropping acid through the box," she recalled afterwards. "As the women passed a pillar box they dropped in a lighted match or a wee drop of acid. Who would have suspected those timid downstairs maids of doing such a thing?"

When Jessie heard that one of the WSPU's leaders Sylvia Pankhurst was heading to Glasgow to set up a branch of the Workers' Suffrage Federation, she made it her business to be introduced to the famous suffragette and was rewarded with an invitation to work with Sylvia in London.

Working in the front line of the suffragette movement with the WSPU's leaders, Jessie managed to avoid imprisonment despite her involvement with schemes such as smuggling Emmeline Pankhurst past a police blockade to speak at a rally. "Police, five deep, had surrounded St Andrew's Hall in Glasgow. They were on the roof and posted at every door and window. The objective was to prevent Emily [sic] Pankhurst from addressing a packed meeting," wrote the *Bristol Evening Post*, who interviewed Jessie in 1978. "The meeting began with the police confident that

Jessie Stephen illustration by Jenny Howe

they had reached their objective. Then Jessie announced, 'Ladies! Our leader!' And out of the wings stepped Emily [sic]. They had smuggled her past the police in the laundry basket where she remained on stage all day as the police searched for her."[310]

Although Emmeline attempted to call a halt to all suffragette activities once war was declared in 1914, Jessie was reluctant to stop. She promptly left the WSPU and went to work full-time with Sylvia's East London Workers' Suffrage Federation. One of Jessie's first tasks was to organise an open-air meeting in Hackney. "After half an hour of throwing my voice into space, very slowly passers-by came closer to the platform, usually a chair or box borrowed from a shopkeeper," remembered Jessie.

Sylvia soon dispatched the Glaswegian into the provinces to rally yet more troops to the cause of female emancipation. The constant police surveillance failed to ruffle Jessie's feathers and she shrugged off the ready attendance of officers at her rallies saying: "Detectives attended all meetings and took shorthand notes of the speeches ... One of them always approached the speaker to ask for one's name and address and permanent place of abode."

Jessie believed that mass canvassing via open-air meetings was a way to reach the working women who might feel intimidated by attending more formal political meetings in halls. She wanted to reach "women who are so poverty stricken that they have not the necessary clothes to go out in ... This group is larger than many suppose"[311].

She was adamant that the impression that the suffrage movement and its successors were largely middle class was a "distortion", stressing that there were "a tremendous number of

310 Ian Onions (1978), 'When Premier Jim Ran My Errands' in *Bristol Evening Post*. Photocopy.
311 Maroula Joannou, June Purvis (1998). *The Women's Suffrage Movement: New Feminist Perspectives*. Manchester: Manchester University Press. 47.

working-class women". However, just as Jessie herself is excluded from the vast majority of suffrage histories, so are many of her working-class sisters. It was only via her subsequent work with the trades unions that the scale of Jessie's work as a suffragette came to light. In 1978, she stated: "It was the working women of Britain who were the driving force that led to the vote. But those who thought equality would come with the vote were wrong."[312]

Jessie's many roles included Organiser of the Bermondsey Independent Labour Party, Secretary of the National Federation of Women Workers and Vice Chair of the Ministry of Reconstruction. In 1922, she was the elected Labour Councillor for Bermondsey and worked to improve public health in the borough. She was still only 29.

Not forgetting her roots, Jessie remained committed to improving the lot of domestic staff, and was the General Secretary of the Domestic and Hotel Workers' Union. At the 1923 Domestic Service Inquiry, Jessie was a witness and "made a definite charge that domestic service as organised was an unhealthy occupation. Constant confinement and overwork contributed to this. She also declared that a number of employers were committing a gross breach of contract by supplying inferior food and providing bedrooms in which they would not house their pet dogs."[313]

Four years later in 1927, Jessie – now Area Organiser of the Clerical and Administrative Workers' Union – had progressed to fighting the corner of office workers stuck in appalling conditions. At a meeting at Bristol's Grand Hotel on Broad Street (now the Mercure Grand Hotel), the *Western Daily Press* reported: "'If the average citizen knew of the appalling conditions which exist in many offices in the city he would be disgusted,' declared Miss Jessie Stephen. People were apt to judge these by the high

312 Ian Onions (1978), 'When Premier Jim Ran My Errands' in *Bristol Evening Post*. Photocopy.
313 *Western Daily Press*, 1923, 14 June, 'Domestic Service: More Spare Time Wanted'. 10.

standards set in the more modern establishments, but in the centre of the city some of the offices were not much better than pig sties."[314]

By 1930, Jessie was still going strong for domestic workers. At the Spring Conference of London Labour Women, she asserted: "A maid has artistic perceptions and aspirations just the same as anyone else, and a mistress has no right to give her inferior sticks of furniture or a damp room in the basement, or a lumber room at the top of the house. A girl, too, needs a certain amount of liberty and recreation. She wants to dance and sing and kick up a row occasionally."[315] And at the National Conference of Labour Women a few days later, the following report confirms: "Miss Jessie Stephen said that they heard a lot of nonsense about what was being done for domestic servants in regard to supplying them with wireless sets and so on, but nothing was said about their conditions of work and about the horrible servility that employers expected."

The report continued: "They were expected to be on duty 16 and 18 hours a day. People said the girls were not working all this time, yet they were on duty and were liable to be called upon. 'I was a domestic servant for many years, and I became a councillor at the age of 22,' said Miss Stephen. 'I hope I shall be the first domestic servant to enter the House of Commons.'"[316]

Her work took her all over the globe. During 1926, Jessie toured the United States to explain the trades union position to workers there. She also spoke to groups including immigrant workers from Europe, the National Union of Mineworkers and the Socialist Party of America, and she was instrumental in the formation of the Canadian Union of Domestic Workers.

314 *Western Daily Press*, 1947, 3 December, 'City Offices Like "Pig Sties": Complain Clerical Workers'. 3.

315 *Western Daily Press*, 1930, 26 May, 'A Lady With A Duster'. 7.

316 *Western Daily Press*, 1930, 6 June, '"A Lot of Nonsense"'. 7.

Once back in the UK, Jessie widened her talents. As well as establishing herself as a freelance journalist, she also set up a secretarial agency and joined the National Union of Clerks in 1938. By 1944, she was appointed the first female Area Union Organiser of the National Clerical and Administrative Workers' Union for South Wales and the West of England, and it was this role that brought her to Bristol where she would become the first-ever woman president of the Trades Union Council. Jessie was elected as a City Councillor of Bristol in 1952 and used this as an opportunity to speak widely and loudly about birth control.

In 1978, Jessie received the MBE for her trades union work. However, she died of pneumonia and heart failure at Bristol's General Hospital on 12 June 1979, aged 86. Jessie's last address on Chessel Street is honored with a blue plaque and her (as yet) unpublished autobiography is kept at the People's History Library in Manchester.

ELSIE STEVENS and VIOLET FRAMPTON

dates unknown, NURSES

During World War Two, Bristol felt the force of 6,184 high explosive bombs.[317] And in March 1941, Bristol suffered its worst loss of life from one single wartime air raid; it was an event that triggered some truly heroic actions. Two such sheroes were Assistant Matron Elsie Stevens and Nursing Sister Violet Frampton, who worked at the Bristol Maternity Hospital. They had no second thoughts about going to the aid of a pregnant woman – Lilian Braund – who was in labour and trapped in the basement of her house, caught under the rubble caused by the

317 Bronwen Weatherby, 'On That Bombshell… The Deadly Reminders of War Beneath Our Feet.' In *Bristol Post*, 5 September 2017. 9.

Blitz. To make matters worse, Lilian's husband and an older child had just been killed in the blast and their bodies were lying beside her. She was understandably distraught.

Elsie and Violet bravely volunteered to navigate the falling bombs and broken gas mains (which could have exploded at any second) and rescue the trapped woman, despite the air raid very much continuing all around them.

The *London Gazette* reported in May 1941 that: "Sister Stevens was lowered into a narrow opening and found it necessary to lie flat to reach one casualty. The Rescue Party and the two Sisters succeeded in releasing an old lady and two children [Lilian's mother and two surviving elder children]. Sister Stevens then returned to the cellar where her patient was lying entirely covered by debris. There was considerable danger as the whole building was liable to collapse. Despite this and in an atmosphere made poisonous by an escape of gas, the Sisters carried on."[318]

Violet and Elsie stayed in the crumbling basement with Lilian as her labour progressed, working carefully to try and release her. It was 3am before they had even freed the woman's head. Meanwhile, the rescue crew above the three women was working frantically to get them all out. Lilian finally gave birth in the rubble at 8am but remained trapped in the basement until 1pm the following day, when she and her new baby were taken to the hospital and fortunately announced to be in good health.

Both Elsie and Violet were deservedly awarded the George Medal for bravery a few months later for their extremely sheroic efforts that night.

318 https://www.thegazette.co.uk/London/issue/35174/supplement/3066/data.pdf

JOYCE STOREY
1917-2001, WRITER

Joyce Storey was a success of the Bristol Broadsides publishing project, which ran writing workshops around the city to encourage anyone who thought they had a story in them to get it out on paper. Joyce went blind in her mid-60s, yet she took this as an opportunity to learn new skills and attended the Blind School in Henleaze, where she was taught to touch type. Her blindness understandably made the writing process much more difficult: "It's a long and painful process, trying to write when you can't see your words and having to wait until someone comes in to read it back to you."[319]

With three volumes of autobiography to her name, Joyce's stories about her life in Bristol before, during and after World War Two certainly caught people's imagination both locally and nationally. Joyce was an ordinary working-class girl, woman and mother from Bristol who experienced everything from work at Langridge's corset factory on Two Mile Hill Road to struggling to bring up her children while her husband was away at war, and then moving into a prefab house in Southmead post-war, of which she felt very proud... and where she had one of those rare creatures, a 'lady doctor'. Joyce's stories are important testimonies because they are not exclusive to her alone; what Joyce experienced was what countless other working-class women experienced and that is what the following examples from her life illustrate.

Describing her first day of work at the corset factory, which filled the 14-year-old Joyce with dread, she wrote: "The noise of the machines, all whirring incessantly, and the white-aproned girls with arms full of half-finished garments, and other girls

319 Joyce Storey (2004), *The House in South Road*. London: Virago. 430.

bent low over the machines, hardly daring to lift their eyes for fear of losing precious seconds in piece-time rates, dismayed and appalled me."[320] A few years later in the mid-1930s, Joyce's friend Barbie persuaded her to attend a meeting where other factory workers were attempting to form a union to challenge their bosses over their working conditions and low pay. It has strong echoes of Bristol's socialist history of unionisation that extends back to the Victorian factory strikers who had been led by middle-class women such as Miriam Daniell and Helena Born, except this time we are hearing an account from one of the workers.

Joyce describes the occasion here: "The meeting was a noisy one, with a lot of heckling from a crowd of youths at the back of the hall near the door. Several speakers expressed in their own way what they thought was an immoral system that extracted huge profits at the expense of the working class, and until we all had the strength of a union around us the capitalists would go on exploiting us. We must all stick together, for unity is strength."[321] Joyce ended up so inspired by the meeting that, despite the risk of losing her job for being an agitator, she started handing out leaflets to her colleagues urging them to unionise as well. After Barbie was sacked for doing the same, Joyce was called to the manager's office and subjected to a long lecture about the wonderful working conditions the staff apparently already enjoyed and was allowed to keep her job: "Once outside in the street, I gulped great breaths of air until the frantic shaking stopped and I retraced my steps to the packing department. I found the rack where Barbie and I had talked about striking a blow for socialism and I suddenly burst into tears."[322] This would not be the last time that Joyce would take a stand.

320 Ibid. 93.
321 Ibid. 122.
322 Ibid. 127-128.

On the eve of World War Two, Joyce and her Royal Air Force sweetheart Bert Storey were granted a special licence to marry, and like many in the same circumstances, they had a rushed ceremony one afternoon with only two witnesses. Just as many women like her must have done, Joyce describes her dismay at finding herself pregnant soon after war is announced and how helpless it made her feel: "I [told Bert] that in my considered opinion women had no control over their own bodies, and if only he had used the 'thingies' that the services dished out so easily, and had a bit more respect for me, none of this would have happened."[323] And while this might seem trivial and domestic, it is an excellent example of the lack of choice that women had over planning whether or not to start a family, and the way that women were expected to do merely what was expected of them – ie have a baby – rather than what they wanted. Which is further illustrated a few years later when, following the birth of her second daughter, Joyce's doctor advises her that for her health she should consider having no more children… something she desperately wants to agree to if only she knew how: "I felt embarrassed. I wanted to tell [the doctor] that two babies were more than enough for me, and what could I do to prevent another pregnancy? But I felt myself blushing. I could not talk about these things, not even to a doctor."[324]

After she became pregnant for a third time, a desperately unhappy Joyce tried everything to end the pregnancy: "Take a load of Beecham's Pills. Have a mustard bath. Drink loads of gin. Move all the furniture. Mangle a wet blanket. I tried it all and nothing worked."[325] In desperation, she visited her male doctor requesting an abortion and tried to make him see how having a third baby would be "detrimental to my health". However, "completely

323 Ibid. 171-172.
324 Ibid. 237.
325 Ibid. 258.

unmoved by my sad saga" the male doctor referred Joyce to a female gynaecologist who, without raising her eyes to look at Joyce, coldly said: "Mrs Storey, what you are asking me to do amounts to murder", before she added: "As far as I am concerned, you are going to have a baby, and that is precisely what you will go home to do. Should any foolish action of yours bring about an abortion, may I point out that you are liable for prosecution? I shall write to your doctor and your husband to make sure that they, too, are in possession of the facts."[326] This was the 1940s and it stands as a stark reminder of how little control women were allowed about their own bodies and choices. When Joyce experienced a miscarriage at four months, she was treated with utter contempt by hospital staff and her family, who all believed she had deliberately brought on the miscarriage and did nothing to comfort her in her grief and pain.

When the National Health Service was launched in 1948 it changed everything, especially for women. As Joyce explained: "For the first time, women visited the doctor on their own account. Before, it was all they could afford to get the kids there in emergencies, and it was common to see women almost limping with the pain of untreated ulcers, bad veins and worse." She added: "Minor ailments would drag on and on, dosed up with home remedies or ineffective commercial preparations. Now we had free hospital and dental treatments, free glasses and the Family Allowance."[327]

Joyce lived long enough to see many changes for women that brought about freedom and opened doors to a way of life that wasn't dependent on a man. When the 1970s came and brought with them the second wave of women's liberation, Joyce wrote: "There was a massive swing of the pendulum, away from the

326 Ibid. 259.
327 Ibid. 291.

repressive Victorian values of our youth and the dominant male role. It was not enough any more for women to remain passive, to endure what had always been and think things could not be changed."[328] She added: "Perhaps my dream of equality for all women will become a reality now that the torch has been truly lit and there are so many of us working towards that end. That's all I ever wanted, all I ever fought for. The most important things in life are equality and freedom."[329]

Joyce's three books really throw open the reality of being a working-class woman in 20th-century Bristol and can be read in a collected anthology re-published by Virago in *The House in South Road*. As Joyce's daughter Pat Thorne said: "Joyce's story is riveting ... because she tells it with such brutal honesty and self-deprecating humour."[330]

CAROLINE STURGE

1861-1922, DOCTOR

Inspired by her brother William Sturge and his wife, Caroline Sturge (known as Dot) was drawn to medicine from an early age. William was a lecturer at the distinguished London School of Medicine for Women and Dot also wanted to be a doctor. However, her parents would not agree to her leaving home to study medicine and she had to wait until, in 1883, she received an annuity from an uncle and could fund her own studies.

After qualification, Dot worked in the New Hospital for Women, then ran a midwifery practice in London and worked as a consultant at the Elizabeth Garrett Anderson Hospital.

328 Ibid. 400.
329 Ibid. 431.
330 Pat Thorne in Joyce Storey (2004), *The House in South Road*. London: Virago. 435.

In her later years, she moved to the Quaker village of Winscombe, Somerset, and used her inheritance to hire an architect to build a house for her and her friend Jane Gay to retire in. Dot was never fully retired though, and continued to work at the District Nursing Society, the Committee of the County Institutions for Mentally Handicapped Children and as an examiner on the Central Midwives' Board.

Please also see the entries for: Elizabeth Sturge, Emily Sturge, Helen Sturge and Mary Sturge.

ELIZABETH STURGE

1849-1944, PHILANTHROPIST

In line with the rest of her kind-hearted Quaker family, Elizabeth Sturge also took up a wide number of positions to further the welfare of those less fortunate. Among her roles, she was a Manager and Honorary Secretary of her friend Mary Carpenter's Red Lodge (and assumed more authority at the Lodge after Mary's death in 1877) and a co-founder of Redland High School for Girls (of which her sister Emily was on the committee). Elizabeth was very involved with charitable organisations, and her 1898 article 'The Charities of Bristol' was published in the journal *Charity Organisation Review*. She became the first of her sisters to find regular paid work when she began teaching at the Friends' Sunday School.

Elizabeth and Emily attended the Lectures for Ladies series in Clifton at the University College from 1876. Elizabeth wrote: "There were a large number of young women who could never hope to become students at Oxford or Cambridge – for their benefit a system of local lectures to ladies was established. We were fortunate in having in Clifton a circle of enlightened men and women [among] whom the idea was warmly taken up ... Of course such a method of study was very unsystematic, one jumped from one subject to another, but the mental stimulus was of lasting value. We read diligently and every week handed in papers signed by a number of pseudonyms – such was the dread at that time of having your name known in such a connection. There was great excitement when the [marks] were read out – some, who had not attained the position they hoped for, were even known to weep!"[331]

After hearing of a post assisting housing reformer Octavia Hill in London, Elizabeth moved to the capital for a few years and the experience gave her a great understanding of the need to replace slum housing with homes that were fit for purpose. When property in Bristol's Barton Hill was bought with the intention of forming a University Settlement and repairing old cottages on the site, Elizabeth oversaw the project to ensure it was done well.

Emboldened by this, in 1907 Elizabeth and Dr Eliza Walker Dunbar teamed up to provide a garden suburb in Bristol; an initiative that had been successful in other cities. The idea was to provide low-cost housing in pleasant suburban surroundings, with the aim that living comfortably and in fresh air would improve the health and lives of the workers who lived in the houses. A 26-acre site was found in Shirehampton and 14 houses were built there.

Please also see the entries for: Mary Carpenter, Eliza Walker Dunbar, Caroline Sturge, Emily Sturge, Helen Sturge and Mary Sturge.

331 Elizabeth Sturge (1878) in Helen Reid, (2005). *Life in Victorian Bristol*. Bristol: Redcliffe Press. 49.

EMILY STURGE

1847-1892, PHILANTHROPIST, SUFFRAGIST

You may think that the Women's Equality Party (founded in 2015) was the first women-only political organisation but you would think wrong. Because the Bristol Women's Liberal Association, founded in 1881 by 34-year-old Emily Sturge, actually claims this honour. The Association aimed to "diffuse knowledge on political questions of general and local interest" and to engage women in politics. It also had no truck with any political candidates who did not support women's suffrage, a topic on which Emily lectured around the country for ten years.

Emily was one of several sisters in the large Sturge family, who were a prominent Quaker family throughout the Victorian United Kingdom, especially Bristol. Emily and her sister Elizabeth were the most active in terms of philanthropy but all of the sisters were concerned with women's suffrage and with improving the quality of life for those less fortunate than themselves.

Along with Lilias Ashworth Hallett and Helen Blackburn, Emily was a member of the League of the Unrepresented, which was on the conservative end of the liberal spectrum. Elizabeth Crawford writes: "The intention may have been to unite opinion in a city where support for women's suffrage was particularly associated with the Liberal Party and also to broaden the appeal of the suffrage society to include all women ratepayers."[332] However, the League was not able to hold the middle ground it wanted and by the end of 1888 Bristol remained affiliated to Millicent Fawcett's burgeoning Central Committee, of which the many Sturge sisters stayed supporters.

The year before this, Emily had become the youngest person

332 Elizabeth Crawford (2006), *The Women's Suffrage Movement in Britain and Ireland: A Regional Survey*. London: Routledge. 131.

ever to be voted onto the Bristol School Board, a position she held until her death in 1892. She was also (take a deep breath) a founder of the Bristol Educational Council, on the committee for the Redland High School for Girls (where she was described as "a tower of strength"[333]), Honorary Secretary of the Bristol Society for Women's Suffrage, and she organised fundraising campaigns to help save the University College's English and History departments when they were under threat. Quite when she found time to sleep is unknown.

Emily tragically died aged just 45 after fracturing her skull while out horse-riding with her sister Helen. Emily's death had a devastating impact on Bristol and her sister Elizabeth later wrote that it was felt to be a great loss for everyone due to the wide range of good works that Emily had been involved with.

Please also see the entries for: Helen Blackburn, Lilias Ashworth Hallett, Caroline Sturge, Elizabeth Sturge, Helen Sturge and Mary Sturge.

HELEN STURGE

1858-1945, SUFFRAGIST, EDUCATIONALIST

As with many Victorian spinsters, Helen Maria Sturge was a 'home daughter', which is a polite way of saying she was expected to remain a spinster and care for her parents in lieu of having her own family. But Helen was keen to improve herself and followed her home education with the Lectures for Ladies series in Clifton and by taking a course at the University College. Egyptology and the Orient particularly interested Helen and she took a solo trip

333 Lorna Brierley, Helen Reid, (2000). *Go Home and Do the Washing!* Bristol: Broadcast. 65.

to Cairo and the Nile, which was extraordinarily bold for the time. A few years later, Helen and her sister Elizabeth would take a trip to Sudan.

Back in Bristol, Helen became Assistant Honorary Secretary of the Bristol Women's Liberal Association in 1890, alongside her sister Emily. She also became involved with work to improve the welfare of shop and factory girls via the Preventative Mission. Following her father's death (and despite their mother's disapproval), Helen and her sisters were able to devote themselves to the cause of women's suffrage full time, becoming the third generation of Sturge women to campaign for votes for women.

True to her political beliefs Helen stood in the 1908 elections, which were the first city council elections in which women were eligible to stand. However, she was unsuccessful. But what she *was* successful at was more significant than what she was not. Among her other achievements, Helen was a committee member of the Bristol branch of the National Union of Women Workers which, in the dawn of World War One, helped to implement the country's first-ever women's police training school in Bristol.

Please also see the entry for: Rosa Pease, Caroline Sturge, Elizabeth Sturge, Emily Sturge and Mary Sturge.

MARY STURGE

1852-1929, TEACHER

Known affectionately as Carta, the fourth Sturge sister was considered the most intelligent. This might have set Mary Charlotte Sturge up for her future role as a teacher, whether at the Friends' Sunday School or as a governess. Regretting her lack of formal qualifications, Carta enrolled at the University College to study for the Cambridge Higher Local exams, which she passed after three years.

With an enthusiastic report from her tutor Mary Paley Marshall, Carta was able to go to Newnham College at Cambridge and study Moral Sciences, which she passed in 1887 – although she was not awarded her degree until 1923 because, well, she was a woman. After studying at Cambridge, Carta was able to lecture on moral philosophy at universities all around the country.

Please also see the entry for: Mary Paley Marshall, Caroline Sturge, Elizabeth Sturge, Helen Sturge and Emily Sturge.

MARY TALBOT

1690-1735, MOTHER

The mistress of Lacock Abbey following her marriage to John Ivory MP, long-suffering Mary Talbot spent much of her marriage in an invalided state as she bore him child after child, despite the fact that each pregnancy made her weaker and weaker… leading ultimately to her early death at the age of 45, and leaving behind four surviving children.

John's letters frequently refer to his wife having a "disorder", "fits" and being "weak in her limbs". Regular relapses occurred and medical bills were racked up, plus a move to Bath where John hoped the city's famous spa waters might help his ailing wife who was prone to "giddiness" and "fainting". Despite her chronic illnesses, John continued to father children with Mary, which put a further strain on her health, and this time the couple moved to Bristol for better medical care. A string of miscarriages are then referred to in John's letters, and the reader cannot help but feel sorry for his poor wife and the continued pressure she was under to keep bearing children despite being so unwell. On 17 October 1735, John wrote: "My poor dear Wife that was so unfortunate as to lose her senses by a fever ten years and half ago dyed of a mortification in four days occasioned by Pricking a Tendon in her arm in bleeding." Mary's story is, if anything, an example that despite wealth and luxury, a woman's role in the 18th century was seen chiefly as child-bearer.[334]

MARGARET PRIESTMAN TANNER
1817-1905, SUFFRAGIST, CAMPAIGNER

Margaret Tanner was born into a Quaker family in Newcastle and was the sister of Anna Maria and Mary Priestman. She joined an extensive network of family members, including the Clarks, the McLarens and the Brights, who were active in women's rights campaigns in the 19th century. She moved to the south in 1846 when she married Bristol Quaker Daniel Wheeler who died in 1848. In 1855 she married Arthur Tanner of Sidcot but was again widowed in 1869. She then spent part of each year living with her sisters in Bristol and was involved in the same radical causes.

Margaret signed the 1866 petition for women's suffrage and by 1872 was a member of the committee of the West of England branch of the National Society for Women's Suffrage. She also took part in the Bristol Women's Liberal Association, which had been founded by her sister Anna Maria in 1881. Most of her energies, however, went into the campaign for the repeal of the Contagious Diseases Acts, passed in the 1860s to regulate prostitution in garrison towns. She was a member of the Bristol branch of the Ladies' National Association (LNA) but, as with her

334 http://www.wshc.eu/blog/item/insanity-and-inebriation.html

sisters, was also active at a national level.[335] She was Treasurer of the LNA and when its leader Josephine Butler was ill, Margaret worked with her sister Mary to sort out problems with the paid agents. After the repeal of the Acts in 1886, Margaret continued to take an interest in the state regulation of prostitution in other countries and attended an international meeting on the subject in 1895. She was also, from 1890, a member of the executive committee of the Central National Society for Women's Suffrage.

Margaret also pursued her feminist aims in other parts of her life. For example, she spoke in support of the claim of women members of the Society of Friends to be accepted as an integral part of the Yearly Meeting.

Another of her interests was temperance reform. Her father had been President of the Newcastle Total Abstinence Association and his daughters remained total abstainers throughout their lives. In the 1890s, Margaret was President of the Western Temperance League and was also elected to the parish council of Winscombe.

Margaret was one of an influential group of women in Bristol that was active in a wide range of women's rights campaigns in the 19th century, not just at a local but also at a national level.

Written by June Hannam, who is Professor Emerita of Modern British History at the University of the West of England. June has written extensively on the relationship between socialism and feminism in the late 19th and early 20th centuries.

Please also see the entries for: Josephine Butler, Anna Maria Priestman and Mary Priestman.

335 Walkowitz, J (1980). *Prostitution and Victorian Society: Women, Class and the State.* Cambridge: Cambridge University Press.

SARAH TERRETT
1836-1889, TEMPERANCE CAMPAIGNER

As the wife of Bedminster East councillor William Terrett, Sarah Mary Terret (née Babbage) was in a prominent social position from which to do good deeds. And there were many good deeds to be done. Most notably, this staunch Methodist was the founder in 1878 of the White Ribbon Gospel Temperance Army, which she formed after being disgusted at the open displays of drunkenness near her home in Bedminster.

After buying a disused chapel and appointing officers, Sarah soon had 44 'battalions' of her Army in Bristol and the surrounding area. Thanks to Sarah's charisma and her skill at public speaking, the Army quickly grew, as did her reputation for "intuitive sagacity, her sanctified common sense and her unfailing good humour"[336]. Ironically, this is also where she was when she died suddenly in 1889 after falling off the platform from which she was giving a speech. Sarah was just 53 when she passed away but at least she had died "while engaged in her best loved work of rescuing the perishing from drunkenness and sin".[337]

The Terretts had lived at Church House, Bedminster, where they endured the incomprehensible grief of seven of their nine children dying in infancy. Perhaps it was in an effort to distract herself from her losses that Sarah turned to campaigning to save the souls of others; Sarah was also a Poor Law Guardian of the Bedminster Union Workhouse and an advocate for women to train as teachers. One of her surviving children, a daughter known as Sunshine, went on to do good work in her mother's memory before her own untimely death in 1903.

336 Jennifer Lloyd, (2009). *Women and the Shaping of British Methodism: Persistent Preachers 1807-1907*. Oxford: Oxford University Press.

337 Barb Drummond, (2008). *Victoria Park: The People's Park*. Bristol: Barb Drummond. 9.

KATE TERRY and ELLEN TERRY
1847-1928 and 1844-1924, ACTORS

Bristol is associated with the early careers of two rising stars of the 19th-century stage, Ellen Terry and her older sister Kate. Training for the stage began at a very young age and their parents took them on theatrical tours to many different towns and cities. In 1856, Ellen made her stage debut at the age of nine years with the role of Mamillius in Charles Kean's production of *The Winter's Tale*. In 1861, five years later, she joined her sister Kate at the Theatre Royal (now the Bristol Old Vic), which was then under the management of James Henry Chute.

Bristol was a very special place for Ellen in other ways. It was where she met the charismatic Edward Godwin, who was to become one of the most influential figures in her life. He was trained as an architect but had an avid interest in the theatre and other arts. Both Terry sisters visited Godwin's house in Portland Square, St Paul's, in the early 1860s for Shakespeare readings.

A few years later, marriage brought a temporary end to both Terry sisters' stage careers and an entrance into a different social circle. Ellen's marriage in 1864 to the artist George Frederic Watts was short-lived. In 1867, Kate married Arthur Lewis and their grand house, Moray Lodge in Kensington, London, became a vibrant cultural salon. Meanwhile, Ellen was effectively in exile from polite society when she set up home with Godwin in Hertfordshire and raised their two children Edith and Edward. In 1874, when the relationship with Godwin came to an end, Ellen was obliged to return to work.

In 1878, she joined Henry Irving's Lyceum Theatre Company and developed an international reputation as a Shakespearean actor. She achieved great success and great wealth, which enabled her to support her children and the extended family. She was in a position to help when, in 1893, Kate asked to borrow £5,000 (approximately £300,000 in contemporary money) when Lewis's business was failing and Kate was briefly obliged to resume her stage career. Ellen's generosity and various unforeseen difficulties meant that retirement was never a possibility for her. However, both Ellen and Kate became role models for the younger generation, notably Kate's grandson Sir John Gielgud, who became one of the leading actors of the 20th century.

When Ellen went on tour, Bristol was one of her favoured destinations. In the summer of 1904, the financial success of the tour was urgently required to recoup the losses incurred after her brief management of the Imperial Theatre in London. Ellen must have felt confident that her productions at the Prince's Theatre in Bristol would attract a large and sympathetic audience. The plays were well-chosen to enhance Ellen's emotional appeal. She played the title role in Charles Reade's play *Nance Oldfield,* about the 18th-century performer who was noted for her success on stage and her independence in her personal relationships. Ellen also played the long-suffering Kniertje in the Dutch play by Herman Heijermans, *The Good Hope,* about a maritime disaster in which a fishing community is devastated by a tragic loss.

Ellen's two children trained as performers with the Lyceum Theatre company before they found their niche. They both turned towards the emerging role of the director and the artistic design of the overall theatre production. In Ellen's 1904 tour, her son Edward Gordon Craig produced *Much Ado About Nothing* at the Prince's Theatre. Less than a decade later, he designed *Hamlet* for Konstantin Stanislavsky's influential production at the Moscow Art Theatre.

Meanwhile, her daughter Edith Craig found new opportunities with the women's suffrage movement. She became renowned for the productions of women's suffrage plays. One

Ellen Terry illustration by Carrie Love

of the most successful was Cicely Hamilton's play *A Pageant of Great Women*. Edith staged it at least 13 times all over the United Kingdom between 1909-12. It was produced in Bristol at the Princes' Theatre on 5 November 1910 for the Women's Social and Political Union (WSPU). Annie Kenney was the principal WSPU Organiser in Bristol at this time and was involved in correspondence with Edith about the production, and she sent a letter of thanks afterwards. As a major city and centre for cultural and political innovation, Bristol attracted such events and had a secure place in the schedules of theatrical tours. For the Terry family, Bristol held special memories as it was associated with the early days of their remarkable family history.

Written by Professor Katharine Cockin, who works in the Department of Literature, Film and Theatre Studies at the University of Essex. She has been researching Ellen Terry and her daughter Edith Craig for more than 20 years. Katharine is also the editor of *The Collected Letters of Ellen Terry* (Taylor & Francis, 2010-) and, most recently, *Edith Craig and the Theatres of Art* (Methuen Drama, 2017).

Please also see the entries for: Annie Kenney, Sarah Macready and Marguerite Steen.

ANNA THOMAS

born 1810, EDUCATIONALIST

Mary Carpenter's sister Anna Thomas married a philanthropist and member of an established Bristol manufacturing family. Consequently, with a supportive husband, Anna became a member of several committees, including those running Park

Row Industrial School and Red Lodge. Following Mary's death, Anna also became involved in the running of the memorial Mary Carpenter Working Women's Home. By 1880, Anna was a Vice President of the Bristol Women's Liberal Association and was active in the campaign to repeal the Contagious Diseases Acts.

Please also see the entry for: Mary Carpenter.

ETHEL THOMAS

1925-2008, HISTORIAN

Keen local historian Ethel Annie Thomas moved to Dursley Road, Shirehampton in 1937, when her father got a job at the Avonmouth Dock Junction Signalbox. Following an education at Portway Senior Girls' School, Ethel found work at the CWS Flour Mills in Avonmouth and moved to 55 Cook Street with her new husband. Ethel wrote short articles about the history of Avonmouth, Shirehampton and Sea Mills for the local newspaper, and used these articles as the basis for a number of popular books about the history of the area, several of which went into re-prints because they kept selling out.

KATHLEEN THOMAS

1906-1987, SWIMMER

Although many men had attempted it, by 1927 nobody had successfully swum across the Bristol Channel between Penarth, Wales, and Weston-super-Mare, England. That all changed on 5 September 1927 at 4.15am, when 21-year-old Kathleen Thomas from Penarth put on her swimming cap and plunged into the icy waters. With the wetsuit yet to be invented, Kathleen wore only a swimming costume, goggles and cap, and she was sustained simply by hot beef tea and chunks of chocolate handed to her from a support boat. Rousing music was played to her via a cranked-up gramophone onboard the boat.

While the journey is technically 11 miles, by the time treacherous tidal flows are accounted for the distance covered is equivalent to 22 miles. And it is not a smooth journey: with an assortment of headlands, islands and sandbanks all jostling for space in the same stretch of water, there is a real risk that if the strong current hurls a swimmer the wrong way, then the swimmer will be very badly injured. In a press conference immediately after the swim, Kathleen told reporters: "It was very hard going all the way, but the most difficult struggle came near the Holms [islands], when I appeared to be taking one strong forward and being dragged back two."[338]

Already a champion swimmer, Kathleen had spent months preparing herself for the challenge, despite a lack of support from those around her. She later said of the swim, which took her seven hours and 20 minutes: "The experts said it was an impossibility. And I am afraid I got very little encouragement. I knew well the difficulties that I should have to conquer. It was an eerie and creepy experience stepping into the water at zero hour, but I soon became used to the darkness."[339] Indeed, there were those who were so unbelieving that Kathleen had achieved this seemingly impossible feat that the *South Wales Echo* had to follow up its initial story about her triumph with a second story the next day confirming that it definitely was true.

Her great swim propelled Kathleen to the status of celebrity

338 Eugene Byrne, 'The Experts Said it Was Impossible, Kathleen Proved Them All Wrong' in *Bristol Times*, 5 September 2017. 2-3.
339 Ibid. 2-3.

and she became a much sought-after swimming teacher and even occupied the support boat that later assisted other women who attempted to follow in her own waves. Following her death in 1987, Kathleen's ashes were scattered in the Bristol Channel, while her record for swimming the Channel remained unbroken until the 1990s.

SYBIL THORNDIKE

1882-1976, ACTOR

National treasure Dame Sybil Thorndike's links to Bristol Old Vic go back decades, despite her really being a Londoner. After being evacuated to Bristol during World War Two, Dame Sybil underscored her love for the city by not only being a regular performer at the Bristol Old Vic but also by officially opening the new Bristol Old Vic Theatre School in 1956.

Please also see the entry for: Elizabeth Casson.

HESTER LYNCH THRALE

1741-1821, WRITER

Diarist, author and all-round patron of the arts, Hester Lynch Salusbury was born into the Welsh, land-owning Salusbury family. She married well, with her first husband being the wealthy brewer Henry Thrale, with whom she had an astonishing 12 children. As a respected member of London society, Hester mixed with high fliers including Samuel Johnson, James Boswell and Bishop Thomas Percy, as well as the young Fanny Burney. Hester's diaries of these years have become valuable sources of

English social history. After Henry's death in 1781, Hester married the relatively impoverished Italian music teacher Gabriel Mario Piozzi in 1784, which caused feathers at the snobbier end of society to ruffle. As Mrs Piozzi, Hester died in 1821 while at Sion Hill, Hotwells, where she suffered complications following a fall. Her diaries have subsequently been used as inspiration by writers including Samuel Johnson and Samuel Beckett.

Please also see the entry for: Fanny Burney.

JACKIE THRUPP

1941-1991, WRITER, PERFORMER

Exeter-born, art school educated Jackie Thrupp was wildly influenced by Dada and agitprop. Recalling their first meeting, her friend Pat VT West said Jackie had "covered a hill in the harbour with polystyrene flowers, different coloured flowers, and looked very elegant wafting about. I asked her what they were for, and she said they were there for themselves".[340] Jackie and Pat later founded the feminist theatre collaboration Sistershow.[341]

Author Nell Dunn, who wrote the 1963 short story collection *Up The Junction*, was friends with Jackie and described her as "exotic, astonishingly courageous, open and immensely creative", adding that Jackie often appeared "to live on nothing, yet was never drab or crushed".[342] Jackie featured in Nell's 1978 collection of real women talking about their alternatives to the nuclear family, *Living Like I Do*, in which Jackie speaks about the

340 Deborah M Withers, (2011). *Sistershow Revisited: Feminism in Bristol 1973-1975*. Bristol: Hammer-On. 29.
341 Please see Angela Rodaway's entry in this book for more information about Sistershow.
342 Deborah M Withers, (2011). *Sistershow Revisited: Feminism in Bristol 1973-1975*. Bristol: Hammer-On. 29.

gendered power struggles in a marriage and how she was finding new freedom in her relationships with women.

Jackie is survived by her son Dominic, who said in 2011 that his mother was someone "who did what she felt she wanted to do. She was never afraid not to conform and influenced people to do what they wanted to do in their lives. It's a wonderful legacy."[343]

Please also see the entries for: Angela Rodaway, Monica Sjöö, Beverley Skinner and Pat VT West.

JANE TILLETT

1859-1936, POOR LAW GUARDIAN

Jane Tillett became a Poor Law Guardian in the pre-war years and helped influence civic life. Jane was a working-class woman whose Bristol-born husband Ben Tillett was a socialist, trades union leader and founding member of the Independent Labour Party. This put her in an informed position to sit on the Poor Law's Board of Guardians and to be involved with its Right to Work committee, where she counted the nourishment of schoolchildren as one of her interests.

GRACE TOLLEMACHE, AETHEL TOLLEMACHE and BALOO

1870-1952 and 1874-1955, SUFFRAGETTES

The Tollemache family of Batheaston Villa (Grace and Aethel plus married sister Mary Everett and their mother, Frances) were

343 Ibid. 32.

great friends with the nearby Blathwayt family. In the same way that the Blathwayts offered hospitality to suffragettes in need of recuperation, the Tollemache house was also open to visitors requiring a rest. For instance, Henry Nevinson (suffragist, war correspondent and founder of the Men's League for Women's Suffrage, whose wife was a suffragette) wrote in his diary: "To Batheaston beyond Bath and house called the Villa. Mrs Tollemache received me (lived 16 years Burma) – now courageous suffragette with two suffragette daughters. Another married at Windsor."[344]

Aethel, Grace and their mother Frances marched behind the Bath Women's Social and Political Union (WSPU) banner at a colourful procession to the Albert Hall, London, on 18 June 1910. But they had been involved with the WSPU since hearing Emmeline and Christabel Pankhurst speak with Annie Kenney at the Victoria Rooms in Bristol in 1907. Consequently, the Tollemaches worked almost as much for the cause in Bristol as they did in Bath.[345]

On the night of the census evasion on 2 April 1911, the Tollemaches hosted the local women who wished to hide at 12 Lansdown Crescent, Bath, and kept the women entertained throughout the night: Grace was a violinist and Aethel a pianist.[346]

The Tollemaches were among those who refused to pay their taxes in protest at women's unenfranchised position and joined the newly formed Women's Tax Resistance League in 1910. Consequently, their property was seized by the authorities and

344 June Hannam, (2000), 'Suffragettes are Splendid for Any Work: The Blathwayt Diaries as a Source for Suffrage History' in Claire Eustance, Joan Ryan, Laura Ugolini (eds), (2000), *A Suffrage Reader: Charting Directions in British Suffrage History*. London: Leicester University Press. 57.

345 Elizabeth Crawford, (1999). *The Women's Suffrage Movement: A Reference Guide 1866-1928*. London: University College London Press. 688.

346 Jill Liddington, (2014), *Vanishing For the Vote*. Manchester: Manchester University Press. 162. For more information about the Tollemaches on census evasion night, please see the entry in *The Women Who Built Bristol* for Mary and Emily Blathwayt.

auctioned annually at the White Hart pub, Batheaston, in 1911, 1912, 1913 and 1914 as payment for their rates. Each year that this happened, their property would be bought back by sympathisers who immediately returned the things to their rightful owners. While the auctions were taking place, Frances would quietly hold a banner that simply said: 'No Vote, No Tax'.[347]

Under the headline 'Tax Resistance Sale at Bath' the *Western Daily Press* wrote in 1914: "A sale of articles seized from Batheaston Villas, the residence of Mrs CR Tollemache, an advocate of Votes for Women who refuses to pay income tax on the grounds that there should be no taxation without representation, took place at Batheaston yesterday. The amount of taxes required was £15 8s 9d, but the costs had brought up the total to nearly £20. Mr AC Turpin conducted the sale and the first and only bid was made by Mrs Cave[348], who offered £21. After the sale a meeting of protest was held, and was addressed by Mrs Gladys Hazel."[349]

In her diary, Emily Blathwayt records how during self-denial week, Aethel left no stone unturned in her efforts to fundraise. This included putting a collecting tin around her dog Baloo's neck with a sign in green and purple ink that urged: "Please give Baloo something to help the women's movement. Votes for Women".[350]

But as their tax resistance effort showed, the Tollemaches were not afraid of militancy in the name of votes for women. Aethel and Grace were both imprisoned numerous times for various actions, such as pouring tar into postboxes, smashing windows and cutting telephone wires.[351] Aethel and Grace were also linked

347 Lucienne Boyce, (2013). *The Bristol Suffragettes*. Bristol: SilverWood. 42.
348 Presumably, this is the same Mrs Cave who we met in the Blathwayts' entry and who "arranged everything very well" on the night of the census evasion in Bath.
349 *Western Daily Press*, 1914, 13 March, 'Tax Resistance Sale at Bath'. 7.
350 June Hannam, (2000), 'Suffragettes are Splendid for Any Work: The Blathwayt Diaries as a Source for Suffrage History' in Claire Eustance, Joan Ryan, Laura Ugolini (eds), (2000), *A Suffrage Reader: Charting Directions in British Suffrage History*. London: Leicester University Press. 56.
351 Ibid. 63.

to an arson attack that destroyed a house on Lansdown Hill.

The two sisters were among the 68 arrested on 21 May 1914 during a deputation led by Emmeline Pankhurst to the King at Buckingham Palace. The King refused to grant them an audience and so violence broke out, with mounted police charging the crowd and using whips and clubs to attack women, causing horrific injuries. Grace was released from her cell, only to smash windows at Buckingham Palace a few days later. But Aethel stayed put and endured a six-day hunger and thirst strike.

Please also see the entries for: Mary and Emily Blathwayt and Gladys Hazel.

MABEL TOTHILL

1869-1931, POLITICIAN, SUFFRAGIST[352]

Born into a wealthy Liverpudlian Quaker family, Mabel Tothill was an active member of the Independent Labour Party (ILP). Mabel assisted Annie Townley to garner support for the trades unions in east Bristol. They came from different backgrounds but shared a passion for women's rights, socialism and peace. Mabel became the Honorary Secretary of the East Bristol branch of the Civic League, acting as a bridge between voluntary social actions and the state. But she wanted to work more directly with working-class people, so used some of her inheritance after her father died to establish the University Settlement (an adult education centre) at Barton Hill, where she lived with sister Quakers Hilda Cashmore and Lettice Jowitt.

Following a suffrage meeting at the Barton Hill baths in

352 With thanks to June Hannam, (2014). *Bristol Independent Labour Party: Men, Women and the Opposition to War*. Bristol Radical Pamphleteer 31. Bristol: Bristol Radical History Group.

January 1912, Mabel began working closely with fellow ILP members Walter and Bertha Ayles, soon becoming President of the East Bristol Women's Suffrage Society. Here she met Hannah Higgins, who was strongly opposed to the looming war and evidently had an influence on Mabel, who would later become one of the leading voices in the anti-conscription campaign.

The National Union of Women's Suffrage Societies had suspended activities once war was declared, so Mabel instead focussed her energies on relief work with women and children, becoming Treasurer of the Sub-Committee for Women's Employment and the Prince of Wales Fund, which had set up a training centre for unemployed women at the Barton Hill settlement. In this way, she helped women train as seamstresses to make garments for less-fortunate people in Belgium and France.

In Bristol, Mabel was the Honorary Secretary of the Joint Advisory Committee for Conscientious Objectors, which was established by the ILP to support those who were victimised for their stance. One of her actions was to highlight the mistreatment of objectors who had been sent to Horfield Gaol and who were forced into solitary confinement, denied access to Bibles, fed a diet of bread and water, and forced to wear khaki (the colour of military uniforms). Mabel believed that highlighting what the men were enduring was a way of showing how much their anti-war beliefs mattered to them. After the war ended, Mabel worked to free the imprisoned conscientious objectors and helped rally 90 MPs to sign a petition calling for their freedom. She also read letters of support from politicians across the entire political spectrum and in her own speech she made clear what a disgrace she felt it to be that Britain was operating on a lower basis than Germany, since Germany had opened the doors of its prisons when peace was declared. It took a further year for the British conscientious objectors to be released.

After the war, Mabel became the first woman councillor in Bristol for the Easton ward in 1919, a position she held for 18 months despite the press writing her up as a "troublemaker".[353]

Please also see the entry for: Annie Townley.

ANNIE TOWNLEY

born 1875, SUFFRAGIST, LABOUR CAMPAIGNER

Annie Townley, born in Lancashire in 1875, first came to Bristol in 1913 as a paid Organiser for the National Union of Women's Suffrage Societies (NUWSS). She was married to Ernest Townley, a textile worker from Blackburn, and had two young daughters at the time of the family's move to Bristol.[354] The NUWSS had recently changed its policy to give support to Labour candidates through an Election Fighting Fund for seats where Liberal Party MPs were hostile to women's suffrage. Annie was one of the working-class women recruited to carry out this policy and was sent to East Bristol to campaign for suffrage and labour.

Finding that the local NUWSS was unsympathetic to the new policy, Annie worked via the East Bristol Women's Suffrage Society, a group composed largely of socialists and working women. She formed strong friendships with socialists from the Independent Labour Party (ILP) that were to sustain her in the difficult years ahead. They included Mabel Tothill, a middle-class Quaker who lived and worked in the local University Settlement and was Secretary of the East Bristol Women's Suffrage Society,

353 Eugene Byrne, Clive Burlton, (2014). *Bravo, Bristol! The City at War 1914-1918*. Bristol: Redcliffe Press. 76.

354 Her role as a suffrage organiser is discussed in June Hannam (2007). 'To Make the World A Better Place: Socialist Women and Women's Suffrage in Bristol, 1910-20'. In Myriam Bousshba-Bravard, ed. *Suffrage Outside Suffragism, Women's Vote in Britain, 1880-1914*. Houndmills, Basingstoke: Palgrave Macmillan. 157-179.

and Walter and Bertha Ayles, who were committed campaigners for women's suffrage and who were prominent in the ILP and Women's Labour League (WLL) respectively.

Annie demonstrated her organising talents as soon as she arrived. She made contact with numerous labour groups, including trades unions, the Labour Representation Committee and the Women's Cooperative Guild as well as organising suffrage meetings in East Bristol. By May 1913, 200 friends of suffrage had been enrolled. The campaign intensified in 1914 when Walter, who was Organising Secretary of the Bristol ILP and a City Councillor, was selected as the Labour candidate for East Bristol. His personal identification with women's emancipation was important in gaining the support of local labour organisations but there was also praise for Annie "whose tact and ability have won her golden opinions from all sorts of people".[355]

Suffrage campaigning ceased with the outbreak of war but Annie continued to work closely with Mabel, Walter and other ILP socialists in opposition to the war and to conscription.[356] Using the ILP as a base, Annie found many different spaces to express her peace activism including the WLL, where she was President of the Bristol branch. She attended the WLL annual conference in 1916 to express her "hatred of war" and to urge the Labour Party to take more definite action to stop the war and to press for peace by negotiation.

Annie's focus was always on the needs of working-class women. She was the Regional Organiser for the Women's Peace Crusade – a series of mass demonstrations throughout the country in 1917 involving working-class women that were organised largely by ILP members. She used her column in the

355 *Common Cause* (1913) 23 May.
356 June Hannam (2014). *Bristol Independent Labour Party. Men, Women and the Opposition to War. Pamphlet 31.* Bristol: Bristol Radical History Group.

local ILP paper *Bristol Forward* to draw attention to the impact of war on women's work and wages, and argued that mothers should be represented on committees dealing with maternity and babies. Annie found it humiliating that women's groups, who lacked the power of the vote, had to appeal to a male parliament in order to be consulted about such obvious women's work.

She also took a more prominent role in the ILP when key leaders such as Walter were imprisoned as conscientious objectors. She became Chair of the branch in 1916 and took on Walter's organising work, receiving a vote of thanks at the AGM in 1917. All this was done at a time of personal anxiety about her husband. In 1916, Ernest was "knocked about" at a demonstration in London against conscription and it was reported in the *Labour Leader* that "he has never been quite well since". He was arrested as a conscientious objector in January 1918 and asked for a few hours' remand because Annie was attending an ILP conference in Nottingham. He was granted 24 hours.

By the end of the war, Annie was a well-known figure in the labour movement with a reputation as a good organiser. She was Vice Chair of the Bristol Labour Party in 1920 as well as continuing as Chair of the ILP. It is perhaps not surprising, therefore, that she was appointed as Labour Party Women's Organiser for the South West in 1920, a job she was to hold until her retirement in 1943. Writing in *Labour Woman* in September of that year, Annie summarised the work she had undertaken in the South West. This involved her travelling long distances to speak at meetings and to promote the formation of women's sections.

Bristol was a key site for such work and here, Annie was instrumental in organising structures that would bring women's sections together, such as the Bristol Labour Women's Advisory Council (Bristol LWAC). She was also tireless in organising women's weeks and women's summer schools that provided members with education and training. Although it was difficult for women to exert real influence over the direction and policies of the local Labour Party, Annie's work with local women's sections did provide an important space for women who were less confident to enter the public sphere and to gain experience as speakers and propagandists.[357]

There is little information about her private life in these years. Ernest was still active in the ILP in the 1920s but his role was never as prominent as that of his wife. Annie's daughter Kathleen, who still lived at home, was Secretary of the Bristol LWAC for most of the inter-war years and edited the women's column in *Bristol Labour Weekly*. What we do know is that Annie spent most of her adult life campaigning for socialism, peace and for improvements to the lives of working women in Bristol and the South West. She was still active in her local women's section and was in demand as a speaker well into the 1950s.

Written by June Hannam, who is Professor Emerita of Modern British History at the University of the West of England. June has written extensively on the relationship between socialism and feminism in the late 19th and early 20th centuries.

Please also see the entries for: Bertha Ayles and Mabel Tothill.

EVA TRIBE

dates unknown, SECRETARY OF BRISTOL WLA

Along with Helen Sturge, Eva Tribe was a Secretary of the Bristol Women's Liberal Association, which was the first in the country.

357 A key source for her activities as a LP organiser is *Labour Woman* in the 1920s and 1930s

The Association aimed to educate women on political matters and put pressure on the Liberal Party to grant women the vote.

Please also see the entry for: Helen Sturge.

FRANCES MILTON TROLLOPE

1779-1863, NOVELIST

A successful novelist in her own right, it is frustrating that Frances Milton is perhaps better known for being the mother of novelist Anthony Trollope. Regardless, Frances was born in Stapleton where she remained until she married at the age of 30. After her husband struggled financially, Frances decided to move the family to the utopian ideal of the Nashoba Commune in the United States for a while, and on her return to England she picked up her pen and began her illustrious writing career.

Domestic Manners of the Americans was Frances' first book in 1832, followed swiftly by *The Refugee in America* the same year. Her book *The Widow Barnaby* (1839) draws on Clifton for its locations. She became known for her novels of social protest and wrote the first anti-slavery novel – *Jonathan Jefferson Whitlaw* – in 1836. Fanny had visited a plantation at Nashoba, which had been set up as an experiment by the Scottish activist Fanny Wright as a place for former enslaved Africans to move to. Despite the good intentions of Fanny's plan for Nashoba, the reality that Frances found was disheartening. Frances saw desolation, disease and disorder, and she stayed for only ten days. *Jonathan Jefferson Whitlaw* was born out of this experience.

VICKY TRYON
1897-1977, DOCTOR

For more than 40 years, Dr Vicky Tryon cycled around Bristol doing her rounds. When thick snow prevented her from getting her bicycle out, the committed General Practitioner simply put on her heavy boots and trudged around the city with her doctor's bag in hand.

Vicky was on call 24/7, and when she had a pregnant patient due to go into labour at any moment, Vicky would sleep on a couch by her hall telephone, so that she would be ready to spring out of the door and deliver the baby the second the phone rang.

One patient of Dr Tryon's recalled: "I ran across Clifton Down with my coat over my nightdress as my flatmate was desperately ill with an asthma attack. Vicky did not hesitate. She grabbed her bag and ran back with me at full speed, and on up five flights of stairs. She saved my friend's life."[358] Such was Vicky's impatience to get to her patients that on another occasion in 1920, while stuck in a car behind a large group of male students cycling slowly near the Clifton Suspension Bridge, "Vicky became exasperated by the hold-up, leapt out of the car, picked up one of the obstructing cyclists, deposited him in a ditch and jumped back into the car to complete the journey."[359] This is remarkable for numerous reasons: cars were rare in 1920, a woman with a car was even more rare, plus the strength and audacity to physically remove the male cyclist is impressive. Bravo, Dr Tryon.

Vicky had been born in Bristol and attended Clifton High School before studying at the University of Bristol, where she became Woman President of the Union in 1919 (there was both

358 Lorna Brierley, Helen Reid, (2000). *Go Home and Do the Washing!* Bristol: Broadcast. 82-83.

359 Ibid. 83.

a male and female President at that time). However, she was far from a demure and retiring character, and had something of a reputation for being a tad rowdy at times. This is one description of a degree ceremony Vicky attended: "Singing and shouting interrupted the proceedings and on one occasion a hen was let loose to fly over the heads of the assembled students and dignitaries."[360]

Like other women who were attempting to forge careers in medicine in the early 1920s, Vicky was met with misogyny upon graduation. After applying for the post of House Surgeon at the General Hospital, Vicky was only granted an interview for the job if she promised to call one of the male doctors if there was any difficulty. It took 24 hours of hand-wringing and foot stamping before Vicky reluctantly agreed to this archaic condition. However, Vicky was to prove herself so capable and skilled in the role that the hospital then made a point of only appointing women to that position in the future.[361]

As President of the Institute of Voluntary Welfare Workers and the Venture Club, Vicky encouraged members to help the unemployed, to assist homeless women in Bedminster and to support children who had lost their mothers.[362]

JOAN TUCKETT and ANGELA TUCKETT

1895-1957 and 1906-1994, SOLICITORS

The Tuckett sisters were nieces of Bristol socialist Enid Stacey and the daughters of a prominent Bristol solicitor. They followed their father's lead by qualifying as solicitors themselves – with

360 Ibid. 83.
361 Ibid. 83-84.
362 Madge Dresser, (2016). *Women and the City: Bristol 1373-2000*. Bristol: Redcliffe Press. 149.

Vicky Tryon illustration by Jenny Howe

Angela becoming the first female solicitor in Bristol in the process in 1929 and Joan qualifying shortly after.

Like their aunt Enid, both Joan and Angela were involved with progressive politics in the city and joined the Communist Party. Angela demonstrated a lifelong commitment to radical politics and supported the Welsh contingent of the 1931 Hunger Strike by bringing food and copies of the *Daily Worker* (for which she worked as both a solicitor and a reporter) to the striking marchers every day.

Joan and Angela would add theatre to their repertoire by establishing and running the left-wing Bristol Unity Players' Club, and a production in 1942 raised an impressive £80 (approximately £2,300 in contemporary money) to go towards the fund to help save Bristol's Theatre Royal (now Bristol Old Vic). The Unity Players' Club managed to continue during World War Two despite disruptions from air raids and several key cast members becoming injured. Together, the sisters wrote plays including *The Bulls See Red*, *Passing Unnoticed* and *Smash and Grab*. They were members of the League of Progressive Writers but, although they clung onto it throughout the difficult war years, the theatre closed in 1946 once Joan's health began to fail.

To add variety to her life, Angela could claim concertina player as another string to her bow, plus being a member of the English Folk Dance and Song Society. Refusing to let age be any kind of barrier, Angela could be found out busking with her concertina when she was well into her 80s… with the proceeds continuing to go towards the striking miners.

Meanwhile, Joan was able to supplement her already bursting CV by adding that she was a qualified pilot and an international hockey player. Just extraordinary. What women!

Please also see the entries for: Doris Flinn and Enid Stacey.

LIZZIE TUCKETT
1837-1872, EXPLORER

In 1870, wearing white face masks, broad-brimmed hats and veils to prevent their faces from acquiring unfashionable tans, Lizzie Tuckett and her female companions travelled through the Italian Dolomites with Lizzie's brother's mountaineering party.

Her brother Francis Fox Tuckett was a renowned Alpinist and had a peak named after him. He and several other male mountaineers scaled mountains, while the ladies rode horses through the tracks and passes. This all-female party included sisters Lizzie and Charlotte Tuckett, Miss Pease and Miss Hustler, who was the chaperone. Judging by her illustrated letters home, Lizzie clearly enjoyed herself, describing beauty and humour in everything she saw. Even restrictive clothing of long skirts and petticoats and having to ride sidesaddle did not deter her enthusiasm. "I think it is perfectly easy to travel without gentlemen," she announced.

In her earlier years, Lizzie, a Quaker from Frenchay, helped in the large Clifton and Bristol workhouses by organising entertainment and befriending the inmates. She sketched skilfully and delightfully and was mentored in 1869 by the Pre-Raphaelite painter William Holman Hunt. Her illustrated children's stories were published and proved successful.

During the journey through the Dolomites, Lizzie drew the mountain views, the people they met, the accommodation they slept in and the party members themselves. Her charming sketches depict softly and enticingly everything she saw, with descriptive captions of tender humour. In the days before en-suite bathrooms, they carried with them a folding Indian rubber bath, which Lizzie also portrays amusingly. The subject of one of her sketches shows the scene when, maddened by flies, the chaperone's horse rears on a steep and narrow mountain track, an episode that amused Lizzie somewhat.

Admired by art critic John Ruskin, her book about her travels, *Zigzagging Amongst Dolomites,* is presented in picture storyboard style. Her book is still in print in Italy, where it is called *Zigzagando tra le Dolomiti,* and in 2012 it became the core of a European Union high school lifelong-learning programme. Lizzie married in 1871 but tragically died in childbirth in 1872.

Written by Jacqui Furneaux, who has been exploring the world on the back of her motorbike since 2000. Her memoir *Hit The Road, Jac!* was published in 2017.

HELEN TUFTS
1874-1962, SOCIALIST

American activist and writer Helen Tufts made a big impression on the Bristolian Helena Born, following their chance meeting in Boston, United States, in 1895. As such, Helen was inspired to follow in four of Helena's footsteps and become a vegetarian, anarchist, communist and socialist. Indeed, such was the two women's closeness that, following Helena's death from cancer in 1902, Helen went on to marry Helena's widower, William Bailie. In 1914, Helen and William had a daughter whom they named Helena in honour of the woman who had meant so much to both of them.

Helen did not visit Bristol until 1907, when she came with her friend Beatrice Taylor for a six-week visit to the United Kingdom. When her trip brought her to Bristol, Helen and Beatrice met with the socialist Robert Gilliard, with whom Helen had corresponded. During this visit, Robert took Helen on a tour of all of Helena's (and her friend Miriam Daniells') old haunts, including their former home at 9 Louisa Street in St Phillips, where "she peeped in at the window of the house where they lived". Robert also introduced Helen to Helena's estranged father Richard Born, hoping to heal some of the pain he had felt at his now-deceased daughter's emigration… but unfortunately it was not to be.[363]

EVA TURNER

1892-1990, OPERA SINGER

Mary Rose White was born in Oldham but grew up in Bristol. Dame Clara Butt's singing teacher Daniel Rootham trained young Mary for a scholarship at the Royal Academy, where she studied from 1911 to 1915 and changed her name to Eva Turner. After hearing the Carl Rosa Opera Company perform in Bristol, Eva was determined to become an opera singer herself and joined the chorus in 1915 before making her solo debut in *Tannhäuser* in 1916. By 1924, she was the leading dramatic soprano in the La Scala Milan company. Old recordings exist on CD of Eva singing around this time, and some clips on YouTube show her to be not only an extremely talented performer but also a naturally funny woman.

ADA VACHELL

1866-1924, DISABILITY CAMPAIGNER,

Until the Victorian era, blind, deaf and otherwise disabled children were poorly provided for. So badly so that by the time they reached adulthood they had often not been taught how

363 Sheila Rowbotham, (2016), *Rebel Crossings*. Verso: London. 341.

to adequately look after themselves. Although Bristol had seen one or two schools specifically for deaf or blind children, there was next to no provision for a child with any other disability. Consequently, the dreaded workhouses were often the only destination for the disabled poor.

Ada Vachell of Sneyd Park had developed a degree of deafness following a case of scarlet fever as a child and her deafness grew worse as she got older. Not having had much of a formal education, Ada educated herself by attending university lectures, playing chess and going on walking tours. She loved to experience life and once spent a few nights sleeping outside, just to see what it felt like. All of this gave Ada a natural affinity to care for others and she began visiting families in poor areas of Bristol, offering help to those with sick children, and she eventually became known in the city as 'Sister Ada'.

Writing in 1896 of her visits to the slums, she said: "Neglected [children] lurked in dark corners, and at their relations' call, crept timidly into the light. Poor, pitiful objects with paralysed or distorted limbs sat dully as they had sat, year in and year out, doing nothing and having nothing done for them." She continued: "I dipped my head under the clothes lines, and stepped over refuse heaps that waited at the roadside to be carted away. At the end of one court a thin, sorrowful-looking girl, with a sack tied over her clothes, was scrubbing out pots and pans by a pump. She was deaf and dumb, with curious shifting eyes, behind which lurked fear. You wondered what her life had been – how much suffering had been pressed in. 'She's very stubborn. Them afflicted ones often is,' the hard-featured woman with whom she lived told me. I held out a few flowers I had in my hands, which she took eagerly."[364]

Seeing this huge neglect, Ada decided to take action and in

364 Eugene Byrne, http://historyof.place/ada-vachell-a-life/

1895 she opened the Guild of the Brave Poor Things in Broad Plain (renamed the Guild of the Handicapped after a few years). The Guild moved to a building on Braggs Lane, Old Market, in 1913; this was one of Britain's very first purpose-built accessible buildings and still stands today. "Not just a building, Heritage House provided a centre for the isolated members of Bristol's disabled community and became a lifeline for the disabled poor," wrote Edson Burton and Mike Manson in their history of Old Market. "Each floor offered a range of different activities ranging from gym classes, to woodwork and reading. Bristol's Guild members were each given a bright red membership card emblazoned with their logo – a crutch crossed with a sword – and the motto 'Laetus Sorte Mea' which, translated from the Latin, means 'happy in my lot'."[365]

The Guild offered disabled people a chance to meet others who shared their experiences, to make new friends and to learn new skills. Ada encouraged the children at the Guild to see themselves as soldiers who were being armed with the tools they needed to cheerfully take on the fight against the judgemental adult world. As well as running the Guild, Ada also organised country holidays for the children and helped them to find apprenticeships and work when they got older. In addition, she was a staunch supporter of votes for women and an ardent temperance campaigner.

The Guild operated on Old Market until 1987 and the building now, appropriately, houses the National Society for the Prevention of Cruelty to Children.

365 Edson Burton, Mike Manson, (2015). *Vice and Virtue: Discovering the Story of Old Market, Bristol*. Bristol: Bristol Books. 23.

JANET VAUGHAN
1899-1993, HAEMATOLOGIST

The food at Somerville College, at the University of Oxford, was nothing special, so sometimes my attention would wander. There were portraits on the walls to look at and one was of a woman with dark hair, the style modernist, the colours bold. The plaque beneath said the subject was Dame Janet Vaughan and that explained the name of the first-year residence I was living in. But beyond looking at her portrait when I needed distraction, I knew nothing about Janet until I read a line in a book that said a bottle used to collect blood donations was named for her. I read on and learned about an extraordinary woman, a scientist who had dealt with profound sexism during her career, including being told she was a "very naughty little girl" when she wanted to test whether arsenic was not, perhaps, the best way to treat anaemia.

Janet was born in Bristol to privilege but not riches. Her ancestors had been surgeons to royalty. Her father, William Wyamar Vaughan, was a schoolmaster; her mother was Madge Symonds, a great beauty from an eccentric family who had grown up in Italy. Janet, one of three children, was not considered worthy of education, though her two brothers were, only finally being sent to Miss Wolseley-Lewis at North Foreland Lodge in Kent, which was "an excellent school for young ladies". There was poetry and more poetry but not much else, and Miss Wolseley-Lewis thought Janet "too stupid to be educated". Janet didn't pay heed, studying on her own to pass the entrance exam for the University of Oxford and succeeding on the third attempt (she was probably dyslexic). She studied medicine, despite only knowing "a little lady-like botany", and got a first, despite apparently being too stupid to be educated. She then set about becoming a doctor, working in London's slums and developing her lifelong conviction that poverty is a healthcare emergency. "How anyone could do medicine in those days," she wrote, "and not become a socialist I find hard to understand."

But she also developed a lifelong passion for blood, especially after she switched to pathology, reasoning that the more stable hours would enable her to care for her now-widowed father. She won a scholarship to Harvard University in the United States where she wanted to study mice but wasn't permitted, so she studied anaemia in pigeons instead. She called them her 'Bloody Pigeons' and wrote a paper on B12 deficiency that became a textbook standard. She did that research into anaemia, borrowing a mincer from her cousin Virginia Woolf to mince raw liver, then taking it herself as a test. She survived and so did the patients (of course a male doctor took all the credit).

Then there was marriage – to a kind man who ran a travel agency – and children. Janet was happy but then war began to brew and Janet found another vocation. She had read about efforts to revolutionise the blood supply in Barcelona during the Spanish Civil War. Before that, blood donation was 'on the hoof': doctors who needed blood would phone the Red Cross, for example, who would send a living donor with the right blood type. A Barcelona doctor named Frederic Durán-Jordà instead learned how to store donated blood and took the blood – rather than a living donor – to the injured.

When World War Two approached, Janet thought of this and knew that no provision had been made for an emergency blood supply, even though massive casualties were being predicted. A total of eight pints of blood was stored and most of that was in maternity units. Janet, undaunted, organised an informal committee of peers in her Bloomsbury, London, sitting room, and devised a system of mass donation and supply. When war broke out, she ran one of four blood supply depots, at Slough, using a fleet of women drivers to transport blood all over London. At the end of the war, she went to Belsen, Germany, briefly to "do science in hell", then became a popular and well-loved Principal of Somerville College, her alma mater. Even that job did not keep her from science: after rising early to deal with college business, she spent all day in her lab researching the metabolism of nuclear fission on rabbits. Janet retired in 1967 but kept writing books and papers into her 80s. She died in 1993, a very naughty little girl who had changed the world.

Written by Rose George, who is an author and journalist. Her most recent book *Nine Pints*, about our relationship with blood, is published by Portobello Books in 2018.

'PAULE VÉZELAY'

1892-1984, ARTIST

Bristol was the birthplace of a woman as amorphous as one of the shapes in her artworks: the person who can quite properly be thought of as Britain's very first abstract artist was variously in her life a painter, sculptor, etcher, illustrator and fabric designer. Even Paule Vézelay's name changed shape.

She was born Marjorie Watson-Williams in 1892, daughter of a groundbreaking ear, nose and throat surgeon. At school, she excelled at art and in 1911 went to the Slade School of Fine Art, London. She did not thrive there, feeling restricted by life-drawing and the conventionality of her classes. She soon left and went to the London School of Art instead, where she was taught by cartoonist George Belcher, who encouraged her to draw from life around her. She became a success: her professional career began with illustrations for a pastiche of Samuel Pepys' diaries;

she exhibited several times and was invited to join the London Group in 1922.

Marjorie's head, however, had been turned by a different city: Paris, which she first visited in 1920 and moved to in 1926, enabled by a small allowance from her father, who admired and encouraged her art. She lived at the epicentre of the Parisian art world: her studio was on the next street to Pablo Picasso's and Georges Braque's, and she mixed with the likes of Jean Arp, Joan Miró, Wassily Kandinsky and Henri Matisse.

It was then that Marjorie became Paule, changing her last name in honour of a Romanesque church in the town of Vézelay. Although some have hinted there was deliberate masculinity about the name, she denied it. "I've never pretended to be a man," she said, stating that the 'e' on the end made it clear she was a woman.

In France, Paule's work continually developed. In 1928 she dedicated herself to abstraction, exploring what she called "living lines" and experimenting with mixed media and three dimensions, using wire to suspend her lines (the first artist to do this), then plastic to bend them.

Her close friend Arp encouraged her into sculpture in the 1930s, the decade she was elected to Abstraction-Création, the French abstract movement. And then World War Two broke out.

Paule left France to avoid internment in occupied Paris, moving back in with her parents in Rodney Place, Clifton (there's a plaque on the house, which is now owned by the University of Bristol). Naturally, she began making what was happening around her into art. Although not an official war artist, Paule nevertheless gained a permit to draw damage around the city: works including 'Bomb Damage at a Bristol Store', 'Twisted Girders' and 'A Church Steeple Amongst Bombed Houses' are owned by the Bristol Museum and Art Gallery. She also did wonderful drawings of Bristol's barrage balloon centre, staffed by women; she observed that the balloons, like paintings, were "full of air".

After the war, Paule moved back to Paris but the moment had gone. She did not prosper and she couldn't afford a studio, so she came back to London. However, she did not get the recognition that she deserved there, partly because she was so identified with France and partly because her work was still too modern for post-war London.

Paule carried on working and showing and set up a London branch of Groupe Espace, which exhibited at the Royal Festival Hall in 1955. She also changed again, morphing this time into a successful textile designer for the scarf manufacturer Ascher (her floating shapes lending themselves well to floaty silks) and worked with upmarket department stores: Heals in London and Metz in Amsterdam.

Paule worked right up until her death in 1984. She craved recognition for her pioneering role in abstract art and she got it, albeit late in life. The Tate gallery held a retrospective in 1983 and she was the subject of a BBC TV documentary called *Women of the Century* the year she died. Paule's creations are in collections of British Museum, Imperial War Museum, Victoria & Albert Museum, Ashmolean, Basel, Australian National Museum and, of course, Bristol. Tate Britain held another exhibition in her name in 2017.

Written by Kim Renfrew, who is a South Walian, ex-Amsterdammer and adopted Bristolian who writes (especially from an LGBT angle) and edits things.

ALICE WALTERS and DANIEL
born 1859, SUFFRAGETTE

Describing the Bristol Women's Social and Political Union (WSPU) shop, where Alice Mary Walters was one of the staff members, Annie Kenney wrote in *Votes For Women* magazine in 1908: "We have a list of all our meetings in one window, and in the other the big photo of Mrs Pankhurst in the centre. In the glass door we have our Votes for Women poster – we show our pamphlets and books, display our colours and scarves, ties, ribbons etc in the big window. Inside we have our banners and our literature beautifully set out on nice shelves around the shop … Miss St John and Miss [Mary] Blathwayt are the ones who have done the decorating of the shop."[366]

The WSPU shop on Park Street was famously trashed by male university students on 24 October 1913, in what the men saw as retaliation for the suffragettes burning down their sports pavilion at Coombe Dingle, as part of a spate of suffragette arson attacks on property. Armed with bricks, sticks, hatchets and more, about 300 students set off for the Park Street shop, divided into two groups. They smashed their way into the shop, looting and wrecking as they made their way up to the offices on the top floor, where they threw everything from typewriters to desks out of the windows. It only took them eight minutes to destroy the building and begin a bonfire of suffrage paraphernalia on Park Street outside.

There were two women in the building at the time of the attack, one of whom was Alice. The promised police protection never came and when women returned to the shop the next day to start clearing up, the students launched a second attack that

366 Cited in Lucienne Boyce, (2013). *The Bristol Suffragettes*. Bristol: SilverWood. 24.

culminated in overpainting the 'Votes For Women' shop sign with the single word 'Varsity'. Out of the 300 men involved, only one student was arrested and this was for assaulting an officer not for destruction of property. The students were largely celebrated nationwide for their actions. The University of Bristol also did not punish the offenders.

Taking inspiration from the Priestman sisters who had refused to pay their taxes given they did not have the vote, teacher Alice made a similar stand by refusing to pay her dog licence for her pet hound Daniel. Alice was imprisoned for seven days as punishment. However, this did not deter her from refusing to pay her dog licence for three consecutive months… and spending a week in prison for each of the three months. Alice later changed Daniel's name to Peg "because I use him to hang my protest on"[367].

Later, Alice was arrested for window smashing in London, and while in prison she went on hunger strike and survived force feeding: "Numerous wardresses sat on her, bending her backwards, tearing out her hair and beating her with their fists. Her mouth was so badly damaged that she could not speak afterwards."[368] Fearing for her sanity, the prison authorities immediately released Alice and escorted her back to the comfort of her home in Bristol. She later became Honorary Secretary of the Bristol branch of the WSPU.

Alice was also an aspiring actor. In 1910, she played Maudie Spark in the Cicely Hamilton play *How The Vote Was Won* at Prince's Theatre in Park Row, in the grand pageant organised by Annie Kenney. And in March 1913 she played Miss Walters in the Evelyn Glover play *A Chat With Miss Chicky* at the Co-operative Hall in Fishponds.

367 Valerie Pitt, (2015). *Bloody Bristol*. Stroud: The History Press. 112.
368 Ibid. 112.

EMILY WEBB

dates unknown, POOR LAW GUARDIAN

Emily Webb was appointed as a Bristol Poor Law Guardian before the outset of World War One, and was committed to improving conditions for the poor and unemployed. These experiences made her an excellent candidate when she sought election to Bristol City Council in 1929.[369]

'VERA WENTWORTH'

1890-1957, SUFFRAGETTE

Jessie Spinks was an ordinary shop girl who turned herself into the super suffragette 'Vera Wentworth' in 1908 after joining the Women's Social and Political Union (WSPU). Why Jessie changed her name is unclear, especially given her brother was also active for women's suffrage under his given name of Wilfred Spinks. As Vera, Jessie was arrested for the first time in February 1908 and sentenced to six weeks in Holloway for taking part in a WSPU raid on the House of Commons: after carving 'Votes for Women' into the wall of her cell, she had an extra day added to her sentence. Newly released, Vera promptly joined another WSPU raid on the House of Commons and went straight back to prison, this time for three months. Vera wrote about her experiences in prison in the article 'Three Months in Holloway' published in the *Christian Commonwealth* journal.[370]

Following her release from prison, Vera moved to Bristol to help Annie Kenney and Elsie Howey with the Bristol branch of

369 Julie V Gottlieb, Richard Toye, (2013), *The Aftermath of Suffrage: Women, Gender and Politics in Britain 1918-1945*. London: Palgrave Macmillan. 230.
370 Elizabeth Crawford, (1999). *The Women's Suffrage Movement: A Reference Guide 1866-1928*. London: University College London Press. 704.

the WSPU, and she wholeheartedly threw herself into activities in the South West. The three women were all under the age of 30 and, along with Annie's sister Jessie Kenney and friend Grace Roe, they formed a top-secret spin-off group called the Young Hot Bloods and pledged to undertake "danger duty" in the name of women's suffrage. Of the older WSPU members, only their leader Emmeline Pankhurst was permitted to sit in on their meetings, which were held in a tea shop on the Strand, London.[371] Indeed, Emily Blathwayt found Vera and Elsie so charming but wayward that she affectionately referred to them as "the two Hooligans we know"[372].

As well as Bristol and Bath, Vera, Annie and Elsie's patch covered most of the South West, and one meeting in Weston-super-Mare in March 1909 was particularly rowdy: "Probably the most uproarious meeting ever held in Weston-super-Mare was that which took place in the Town Hall last evening, where Miss Annie Kenney was announced to give an address," worried the *Western Daily Press*. "Almost every inch of seating and standing room appeared to have been monopolised when the meeting commenced, but nevertheless room was found for some 200 or 300 others who – having been unable to gain admittance in the ordinary manner – eventually solved the matter by breaking in the doors."

The article continued: "Miss Vera Wentworth, who took the chair, gave an address in dumb-show [mime] to the wildly shouting and ironically cheering audience, but her reception was graciousness itself compared with that accorded Miss Kenney. The audience was good humoured, buts its intolerance of Miss Kenney's views – which, unfortunately, had to be taken for granted, as they could not be heard – was marked by the

371 Ibid. 765.
372 Ibid. 297.

creation of an indescribable babel, songs (patriotic, comic and sentimental), dog whistles and rattles being brought to bear with ear-splitting effect. Miss Kenney faced the situation for 50 minutes, but was presumably at length persuaded to desist by Sergt T Brown and after a tumultuous dispersal of the attendance she and Miss Wentworth repaired to the railway station under police protection and followed by a yelling mob."[373]

Vera was relentless in her activities and her militancy in the name of votes for women. On 27 November 1909 she was released from Horfield Gaol at the same time as Mary Sophia Allen. Speaking to the *Western Daily Press*, Vera recounted her experiences of being fed by force, which began after she had been on hunger strike for four days: "At four o'clock on Tuesday afternoon they brought a nasal tube. They forced me onto my bed and six wardresses held me down. I resisted all I could but it was impossible to hold out against them. That was done twice a day until I came out." Extraordinarily, Vera added: "The wardresses were really kind to me, as kind as they possibly could be."[374]

A week or so later, Vera addressed a meeting and talked further about her experiences in Horfield Gaol. The *Western Daily Press* reported: "She remarked that there were a great many things which happened in prison which were both annoying and painful, but there were also other things which were very funny. She broke her cell windows in protest against the forcible feeding of Miss [Theresa] Garnett, whose cries she could hear. For that she was placed in the punishment cell and handcuffed. In the daytime her hands were secured behind her and at night they were fastened in front. The handcuffs used were those with which prisoners who threatened suicide were secured." The newspaper continued: "They had some special cells for Suffragettes, and two

373 *Western Daily Press*, 1909, 9 March, 'Noisy Meeting at Weston-super-Mare'. 5.
374 *Western Daily Press*, 1909, 27 November, 'Suffragettes Leave Horfield Prison'. 9.

wardresses were specially brought from Holloway Prison to deal with the Bristol prisoners ... With regard to forcible feeding, [Vera] reminded [the audience] that doctors disagreed as to whether it was painful or dangerous. They at Horfield certainly found it was exceedingly painful."[375]

In August 1910, the WSPU held a demonstration on the Downs with four platforms of speakers including Vera, Annie, Elsie, Dorothy Pethick (sister of Emmeline Pethick Lawrence) and Adela Pankhurst among others. The following resolution was duly proposed and seconded: "This meeting rejoices that the Woman Suffrage Bill has passed its second reading with 110 votes, a majority larger than that accorded to the Government Veto resolution." It continued: "The meeting further calls upon the Government to bow to the will the people expressed to their elected representatives in the House of Commons and to provide the facilities necessary to enable the bill to pass into law."[376]

Please also see the entries for: Emily and Mary Blathwayt, Theresa Garnett, Elsie Howey, Annie Kenney and Adela Pankhurst.

PAT VT WEST

1938-2008, PERFORMER, WRITER

"Tall and striking," wrote Sheila Yeger in her obituary for her friend Pat VT West in *The Guardian*. "She dressed for effect in flowing clothes, adorned with vivid scarves and huge necklaces."[377] It seems fair to say that everything Pat did, she did both for effect and with effect.

375 *Western Daily Press*, 1909, 7 December, 'News'. 3.
376 *Western Daily Press*, 1910, 1 August, 'Demonstration on the Downs'. 7.
377 https://www.theguardian.com/theguardian/2008/jul/18/5

Pat VT West illustration by Carrie Love

The Bristol feminist theatre production Sistershow, which ran from 1973-1974, is perhaps Pat's greatest legacy but there was much more to Pat than theatre.[378] Indeed, she described herself as "a hothead with revolutionary ideas".[379]

After arriving in Bristol in 1967 as a divorced single mother, Pat quickly became involved with the Bristol performance poetry scene, such as at Hydrogen Jukebox and later with the all-women poetry yurt she set up at the Glastonbury Festival (which was the only all-women space at the entire festival). Pat also started attending the consciousness-raising meetings held at Ellen Malos' flat and found this a revolutionary experience, telling interviewer Viv Honeybourne: "It was hard to find the language, we didn't know how to give voice to what we were feeling."[380]

At the St Ives Festival in 1970, she met Jackie Thrupp who was to become her Sistershow partner in crime back home in Bristol. Tired of just talking about women's liberation, Pat and Jackie decided to "move out of dull meetings [and] use art to show what we meant"[381]. The pair had attended a variety of national feminist protests and marches, and in response to these they began to create their own 'happenings'. Their first happening was at the Acton Women's Conference where they arrived in drag and were initially turned away, which Pat explained supported their argument that "you didn't have to dress in dungarees to be a feminist". They were a disruptive force, often just turning up at meetings, throwing leaflets into the crowd and constantly questioning gender stereotypes. It seemed obvious to both Pat and Jackie that theatre was the logical next step. And perhaps never more so than when they gatecrashed a Women's Institute

378 Please see Angela Rodaway's entry in this book for more information about Sistershow.
379 http://feministarchivesouth.org.uk/wp-content/uploads/2013/02/Personal-Histories-of-the-Second-Wave-of-Feminism.pdf
380 Ibid
381 Deborah M Withers, (2011). *Sistershow Revisited: Feminism in Bristol 1973-1975*. Bristol: Hammer-On. 32.

lunch in Bristol, where they marched through the doors while dressed in French maid outfits, dished out spoons of alphabetti spaghetti into the stunned guests' plates and told them to "eat their words"[382].

One of the leaflets thrown into the crowd sums up neatly the way that Pat and Jackie worked together: "Fidgeting one day in a Women's Lib Meeting, I woke up to realise that the revolution is what we do on the way to getting it ... I got up and left, hand-in-hand with Jackie, the most devastating lady in Bristol."[383]

Remembering the National Women's Liberation Conference held at Acton Town Hall in February 1972, attendee Judith Barrington was struck by the rude interruption from Pat and Jackie. An afternoon workshop was disturbed by a kerfuffle at the door and two figures in extraordinary dress made their entrances. Judith recalled: "They both wore long, elaborate gowns that hugged their bodies, elegant high-heeled shoes, enormous, sweeping hats and elbow-length white gloves, and they both carried parasols … They paraded in a circle, stepping out with pointed toes, swiveling their upper torsos to the left and right. Monica [Sjöö], however, started nudging me in the ribs. 'I know them,' she hissed. 'It's Jackie and Pat. I know them.' 'Jackie and Pat?' I repeated stupidly, having only a vague idea that gay men sometimes used women's names. 'But... they're men.' 'No they're not,' Monica said firmly. 'They're women. I know them. They live near me in Bristol. This is an action.'" Judith goes on to explain how after Jackie and Pat had made their way around the silenced room, they threw some cards into the air: "I walked out onto the dance floor and picked one up. 'Sistershow' it said. 'Feminist political theatre by Jackie Thrupp and Pat Van Twest

382 Ibid. 33
383 https://sistershowrevisited.wordpress.com/2010/10/24/pat-vt-west-and-jackie-thrupp-gender-troubling-the-wlm/

[sic[384]].' When I looked up again, they had gone and there was a buzz going around the room."[385]

Thinking about the Sistershow performance in the evening of the Bristol Women's Liberation Conference at the Anson Rooms, Clifton, Pat said it was "mind-blowing, it was wild and women were making love on the dance floor".[386] After the break-up of Sistershow, Pat continued to perform as a solo artist... in both conventional forms (eg at the Edinburgh Fringe) or less conventional forms (eg in court). Pat, who was vehemently anti-nuclear, gave evidence at the Hinkley Enquiry, which she billed as a "stand-up comic piece". Dressed as an elderly lady, Pat nervously delivered her evidence to the court, with the onlookers slowly realising that what was happening was a piece of theatre and bursting into laughter. Despite the chairman berating the crowd for the laughter, Pat claims she left the stand to "riotous applause" and considered it a triumph.[387]

After spending time at Greenham Common Women's Peace Camp, where she was a frequent nightwatcher of the Orange Gate, Pat began writing a novel and leading creative writing workshops for women in Bristol. She told Viv Honeybourne that "women had been held back for so long that when the lid was taken off, there was an explosion! We were challenging all the time".[388]

Please also see the entries for: Joan Hammond, Angela Rodaway, Monica Sjöö, Beverley Skinner and Jackie Thrupp.

384 For a period, Pat VT West was also known as Pat Van Twest.

385 Judith Barrington (2008) in Linda Joy Myers, Kate Farrell et al (2013), *The Times They Were A-Changing: Women Remember the '60s and '70s*. US: She Writes Press. 225-226.

386 http://feministarchivesouth.org.uk/wp-content/uploads/2013/02/Personal-Histories-of-the-Second-Wave-of-Feminism.pdf

387 Ibid

388 Ibid

HANNAH WILTSHIRE
1833-1855, WORKHOUSE INMATE

During the year 1855, rumours of murder and cover up were circulating in the small North Somerset village of Walton-in-Gordano. The allegations were that in Bedminster Union Workhouse[389], a 22-year-old female inmate who suffered from epilepsy had been murdered. The victim's name was Hannah Wiltshire. Within a few months of entering the workhouse, Hannah died a violent, neglected death after an altercation with the woman in charge of the workhouse dining room, Mrs Cavil. Her premature death caused local public outrage in the media at the time, instigated by her pauper aunt, Ann Howe. Ann was Hannah's only guardian before she had to enter the workhouse. Ann was illiterate and the homeless daughter of impoverished farm labourers. However, this did not stop her from attempting to expose how Hannah had died, which was through neglect and medical negligence. With the help of friends, Ann embarked on a letter-writing campaign to the local newspapers for justice. The accusation being that the Poor Law Guardians of the Workhouse had concealed the extent of neglect that existed within the walls of Bedminster Union Workhouse.

To add to her distress, Ann was not convinced that Hannah's body was even in the coffin, because she was not given the chance to view her niece's body before she was buried in the local churchyard. Her suspicions were valid because the Workhouse Guardians had the right, under law, to hand over dead bodies to medical schools for dissection if a body remained uncollected by family or friends, leading to a financial gain for the workhouse.

389 Bedminster Poor Law Union Workhouse was built at Flax Burton during 1837 and 1838 in south Bristol. The design was based on Victorian prison plans and originally was intended to house 300 inmates. Part of the building remains to this day and has been converted for office use. The "young, old, feeble minded [sic] and invalids" were mixed together.

Due to public pressure, an inquest opened on 11 October 1855 in the village schoolhouse situated next to St Paul's Church, Walton-in-Gordano. The Coroner agreed that Hannah's coffin should be opened for inspection, with the jury and those who knew her to be present. The coffin was exhumed on the day of the inquest and when it was opened the female body inside was recognisable as the deceased Hannah Wiltshire. The local surgeon who carried out the autopsy stated that although her skull had not been fractured, there was a sign of a bleed under her skull. Surprisingly the workhouse doctor, Mr Massey, as well as the Master and Matron of the workhouse, were not required to be present at the inquest.

Many pauper witnesses were called. A key witness, Mary Jane Tyler, gave evidence of what she had seen. "Mrs Cavil struck her three blows under the right ear, and then got up; deceased then had a fit and got up, and attempted to put her hands into the fire [Hannah had been attempting to warm water on the fire], but was prevented; she then again lay down in the fits … and then Sexa Marshall [a pauper nurse] and other persons took her into the Infirmary and put her to bed; on the following Monday morning I saw deceased lying dead in the Infirmary; the doctor [Mr Massey] was at the union on Saturday, and might, perhaps have seen her … but I do not think so, neither the master nor the matron of the house was present at the time, but hearing the alarm they inquired about it afterwards."[390]

After hearing all the evidence, the jurors took only 15 minutes to return the following verdict: "That the deceased's death was caused by apoplexy, but that sufficient care was not taken by the authorities of the Bedminster Union Workhouse to separate the deceased from the other inmates of the establishment, knowing,

390 *The Bristol Mercury*, 1855.

as they did, the very peculiar liabilities of the deceased to fit, upon being thwarted. The jury are also of the opinion of the peculiar circumstances under which the deceased on this occasion, came by her death. This verdict was dissented from by one or two jurors, who were for one of 'Manslaughter'".

Following the verdict, a public outcry ensued which resulted in numerous letters of complaint and dissatisfaction directed towards the Board of Guardians. The writers were outraged that a unanimous verdict of manslaughter was not reached and they demanded a public enquiry. Instead the Board of Guardians agreed to hold an enquiry in private, behind closed doors.

Ann Howe persisted in attempting to bring those to blame for the death of her niece to trial, with the possibility of them being charged with manslaughter. Although she was ultimately not successful in provoking a trial or even a public enquiry, her campaign did instigate a coroner's inquest and ultimately a private investigation by the governors' of the Bedminster Union Workhouse. This was quite a remarkable achievement for an impoverished daughter from the labouring classes and as a woman who had very few rights. The case of Hannah Wiltshire also demonstrated disquiet in the community at large regarding the treatment of epileptic paupers.

During this period, the government decreed that each county should build a lunatic asylum where the disadvantaged classes who suffered with epilepsy and other mental health issues could be sent.[391] Perceptions of epilepsy among Victorian medical practitioners were formed by consideration of class and social status, a view that dramatically affected the treatment of the disease. The condition was believed to be a social stigma

391 During the Victorian era, the understanding of 'lunatic' was a person who had episodes of mental illness with a hope of recovery. 'Idiot' and 'imbecile' referred to those who were permanently afflicted with some form of mental illness with no hope of improvement in their condition.

and the social characteristics of the patient often determined medical diagnosis. Victorians saw the working-class epileptic as a burden on society, and viewed epilepsy as a dangerous character flaw among the labouring poor. On the other hand, epilepsy was characterised as a private misfortune among the wealthy. Although doctors had a basic understanding of what epilepsy was, they were unable to detach themselves from the social attitudes towards epilepsy.

The life and nature of Hannah's death illustrates the typical treatment imposed upon the vulnerable poor living in England during the mid-19th century. Yet, despite class-based medical discrimination towards the treatment of epileptics in Victorian England, Ann and her supporters succeeded in provoking a legal obligation for accountability from the Guardians of Bedminster Union Workhouse.

The case of Hannah Wiltshire illustrates many of the significant discriminatory failings of Victorian society, mainly those of stigma and social class discrimination. The inquest exposed many fundamental issues: that key people and witnesses were not answerable to an inquest court; that the treatment of epileptics was class based; and that institutions were not sufficiently transparent and accountable to the public. The revelations from this case began a public shift of attitude towards the treatment of epileptic paupers, as well as a heightened suspicion of the management practices inside England's workhouses.

Hannah did not have a remarkable life, but her death was remarkable because the case exposed to the public the lack of treatment and absence of any compassionate care for epileptic paupers in Bristol.

Written by Rosemary Caldicott, who is a historian and the author of a number of books including *The Life and Death of Hannah Wiltshire*.

CATHERINE WINKWORTH
1827-1878, EDUCATIONALIST

Passionate about education for girls, Catherine Winkworth worked herself ragged to set up the Clifton High School after moving to Bristol with her sister Susanna in 1864, where they were attracted by the intellectual and literary circle. Catherine and Susanna had already met and befriended Mary Carpenter before they came to Bristol, and Mary's philanthropic work surely had a strong influence upon them.

In addition to establishing Clifton High School, Catherine also joined the Clifton Association for the Higher Education of Women in 1868, and the Association played a key role in establishing University College, Bristol. As if that wasn't enough, Catherine was also a Governor of Red Maids' school and a member of the Council of Cheltenham Ladies' College.

With Susanna, Catherine was a passionate supporter of women's suffrage and the Winkworths, along with Anna Maria and Mary Priestman, were signatories on the groundbreaking petition presented to Parliament by John Stuart Mill in 1866.

When Clifton College's headmaster John Percival began to take an interest in the education of women in 1868, middle-class women were suddenly allowed to attend morning lectures, as well as evening classes on topics as diverse as logic, political economy, Latin and geography, and the Winkworth sisters took full advantage. Building on her enthusiasm for learning, Catherine became Honorary Secretary of the Association for Promoting the Higher Education of Women, and organised her own lectures and talks for women, which by the 1870s were designed to prepare girls to sit the Higher Cambridge Examination.

SUSANNA WINKWORTH

1820-1884, PHILANTHROPIST

Born into an Evangelical household in London, the Winkworth sisters (Susanna, Catherine and their lesser-known sibling Alice) regularly attended three church services on a Sunday, as well as going to Sunday School (initially as students and later as teachers) and missionary meetings. Theirs was a strict family with no acceptance for fairy tales, meaning the sisters conjured up an imaginary world inhabited by sprites and fairy folk.

In 1864, Susanna and Catherine moved to Bristol where they set up home at 31 Cornwallis Crescent in Clifton, and took to visiting the poor district of Hotwells, which prompted Susanna to seek better accommodation for the families and to improve the area. A biographer wrote: "[Susanna] took several houses in Dowry Square, which were at that time inhabited by a very rough and low set of people, put them into a thorough state of repair at a great expense, and placed in each a superintendent to let the rooms, collect the rents and enforce order in the house."[392] These 90 apartments instantly raised the tone of the neighbourhood.

Building on this work and learning from one or two mistakes made, Susanna undertook the management of a Sanitary Mission in 1872, employing a woman to visit the homes of the poor, and teach them how to clean and improve their homes to better their health. As a result, she began to lecture and write on the subject of sanitation to spread the word.

Shortly after, in 1874, she formed a company with members of the Fry and Wills families to buy a plot of land and build model dwellings. The Jacobs' Wells Buildings were based on blocks of model homes in London and were revolutionary at the time.

392 Lorna Brierley, Helen Reid, (2000). *Go Home and Do the Washing!* Bristol: Broadcast. 38.

The low-rent flats (demolished in the 1960s) had water, gas and a balcony, and consequently a low rate of infectious diseases. They were a big success.

Please also see the entry for: Catherine Winkworth.

MARY WOLLSTONECRAFT

1759-1797, WRITER

Yes, she famously wrote what is widely perceived to be the first feminist tract in *A Vindication of the Rights of Woman* (1792) but did you know that before then Mary Wollstonecraft wrote her first – and only – novel, *Mary: A Fiction (1788)*, while living on Sion Hill, Hotwells? At the time, Mary was working as a governess for the Kingsborough family and used her experiences with them as the basis for her book; for example, the character Eliza is reportedly based upon Lady Kingsborough, whom Mary felt took more interest in her dogs than she did in her children. Mary did begin writing a second novel while in Bristol, which was to be called *The Cave of Fancy*. However, after the Kingsborough family dismissed Mary she returned to London and the second novel was never completed. That's not to say she didn't go on to write many other important works, however. Because she certainly did.

Please also see the entry for: Mary Shelley

PEGGY ANN WOOD
1912-1998, ACTOR, THEATRE MANAGER

Peggy Ann Wood is a true Bristol treasure. Her work in the arts, both in the city and beyond, is prolific and completely badass. Alongside her husband Ronald Russell, she ran The Rapier Players; from the mid 1930s to the early 1960s her company staged nearly 1,000 productions, which is pretty much a new show every single week for three decades… that ain't bad going by anyone's standards, especially when you know nearly 50 of these productions were world premieres.

With Ronald serving in the Police War Reserves, Peggy supported the morale of the city by keeping the doors of the Little Theatre at the Colston Hall open and the place jumping. At one point during the war, with the Blitz destroying much of the city, this was the only live theatre available to Bristolians. Air raid sirens would blast, the audience would be consulted, "Do you want to continue?" and, of course, the response was a resounding "Yes!". The Rapier Players were a beacon of light, a morsel of hope among some very dark days. If the Rapier Players were still going, so could the rest of the city continue. Peggy said: "If you determine to do something well, you determine to do it."

When the company's home in the Colston Hall burnt down in 1945 – all records, scripts, costumes gone with it – the Little Theatre was somehow reopened just five days later. This is a tribute to Peggy's tenacity, her dedication to her art and her sheer determination to provide Bristol with a constant stream of affordable, consumable live performance. Peggy was busy running her company but she also found time to direct, write and even star in lots of these productions. A talented actor, she was a recognisable face in homes up and down the country, working steadily and prolifically in TV until the mid-1990s.

Peggy Ann Wood illustration by Jenny Howe

When Peggy died in 2008, actor, ex-Rapier company member and Bristol-boy Timothy West said: "We've lost an important link with a theatrical past that young people can hardly recognise or scarcely believe in." He was right. It's almost impossible to imagine working like you're running out of time, delivering a new, high-quality, entertaining show for a hungry audience every single week. Peggy was magical. The driving force behind this decades-long artistic endeavour and its triumph was Peggy herself. Described in the 1950s as "a rapid, energetic talker with a friendly, vivid personality, this woman has a flare for imparting the excitement she feels in working in the theatre to others".

If you're walking past the Colston Hall today, take a moment to look for Peggy's blue plaque. We need to remember her name because it whispers in the wings of our city's most iconic venues and it calls to us every single day: the show must go on.[393]

Written by Charlie Coombes, who is Communications Officer at Bristol Old Vic. She is almost always reading post-apocalyptic books written by badass women, or watching horror movies.

Please also see the entry for: Violet Lamb.

CATHARINE WOOLLAM

1830-1909, POOR LAW REFORMER

Catharine Woollam was a committed campaigner for better conditions for Bristol's poor and sick. In 1882, she was one of the first women elected onto the Bristol Poor Law Board of Guardians, at a time in which it was still unusual for women to

393 With huge thanks to the University of Bristol Theatre Collection, where the Peggy Ann Wood Archive proved invaluable in researching this remarkable woman.

take up such a position. She served on the Board for 27 years. Catharine was Head of the Clifton District Nurses' Society and insisted on replacing 'pauper nurses' (unpaid workhouse inmates) with paid professional nursing staff. The *Western Daily Press* wrote: "She was always the friend of the nurses as well as of the sick, and sought to bring brightness and interest into their work, which is necessarily of a more monotonous character than that of ordinary nurses."[394]

In her obituary, the *Western Daily Press* wrote: "From the first, Miss Woollam took up her duties with that whole-hearted devotion which characterised all her many sided work. She hardly ever allowed herself any holiday, but was always in her place at board meetings and committee meetings, and was one of the first to come and the last to leave." It continued: "Every week she was with the imbecile boys, endeavouring to interest them and to bring out any spark of intellect which they might possess."[395] She is celebrated with a brass plaque in Bristol Cathedral.

DOROTHY WOOLLARD
1886-1986, ARTIST

Etcher and printmaker Dorothy Woollard created a series of images of Bristol that were published by AC Black in its Sketch Book series. Dorothy had studied and later taught at the Bristol Municipal School of Art, before winning a scholarship to the Royal College of Art in London.

Dorothy stayed in London after the war, where she had worked for the Admiralty drawing maps, and in 1914 *The Times*

394 *Western Daily Press*, 1909, 25 October, 'Death of Miss Woollam'. 5.
395 Ibid. 5.

rated her work as on a par with that of DY Cameron.[396] Dorothy exhibited regularly at the Royal Academy, the Royal Society of Painter Etchers and the Royal West of England Academy. But while her body was in London, her heart remained in Bristol and she relished commissions from her home city.

Dorothy's career suffered when the popularity for black-and-white etchings faded and she slipped out of the public view, although even in 1930 she was still being exhibited in Bristol and it was "hoped that the works, being purely of local interest, will find permanent homes in Bristol"[397]. That said, collections of her work can be found in both the Victoria and Albert Museum and British Museum in London, as well as the Bristol Museum and Art Gallery on Queens Road.

ANN YEARSLEY

1752-1806, MILKMAID, POET

With the respected bluestocking writer Hannah More as her patron, impoverished peasant woman Ann Yearsley, who was married to a smallholder in Clifton, was dealt both a good hand and a bad hand at the same time. Ann grew up in extreme poverty but despite her lack of education she had a passion for poetry that was picked up by Hannah. Such was Ann's talent for the written word that she succeeded in getting a collection of her verses, *Poems: On Several Occasions*, published in 1785 that sold very well.

Due to Ann's day job as a milkmaid, the rather snobby bluestockings referred to her unkindly as 'Lactilla'. Novelist Fanny Burney described Ann saying: "She is plain but not disagreeable

396 http://www.dorothywoollard.com/

397 *Western Daily Press*, 1930, 8 July, 'Exhibition of Drawings and Etchings'. 8.

to look at and has a good singing voice"[398], as if either point had an impact on Ann's skill as a poet.

Thanks to Hannah's tutoring, Ann's poetry was a good interpretation of the "high-flown 18th century verse style, full of abstractions and lofty sentiments".[399] The subject matter was frequently self-indulgent and self-pitying, which was typical of Ann's attitude to her life, although she also used her poetry to vociferously express her opposition to the slave trade, for example in 'A Poem on the Inhumanity of the Slave-Trade'. Indeed, such was the size of Ann's chip on her shoulder that she subsequently had a flamboyant falling out with Hannah over some money of Ann's that Hannah had invested for her... a disagreement that turned into a lengthy feud. Once she had control of her own funds, Ann used the money to open a library at the Colonnade at Hotwells, despite Hannah's derision for the plan.

Please also see the entries for: Fanny Burney and Hannah More.

EMILY HILDA YOUNG

1880-1949, NOVELIST, SUFFRAGIST

They say that you should write about what you know and that's exactly what Emily Hilda Young did. She had spent most of her life living in Bristol with her solicitor husband Arthur Daniell, so for her best-selling novels she created a fictionalised version of Clifton that she called Upper Radstowe: many of these novels were republished by the feminist publisher Virago in the 1980s.

Unlike some of the novelists in this book who took to writing

398 Lorna Brierley, Helen Reid, (2000). *Go Home and Do the Washing!* Bristol: Broadcast. 116-117.
399 Ibid. 117.

simply out of a necessity to earn a living, Emily possessed a genuine skill for writing fiction with a sense of wit, irony and sharp observation. So much so that she won the James Tait Black Memorial Prize in 1930 for *Miss Mole* (about a poor spinster living at the mercy of a mean clergyman), and her 1925 novel *William* (set in Hotwells, Clifton and the docks, which followed a marriage rocked by scandal) was one of the first ten books to be published in paperback by the newly formed Penguin Books in 1935; Penguin having a Bristol connection as its founder Allen Lane was born and attended school here.

Alongside writing, Emily became an active supporter of the women's suffrage movement, as was her husband, and they organised an evening of feminist theatre in Bristol one night as a fundraiser for the cause. Emily's sister Gladys Young was a popular actor who enjoyed a long career on television into the 1960s and she performed at the show.

World War One saw Arthur killed in Ypres, Belgium, in 1917, while Emily worked in a munitions factory and later as a groom in a stable. After the war, the widowed Emily moved to London but the affluent suburb of Clifton never left her novels.

Unusually, Emily was a pioneer of women's climbing, having developed an interest for the hobby in 1906 when a friend, Ralph Bushell Henderson, had introduced her to the activity. Ralph had been a friend of Arthur's and, once in London, Emily moved in with Ralph and his wife Beatrice, and they lived ménage-à-trois until 1940 when Emily and Ralph moved to Bradford-on-Avon to live as a couple. After Emily's death from lung cancer in 1949, a grieving Ralph wrote to his sister: "Life without Emily is just one long, long pain."[400]

400 Ibid. 133.

WOMEN'S WORK

INTRODUCTION

"Get leave to work,
In this world, 'tis the best you get at all."

From the Elizabeth Barrett Browning poem 'Aurora Leigh' which was used as the motto for The Loan Exhibition of Women's Industries in Clifton, 1885

The women of Bristol could never be accused of being workshy layabouts. Since the beginning of time, they have worked conscientiously and constructively in all manner of fields, yet all too often their efforts have gone unnoticed or, worse, been attributed to a man.

Well, no more. Because you've got this far, you will have already read about scores of wonderful women who contributed so much to Bristol and the wider world as everything from sculptors to doctors to architects to politicians to painters to teachers to spies... here we will look at the largely unthanked women who worked in the factories, of which Bristol had – and still has – plenty. And in which women made up – and still make up – the bulk of the workforce.

Although it was mostly the working-class, poorer women toiling in the factories, their better off middle- and upper-class sisters still had their backs. Without needing to be told to check their privilege, the wealthier women of Bristol used their powers for good and frequently worked to improve the lot of the less-fortunate women.

For instance, in 1875, the Bristol National Union of Working Women had been the first women's union to gain admittance to the Trades Union Congress. And by 1881 the reformers in that same Union were to be found on the executive of the Bristol Association of Working Women; this included **Agnes Beddoe**, who in May 1879 was President. The unions were supportive of women's welfare and wanted to encourage a good relationship with employers.[401]

South Bristol has a long history of mining dating back to 1748 and there were 18 collieries around Bedminster alone, providing fuel for the city's factories and homes. And while the dirty, poorly paid and extremely dangerous work was largely done by men and boys, there were also some women and girls working underground in the mines. Indeed, until the law was changed in the 1840s – to prevent children under ten and all women from working in the mines – it was not uncommon to see women and girls in the mines because they were even cheaper labour than men and boys. In 2017, Bedminster's acta Community Theatre created the play *Blood On The Coal* to share the stories of the families whose lives revolved around the treacherous mines, particularly focussing on the stress mining placed on the wives of the miners.[402] The final Bedminster mine to close was the one on South Liberty Lane, Ashton Vale, in 1925.

Above ground, things were moving at a rapid pace due in no small part to the aftereffects of the Industrial Revolution. In 1927, for example, 50 years of the Fear family's watch- and clock-making business on Bristol Bridge was celebrated with a special article in *The Evening News* and an interview with managing director **Amos Fear**. Among the many things Amos noticed as having changed in the previous 50 years, one advancement he especially welcomed was the number of women who were now on his staff. The *Evening News* reporter stated: "Mr Fear remarked

401 Mike Richardson, (2012). *The Bristol Strike Wave of 1889-1890: Socialists, New Unionists and New Women. Part 1: Days of Hope*. Bristol Radical Pamphleteer 21. Bristol: Bristol Radical History Group. 18.
402 https://www.acta-bristol.com/blood-on-the-coal/

that one of the outstanding features of business today was the number of women employed, but he thought that the introduction of typewriters with of course shorthand writers and typists had increased the capacity of the ordinary business man about three times."[403] Well done, women.

Factories such as those producing cotton, tobacco, chocolate and corsets provided many opportunities for women's employment after the Industrial Revolution came into effect and began the process of mechanising certain tasks that had previously been done by hand. Between 1915 and 1955, 36 per cent of all female school leavers in Bristol went to work in the industries of paper and printing (such as at ES & A Robinson's factory in Bedminster), and for the Fry and Wills factories that we will encounter in the coming pages.[404] By 1956, there were still more than 500 Bristolian women and girls employed by the big factories mentioned above.

Some places were more entertaining to work at than others, and **Pat Pearce** made the most of her job as a cleaner at the Bristol Hippodrome. Pat, who lived in Totterdown, spent 20 years working at the theatre until she was well into her 60s and during that time she amassed 15 albums full of photographs of her with the stars who came to perform there. After being made redundant by Wills, Pat popped into the Hippodrome on the off-chance that there was a job going and it worked out well for her: "My aunt and uncle used to take me to variety shows there when I was young. It was a magical place for me." But the job itself wasn't very glamorous and Pat says it was the hardest job she had ever had: "I was up every weekday ay 6am, and at 4am on a Sunday, to get into town and start cleaning the theatre from

403 *Evening News*, 25 May 1927, Bristol

404 Hilda Jennings, (1968, rep 2001), *Societies In The Making: A Study of Development and Redevelopment Within a County Borough. London: Routledge.* 38-39.

the night before. I would have to clean beneath 508 chairs in the Circle every shift. Sometimes I'd have to clean the stars' dressing rooms."[405]

In the following pages, we will meet women who set up an early female employment agency in the city with the intention of saving 'fallen' girls from prostitution. We will meet women who worked in some of the city's better known factories. And we will meet an army of resourceful, resilient and strong women who endured grim hardships simply because they had to in order to support their families. All of these women helped to build the Bristol we know and love today.

THE BRISTOL FEMALE MISSION SOCIETY

Bristol in the 1820s was one of the most overcrowded cities in England and consequently the poorest people in the city lived in utterly uninhabitable conditions. In response, the City Mission was founded in 1827 with well-intentioned middle-class men attempting to find a solution to the poor housing problem. The wives of these men formed a Ladies' Committee and in 1851 appointed a female missionary to work among the poor women in St Judes. After 1859, the women of the Ladies' Committee separated from the City Mission, re-named themselves the Bristol Female Mission Society and widened their remit.[406]

This was an organisation run by women for women, without the involvement of men. One of the aims of the Mission was to prevent young girls from selling sex for money and this was done via a programme of education and training, and by providing

405 Gerry Parker, John Hudson, (2014). *Stage Door: The Bristol Hippodrome 100 Years*. Bristol: Redcliffe Press. 12-13.
406 Gill James, (2003, September), 'The Bristol Female Mission Society, 1859-1884: Prevention or Cure?' Academic paper, University of the West of England.

a support network for young women. In a paper she gave at a meeting in Dublin, Ireland, in August 1861, Bristolian stalwart **Frances Power Cobbe** described the work being done at the Bristol Mission as revolutionary in the preventative way it aimed to save young women from 'falling' into sex work, rather than reactively helping those who had already 'fallen'.[407]

The women on the committee of the Bristol Mission Society were drawn from the upper and middle classes and included founding member **Annie May**, plus **Mrs JP Budgett**, **Miss Leonard** and **Miss Marriott**, who were also on the Lock Hospital Committee (please see the entries for **Josephine Butler** and **Ellen Cullinane** for more information about the Bristol Lock Hospital). The longest-serving Bristol missionary was **Hannah Denyer** who worked from 1858 until 1864, when ill-health forced her to resign. Failing health was often a reason that women had to stand down from their charitable duties, because they regularly worked without end and often in the face of much hostility, so inevitably it would take its toll on the women's mental and physical health, including their eyesight in numerous cases.

A female penitentiary was established on Upper Maudlin Street, City Centre, in 1800 for women who had "strayed from the paths of virtue [and] desire to recover their lost character"[408], with a similar home also opening on Marlborough Hill, Cotham, in 1813. The main goal of these institutions was to provide an alternative to the streets, prison or the workhouse for the women who had recently had to turn to sex work. However, women who had been involved in prostitution for a number of years and/or who had criminal records were considered beyond help.

The Bristol Female Mission Society decided that one way to prevent young women from 'falling' was to help them find

407 Ibid.
408 Ibid.

alternative work and so, in January 1859, they set up the Free Register Office at 3 Park Row to operate as an employment agency. This typically meant placing women in big houses as domestic servants, owing to the huge demand for servants in the Victorian era. However, it is odd that domestic service was seen as appropriate work for these 'at risk' young women given that research in London between 1870-1890 showed that 40-50 per cent of women in Lock Hospitals had previously been domestic servants. Granted, this research was carried out after the time we are talking about for the Bristol Female Mission Society but presumably the link was already clear for anyone who wanted to see it.[409] However, given that factory work was irregular and badly paid (akin to contemporary zero hours contracts) and shop work often meant women were unsupervised in the evenings (the time of day they were felt to be most at risk), domestic service did offer certain advantages.

The Mission did more than find young women suitable work because it also offered them a place to receive continued moral support and encouragement, as well as a place to buy affordable clothing and to gain access to training to boost their employability. It was felt this was important to stop the young women from succumbing to 'temptation'. The team at the Mission also paid a monthly visit to the young women they had placed in work to ensure that they were being well treated by their employers.

By 1862, the house at Lower College Green had become too small for the numbers applying for admittance. So the Mission purchased larger premises on Fort Lane off St Michael's Hill. Royal Fort House (now part of the University of Bristol) could accommodate 42 young women and remained open until 1937. To gain admittance, girls were either recommended to the home

409 Ibid.

by a third party or they attended a probationary sewing class (an attempt to assess their skills and ability to learn). The average age of the girls received into Royal Fort House was just 13 years and one month, and the average stay in the home was a little under six months. Also in 1862, the Register Office moved to larger premises at 8 Lower Park Row, which became Free Lodging House and provided accommodation between jobs or in times of sickness for the Mission's young women. Once in the Home, girls stayed until they had been taught enough to "fit them for humble service" and until they were found suitable work.[410]

THE LOAN EXHIBITION OF WOMEN'S INDUSTRIES

"Bristol may take credit to itself for having devised a novelty among Exhibitions. The present is peculiarly an exhibiting age, but there has not been till now an Exhibition devoted exclusively to women's industries. Bristol has, however, led the way, and the Exhibition just opened is so successful and so interesting that it will be surprising if the example is not rapidly followed in other places."[411]

On 26 February 1885, an extraordinary exhibition celebrating women's industries was opened at the Queen's Villa on Queen's Road, Clifton, and ran until the end of April. The Loan Exhibition of Women's Industries was believed to be the first such exhibition ever held in the United Kingdom. In an effusive article, the *Western Daily Press* summarised: "Time was when a strictly representative collection of women's industries would have presented very few features of interest."[412] The aim of the exhibition, which featured

410 Ibid.

411 *Pall Mall Gazette*, (1885, February 26). 'A Novelty in Exhibitions.' 4.

412 *Western Daily Press*, (1885, February 27). 'Loan Exhibition of Women's Industries at Clifton: Opening Ceremony'. 6.

a whopping 330 exhibitors, was to highlight the work of women, to give women's work improved representation and to encourage others to better appreciate the work of women despite them being, as one wag commented to the press, "not even men"[413]. More than 18,000 people attended the exhibition over the course of its run, with several complaining of over-crowding due to its phenomenal popularity. The fact it was housed in a disused residential property rather than a formal exhibition space no doubt added to the cramped conditions.

The brains behind the exhibition was **Helen Blackburn**, who we met earlier in this book. She was inspired by an exhibition held in Bristol the previous autumn called the Industrial and Fine Art Exhibition, and promptly formed a committee to encourage "opportunities afforded women for scientific study and technical training", and she began contacting local women's societies and employers around the country to gather support for her new exhibition. The University College, Bristol, had been a benefactor of the Industrial and Fine Art Exhibition and it welcomed the opportunity to be more heavily involved in the new trades exhibition. Historian Emma Ferry writes: "[The Women's Employment Society in London, the Female School of Art, the School of Wood Carving] and others involved with the training and employment of women, submitted exhibits to advertise their activities, to demonstrate the benefits of technical education, and 'to make access to those paths of appropriate work more plain and obvious'."[414] Helen was assisted in her work for the new exhibition by a lot of women who we have become familiar with throughout this book, including: **Agnes Beddoe**, **Georgina Budgett**, **Mary Clifford**, **Eliza Walker Dunbar**, **Lilias Ashworth Hallett**,

413 *Pall Mall Gazette*, (1885, February 26). 'A Novelty in Exhibitions.' 4.

414 Emma Ferry, '"A Novelty Among Exhibitions": The Loan Exhibition of Women's Industries, Bristol, 1885' in Elizabeth Darling, Lesley Whitworth (eds), (2007), *Women and the Making of Built Space in England, 1870-1950*. Hants: Ashgate. 53.

Emma Marshall, the many **Sturge** sisters, **Mabel Tothill** and **Dorothy Woollam.**

The Loan Exhibition of Women's Industries included a room of "consciousness-raising displays of portraits of women who led the way in opening new fields for the employment of women, or who had shown special excellence in work already done by women".[415] More than 90 women "who have left their mark on the world remind us of many efforts for progress in society, which can neither be engraved nor embroidered, in stone or tissue, but in the fabrics of society and the memories of history"[416] were celebrated in this way, including **Mary Carpenter, Millicent Fawcett, Lady Gore Langton, Florence Nightingale** and **Susannah Winkworth.**

As well as highlighting older trades that were going out of fashion or being replaced by industrialised versions, such as weaving on looms or spinning thread on spinning wheels, the exhibition also profiled newer work for women that required training and qualification, such as medicine. The *Western Daily Press* wrote that the organisers "would remind their visitors that all the modern work they will see in this exhibition is done by women who make a profession of their pursuit, either for the arts' sake, for the sake of earning a livelihood. No work is shown done for recreation or amusement only".[417] There was also room for the newer trades that were emerging thanks to the invention of various newfangled machines such as typewriters and sewing machines (although sewing machines had been around in various guises since 1790, they took a fair while to become commonly used in tailoring). There was a display focussed on women's domestic

415 Elizabeth Crawford, (1999). *The Women's Suffrage Movement: A Reference Guide 1866-1928*. London: University College London Press. 61.
416 *Western Daily Press*, (1885, February 27). 'Loan Exhibition of Women's Industries at Clifton: Opening Ceremony'. 6.
417 Ibid. 6.

work, which included a life-size wax model of a baby: "The chief of women's industries!" chuckled the *Pall Mall Gazette*, believing itself to be clever.[418] Meanwhile, girls from the nearby Red Maids' School were on hand to demonstrate the new opportunities offered to workers by telegraphs and typewriters.

It is no coincidence that the Loan Exhibition of Women's Industries was conceived at a time when women were beginning to mobilise in great force for the vote and it is also no surprise that this exhibition should happen in Bristol: a city that, outside of London, demonstrated (and continues to demonstrate in 2018) the highest volume of women's campaigning in all of the United Kingdom. Inevitably, there were criticisms that the exhibition was focussed towards middle- and upper-class women, and that its Clifton location and entry charge made it inaccessible to working-class women but a placatory reduced charge of 6d was levied on Saturdays to try and counter this.[419]

In his opening speech, the former Bristol mayor **Sir Joseph Dodge Weston** complimented the committee on its hard work in creating the exhibition and pointed out that although there were women who had been praised for their achievements in music or literature, he was "very much afraid that [we] have been accustomed to regard these as phenomenal instances, and whether this arose from the self conceit of the harder sex he did not know, but he was afraid that the general opinion was that for all the higher pursuits in life, woman was not equal to man". He added that "the exhibition with all its variety, all its beautiful and excellent objects, the work of women's hands, would at least have this result: a higher appreciation, a higher general appreciation, of the skill, the talent and the genius of woman.

418 *Pall Mall Gazette*, (1885, February 26). 'A Novelty in Exhibitions.' 4.

419 Emma Ferry, '"A Novelty Among Exhibitions": The Loan Exhibition of Women's Industries, Bristol, 1885' in Elizabeth Darling, Lesley Whitworth (eds), (2007), *Women and the Making of Built Space in England, 1870-1950*. Hants: Ashgate. 54.

And if, then, with increased appreciation there would naturally be some added energy to give rise to a movement for increased scholastic establishments that should have for their special object to technical training of women then, indeed, that exhibition would have accomplished a very great result".[420] He added that he hoped the proceeds from the exhibition would go towards the National Society for the Promotion of the Franchise of Women and therefore help women to secure the vote. When Sir Joseph finished his speech, **Agnes Beddoe** handed him a bouquet of flowers and said, with her tongue wedged firmly in her cheek, that as he had done so much for the rights of women it was only proper that he should enjoy some of their privileges and receive the delicate flowers normally given to a female speaker.

Summing up the value of the Loan Exhibition of Women's Industries as a predictor of the future as well as a retrospective of women's work, Emma Ferry writes: "Functioning as a contemporary trade exhibition and producing ephemeral knowledge too, the exhibits at Queen's Villa celebrated current examples of women's work and indicated what might be achieved in the future, given access to technical education." She adds: "Many of the objects at Queen's Villa were displayed to demonstrate the contribution women could make to British trade, which no doubt had particular significance given the economic depression of the 1880s and the falling value of British exports."[421] Showing that, given half a chance, women really would be the future.

420 *Western Daily Press*, (1885, February 27). 'Loan Exhibition of Women's Industries at Clifton: Opening Ceremony'. 6.
421 Emma Ferry, '"A Novelty Among Exhibitions": The Loan Exhibition of Women's Industries, Bristol, 1885' in Elizabeth Darling, Lesley Whitworth (eds), (2007), *Women and the Making of Built Space in England, 1870-1950*. Hants: Ashgate. 60.

THE CHOCOLATE FACTORY

Joseph Fry was an apothecary with a shop on Small Street, and in 1756 he was making his own chocolate for the purpose of brewing a hot chocolate drink. But such was the popularity of his hot chocolate drink that in 1777 Joseph moved to Union Street "where he keeps sorts of Chocolate Nibs and Cocoa"[422] and before long, Joseph had made his first block of chocolate... and hurray, the city's favourite treat was created. After Joseph died in 1787, his widow **Anna Fry** took over the business and ran it with their son under the name 'Anna Fry and Son' until her own death in 1803.

In 1820, female employees at Fry's outnumbered males by 2:1 and they were often the daughters of the older male employees already working there. By 1850, the women were given overalls to wear at work, although they were expected to contribute to the cost themselves. However, a visitor to the factory in 1890 commented on the "hundreds of neatly dressed girls preparing fancy chocolates, filling fancy boxes, wrapping chocolates in pretty tinfoil, weighing cocoa, or covering little balls of cream with chocolate".[423] But it wasn't all about appearances. For the women who worked there it was a hard job for little financial reward. They were largely on piecework and, for example, received three farthings (about 0.3p in contemporary money) for filling a tin of 140 creams and were liable to be fined for poor work, dropping work or wasting raw materials. And because only unmarried women were employed, there was a high turnover of staff; because once a woman got married she was expected to leave her job.

The welfare conditions in the Fry's factory were praised in

422 Keynsham & Saltford Local History Society, (2010). 'Around Keynsham and Saltford: Remembering Somerdale'. Keynsham & Saltford Local History Society. PDF download from: http://www.keysalthist.org.uk/Journal%20of%20the%20Key%20Hist%20Soc%202010.pdf
423 Ibid

an 1883 report by the Royal Commission on Labour. The report wrote: "Every girl changes her dress before she goes home, with the result that both outside and inside the factory she is neater and better dressed and distinctly superior in appearance to those in any of the other factories visited." It was also commented upon that the wages at Fry's were comparatively high for the work done, and that this was the only Bristol factory where girls under the age of 25 could expect to earn more than 12 shillings a week.[424]

Fry's had seven chocolate factories located in the central shopping area of Bristol (adjacent to where Broadmead and The Galleries are now), before moving seven miles out to a large factory in Somerdale in 1936. There remains a plaque up in Union Street (outside what is now a branch of Subway) marking the spot where the central factory used to stand.

Built on Quaker roots, all of Fry's staff were expected to attend a church service at the start of each working day, and hymn singing was encouraged to keep the staff motivated and uplifted during their 12-hour shifts. At the height of Fry's chocolate production they employed 4,600 staff, mostly women, who were known locally as Fry's Angels.

Perhaps the most well-known Fry's Angel was **Elsie Griffin**, who we met earlier in this book. Elsie joined Fry's in 1910 at the age of 14 as a chocolate packer and would sing at the factory's church service every morning before work. Such was her talent for soprano that she performed widely in concerts around Bristol, including as a soloist in front of a 500-strong temperance choir at the Colston Hall. When World War One broke out, Elsie's talents were called on to entertain the troops but she never forgot her time at Fry's and would come back to visit her former colleagues whenever she was in Bristol.

424 Hilda Jennings, (1968, rep 2001), *Societies In The Making: A Study of Development and Redevelopment Within a County Borough. London: Routledge.* 37.

On 19 October 1889, the female workforce at Fry's chocolate factory was addressed by **Miriam Daniell** of the Bristol Trades Council and the Bristol Socialist Society. Fry's staff was not unionised and Miriam wanted them to consider how unionisation would improve their wages and working conditions. There were around 900 women and girls working at Fry's at this time, alongside a much smaller number of male workers, and collectively they were unhappy about the length of their working day and the unfair distribution of a recent pay award.[425] The Quaker establishment that ran Fry's was attacked with the rhetorical question of whether the "rich Cliftonians, some of whom live on the labour of these girls, [would] allow their daughters to run such risks?": those risks being the "deplorable" and "white slavery" conditions they were forced to work in.[426] Fry's acted fast. On 22 October 1889 they announced staff would receive an advance of 1s per week, although it did not give in to the demand for shorter hours, and their spokesman said staff were free to join a union if they wished.[427]

When World War One commenced in 1914, many of Fry's younger male employees were called up to join the armed forces but were promised that their jobs would still be there for them on their return. With an absence of men, in 1917 Fry's was employing more than 2,500 women in the Union Street factories, along with a number of "clerks, lady clerks, typists and travellers in the offices". (Quite how a 'clerk' and a 'lady clerk' are different, nobody is sure. Nor are we clear how a traveller could work in an office.)

Bertha Milton began working at Fry's when she was just 14

425 Mike Richardson, (2012). *The Bristol Strike Wave of 1889-1890: Socialists, New Unionists and New Women. Part 1: Days of Hope*. Bristol Radical Pamphleteer 21. Bristol: Bristol Radical History Group. 19.
426 Ibid. 20.
427 Ibid. 21.

years old and explained the process of getting a job there: "You had to go through a thorough examination by a doctor and they wanted to know if you went to church or chapel or if you were good or no. So I had to have a tooth out and I didn't like that very much. I had to have the tooth out or else I wouldn't have gone into Fry's. I wanted to be one of their 'Angels'. If you were a 'Fry's Angel' in them days you were somebody. At Packers, the other chocolate place here, they were called 'Packer's Devils'."

Bertha initially worked in the weight room and then she learned how to cover chocolate, which was piece work. "It was to cover little creams which were called tens," she said. "We used to have to cover 120 for three farthings. A couple of weeks after they put it up to a penny. I didn't like it ... but of course you couldn't leave. ... In those days, during the hot weather, if the work [was ruined in the heat] you didn't get any money and you were sent home. In the summer I was at home more often than I was at work ... Finally I got onto chocolate creams, which are still made to this day [1977], but today it's all done by machinery. We daren't talk and we daren't laugh. If we laughed or if we talked we had to leave off. She'd tell you, 'Leave off and sit'. We had to sit on our stools and wait half an hour and then we'd start work again."

True to the Quaker origins of the Fry's factory, Bertha recalled how every day there was a service with hymns, prayers and a doxology (a form of religious praise). While Bertha didn't seem to think much of the enforced worship, she did admit that the bosses – if eccentric – were at least kind. "[The boss] used to look a real sight. With a frock tail coat and a pair of boots on that were never done up," she said. "But I must say, when he died he left us all a bit of money, so I was alright then. If you worked there five years you had £5, and for every year over that number you had an extra pound. So I had £5 and I thought it was lovely. I was very happy in Fry's but I was glad to leave."[428]

The bicentenary of Fry's was celebrated in 1928 with a special edition of the staff magazine and an article entitled 'Eve Comes To Stay', which was a comment on the number of women who had moved from the factory floor to office jobs at Fry's... and seemingly were not going anywhere. Of course, 1928 was the year in which all women over 21 were finally entitled to vote and the upset this caused some people can be sensed in the tone of the Fry's article, which explained that the company had previously only had two women in office jobs (both secretaries) prior to 1914 but that Fry's had been "compelled" to employ more women in office roles while the men were away in the war.[429] The article said: "And when the war was over, although every gallant soldier who returned was re-instated, the sweeping changes which took place in the Offices and the wholesale mechanisation of invoicing and accounting processes made it necessary for the Firm not only to retain the ladies they had, but also to engage a large number of others. And so Eve came into our Offices, first in ones and twos, then in dozens, scores and hundreds."

The prejudice that women in the office had to endure was evident and it is a sad reflection of our times that even in 2018 women still have to work three times as hard as their male colleagues to be treated equally. The article continued: "At first we were inclined not to take her very seriously. We thought that after a few days' steady work Eve would be probably knocked up

428 Bertha Milton in Bristol Broadsides, (1977), *Bristol as We Remember It*. Bristol: Broadsides. 15-16.

429 Of course, the same was true in all types of factories not just at Fry's. For instance, Joyce Storey (who has her own entry in this book) found work at an engineering factory called Magna Products in Warmley during World War Two when all the young men were called up. Her father, who was too old to go to war, talked to Joyce about the new wave of women workers: "He said that because of the war they could not get the young lads to make the cores for the moulds, but they had taken on women for the work. He looked down at the floor before admitting that they were far better at it than any of the men, with far fewer 'wasters'." In Joyce Storey (2004), *The House in South Road*. London: Virago. 210.

and absent with an attack of hysteria, the megrims or the vapours ... Eve has been with us several years now and we have become quite attached to her. For she has done her job both in Peace and in War. So Eve has come to stay."[430] I repeat, *"probably knocked up and absent with an attack of hysteria"*. In 2018, it's hard to say with certainty whether this comment from 90 years ago was intended to be flippant or serious but either way it smacks of the sense that there was truth in the idea that some people (ie some men) believed it to be fact.

Another woman who worked at the Fry's factory in Pithay was **Olive Knowland**, who joined in 1930 when she was 14. "I started in the foiling department, hand wrapping small chocolates in tin foil to go into fancy boxes," she said. "I liked this work but after a while I was sent to work at the new factory in Somerdale. There I worked on a conveyor belt taking bars of chocolate off and putting them into trays. This to me was very boring. I hated it there and I left 11 months after."[431]

The move in 1936 out to a 228-acre site in Somerdale, near Keynsham, was the result of the company merging with rival chocolate manufacturer Cadbury in 1919. But it was a nuisance for the Fry's and Cadbury's workers who had previously enjoyed a cost-free short walk or cycle to work in the city centre. Suddenly there was a price involved with getting to work, which had an immediate impact on the largely female workforce of 5,000 staff. There were three morning trains from Bristol to Keynsham that the staff could take but this took a huge bite out of the workers' weekly earnings and, given their already low wages, this was a charge they could ill afford. But presented with little other choice, the women had to use the trains. A local newspaper commented

430 Keynsham & Saltford Local History Society, (2010). 'Around Keynsham and Saltford: Remembering Somerdale'. Keynsham & Saltford Local History Society. PDF download from: http://www.keysalthist.org.uk/Journal%20of%20the%20Key%20Hist%20Soc%202010.pdf
431 Olive Knowland in Bristol Broadsides, (1987), *Bristol Lives*. Bristol: Broadsides. 72.

at the time: "At present it is costing some of these girls as much as 4s. 0d. (20p) to 4s. 6d. (22½p) of their weekly earnings, and often they have to be content to ride in the milk or guards van at that."[432]

The Cadbury factory at Somerdale, as it was known after 1981, closed for good in March 2011 after the company was bought out by Kraft Foods and production moved to Poland. However, while much of the factory buildings have since been demolished and replaced with housing, the Fry Club remains as a social centre for the new community that has set up there.

THE PIN FACTORIES

Pin making was a major industry in Bristol from the middle of the 16th century until the end of the 19th century, employing mostly women and girls. It was an example of a pre-industrial outworking system that survived into the Victorian era of factory-based industrialisation. Outwork (that being work done at home rather than in the factory) was popular since it did not undermine a woman's domestic role: because although engaged in paid labour, she was still at home with her children and away from the temptations of men.

One of the largest pin-making factories in East Bristol was **Robert Charleton**'s factory at Two Mile Hill, Kingswood, which opened in 1831. There was also **James Dobson**'s factory at Soundwell and **Thomas Rawbone**'s factory at Staple Hill, and it is thought pins were also made at a factory in Downend, as well as at various workhouses around Bristol.

432 Keynsham & Saltford Local History Society, (2010). 'Around Keynsham and Saltford: Remembering Somerdale'. Keynsham & Saltford Local History Society. PDF download from: http://www.keysalthist.org.uk/Journal%20of%20the%20Key%20Hist%20Soc%202010.pdf

In 1841, the Children's Employment Commission (CEC) compiled a report into the factories that showed there were 110 women and girls plus 50 men and boys working at Charleton's factory, as well as 500 female outworkers who did 'heading' and 'sticking'. While the CEC report primarily focussed on children, a sub-commission also reported on women's employment. The CEC visited the factories of Charleton and Dobson and reported that the majority of employees in these two factories were young girls from 14-18 years old. The women and girls worked 12 hours a day and they earned 2/6d to 7/- a week; the boys earned 1/- to 8/- a week. The report rightly noted: "There is a great disproportion between the wages of the men and the females." Yet nothing was done to affect change.

Pointing the pins was dangerous because the fine brass dust was breathed in by the grinding operators. Despite this, report writer **Elijah Waring** stated that he "observed no unhealthy appearances" among the pin makers. He added: "Many of the girls are even remarkably blooming, and their persons and dress particularly clean and neat. I saw no curvature of the spine, or other deformity; and, judging from their merry carolling whilst at their work, they do not feel oppressed by it."

Waring reported on six individual young women at Charleton's factory: **Eliza Lewis**, 17; **Elizabeth Palmer**, 17; **Martha Pearce**, 16; **Fanny Britton**, 17; **Ann Green**, 16; and **Sarah Shepherd**, 16. They had all worked for between six months and five years at the factory and could all read, except for Fanny. They lived with parents or friends and received their own wages, and Waring reported they were in good health. However, Waring did note the dangers posed by the machines used: "The old-fashioned heading-machines are semi-barbarous contrivances, which it would be desirable to see annihilated. They require a close and continuous application of the sight, a protracted action of the feet, and an inclination of the whole body unfavourable to health."

Indeed, the *Gloucester Journal* of 3 February 1838 records at least one death at a Bristol pin factory: "A sad accident occurred at the pin manufactory of Mr Dobson, near Bristol, on Tuesday last, to a young female named **Sarah Taylor**, who was standing near to a part of the machinery, when the corner of her shawl was caught by it, and she was instantly drawn in, and before the engine could be stopped, she was dreadfully injured and fell dead on the floor. A young woman standing near to Sarah Taylor was seized by her at the instant the machinery caught her, and was most providentially saved with some lacerations."

Charleton believed the women he employed were "respectable" and mostly "virtuous girls". And Waring noted: "They work 6am-6pm and in the factory a fine of 3d is inflicted on any female who uses bad language or sings a profane song; they sing a good deal but are permitted only hymn tunes, of which there is a great variety."[433]

Once the Victorian trend for industrialisation crept into the pin factories, opportunities for working at home declined and the wage-based economy became more firmly established, and therefore girls and women were forced to seek work in factories instead of the home. By 1871, the census recorded just 27 female pin makers in Kingswood. The decline of the pin industry in East Bristol mirrored the decrease of outwork in British industry generally and there is now almost no trace left in the city as a reminder of the thousands of women and girls who worked tirelessly for next to nothing making pins and money for their masters. The buildings in which these great factories once stood are now almost entirely demolished.[434]

433 Helen Reid, (2005). *Life in Victorian Bristol*. Bristol: Redcliffe Press. 25.
434 With thanks to Myna Trustram, (1986), 'Pin Money: Pin Making in East Bristol in the 18th and 19th Centuries', in Bristol Broadsides, *Placards and Pin Money: Another Look at Bristol's Other History*. Bristol: Broadsides. 24-44.

THE COTTON FACTORY

The Great Western Cotton Factory, designed by **Isambard Kingdom Brunel**, opened its doors with much fanfare in 1838 and by June 1839, the factory on Maze Street, Barton Hill, had 958 employees, of whom 609 were girls aged just 13-14 years old. There were also 113 boys, 117 men and 119 women.[435] Indeed, such was the factory's dependence on child labour that until 1845 any child who missed a day of work could be imprisoned, although in 1845 local people organised to get this barbaric rule overturned.[436]

Chilcott's Guide of 1846 describes the factory as: "An immense pile of building, for the purpose of cotton spinning and weaving has been erected on the margin of the Avon and the works are now in full operation having engines of 80 horsepower each and two of 20 each, constantly at work. The room at the front of the mills is the weaving room where about 700 persons chiefly young girls are employed making the yarn spun in the mill into cloth. The whole establishment is a perfect model of comfort and good arrangement and employs about 1,700 hands."[437] By 1883, the reports stated there were 1,000 people working at the factory, of which about 75 per cent were female.[438]

Inside the Great Western Cotton Factory, the writer known as **Lesser Columbus** reported on what he saw after visiting in 1893: "Hundred upon hundreds of women and girls, with headgear consisting of shawls, mostly of a red and white plaid, but hanging over the shoulders, the quaint style of dress peculiar to their calling and formerly with wooden shoes, pattens on the pavement making the air merry with their peculiar sound. Such gigantic works as these, affording employment to so many

435 http://www.bhhg.co.uk/showfiles.php?files=Cotton%20Factory
436 http://www.brh.org.uk/site/articles/great-western-cotton-works-barton-hill/
437 Helen Reid, (2005). *Life in Victorian Bristol*. Bristol: Redcliffe Press. 34.
438 http://www.brh.org.uk/site/articles/great-western-cotton-works-barton-hill/

females who might otherwise find it difficult to obtain work of a suitable character, cannot but be a very good direct benefit to the hands themselves while the indirect good resulting therefrom cannot be gauged."[439]

The workforce at the Great Western Cotton Factory was mainly low-paid women and children, who endured long hours, wage cuts and a stratospheric rate of industrial accidents and ill-health due to the cotton dust, humidity and machinery. Consequently, there were a number of acts of worker-led rebellion from the women, who were often forced to steal cotton from their employer to sell on the black market to supplement their meagre wages.

Bertha Milton's aunts all worked at the cotton factory or "down the back lane" as it was referred to locally. Bertha said: "They'd always look lovely and clean. White aprons, just a shawl around the shoulders in the first days. Long hours, not much pay. Our sisters worked in what they called the weaving. And on occasions when they had four looms they had what they called a helper, which was a very young girl. And of course she was paid a very small wage. It was a really busy place."[440]

In 1889, there was a month of "wearisome" striking and the organisers enlisted the support of the also-striking Bristol dockers which bolstered morale.[441] By this time, the women had unionised as the Cotton Workers' Bristol Branch of the Gas Workers' and General Labourers' Union. The strike was focussed around the attempt by factory managing director **George Spafford** to reintroduce a ten per cent wage cut on the women, which had been applied by the factory during a trade recession five years before. Once negotiations between Spafford, socialist **Miriam**

439 Helen Reid, (2005). *Life in Victorian Bristol*. Bristol: Redcliffe Press. 34.
440 Bertha Milton in Bristol Broadsides, (1977), *Bristol as We Remember It*. Bristol: Broadsides. 12.
441 http://www.brh.org.uk/site/articles/great-western-cotton-works-barton-hill/

Daniell and the women broke down, the 1,700-strong workforce had already walked out… and kept walking the two miles to Bristol city centre where they publicly demonstrated their anger. Spafford became so unwilling to relent to the workers' demands that he instead threatened to close the factory entirely if they did not return to work – meaning the women would be permanently out of a job.[442]

Miriam, **Helena Born** and other Bristol Socialist Society members formed a committee to fundraise in support of the striking women who were now entirely without a wage. Their comrade **Helena Tufts** wrote: "Night upon night, after days of unremitting activity, into the small hours they sat counting the pennies taken up at local meetings and strike parades and planning the judicious disbursement of the money among the needy strikers."[443]

Another action taken by the women was to march to the affluent area of Clifton on Sundays and visit all of the church services where their employers would be, and once inside the churches they would peacefully and quietly walk around with their strike banners clearly on display in an effort to embarrass their employers in front of their wealthy chums. In this way, around 400 women collected in All Saints Church on Pembroke Road and another 300 in Tyndale Baptist Church on Whiteladies Road (as well as other churches in other weeks). The strikers made clear that "they would rather go to the [workhouse], or to prison, or starve, than go back to work under the old conditions".[444]

442 Mike Richardson, (2012). *The Bristol Strike Wave of 1889-1890: Socialists, New Unionists and New Women. Part 1: Days of Hope*. Bristol Radical Pamphleteer 21. Bristol: Bristol Radical History Group. 25.
443 Ellen Malos, (1983), 'Bristol Women in Action 1839-1919: The Right to Vote and the Need to Earn a Living' in Bristol Broadsides, (1983). *Bristol's Other History*. Bristol: Broadsides. 118.
444 Mike Richardson, (2012). *The Bristol Strike Wave of 1889-1890: Socialists, New Unionists and New Women. Part 1: Days of Hope*. Bristol Radical Pamphleteer 21. Bristol: Bristol Radical History Group. 31.

The situation looked pretty damning for the factory bosses. Yet still Spafford and his fellow managers refused to budge on the workers' demands. So in a show of support, dockers in both Bristol and Liverpool refused to handle cotton produced by the factory, hampering trade and business for the factory owners. More support came from **Anna Priestman** of the Women's Liberal Association, who opened a soup kitchen to feed the strikers and their families.

The strike came to an end on 28 November 1889 when, despite Spafford refusing to budge on the pay cut, he relented on: abolishing fines for breakages, opening windows to reduce temperatures, allowing three meal breaks a day and paid overtime. Writing to a friend about the end of the strike, **Mary Clifford** said: "The cotton people went to work this morning. No increase in wages, but many grievances redressed. We are having a heavy time tackling these huge labour questions and have been meeting some of the men and women privately. The women are at present very open to being led … I think there is much more to come on all hands. They have offered to take us into their counsel … My mind goes out to these women and girls. I am going over to see some of them on Saturday. One can only pray."[445]

Barton Hill resident **Flo Melhuish** worked at the Great Western Cotton Factory as a 14-year-old. She had only been working at the factory for a few days when her supervisor told Flo that she was heading to the pub for a while and she asked the young girl to just carry on with her work. But when the supervisor returned, she was furious to see a streak had developed on the calico Flo's loom had been producing and told the teenager it would need to be re-done or she wouldn't be paid. Flo recalled: "She got in a temper, slapped my face and left her finger marks

445 Ellen Malos, (1983), 'Bristol Women in Action 1839-1919: The Right to Vote and the Need to Earn a Living' in Bristol Broadsides, (1983). *Bristol's Other History*. Bristol: Broadsides. 115.

on my face. So I thought, well the only thing I can do now is give her one back. So I picked up the bobbin and let her have one back see. So the foreman says, 'What's going on here?' So I said, 'Well, she slapped me across the face, you can still see the marks. So I got into a bit of a paddy and hit her one with this bobbin.' So he said, 'That's enough of that then. You go to the office and get your cards. You're finished.'"[446]

Seemingly, Flo didn't really lose her job or else she returned to the cotton factory at a future date, because she later writes that she worked there for several years and describes the conditions as such: "We didn't have any canteen there to eat our food. You'd sit down in the alleyways. There was nowhere to wash your hands or anything like that. I stayed there for four or five years amongst the cotton workers. I started about 1918 just after the war. Now all the women there worked very hard."[447]

Alice Price, born 1898, had had an awful start to life. Her father was driven insane by lead poisoning from his job as a smelter and attempted suicide numerous times as well as threatening to slash the throat of Alice's older sister. In addition, several of her many siblings died in infancy, her mother died when Alice was just 13 and, as a result, in 1911 Alice was removed from school and told to seek work by her father, who then threatened to kill her in one of his rages. Alice, aged 13, promptly ran away from home. Having no money, the child slept rough in some washhouses backing onto the Feeder Canal waiting for Monday morning when she could present herself at the Great Western Cotton Factory as looking for work.

Alice recounted: "To my surprise I was taken on, mainly for the cheek I think, at the princely sum of three shillings and sixpence

446 Flo Melhuish in Bristol Broadsides, (1977), *Bristol as We Remember It*. Bristol: Broadsides. 10-11.
447 Ibid. 12.

... But the clothes I was wearing were my entire wardrobe until I could sneak back and get some more. I had not eaten since Saturday, except for bread thrown out for the birds; payday was a long way off and I was homeless."

Alice continued to sleep out in the washhouses until her first payday and some of the sympathetic loom women gave her leftover food and tea to keep her from starving. But despite all this, when she finally received her first pay packet, Alice's furious father found her and demanded she hand over the money. Thanks to the sisterhood of older women from the factory, Alice was saved: "I shouted and screamed for help – and it came. A solid body of women from the looms bore down on us, pulled me out of his grasp, and tore into him in a combined fury, which matched anything he could muster. He retreated, shouting, cursing, threatening – but he went. I never saw him again until his death in 1918." One of the women who saved Alice was **Mary Fry** and she invited young Alice home to live with her.[448]

Marjorie Grove also worked at the cotton factory, starting in the 1920s. Marjorie's mother was a single parent to three children and was seemingly an angry woman at the best of times. She dragged Marjorie along to work at the mill, even though the girl was terrified of the prospect. Marjorie (writing in the third person and referring to herself as 'Lottie') explained what it was like: "The rough domineering Judd Haye was teaching her to weave ... He swore and bullied the girl mercilessly each day. He chewed tobacco endlessly and spat it into a pool of slimy brown spittle between the heaving looms ... The din of the endless looms, row upon row in the fluff laden atmosphere, the reek of raw cotton and hot machine oil made Lottie feel sick.

"Several times a day she was expected to carry great laps of

448 Alice Price in Bristol Broadsides, (1987), *Bristol Lives*. Bristol: Broadsides. 5-9.

cloth to the warehouse below, cringing between madly waving picking sticks and flying shuttles, and huge whirring leather fan belts, which it was said had ripped hair from many an unwitting girl's head. She was terrified of the youth whose task it was to sweep beneath the looms. He would have a grimy hand up your drawers before you knew it. He rejoiced in the nickname of 'Pinch Bum'." After being threatened with the sack for lateness by her supervisor, a tearful Marjorie fled the mill to the stream and wept miserably, knowing she would soon have to face her furious mother. But as Marjorie says, she "determined never to enter a mill again" and she never did.[449]

The Great Western Cotton Factory began falling into decline by 1900 and when closure was threatened in 1916, **Annie Townley** rose to action to highlight the plight of the 700 women and girls who would lose their jobs. The factory was saved at that time but finally went into liquidation in 1925, with the building largely demolished in 1968.

THE SWEET FACTORY

By 1890, the Bristol Socialist Society had been busy fighting to try and establish trades unions for the city's unskilled and semi-skilled workers, believing this would help to topple capitalist society. So when the women and girls working at **JA Sanders**' Bristol Confectionery Works at 41 Redcliffe Street went out on strike in December 1892 the socialists were right behind them.

The sweet factory workers protested at Sanders' attempts to enforce an unpaid extra working hour to the day and at Sanders' attempts to quash the women's subsequent efforts to unionise.

449 Marjorie Grove in Bristol Broadsides, (1987), *Bristol Lives*. Bristol: Broadsides. 51-56.

In addition, the women were demanding a 15-minute break each morning. All of this was on top of one particularly petty and controlling rule that Sanders had already enforced: that the women be *locked in* during their lunch breaks, which Sanders couched in such terms as to imply this was for the moral benefit of the women and would therefore save them from falling victim to the perils of potentially meeting any tempting men anywhere.

The Bristol Socialist Society formed a Strike Committee in support of the sweet factory women, who were fighting not only for their right to unionise but also for their independence. They were not yet on strike but when the women and Sanders failed to reach an agreement on any of the above terms, 40 women were given their notice. Sanders still refused to discuss matters with the angered workers and 104 women subsequently went out on strike... for 26 long, cold and hungry weeks.

In a very sniffy statement issued in December 1892, **James Sanders** (son of the factory's owner), said: "One of the girls at the factory was dismissed and this was followed by wholesale dismissal of 30 or 40 girls. The majority of the remainder are determined to work no longer until their comrades are re-instated. They complained of low wages, saying the majority of the girls, many of them grown women, received between three shillings and seven shillings a week and they had been refused the right of combination [joining a union]. So the girls would parade with sandwich boards and collecting boxes around the chapels on Sunday. In all 104 girls went on strike because, in consequence of rearrangements in our departments we gave a girl notice to leave. We have had no difficulty in filling the places of the poor victims who have been induced to throw up their situation."[450]

The striking sweet factory women teamed up with the already

450 Helen Reid, (2005). *Life in Victorian Bristol*. Bristol: Redcliffe Press. 32.

striking deal-runner men from the Bristol docks and collectively marched, wet and hungry, around the affluent areas of Clifton and Cotham every Sunday, sometimes totalling 3,000 in number. On numerous occasions during the 26-week strike, the women clashed with the police. For instance, one woman, **EJ Watson**, was accused in the most vague terms of "unlawfully acting in a disorderly manner" and therefore "disturbing the peace". When the marching women became too vocal or strident, the police responded by pulling them to the ground by their hair and punching them in their breasts; assault the militant suffragettes would unfortunately come to know well in the near future.

In solidarity with the workers, socialists **Enid Stacey** and **Caroline May** took up a regular correspondence with Sanders via the letters pages of the *Bristol Mercury* and *Daily Post*, in which the sweet factory women were sometimes referred to as "Sanders' white slaves" on account of their pitifully low pay, which was often just 3/6d per week. Meanwhile, Clifton-based novelist **Gertrude Dix**, who was actively involved in labour politics, went on to fictionalise a successful strike by female sweet factory workers in her popular 1900 novel *The Image Breakers*.

The real-life strike culminated in what became known as Black Friday on 23 December 1892. The sweet factory women and the striking dockers joined together in a march that became so heated the cavalry was called in to break it up. The intention of the march had initially been to walk from the Grove to the Horsefair and raise funds for the strikers' families at Christmas. But the police objected for safety reasons to the Chinese lanterns carried by the marchers and attempted to re-route the march to avoid the city centre. Consequently and chaotically, the march ended up spreading to three different routes and occupying a far greater space in Bristol than originally planned. The police then batoned protestors when they reached Wine Street, and the great volume of officers riled the strikers up so much that excitement caused passions to overflow and a near riot broke out. There were a huge number of reported injuries and several arrests and the event achieved national news coverage. It was a terrible episode for all concerned.

By the spring of 1893, the sweet workers – cold, hungry and exhausted – were worn down and reluctantly returned to their posts. They achieved a small wage gain but no union recognition. Those strikers who refused the new terms were helped to find alternative and better-paid work by the socialist committee.[451]

THE CORSET FACTORIES

C Bayer & Co's corset factory near Oldham Common, on the edge of Bristol, was one of several spin-off factories set up after the Bath-based business experienced a boom in trade for stays, as corsets were also known. **Charles Bayer** boasted in advertisements that his "super fine British corsets for British wearers" were made with the "daintiest French fabrics" and were "as easy fitting as a perfectly cut kid glove, with a complete absence of pressure upon the respiratory organs"[452]. As with most factories of this type, the workforce was largely female but Bayer provided a rest room, a first aid room and a matron in his factory to assist the wellbeing of his employees. Following the closure of Bayer's factory, by the 1920s the building had become a laundry. However, Bayer's legacy lives on and corsets made at the factories are included in many respected collections, including at the prestigious Victoria

451 Ellen Malos, (1983), 'Bristol Women in Action 1839-1919: The Right to Vote and the Need to Earn a Living' in Bristol Broadsides, (1983). *Bristol's Other History*. Bristol: Broadsides. 71, 120-121. AND with thanks to Sally Mullen, (1986), 'Sweet Girls and Deal-Runners', in Bristol Broadsides, *Placards and Pin Money: Another Look at Bristol's Other History*. Bristol: Broadsides. 112-126.
452 http://cosgb.blogspot.co.uk/2014/03/charles-bayer-co-ltd.html

and Albert Museum in London.

Bayer's was not the only corset factory in Bristol. We have already met **Joyce Storey**, who briefly worked for Langridge's corset factory on Two Mile Hill. And there was also the Chapell Allen Corset Works, which had moved to bigger premises in Redfield (on the corner of Avondale Road and Victoria Avenue) in 1899, after outgrowing its 36 Weare Street site and by 1907 employed around 2,000 staff. Corsets were big business in the Victorian era, there was no doubt about it. The Harris and Tozer department store in Totterdown, for instance, would let its regular customers take corsets home to try on for size. And during a recent exploration of the long-empty shop on Wells Road, an extremely dusty mannequin was uncovered that was sporting a JB Combinaire corset.[453]

With its location directly opposite Redfield School, the Chapell Allen Corset Works was very conveniently situated for the many mothers who worked there. Although the school's headmistress did not appreciate the factory's loud siren that summonsed the women into work as it drowned out her words in the school assembly. The siren was not the only loud thing about the factory. Until the 1930s, the machinery was still steam operated, and the sound of the huge machines, belts and pulleys was deafening. With most of the women employed on piecework, the pace of work was frantic and there was never any let up in the deafening din. When the factory was finally electrified, the new sewing machines offered a much less jarring assault to the ears.

It was a long day for the workers. Shifts started at 8am and went on until 6pm, and even when night-time air raids had taken place during World War Two there was still no excuse to be late – indeed, if you were so much as three minutes late for work you

453 South Bristol Voice. 'Totterdown's Last Eyesore Is About To Be Transformed'. In *South Bristol Voice*, November 2017. 22-29.

had 15 minutes of money stopped from your pay packet.

During World War Two, the the Chapell Allen Corset Works, or Patriotic Corset Works as it was also known, lived up to its name and began making uniforms and armaments for the forces, and the cellars beneath the factory doubled up as shelters during air raids. **Kathleen Burnham** had been working at the factory for just six months when, in 1939, production switched from corsets to parachutes, gas mask cases and gun turret covers. She was only 14 years old at the time, and remembers that Queen Mary came to visit the factory and Kathleen was one of the workers she spoke to: "She said, 'I expect you say, 'Oh bother it', when things go wrong'."[454] Which seems an understatement.

Another teenager working in the factory making parachutes during the war was 15-year-old **Lily Russ**, who remembers the constant fear of air raids. Returning to work from her break one afternoon, Lily describes hearing a German aeroplane attacking the neighbouring roads in St George and suddenly somebody throwing themselves upon her. After the fright, Lily realised it was her father Henry who had leapt from his bike to save his daughter from the machine gun bullets that were being sprayed onto the pavement around them. Fortunately, neither Lily nor Henry was hurt although both were badly shaken up.[455]

When the post-war fashions moved to a more relaxed look than the restrictions offered by stays, the corset factories needed to diversify or sink. In the 1970s, the Chapell Allen Corset Works started to make items for Marks & Spencer under the new name of Celestron Textiles Limited in a bid to move with the times, but it wasn't enough and the company ceased trading entirely in the early 1980s.

454 http://www.bbc.co.uk/history/ww2peopleswar/stories/05/a4022605.shtml
455 http://www.bbc.co.uk/history/ww2peopleswar/stories/80/a2688780.shtml

THE TOBACCO FACTORIES

Bristol has been linked to the tobacco industry since the late 18th century. In 1826, Henry Wills' sons took over what was to become a thriving industry in the city, making its home in Bedminster with four separate factories. By the 1870s, smoking had becoming very popular and consequently by 1901 Wills was the biggest and most prosperous tobacco manufacturer in the whole of the United Kingdom. In the 1960s, there were 6,000 Wills staff in Bristol of whom approximately two-thirds were women.

In 2014, **Helen Thomas**, **Rosie Tomlinson** and **Mavis Zutshi** led a local history project to examine the impact of the tobacco industry on women in Bristol. They talked to many women who had worked in the factories about their experiences and published the results in *Bedminster's Tobacco Women*, and I urge you to seek out the book to get the full story and see all of the fascinating photos.

Annette Pearce worked for Wills, as did her parents, her grandparents and two great aunts. "People were so proud to be able to say that they worked for Wills," she said[456]. While **Jean Hawkins**, who joined Wills in 1939, says her mother felt it was a great achievement to have a child working at the factory: "It was quite a prestigious thing to get your son or daughter into Wills, so she worked hard at it."[457] Given it was such a sought after place to work, having a family member already on the payroll improved your own chances of being accepted.

Why was Wills such a good company to work for? They expected staff to work extremely hard but they also looked after their employees. **Mary Bessell** explained: "When I went to work

456 Helen Thomas, Rosie Tomlinson, Mavis Zutshi, (2015). *Bedminster Tobacco Women: A Local History Project*. Bristol: Fiducia Press. 7.
457 Ibid. 7.

there [aged 14] I was underweight, so I had to have cod liver oil everyday and then I went to keep fit classes because I was only six stone."[458] And as canteen worker **Barbara Giardina** explained, they helped you improve: "They offered me the chance to go to college because I never ever finished my course so I went to college in Bristol and they sent me on day release. They paid for all my stuff."[459]

The Royal Commission on Labour conducted a report on the employment of women in 1893, and Wills came off very well. The inspectors praised the dining room where staff could obtain a "good meat dinner with two vegetables for fourpence", as well as the staff lending library and the provision – which was uncommon – of a woman who "visited the girls in illness and arranged for those who needed it to go to the firm's convalescent home". The report also observed that employees with more than 40 years of service had their pictures hung in the boardroom as a mark of respect for their loyalty.[460]

Perhaps not all of the perks are what 21st-century readers might consider to be good things. Today, perks such as 40 free cigarettes a week would be highly questionable. Although I doubt you would find anyone today who would sniff at paid overtime, staff outings and money for taking part in research, which the Wills workers also benefitted from.

Rather delightfully, the Wills factory workers enjoyed their own in-house DJ in the form of 64-year-old **Kate Milton** at the No 4 Factory. The staff preferred music to listen to while they worked because it was more motivating that the talking on the BBC's radio stations, so DJ Kate filled the role admirably. A 1967 copy of the staff magazine *Wills World* writes: "The BBC's

458 Ibid. 9.
459 Ibid. 10.
460 Hilda Jennings, (1968, rep 2001), *Societies In The Making: A Study of Development and Redevelopment Within a County Borough. London: Routledge.* 37.

Onederful [sic] Radio 1 has proved less than wonderful to listeners during the music periods in the Wills factories. They find the fast talking disc-jockeys with their jokes and comments cannot be heard over the noise of the machinery and long for their old favourite. The factories' own disc jockeys are playing extra sessions of gramophone records to fill the gap. At the No 4 factories at Ashton the regular disc jockey is 64-year-old Mrs Kate Milton, who takes over the turntable for four half-hour sessions and for another hour when evening overtime is being worked."[461]

One woman who remembered the music in the factory was **Ivy Garraway** (née Rogers), who joined Wills in 1939 when she was 14. She said that the job was "relatively well paid and Wills looked after their workers very well". Her working day was from 7.30am until 5pm with an hour for lunch. She added: "Music was played in the factory and the girls working on the cigarette machines sang along with it."[462]

In the 1920s, Wills acquired the concrete Canons Marsh Tobacco Bond Warehouse on the waterfront site that is now the Lloyds Banking Group headquarters but was then known as the Eleven Bond. This was where tobacco leaf was bonded (stored) before being moved to the factories to be made into cigarettes. **Lily Newick** began work there in July 1941, at a time when the warehouse had been requisitioned for war work and was where machinery was taken to be repaired and washed in paraffin. Lily recalled: "I was on the carburetor section assembling the carburetors which I didn't find particularly difficult but I used to be a dressmaker and it was a bit of a shock... especially since I had to get my hands dirty!"[463]

Lily explained that it was a six day week, starting at 7.30am

461 http://www.imagesofengland.org.uk/learningzone/lz/forum_tobacco_67.aspx
462 http://www.bbc.co.uk/history/ww2peopleswar/stories/76/a7217976.shtml
463 http://www.bbc.co.uk/history/ww2peopleswar/stories/16/a4023316.shtml

and going through until 5.30pm every day. With no canteen on site, staff had to rush over to Electricity House in the Centre for lunch and dash back again to pick up their shift, which led to a lot of afternoon indigestion. Being just 19, Lily was paid less than her colleagues who were over 21 "which annoyed me a lot". She added: "The man that was operating the lift only earnt 5 pounds a week which I expect was very frustrating for him and I think he'd have been happy to see the back of us women after the war!"[464]

Because of all the paraffin that had been used to clean machinery while the warehouse had been requisitioned during the war, it couldn't go back to its previous use as a tobacco bond and the building was demolished in 1988. Summing up her experiences there, Lily concluded: "On the whole I enjoyed working there, especially because I was working with lots of people and it was quite good fun. From 3pm until half past we were allowed to listen to *Workers' Playtime* [a BBC radio variety show] so we heard all of the latest songs!"[465]

Derek Knapman runs the Lion hardware store on North Street, which has been there for more than 100 years, and he recalls the Wills' workers coming in on their lunch breaks. He told the *Pigeon* magazine: "The Wills tobacco factory was still working then [1972] and in the lunch hour the street was full of Wills' girls shopping. We used to sell a lot of what we called fancy goods – china figurines, shire horses with a wooden cart, tea sets."[466]

But it wasn't all fun. Wills was a strict employer and, in order to be treated well, staff needed to work hard. "It was very hard to the point where my sister said to my mum, 'You can't let her go in there. It'll kill her!' I was like really puny, a tiny little thing,"

464 Ibid
465 Ibid
466 Nicki Sellars, (2016), 'North Street's Jewel in the Crown' in *The Pigeon*, February 2016, 26.

said **Jackie** (surname unknown), who joined in 1959.[467] The staff magazine *Wills World* had a regular section rather patronisingly called 'Wills Girl' where, as you can imagine, the activities of the female staff were summed up. In one article from 1967, we meet **Joan Daley**, who was 19 when she joined the No 4 factory in 1908 working in the staff kitchens. Looking back on her 59 years at Wills, Joan said: "I used to prepare the meals in the kitchens and I earned eight shillings a week ... I enjoyed it, except for the first few months when we had a new overseer. She made me nearly crazy. I couldn't stick her. She made our lives a misery. The girls were meticulously clean and had to endure inspections by matron."[468]

Showing the old-fashioned attitudes to gendered parental responsibilities that persisted at the time, the November 1972 issue of *Wills World* is at great pains to praise Wills driver **Stephen Loader** for looking after his own son after his working day has ended so that his wife **Sheila** (who has been at home looking after the baby all day so has hardly had the day off) can go and work an evening shift at the factory. Imagine! A man looks after his own child and it makes the news! The magazine reported: "Cigar twilight shift work has created a new routine for housewife Mrs Sheila Loader and her husband Stephen ... Within 20 minutes of getting home Mr Loader is giving their six-month-old baby his bottle and getting him to bed, so that Mrs Loader can start the three-and-a-half hour evening shift as a cigar making examiner at the factory round the corner from their house in Lime Road, Ashton. She is helping to boost production of Castella Panatella cigars during a two month spell with 44 housewives all former cigar factory employees.

"'The extra money helps,' says Mrs Loader. 'I gave up work

467 Helen Tomas, Rosie Tomlinson, Mavis Zutshi, (2015). *Bedminster Tobacco Women: A Local History Project*. Bristol: Fiducia Press. 14.
468 http://www.imagesofengland.org.uk/learningzone/lz/forum_tobacco_67.aspx

in January when I was having [baby] Stuart. During the evening work I meet old friends I have not seen for five years. With the routine we've worked out at home everything is going great.' Mrs Loader is one of many housewives on cigar making, packing or stemming whose husbands arrive home in time to look after the family. Mrs **Kathleen Fowler**, who has returned to No 2 Factory to earn money for Christmas presents, leaves Katie, three, and Timothy, two, to be put to bed by husband Brian. 'They are no problem and he does not mind,' she said. Former factory guide Mrs **Gloria Lambert**, who has a 19-month-old daughter Sharon, is planning to get a colour TV set with her earnings and so is Mrs **Carol Sweet**, a mother of two. For Mrs **Margaret Thomas**, evening work in the stemming room is something of a family affair. She joins her sister Mrs **Josephine Minchin** and sister-in-law Mrs **Jenny Burgess** at work while her mother Mrs **Dorothy Burgess**, who works part-time in cigar packing, looks after her four children until their father gets home. Mrs Thomas says, 'I love being at work anyway and I would like to start part-time on a regular basis in the next year!'"[469]

The Wills staff was unionised but because Wills was a relatively fair employer, there had been no industrial action to speak of among the workforce. It was only in the late 1970s and early 1980s that workers at Wills became more militant. But because there were so few female shop stewards in the union, not many women had any involvement with industrial action.

Another large tobacco company in Bristol was the Imperial Tobacco Company (which joined forces with Wills), which at one point had numerous factories around the city and still maintains a factory on Winterstoke Road. **Miss Clark** remembers working at Mardon (Mardon, Son & Hall was bought out by Imperial

469 Ibid.

Tobacco to do packaging and produce cigarette cards) by Temple Meads for 46 years, where she worked on the machines and says she enjoyed it. In 1979 she recalled: "I worked half past seven in the morning 'til five or half past at night. Then during the war I done shift work. I started at Mardons at the end of the First World War. I can remember when the war finished. We all stood on the steps and watched all the people outside hooraying. I started with 5 shillings a week and I had 6d pocket money. I used to buy stockings and all odds and ends out of that 6d."

She continued: "I done the cartons which the cigarettes go in. When I first started I had to glue up the parcels. They came out of the machine and the girl on the table put them in the parcels and I had to glue them up. Then as I got better I was put on the table where the work came out. And from there I was put on what was called running out. Then I was put on the feeding. That was the tough job – feeding. During the war I done a man's job. Wages went up to 35s during the war. Then when I done a man's job, they gave me an extra 10s a week, but that was took away as soon as I was took off.

"There wasn't a union then. They did try and start one. There was one before I left. I was the mother of the chapel really. I didn't care for it much. There was no-one else to do it. We had to go up in Nicholas Street to the union meetings once a month. I think it changed for the worse. You had incentive schemes. Do so much work and you'd get so much money."[470]

470 Miss Clark in Bristol Broadsides, (1979), *Looking Back on Bristol*. Bristol: Broadsides. 8.

WOMEN IN THE WAR

The dawn of World War Two required women to step up and fill the roles that were now vacated by men who had been called up to fight. We have already seen some examples of women who filled these roles at Fry's chocolate factory and at a requisitioned Wills tobacco warehouse. In this section, we will meet a few other women who capably responded to the call for action. Although it presumably should go without saying that the women mentioned here are but a tiny handful of the legions of women who stepped up and carried out all manner of jobs to assist the country during the war.

Along with women from Birmingham, Devon and Cornwall, **Queenie Coles** began munitions work at the Rolls Royce No 4 Shop in Patchway during the war "entering a man's noisy working world of large machinery". The women were given brown overalls, arm sleeves and wooden clogs to wear, and Queenie's first job was to make spark plugs. Later on, she would become one of the first women to be transferred to a "man's job": grinding huge crank shank sleeves that were part of an engine. "With a man's job came man's wages, which some of the men objected to," remembered Queenie. "They brought in their union who eventually agreed that women could also work on large machines if taught properly. Their loss was my gain and I remained there until the end of the war."[471]

Thanks to her pre-war work as a secretary for Croydon Aerodrome, **Vi Marriott** was well equipped to be transferred to Bristol during the war to deal with military aircraft. Because everything the secretaries did was top secret, the carbon paper that was used in the typewriters to make copies needed to be

471 http://www.bbc.co.uk/history/ww2peopleswar/stories/01/a5206501.shtml

torn into tiny pieces once finished with and then placed in a special sack to be burned. Vi said: "My sense of the ridiculous was enchanted, because these secret sacks came from the ex-German Embassy, and were printed in red and black with the German eagle emblem."

Bristol was heavily blitzed by the Germans, and Vi and her colleagues would keep watch to see whether the enemy planes would turn and fly towards Coventry or the Midlands once they left Bristol. She remembered: "The most spectacular raid was the night the whole of the centre of Bristol went, and the air smelt of mulled ale for the next week as the brewery was burned to the ground." But not all raids happened at night: "The most frightening for me was the daylight raid when one of the escorting fighters was shot down and flew the whole length of Whiteladies Road, emptying his gun and barely skimming the roof of the house where I lived."[472]

When war broke out, 16-year-old **Eileen Phillimore** was required to leave her job at a paint factory and go and work for the Great Western Railway as a telegraphist, sending secret messages in Morse Code. During the war, the telegraph office was moved to the caverns beneath Temple Meads Station to protect the staff from bomb blasts ... although Eileen and the other 'telegraph girls' were afraid of the rats that lurked down there and knew that Temple Meads Station was an obvious target for the bombers. However, because of the importance of the work the telegraphists did and the need for secrecy, armed soldiers were positioned at the doors. Eileen's daughter recounted: "On many occasions, when my father went to meet Eileen so that she would not have to walk home through the darkness alone, he was stopped with a gun in his chest, being challenged 'Halt, who goes there?'"[473]

472 http://www.bbc.co.uk/history/ww2peopleswar/stories/65/a2631665.shtml
473 http://www.bbc.co.uk/history/ww2peopleswar/stories/61/a1961561.shtml

Women who were a part of the Women's Land Army were known as Land Girls. This was a British civilian organisation that sent women out to do the agricultural jobs that had been left empty by male farm workers and land workers who had been called up to fight. Bristolian **Jo Mitchell** was just 17 when she joined the Land Army, which initially sent her to Cheltenham for a month to train as a thatcher. Once she had a grasp of the thatching ropes, Jo was assigned to a job in Almondsbury with a girl from London. She said: "We did threshing in the winter and haymaking and harvesting during the summer." Jo was in the Land Army for three-and-a-half years, saying she enjoyed the experience and it was good fun.[474]

Back in central Bristol, 20-year-old **Jessie Lovell** left her job as a typist to become a clippie (a bus conductor). It was hard work: getting up before dawn, walking several miles to the bus station, ferrying the workers to their jobs at the docks and factories, and walking the several miles home again in the dark at the end of the day. As a young woman of small stature, Jessie was teased mercilessly by the drivers and the passengers on her buses, and her daughter said: "The drivers' favourite trick being to pull away when she was off the bus, and keep just ahead of her chasing down the street. The passengers would love to chat her up, hoping that she wouldn't notice that it was yesterday's ticket in their hand."

But come hell or high water, the buses needed to keep on running, even in the most dangerous of conditions. Jessie's daughter added: "Sometimes, in the blackout, full of fog and smog from the weather and fires, Mum had to walk in front of the bus with a torch, leading the way and looking for bomb craters in the road. Roads were closed from fallen buildings and unexploded bombs, but the buses had to get through." It was brave work.[475]

474 http://www.bbc.co.uk/history/ww2peopleswar/stories/83/a4022083.shtml
475 http://www.bbc.co.uk/history/ww2peopleswar/stories/18/a2857818.shtml

After being widowed and needing to look after her young children, enterprising **Sarah Clark** established a wholesale fish business in Bristol in the 1800s. This was to be a business that the whole family later became involved in, especially the female line. Sarah's son and grandsons took over the business after she retired, but once World War Two broke out and all the men had been called up to fight, it was the turn of the women to return to the fish market, with Sarah's granddaughter **Evelyn Clark** and daughter-in-law **Rose Clark** stepping up to the plate.

Every morning at the break of day, Evelyn and Rose would go from their home in – of course – Fishponds to the market on St Nicholas Street and wait for the deliveries. Evelyn's daughter said: "Fish was boxed in ice and with little in the way of heating in the exposed expanse of the market things were not easy for anyone, especially the 'girls'. It was especially difficult for them with the additional worry of where their husbands were and would they ever see them again this, together with rationing, not to mention bomb attacks on the City made life extremely stressful." When Rose became pregnant, Evelyn was left to cope single-handedly. But cope she admirably did, keeping the business ticking along until the war finally ended.[476]

476 http://www.bbc.co.uk/history/ww2peopleswar/stories/38/a3799038.shtml

FURTHER READING

Lucienne Boyce (2013). *The Bristol Suffragettes*. Bristol: SilverWood Books.

Lorna Brierley, Helen Reid (2000). *Go Home and Do The Washing: Three Centuries of Pioneering Bristol Women*. Bristol: Broadcast Books.

Bristol Broadsides (1977). *Bristol As We Remember it*. Bristol: Broadsides.

Bristol Broadsides (1983). *Bristol's Other History*. Bristol: Broadsides.

Bristol Broadsides (1986). *Placards and Pin Money: Another Look at Bristol's Other History*. Bristol: Broadsides.

Bristol Broadsides (1987). *Bristol Lives: Bristol People Tell Their Own Stories: 1892 to the Present Day*. Bristol: Broadsides.

Dan Brown, Cynthia Hammond (2011). *Suffragettes in Bath: Activism in an Edwardian Arboretum*. Bath: Bath in Time.

Shirley Brown, Dawn Dyer (2002). *100+ Women of Bristol*. Bristol: Bristol City Council.

Eugene Byrne (2017, March 7). 'Bristol's Top 100 Women' in *Bristol Times* supplement in *Bristol Post*. 2-7.

Rosemary Caldicott (2016). *The Life and Death of Hannah Wiltshire: A Case Study of Bedminster Union Workhouse and Victorian Social Attitudes on Epilepsy*. Bristol Radical Pamphleteer 35. Bristol: Bristol Radical History Group.

Elizabeth Crawford (1999). *The Women's Suffrage Movement: A Reference Guide 1866-1928*. London: Routledge.

Elizabeth Crawford (2006). *The Women's Suffrage Movement in Britain and Ireland: A Regional Survey*. London: Routledge.

Madge Dresser (2016). *Women and the City: Bristol 1373-2000*. Bristol: Redcliffe Press.

Margaret Forster (1984). *Significant Sisters: Active Feminism 1839-1939*. London: Secker & Warburg.

June Hannam (2014). *Bristol Independent Labour Party: Men, Women and the Opposition to War*. Bristol Radical Pamphleteer 31. Bristol: Bristol Radical History Group.

Viv Honeybourne, Ilona Singer (2000-2003). *Personal Histories of The Second Wave of Feminism: Volumes One and Two*. The Feminist Archive: PDF download from: http://feministarchivesouth.org.uk/wp-content/uploads/2013/02/Personal-Histories-of-the-Second-Wave-of-Feminism.pdf

Victoria Hughes (1977). *Ladies' Mile: The Remarkable and Shocking Story of Twilight Bristol*. Bristol: Abson.

Jill Liddington (2014). *Vanishing for the Vote: Suffrage, Citizenship and the Battle for the Census*. Manchester: Manchester University Press.

Ellen Malos, Janet Brewer, Sarah Braun (date unknown, circa mid-1970s). *A Bristol Women's History Walk: Central Area 1840-1920*. Bristol: Bristol City Council's Women's Committee. Leaflet.

Marie Mulvey-Roberts (2015). *Literary Bristol: Writers and the City*. Bristol: Redcliffe Press.

Helen Reid (2005). *Life in Victorian Bristol*. Bristol: Redcliffe Press.

Mike Richardson (2016). *The Maltreated and the Malcontents: Working in the Great Western Cotton Factory 1838-1914*. Bristol Radical Pamphleteer 37. Bristol: Bristol Radical History Group.

Sheila Rowbotham (2016). *Rebel Crossings: New Women, Free Lovers and Radicals in Britain and America*. London: Verso.

Joyce Storey (1990). *Joyce's War*. Bristol: Broadsides.

Joyce Storey (2004). *The House in South Road: An Autobiography*. London: Virago Press.

Helen Thomas, Rosie Tomlinson, Mavis Zutshi (2015). *Bedminster Tobacco Women: A Local History Project*. Bristol: Fiducia Press.

Deborah Withers (2011). *Sistershow Revisited: Feminism in Bristol, 1973-1975*. Bristol: HammerOn Press.

ACKNOWLEDGEMENTS

Now that *The Women Who Built Bristol* is completed (although I keep finding new women who deserve to be included... where will it end?), I am looking over the book as a whole and am humbled by the people who have so generously given up their time, skills and knowledge. There is an impressive cast of esteemed contributors to this book, both writers and artists, and I am extremely grateful for their willingness and enthusiasm to get on board.

I am indebted to all of the women who contributed pieces about the 'herstoric' characters of Bristol: proving that deeds *and* words work extremely well together.

I am enormously grateful to Tiitu Takalo for generously donating the wonderful image on the cover of this book. Tiitu is a talented feminist illustrator and comic artist with an extensive back catalogue of work and she welcomes new commissions. Please visit Tiitu's website for more information, further examples of her work and for her contact details: **tiitutakalo.net**

For their illustrations throughout this book, I curtsey before the wonderful artists Jenny Howe (**facebook.com/jennyhoweillustration**) and Carrie Love (**c-love.co.uk**). I thank designer Emily Turner for seamlessly turning Tiitu's strident illustration into the cover of this book, and Joe Burt for designing the interior pages: **wildsparkdesign.com**

For a wide variety of help and advice behind the scenes, from lending books to digging out ancient articles, proofreading chapters, providing advice and everything in between, big thanks to: Michael Beek, Julie Bindel, Eugene Byrne, Elizabeth Crawford, Paul Duffus, Richard Jones, Finn Mackay, Mike Manson, Helen Mott, Helen Pankhurst, Naomi Paxton, Kate Smurthwaite and little Rachel. Sheroic thanks to Kim Renfrew for so many, many things, including going through every single line of this book with the finest of fine-tooth combs, numerous times. And much gratitude to Mark Small for his indefatigable enthusiasm and advice. Needless to say, any errors that do remain in this book are my fault alone.

Publications from Bristol Broadsides have been invaluable in researching this book. This was an independent publisher that operated from the late 1970s to the early 1990s. Bristol Broadsides ran writer workshops with 'ordinary' people at locations all around Bristol, and sought to celebrate the stories of real-life people and their experiences in the city. Although out of print, many of these books can be borrowed from Bristol's libraries and some can be found secondhand online at relatively modest prices. They are highly recommended.

A contemporary Bristol publisher that also seeks to celebrate Bristol's real people and its radical history is Tangent Books, which has published this book. Please visit its website to see the wide range of publications Tangent has produced about amazing people from our city: **tangentbooks.co.uk**